On Kierkegaard and the Truth

The Paul L. Holmer Papers

VOLUME ONE
On Kierkegaard and the Truth

VOLUME TWO
Thinking the Faith with Passion:
Selected Essays
(forthcoming)

VOLUME THREE
Communicating the Faith Indirectly:
Selected Sermons, Addresses, and Prayers
(forthcoming)

On Kierkegaard and the Truth

Paul L. Holmer

Edited by David J. Gouwens and Lee C. Barrett III

Foreword by Stanley Hauerwas

Afterword by David Cain

CASCADE *Books* · Eugene, Oregon

ON KIERKEGAARD AND THE TRUTH

The Paul L. Holmer Papers 1

Copyright © 2012 David J. Gouwens and Lee C. Barrett III. All rights reserved. Except for brief quotations in critical publications or reviews, no part of this book may be reproduced in any manner without prior written permission from the publisher. Write: Permissions, Wipf and Stock Publishers, 199 W. 8th Ave., Suite 3, Eugene, OR 97401.

Cascade Books
An Imprint of Wipf and Stock Publishers
199 W. 8th Ave., Suite 3
Eugene, OR 97401

Revised Standard Version of the Bible, copyright 1952 [2nd edition, 1971] by the Division of Christian Education of the National Council of the Churches of Christ in the United States of America. Used by permission. All rights reserved. Unless otherwise noted, biblical quotations are from this version.

The following previously unpublished manuscript is used by permission of Special Collections, Yale Divinity School Library, Paul L. Holmer Papers.

www.wipfandstock.com

ISBN 13: 978-1-60899-272-0

Cataloging-in-Publication data

Holmer, Paul L.

On Kierkegaard and the truth / Paul L. Holmer ; edited by David J. Gouwens and Lee C. Barrett III ; foreword by Stanley Hauerwas ; afterword by David Cain.

xxviii + 314 pp. ; cm. — Includes bibliographical references and indexes.

The Paul L. Holmer Papers 1

ISBN 13: 978-1-60899-272-0

1. Kierkegaard, Søren, 1813–1855. 2. Theology. I. Gouwens, David Jay. II. Barrett, Lee C. III. Hauerwas, Stanley, 1940–. IV. Cain, David, 1940–. V. Title. VI. Series.

B4377 .H65 2012

Manufactured in the U.S.A.

In Memory of
Paul L. Holmer
1916–2004

Contents

Foreword by Stanley Hauerwas • *ix*

Editors' Preface • *xv*

Acknowledgments • *xxiii*

Abbreviations • *xxiv*

Author's Preface • *xxv*

1 An Introduction to the Problem • 1

2 A Glance at a Contemporary Effort in Danish Philosophy • 18

3 A New Way of Philosophizing • 37

4 The Bible and Christianity • 56

5 History and the Sciences • 79

6 Truth Is Subjectivity: Some Radical Criticisms • 109

7 Truth Is Subjectivity: Some Logical Considerations • 133

8 Some Epistemological Questions • 158

9 Kierkegaard and Metaphysics • 193

10 Kierkegaard and the Nature of Philosophy • 221

11 Indirect Communication • 238

12 Kierkegaard and the Sermon • 260

13 Faith and Christianity • 275

Afterword: Paul L. Holmer: Self-Effacing, Swaggering, Nonpareil—*David Cain* • 296

Appendix—Paul L. Holmer: A Select Bibliography • 299

Bibliography • 303

Index of Names • 309

Index of Subjects • 313

Foreword

I WRITE THIS FOREWORD in "fear and trembling." That may seem an overly dramatic remark, but it is nonetheless true. I have read *On Kierkegaard and the Truth*. In fact, I have read it twice. I also had the advantage of taking Mr. Holmer's Kierkegaard course in 1962. It was my first year at Yale Divinity School, and while I am sure I missed some of the subtle arguments Mr. Holmer was making, I at least got something of the "big picture" he was developing about Kierkegaard's work. That "big picture" is on full display in this book.

So why do I approach this Foreword with trepidation? I do so because it is no easy task to say rightly what Holmer has to say about Kierkegaard. He spent his whole life immersed in the works of Kierkegaard. As this book makes apparent, he had command of the complex authorship that bears the name "Kierkegaard" that few possess. His account of Kierkegaard, moreover, challenges much of the scholarly consensus about Kierkegaard—a consensus not only present at the time Holmer was writing this book but one that largely remains today. This being the case, it's fairly easy to understand why someone like myself, i.e., someone who is not a Kierkegaard scholar, would be fearful of saying something stupid.

Admittedly, although I have read many of Kierkegaard's major works, I do not *know* them well enough to know what I am reading when I am reading Holmer on Kierkegaard. So my main concern in writing this is that I not mislead the reader about Holmer's reading of Kierkegaard. In short, I do not want to write, as Bertrand Russell did in his Introduction to Wittgenstein's *Tractatus Logico-Philosophicus*, a Foreword that suggests I did not understand what Holmer was about in his account of Kierkegaard.

That Russell failed to understand Wittgenstein is understandable given the challenge Wittgenstein presents to most of the ways the work of philosophy was and continues to be understood. Russell's problem was not just that he misunderstood Wittgenstein, but that he had no idea that he misunderstood Wittgenstein. I hope I will not make that mistake. Just as Holmer reminds us that Kierkegaard wrote in a manner to make his reader do intellectually demanding work, so Holmer's way of writing about Kierkegaard is meant to make those who would read Holmer on Kierkegaard do hard work. Holmer assumes it would be a kind of betrayal if he wrote about Kierkegaard in a manner that let those who would read Kierkegaard not do the work required to understand Kierkegaard. So *On Kierkegaard and the Truth* is similarly demanding.

Holmer described the challenge of writing *about* Kierkegaard in a review he wrote in 1970 of Vernard Eller's book *Kierkegaard and Radical Discipleship: A New Perspective*,[1] for the *Journal for the Scientific Study of Religion*. He begins the review by observing that a book on Kierkegaard makes special demands on the author. It does so because few authors are as inquisitive as Kierkegaard, and yet they write at such length and with such virtuosity but finally do not seem to tell you that much. Moreover the demands Kierkegaard makes are of such a variety—intellectual, poetic, ironic, argumentative, humorous—that any attempt at summarization becomes misleading.

Perhaps even more demanding, Holmer observes, is Kierkegaard's use of humor and uncompromising irony to call into question what one may well believe with great seriousness but has not really thought through. Accordingly, Holmer observes that Kierkegaard castigates our assumed competencies that too often reflect the consensus represented by the best intellectual and religious circles. Kierkegaard does so, moreover, because he wants to hit very close to our hearts. His target, however, is not the unsophisticated laity nor the "unwitting fool or obviously second-rate drooling commentator." Rather his foes are the truly distinguished, that is, the best of the religious, the most taxing of the intelligentsia, and the zealous scholar who keeps up with all of "the latest."

Kierkegaard's prose often appears deceptively simple, but as Holmer observes in chapter 9 of this book, in fact, his writing is "aristocratic." It is so because he presupposes that his readers have a certain kind of sophistication formed by the philosophy of the day. Kierkegaard does not, therefore, bother to instruct his readers on ru-

---

1. Vernard Eller, *Kierkegaard and Radical Discipleship: A New Perspective* (Princeton: Princeton University Press, 1968).

dimental metaphysical or logical issues but rather seeks to expose and critique what he regards as clear metaphysical mistakes.

Kierkegaard writes to those he assumes are as well acquainted as he is with Plato, Descartes, Aristotle, Hegel, Kant, as well as biblical writers. Perhaps even more daunting, he assumes his readers suffer from large intellectual problems that he expects the reader will recognize as his own.

So my little worry about writing on Holmer on Kierkegaard does not compare with the challenge Holmer faced by writing on Kierkegaard without betraying Kierkegaard's mode of writing. Holmer knew, moreover, that Kierkegaard knew that his work would often be written about by many who would try to make him but another philosopher or theologian with a "position." Positions give the appearance that the one holding "the position" wants you to agree with his views without having the way you live challenged. In short, Kierkegaard was well aware that many who followed him would try to normalize his work.

Normalization meant that Kierkegaard was thought by many to be an "existentialist." For others, "truth as subjectivity" was used to legitimate positions that Kierkegaard spent a lifetime trying to defeat. It took someone with the philosophical sophistication of Holmer to show, and showing is the right word, that Kierkegaard's philosophical arguments cannot be so easily domesticated. For, as Holmer observes, to write on Kierkegaard knowing what Kierkegaard said about those who would write on him requires a person that is either extremely wise or foolish. Holmer was no fool.

Holmer's account of Kierkegaard is, like Kierkegaard's own work, deceptively straightforward. One is tempted to think you understand what has been said so you can go on to the next chapter. But Holmer has written on Kierkegaard in a manner meant to make you linger on what has been said because what has been said should make us reconsider our fundamental categories of understanding. Kierkegaard was struggling with the difficulty of, as Holmer puts it, writing objectively about subjectivity. The claim that truth is subjectivity, therefore, is an attempt to make us think less about ourselves by directing attention to what such a sentence means for the concept of truth.

What Holmer will not let us forget is that Kierkegaard was a skilled philosopher who practiced his craft in a manner that would force us to recognize that philosophy is about matters of the everyday, that is, matters that entail questions of what it means to "exist." It is not accidental, therefore, that Kierkegaard took Socrates to be the exemplification of the philosophical life. For philosophy is one of the ways, as Holmer observes, that we have to get us back to where we are. That is, philosophy, at least as it was practiced by Kierkegaard, is the difficult work necessary to resist the presumption, a presumption at the heart of the modern philosophical tradition, that the philosopher knows what can be known in a more determinative manner than the person of faith.

Holmer, of course, does not let us forget that Kierkegaard, able philosopher though he may have been, was first and foremost a religious thinker. Kierkegaard took as his task the reintroduction of Christianity into Christendom. Holmer quite rightly argues that contrary to some interpretations of Kierkegaard, Kierkegaard was not calling into question work in biblical criticism. Rather he was rightly reminding his reader that faith cannot be secured by more historical knowledge because we already know all we need to know to be a disciple of Jesus.

Drury reports that he and Wittgenstein once passed a street preacher who was yelling at those who gathered to hear him. Wittgenstein remarked that if the fellow believed what he said he would not use that tone of voice. That seems to me to be a nice description of Kierkegaard's work, and it resonates with Holmer's attempt to help us understand Kierkegaard's work. Kierkegaard, through the development of what Holmer characterizes as a literature of reflection on "vivid examples," was trying to help us discover the tone of voice required by those who seek to live truthful lives.

"Fear and trembling," therefore, seems an appropriate disposition for approaching the work of both Kierkegaard and Holmer. For neither will let us forget that God is not an object to be described but a living reality that would have us worship and love the One alone who should be worshiped and loved. Kierkegaard was only interested in matters that matter. So this is not just another book "about Kierkegaard"; rather, this is a book that forces us to read Kierkegaard as if our lives were at stake. In the process I think you will find that the fear of God makes joy possible.

Stanley Hauerwas
Gilbert T. Rowe Professor of Theological Ethics
Duke Divinity School

Editors' Preface

PAUL L. HOLMER (1916–2004) was a unique and potent theological force. While his own reflections were *sui generis* and extraordinarily elusive, he had a pervasive and significant (but often unacknowledged) impact upon the development of Christian reflection in the United States in the second half of the twentieth century. Holmer served as Professor of Philosophy at the University of Minnesota from 1946 to 1960, and then as the Noah Porter Professor of Philosophical Theology at Yale Divinity School from 1960 to 1987. After his death in 2004, his family gave The Paul L. Holmer Papers, comprising thirty-eight archival boxes, to the Yale University Library, where they form the Holmer Papers Special Collection at Yale Divinity School Library.

Holmer's thought is not as well known as its stature deserves. Holmer published only a few books during his lifetime, and many of his essays appeared in rather hard-to-find journals or only circulated in manuscript form. The editors have carefully reviewed the papers at Yale Divinity School, and have concluded that the publication of three volumes of The Paul L. Holmer Papers will serve to illuminate three important aspects of Holmer's contributions to theology. In volume 1, we have painstakingly reconstructed Holmer's unpublished, and much-rumored, book-length manuscript on Kierkegaard, presented under the title *On Kierkegaard and the Truth*. In volume 2, *Thinking the Faith with Passion: Selected Essays*, we have chosen some of the seminal essays that represent the wide scope of Holmer's thought and interests. In volume 3, *Communicating the Faith Indirectly: Selected Sermons, Addresses, and Prayers*, we present another aspect of Holmer's thought and work as philosopher and theologian, including both his reflections upon, and his practice of, the sermon or religious address.

Paul Holmer's writings about Kierkegaard are almost as peculiar and demanding as Kierkegaard's writings themselves. They defy neat categorization in terms of genre and often defy the conventions of academic scholarship. They are certainly not a linear explication of the texts of the Kierkegaard corpus. Nor are they a sustained effort to illumine the texts by situating them in the complexities of Kierkegaard's historical environment. Moreover, they do not attempt to clarify Kierkegaard's *oeuvre* in the light of their author's odd psychological dynamics. Holmer treats the corpus neither as an extended presentation of a metaphysical "position" nor as a disguised exercise in theological revision or doctrinal repristination. Holmer does not reduce the meaning of the texts to the intentionality of their author, nor does he identify the meaning with any worldview suggested by the texts themselves. Like Kierkegaard, Holmer mixed the citing of evidence and the building of a case with exhortation and solicitude for the moral and religious well-being of his readers. Also like Kierkegaard, Holmer developed his own idiosyncratic vocabulary and quirky style. His sentences have the cadences and punctuation of his speech, and, again like Kierkegaard's own sentences, seem to have been intended to be read aloud. In Holmer's pages philosophical reflection, cultural polemics, and religious edification are curiously mixed.

In spite of this oddness (or perhaps because of it), Holmer was an enormously influential figure in the history of Kierkegaard studies in the United States and Canada. His impact was felt more through his teaching than through his published writings. First at the University of Minnesota and then at Yale, Holmer guided and provoked several new generations of Kierkegaard scholars whose own writing and teaching would shape yet more generations.

Holmer's own approach to Kierkegaard did not spring fully armed from the brow of Zeus. Holmer's engagement with Kierkegaard was deeply indebted to the work of David F. Swenson (1876-1940), a professor of philosophy at the University of Minnesota.[1] By the late nineteenth century, the writings of Kierkegaard were circulating within the Scandinavian immigrant communities of the northern Midwest. In 1898 Swenson discovered a volume by Kierkegaard by accident in a local library, immediately became enamored with it, and by 1914 had begun lecturing on Kierkegaard, transmitting his enthusiasm for the

---

1. See David Swenson, *Something about Kierkegaard* (Minneapolis: Augsburg, 1941); David Swenson, *Kierkegaardian Philosophy in the Faith of a Scholar* (Philadelphia: Westminster, 1941).

Editors' Preface xvii

Danish thinker to his students. For Swenson, Kierkegaard provided a welcome alternative to the two major interpretations of religion available within contemporary American philosophy: the empiricist dismissal of religion, and the idealist assimilation of religion to grand metaphysical systems, mostly of a monistic sort. In the one case religion was deemed irrational, and in the second it was evacuated of personal pathos. Disillusioned with both empiricism and idealism, Swenson was attracted to what he perceived to be Kierkegaard's refusal to divorce matters of passion and matters of reason in his treatment of Christianity. Swenson developed an interpretation of Kierkegaard that differed from that of the existentialists whose influential appropriation of Kierkegaard was beginning to permeate the academy. Swenson's Kierkegaard was no extreme anti-rationalist but rather a Christian philosopher whose work implicitly suggested that belief in a transcendent source of meaning is a legitimate response to the ambiguity and anguish of human life. Of course, this transcendent source of meaning does elude all procedures of objective verification. However, for Swenson, there is a kind of rationality resident in the passional dynamics of human life that becomes evident when an individual begins to strive for personal coherence. The emotions, passions, and feelings that characterize human lives have a type of logic. In light of this, the embrace of Christianity is by no means counter-rational, even though it cannot be justified by the research procedures of empirical scientists.

While an undergraduate at the University of Minnesota, Holmer studied under Swenson during the time that Swenson was preparing his translation of *Concluding Unscientific Postscript*. Holmer met with Swenson once a week to discuss the thought of Nietzsche and Kierkegaard. Moving to Yale for his PhD after Swenson's death, Holmer wrote his dissertation on Kierkegaard's epistemology, a project he described as unabashedly Swensonian. Upon returning to the University of Minnesota to teach in 1946, Holmer saw himself as continuing Swenson's legacy of providing an alternative to the positivism that dominated the philosophy department.

Holmer had enormous respect for the intellectual rigor and precision of the positivist heritage, and was troubled by the suspicion of the truth and meaningfulness of Christian convictions that it spawned. Holmer was intrigued and disturbed by the form of positivism that became popular at the University of Minnesota through the influence of Herbert Feigl, who had joined the philosophy faculty in 1940. He shared positivism's suspicion that metaphysical speculation was nonsense, but recoiled at its equation of meaningfulness with the procedures of verification or falsification. Holmer rejected the suggestion that moral and religious language was nothing more than the expression of affective states or personal preferences with no reference to realities beyond the individual's inner life. Holmer, inspired by Swenson, welcomed what he took to be Kierkegaard's insight that "rationality" is not a homogenous, univocal concept, whose meaning is determined by modern science.

Using his dissertation as a foundation, Holmer began composing a comprehensive book on Kierkegaard's thought. He wrote several different drafts, from the late 1940s through the late 1960s, never entirely satisfied with the results. He was deeply sensitive to the danger of misrepresenting Kierkegaard by paraphrasing his literature as if it were a set of theological or philosophical propositions that could be grasped dispassionately. Such a procedure would subvert Kierkegaard's purpose of occasioning a possible transformation of the reader's passions and dispositions. Consequently, Holmer's work evolved from a summary of Kierkegaard's opinions to a set of suggestions for reading Kierkegaard for one's own self. Holmer was keenly aware that any scholarly writing about Kierkegaard should not function as a substitute for firsthand wrestling with the texts themselves. As he noted, reading Kierkegaard's literature should function as a sort of moral and religious pedagogy. Holmer wanted his book to contribute to Kierkegaard's goal of stimulating the process of becoming a responsible person rather than sabotage that process by communicating results. He did not want to summarize Kierkegaard's thoughts or arrange them in a neat system; he merely sought to coach the reader in the most felicitous ways to engage the literature that would avoid appropriations that sabotaged their edifying purpose. Most of all, Holmer sought to remove the most basic impediment to appropriately reading Kierkegaard that typically afflicts learned people, namely, the tendency to engage a philosophical or theological text as a compendium of "results" that systematically answer all human questions.

In spite of these caveats about the proper way to read Kierkegaard, Holmer did not hesitate to present Kierkegaard as a genuine philosopher. Holmer's sensitivity to Kierkegaard's desire to provoke the reader to a passionate concern about the quality of the reader's own life did not prevent Holmer from realizing that Kierkegaard's literature also served as a clarification of certain perennial conceptual puzzlements. In order to disabuse learned readers of intellectual tendencies that could impede their ability to engage life seriously, Kierkegaard, in Holmer's view, developed a way of doing philosophy as a type of analysis of the concepts that were most basic to various ways of living. According to Holmer, this led Kierkegaard to reflect long and hard on the way that life-shaping concepts come to have meaning. As a result, Kierkegaard recognized the importance of drawing distinctions between different networks of concepts. Holmer's pages trace the ways in which Kierkegaard's corpus can be construed as a type of meta-analysis of the conditions for the appropriate use of existentially relevant concepts. As such, Kierkegaard exhibits all the argumentative rigor and even "objectivity" traditionally associated with philosophical writing. In a way, in Holmer's view Kierkegaard's many volumes implicitly present a sustained argument about the nature and limits of human intelligibility and communication that serves as an alternative to traditional metaphysics.

As the drafts evolved, the influence of Ludwig Wittgenstein became more evident. In Wittgenstein Holmer discerned an illuminating parallel to Kierkegaard's theme that the way of appropriating and using a concept is constitutive of its meaning. Wittgenstein's attention to the particularities of context and purpose seemed to him to clarify Kierkegaard's insistence that the right context of pathos must be present in order for religious and moral discourse to be meaningful. The concept "God" cannot be grasped without imagining the purposes of praising, confessing, and exhorting in which the concept "God" is embedded.

The evolution of the different recensions of the manuscript also shows an increasing sensitivity to the literary qualities of Kierkegaard's work. Holmer realized that the conceptual content of any Kierkegaardian text could not be divorced from its mode of communication. Grasping Kierkegaard's purpose required an appreciation of his literary art. Holmer was keenly aware that Kierkegaard's rhetorical performance contributed so much to their meaning that any purely discursive paraphrase would be a gross distortion of their meaning.

In order to prepare the reader for a potentially edifying encounter with Kierkegaard's texts, Holmer reiterated a few different themes to keep in mind as the texts are being read. One is Kierkegaard's conviction that the objective pursuit of knowledge does not lead to moral or religious growth. There is no necessary connection between scholarship and religious seriousness. The mood of detachment is utterly inappropriate for considering moral and religious matters. Concern for the integrity of the individual's own life must be present in order for moral and religious discourse to be meaningful. An intelligible nexus of passions, emotions, concerns, and purposes is essential for establishing the meaning of authentic ethical and religious communication. Understanding morally and religiously significant language requires the ability to at least imagine the hopes and fears that words are trying to evoke, express, or recommend. This would even lead Holmer to emphasize Kierkegaard's dissatisfaction with the allegedly "scientific" approach to the interpretation of the Bible.

Because of this, no neutral assessment of Christianity's claims is possible. All concepts only make sense within their own domain of discourse, embedded in a network of relationships with other concepts from the same domain, all mutually defining each other. Meaning evaporates when concepts from disparate domains are mixed indiscriminately. Psychological explanations do not make sense in the context of moral responsibility, and notions of historical causality do not make sense when assessing the religious significance of an event. Human beings do not have access to a neutral, omniscient meta-perspective from which all these domains can be coordinated and integrated into a "system." The concepts of Christianity constitute a unique way of life with a distinctive set of virtues, aspirations, dispositions, and passions.

Christianity should not be assimilated to any other academic discipline or cultural sensibility. Christianity is not to be identified with any set of secular political projects, societal values, or popular cosmologies. No meta-perspective is available that could serve as the

Editors' Preface

basis for synthesizing Christianity with some grand vision of the way the universe really is or with some totalizing project of human amelioration. Holmer insisted that Kierkegaard must be read as someone who resisted the accommodation of Christianity to nationalism, generic spirituality, and popular standards of decent behavior.

By stressing these themes in Kierkegaard's literature, Holmer was hoping to warn the reader away from potential ways of misreading Kierkegaard. Kierkegaard should not be read as a rather peculiar and sustained apology for a particular way of life. Nor should Kierkegaard be read as an invitation to indulge in the freeplay of the imagination and make criterionless choices. Kierkegaard should be read neither as an alternative metaphysics, nor as a doctrinal revisionist, nor as an existential irrationalist. Holmer's Kierkegaard is not the Kierkegaard of the ontologists like Paul Tillich, nor the neo-orthodox theologians like Emil Brunner, nor the existentialists like Jean-Paul Sartre. In Holmer's view, Kierkegaard did not simply want to convey information; rather, he sought to foster the possibility that the reader might become a more responsible, coherent self, perhaps even a Christian, through the act of reading. Christian communication must activate self-reflection and concern for the significance of one's own life and provoke a crisis of accountability for the shape of one's own life.

~

A few words of explanation about the editing process are in order. Holmer wrote these drafts before concerns about gender-inclusive language became common. The editors have not attempted to conform Holmer's writings to current practice, but beg the reader's indulgence, and note that Holmer's own practice on this shifted in later years.

Holmer wrote most of these pages before the selections from Kierkegaard's journals and papers edited and translated by Howard and Edna Hong appeared. Consequently, when referring to a journal entry, Holmer cited either Alexander Dru's briefer set of translated selections or, if Dru had not translated a particular entry, the then available Danish edition. Seldom did Holmer cite both. The editors have supplemented Holmer's citations of Dru with the corresponding passages in the Danish edition of the papers that Holmer used.

We have also supplemented his references to the Danish edition with the English translations now available, either from *Søren Kierkegaard's Journals and Papers*, edited and translated by Howard V. Hong and Edna H. Hong, or from *Søren Kierkegaard's Journals and Notebooks*, edited by Niels Jørgen Cappelørn, Alastair Hannay, David Kangas, Bruce H. Kirmmse, George Pattison, Vanessa Rumble, and K. Brian Söderquist.

Acknowledgments

THE EDITORS ACKNOWLEDGE THE following contributors to this project. First, we thank Professor Linnea Wren of Gustavus Adolphus College; it was she who suggested that the editors examine The Paul L. Holmer Papers that had recently been donated by the Holmer family to Special Collections, Yale Divinity School Library. At the YDS Library, Martha L. Smalley, Special Collections Librarian, greatly assisted us in surveying the wide extent of Holmer's papers. Joan Duffy, Archives Assistant, ably helped us in procuring photocopies of selections. Robert Osburn, formerly of the MacLaurin Institute, was helpful in early stages of this project, as he was again, along with Ruth Pszwaro, at its conclusion.

Thanks are due also to Stanley Hauerwas for offering the foreword to this volume. Jack Schwandt and T. Wesley Stewart also provided helpful comments on the project.

Brite Divinity School provided a generous Summer Research Stipend for work on this project. April Bupp of Lancaster Theological Seminary deserves special thanks for preparing the manuscript of volume 1. At Brite Divinity School, Joseph McDonald as graduate assistant provided superb editorial skills, and Karrie Keller, Petite Kirkendoll, and Victoria Robb Powers assisted in typing and proofreading of volumes 2 and 3.

We thank David Cain for writing the afterword and for supplying the photograph of Paul and Phyllis Holmer.

The editors warmly thank their respective spouses for their consistent, gracious support and encouragement as we labored on this project.

Abbreviations

JP   Kierkegaard, Søren. *Søren Kierkegaard's Journals and Papers*. 7 vols. Edited and translated by Howard V. Hong and Edna H. Hong, assisted by Gregor Malantschuk. Bloomington and London: Indiana University Press, 1967–1978. The abbreviation is *JP*, followed by the volume and entry numbers. For example, *JP* 1, 400.

KJN   Kierkegaard, Søren. *Søren Kierkegaard's Journals and Notebooks*. 4 vols. to date. Edited by Niels Jørgen Cappelørn, Alastair Hannay, David Kangas, Bruce H. Kirmmse, George Pattison, Vanessa Rumble, and K. Brian Söderquist. Published in cooperation with the Søren Kierkegaard Research Centre, Copenhagen. Princeton and Oxford: Princeton University Press, 2000–. The abbreviation is *KJN*, followed by the volume and entry numbers. For example, *KJN* 3, Not13:41.a.

Author's Preface

IT IS A LITTLE embarrassing to offer the reading public another book about Søren Kierkegaard, especially when that most singular Dane designed his literature as a tool to personal enrichment and subjective stature. For whatever else might be said about Kierkegaard's literature, it is not ambiguous on this point. With characteristic irony, though, he anticipated our age, the learned corps who would use his writings to get clearer definitions of faith, love, right, and wrong, while remaining the same paltry human subjects.

Perhaps this book will seem to be a betrayal of Kierkegaard's intent and authorship. I hope not. For what I pretend at least is the discovery of all kinds of unsuspected levels of reflection and discourse within Kierkegaard's literature. While I have documented his remarks as best I can and given credit where it is due, still it seems to me that much of what is offered here is the exploitation of neglected aspects of Kierkegaard's reflection. Some suggestions, especially about logic and the limits of logical values, others about the characteristics of propositional truth, and others about ethical choice, seem to have brought me into the middle of both the philosophical tradition and the contemporary discussion. So it is with other matters too. It is with more appreciation, therefore, that I can repeat a remark made about twenty-five years ago by David F. Swenson (reported to me by Professor T. V. Smith) to the effect that the future of American philosophy belonged to Søren Kierkegaard.

A hundred years ago, Kierkegaard suggested that the religious people were so acclimatized to faith and to faith-talk that now was the time to emphasize the minor premise, "works." Today it might be said that the age is full of good works (though the number of saints still seems few) and surely sated with talk again about faith. Perhaps it is time to emphasize reason, reflection, objectivity, and sundry other values. Not because faith abounds—far from it!—but rather because with all the talk and easy accord, almost anything passes for religiousness. The definitions are again blurred and the requisites of systematic consistency, of careful consideration and accuracy, of a weighing of the facts, almost seem to add up to ungodliness. Instead of abandonment to a genuinely ethical enthusiasm and a heartfelt dedication to Christian recklessness, instead of a wanton giving of oneself, the categories become wantonly handled and speech becomes abominably loose. The irony of this is that Kierkegaard is cited as the fountainhead and apogee of the new irrationalism.

At once then there are several difficulties. Kierkegaard is maligned, religion is associated with misology, and the cleft in the person who reads Kierkegaard with concern for both religious stature and intellectual clarity becomes wider. It is true that Kierkegaard opposed philosophical systems but he did not oppose systematic thought; he disparaged talk about the logic of events but not the logicality of argumentative discourse; he minimized the religious importance of discursive reasoning but not by saying that reason was irreligious; he praised subjectivity but not temperamentally; he abjured objectivity as a substitute for enthusiasm but not as a condition for knowledge.

If all this is true it might be well to watch Kierkegaard speak collectedly about paradoxicality, objectively about subjectivity, and detachedly about human interests, without being either intellectually inconsistent or morally reprobate. At the same time he was both reflective and passionately religious. He sought each with diligence, admitting difficulties en route, but never giving up the endeavor to become a living synthesis of aristocratic reflection and religious compassion. His authorship is a calculated attack upon misunderstandings of his day, and, unfortunately, of ours too. The evangelical hope of bringing the reader face to face with the God of Jesus Christ never forsakes him for a moment. But it is for others to say this at length about Kierkegaard. I choose here a more modest task, that of etching out the features of the authorship that give rectitude to his argument, that seem to promise the kind of universality and necessity that any reflection must have if it is to be called valid. This is a kind of scholiast's annotation upon the text, not however undertaken without sympathy and delight. It was Professor David Swenson, who, taking me through Nietzsche's many volumes as an introduction to Kierkegaard's *Philosophical Fragments*, also taught me to respect

Author's Preface

Kierkegaard's logical and reflective acumen. If this book is Swensonian I am neither surprised nor disappointed. My debt to others, including Conger, Hendel, Sheldon, Cassirer, H. R. Niebuhr, Geismar, Lowrie, Thulstrup, Böhlin, and Hirsch, is rather longstanding. I have tried to read the extant literature about Kierkegaard in addition to the vast primary sources. I no longer remember every impetus but I have tried to indicate causes and sources wherever I could. Because of rather strong interests in some of the issues herein involved I have more interest in the validity of the argument than in the source. But this again is no excuse for neglecting the latter.

My thanks are due to Miss Alma Scott, Archivist of the University of Minnesota, for the use of materials in her care, and also to Dr. and Mrs. Lachlan Reed for another kind of solicitude, and to librarians at Yale, the University of Minnesota, and the Royal Library in Copenhagen.

A note concerning the footnote references may also be in order. References to Kierkegaard's collected works are usually to the 1906 edition of the *Samlede Vaerker* (*Saml. Vaerker*); *E. P.* refers to the *Efterladte Papirer* in nine volumes; *Papirer* betokens *Søren Kierkegaards Papirer*, now the standard edition in twenty volumes. Except for special reasons usually noted, references to both the latter and to Alexander Dru's translation of selections from them are to the entry number, not usually to the page. A reference like the following, e.g., *Papirer* X 2 A, 11–13, means volume 10, part two, section A, entries 11–13.

CHAPTER I

An Introduction to the Problem

I

ALL PHILOSOPHICAL WORKS HAVE their genesis in a problem. To this extent at least this volume is philosophical. The problem is deceptively simple in appearance and perhaps seems hardly worth another book. For when an author insists that he is a religious author from first to last and when he proclaims that the movement in his own literature is away from the aesthetic and through the philosophical and reflective and into finally the religious,[1] then it would seem that enough has been said already, that anything else about the author's philosophy will be gratuitous. Appearance also has its structure and there are many readers of Kierkegaard's words who find their anti-intellectual proclivities and judgments strengthened by such remarks. All kinds of existentialists are quick to use Kierkegaard as authority for the view that inferential reasoning is of no avail. With the torrent of praise that Kierkegaard receives from those who are belatedly discovering that biblical religion is serious business, there come also the rejoinders from minorities in philosophy and theology who fear that everything anti-rational and barbaric is being brought back under the aegis of a perverse genius.[2]

---

1. This is asserted in "On My Work as an Author," 145–47.
2. As an excellent example of a clear and forthright statement against contemporary anti-intellectualism, note Blanshard's "Current Strictures on Reason," 345–68.

In one way or another Kierkegaard's disparagement of philosophy is construed to mean something quite different from what was stated within his own authorship. In the contexts of language and reflection in which his strong words are placed and understood by contemporaries, it becomes difficult to make sense of many of his most important remarks. The fact that he eschewed writing a treatise on metaphysics, ethics, logic, or epistemology seems to credit the conviction that he was not a philosopher at all. But, as one reads his voluminous literature, both his published writings and papers, it becomes clear that he is eminently systematic, that every part of his literature expresses an intention. Furthermore, it all belongs together in ways that are very heartening for a philosophically oriented reader. Although there is no treatise on logic, there is a kind of embedded logic, a logical order informing every inquiry and sentence. Although there is no explicit ethical theory there are ample indications of a theory about ethical proposals again informing the entire literature. True, there is no metaphysical system spelled out in detail; but there are numerous statements about metaphysics. Furthermore there are consistent and well-articulated attitudes and convictions that are in the spirit of a "meta-metaphysics," that is, they represent a kind of outlook and language system within which the possibility and limits of metaphysics are seen. Likewise Kierkegaard wrote no extended treatise on epistemology, but when one pieces together all that he said one finds again that only a sustained argument could have produced those somewhat casual appearing remarks.

Those students of Kierkegaard's literature who stress his religious writings all too frequently stress them to the exclusion of his pronounced philosophical abilities. This is easily enough done, especially when Kierkegaard said that he was moving out of philosophy and into the religious. But this was a kind of philosophy, the kind which proposed a set of life-values. The nineteenth century is remarkable for the plentitude of that kind of philosophical system. Kierkegaard did not reject philosophy as a formal enterprise. He was not anti-logic, anti-theory, or anti-consistency, nor did he disparage theories about any of these. His point is rather that the regnant philosophies of his day were full of the self-assertiveness and self-assurance of men and hence acquire their value content, not in virtue of logically necessary

An Introduction to the Problem

reasoning but in virtue of all kinds of social and subjective factors.[3] A more limited scope for philosophy seems called for—this seems to be his plea.

But a warning is in order. Kierkegaard thought that the world of scholarship is quite a humorous spectacle. And it is devoutly hoped that the arrival of the promised philosophical hero will not be accompanied by the tense and varied expectancy Kierkegaard described:

> ... reception committee on its feet ... some with note-books open, pens dripping with ink, minds yearning in systematic instruction; all and sundry awaiting ...[4]

Because Kierkegaard saw clearly that no conviction warranted by detached and rational argument could simultaneously move the thinker from detachment to attachment, from disinterestedness to interestedness, he also believed that it was ridiculously inappropriate to create too wide a concern about epistemological and logical problems. He was engaged as most men are in the pursuit of self-justification and what the theologians call salvation. In this matter he had maximal interest. Furthermore, he believed that the passions ought to be expressed upon such passional matters. But on matters appropriately abstract and detached he was inclined not to be the least bit evocative or persuasive. He was content to think clearly and exactingly for the sake of the clearness and exactness but he refused to give any alien inducements to his readers at this point. The effect of clear expression upon logic and epistemological matters he understood to be regulative and disciplinary, not provident. It was his merit to have seen that the philosophical discourse that tried to get to reality, as he said, "in the last paragraph" or to ascertain the good was a misunderstanding of what reflection and discourse could properly do. Therefore Kierkegaard was most willing to let his readers do without the system—it was only deception that gave systems such importance anyway and such a deception certainly he would not practice.

---

3. Some of Kierkegaard's reflections about philosophers are to the effect that the subjectively derived factors enter reflection and thereafter get a status not quite due them. Note, for example, *Papirer* I A, 72–76 (*JP* 5, 5092, 5093, 22, 5100, 5101), and also V A, 18, 20 (*JP* 1, 622, 47). Professor David Swenson's remarks in his notes to the translation of *Philosophical Fragments*, 99–100, are appropriate too. An earlier reflection, dating from 1840, contrasts Hegel and Kant on this point. See *Papirer*, III A, 3 (*JP* 1, 37).

4. From the preface, *Concluding Unscientific Postscript*, 3.

In a different context, one of Kierkegaard's pseudonymous authors, Johannes Climacus, tries to explain the importance, or rather the unimportance of his huge philosophical work (*Concluding Unscientific Postscript*), and then says:

> If a naked dialectical analysis reveals that no approximation to faith is possible, that an attempt to construct a quantitative approach to faith is a misunderstanding, and that any appearance of success in this endeavor is an illusion; if it seems to be a temptation for the believer. . . . in transforming faith into something else, into a certainty of an entirely different order . . . then everyone who so understands the problem. . . . must feel the difficulty of his position . . .[5]

The difficulty is precisely in loving learning and yet knowing its limits, in admiring scholarship and scholars and yet not crediting them with the fountain of life. The point is that Kierkegaard believed in "a naked dialectical analysis," by which he meant a formal analysis of concepts. The *Postscript* is a study of both passions and concepts. This is why it is called "pathetic-dialectical." The projected title for this largest of his pseudonymous works was originally *Logical Problems* by Johannes Climacus.[6] And the kind of reflection which helped constitute that book is amply illustrated in one hundred pages of his papers. Typical problems adumbrated therein and illustrative of what he meant by dialectical philosophy are questions about the meaning of a category, the difference between a dialectical and pathos-informed analysis, and the status of historical concepts like progress, etc.[7]

Kierkegaard believed that the truth or falsity of claims could be ascertained. To do this was to be dialectical. But there was also a science of ideas, an overview upon ideas and the language stating them. Dialecticians worried their way through such matters. Kierkegaard does not decide with Kant that dialectic is the logic of appearance or with Hegel that it is the logic of reality itself. The dialectical analysis of which Kierkegaard spoke in the passage quoted is "naked" ("*nogne*" in

---

5. *Postscript*, 15.
6. *Papirer* VI B, 89 (*JP* 5, 5850).
7. *Papirer* VI B, 13–99, 89–193; (*JP* 1, 56, 199, 456, 632–35, 925, 926, 1039; *JP* 2, 1344, 1607–610, 1638, 1668, 1746, 2115, 2116, 2235, 2286, 2287; *JP* 3, 2355, 2371, 2372, 2749, 3083–3086, 3307, 3562, 3607, 3654, 3702, 3739; *JP* 4, 4537, *JP* 5, 5778, 5783–797, 5807, 5850, 5851). There are included here many illuminating abstract considerations.

Danish) precisely because it is formal; it has to do with form, not content; it focuses on logical relations, on the limits of valid discourse, not finally on the empirical truth or falsity of what is said except indirectly as this is affected by logical considerations.[8] The dialectician comes to know the rules of discourse. In *Concluding Unscientific Postscript* we see a young dialectician, who, because of philosophical competence, is able to discern the mistakes made by scholars who accumulate evidence for hypotheses that are logically irrelevant to that kind of verification. Philosophers of the non-dialectical and speculative variety are also instances of such mistaken thinkers. To borrow a contemporary expression, it is as if Kierkegaard is saying that there are category mistakes, and not least among the philosophers.

Therefore, the problem with which we are concerned is that of discussing and stating the dialectical and neutral structure within which Kierkegaard believed that he reflected and wrote. It must, of course, first be made clear that he acknowledged such a structure. But beyond this it is essential to state its relation to everything else that he wrote. The fact that this systematic structure of reflection is described as neutral ought to warn the critic who would insist that "now the professors are at him, doing exactly what he said they would, and misunderstanding him completely." The neutrality of the ruled reflection is Kierkegaard's philosophical secret. But to grasp for oneself these rules and forms of reflection, to be clear on the categories, is still to possess no content! So even if this effort is completely successful, nothing ethically or religiously important (as Kierkegaard undertsood such matters) will have been accomplished. Kierkegaard's system will prove to be no palace of reflection with rooms for human occupation! The reality issue—if there is one—is not solved by systematic reflection; neither is the question of right or wrong conduct resolved by systematic thought about ethics. The issue for religious inquiry is certainly not to be resolved by a correct dialectic either. But it is only as we note Kierkegaard's audacious and radical philosophical reflection that we can understand properly why he made the above denials. This is what will be subsequently attempted.

---

8. Readers of the eloquent passages in the author's introduction to *Concluding Unscientific Postscript* will remember the trials faced by the young man who wants to be a thinker!

II

One of the exasperating difficulties in philosophy is to define the word "philosophy" itself. To a surprising extent, the definition of philosophy itself is a problem for philosophy. To the degree that philosophies have included within their limits persuasive and "*lebens*-philosophic" components, i.e., ethical and existential claims, so too have the definitions of philosophy reflected these same components. To determine, therefore, whether a given author was a philosopher or his works philosophical has been a matter most frequently of loud assertion on the part of innovators, on the one side, and a recitation of the precedents on the other. If one were to wait for loud assertions on behalf of Kierkegaard today, one would hear principally the theologians and the men-of-letters. However great their authority, the philosophers perhaps are not persuaded. If one were to wait for the precedents, one waits in vain. Who are the philosophers in the East or West who one would dare to say are the classic instances of what Kierkegaard also did? There are a few, of course, who did some of what he did: Rousseau and Augustine wrote confessional pieces but these are not their principal philosophical writings; Plato and Santayana combine aesthetic appeal and argumentative vigor; many wrote about the religious life, but was it not then theology that they wrote?

Kierkegaard was, in almost every perspective from which he can be read and understood, a most singular person and author. To describe him as a philosopher, whatever else he was, supposes that he had something in common with others called philosophers. As shall be indicated later, many pieces of his writings can be oriented to the elucidation of this issue, but at the outset suffice it to say that Kierkegaard never sought to provide for anyone else a summary of fundamental beliefs. He was not a pontiff philosopher seeking to be anyone else's provident communication of wisdom. He denied his own right to communicate directly any fundamental ethical or religious belief. There was no dialectic establishing an ethical or religious belief anyway. Philosophical dialectic was more important in establishing beliefs about believing, a second-order belief so to speak, than in establishing a primary belief about matters of existence. For reasons which are, therefore, somewhat similar (but if anything much more circumspectly conceived and stated) to those given by logical empiricists and analytical philosophers, Kierkegaard too refrained from providing metaphysical and ethical beliefs in the grand manner.

Much of the history of philosophy is a rather sorry spectacle in which views of the good and the real contend. Even when one finds the occasional author like Plato who can write skillfully while giving contrasting views simultaneous expression in his own work, there is a kind of deception practiced that makes the philosophers suspicious. In Plato's *Gorgias* "the ethical conquers because it is fortunate to have incomparably the abler protagonist; it conquers, and the reader can see the victory achieved and the opponents humbled."[9] Thus it is with most philosophers. A superior dialectical skill wins the plaudits for a point of view for a season and the other philosophical systems are then vanquished, but only until another dialectician arrives who conquers the field again. Metaphysicians who have ruminated about these matters profess to find a kind of depersonalized dialectic shaping the minds of men and predisposing their assent. On the other hand, critics of metaphysics who find such an amplitude of nonsense in philosophy, fittingly enough, use more chaste language and say confidentially, philosophy is analysis. They omit the distressing rubric, "I think," or "I opine that . . ." and without being metaphysical, they still legislate, worse perhaps than the metaphysicians ever did.

It was such a state of affairs that Kierkegaard discovered over one hundred years ago. Instead of thinking for all of humanity and picking up Hegel's burden where he had laid it down, Kierkegaard breaks with the precedence altogether. He refuses to write out still another system of existence—a "*weltanschauung*" for others. "How foolish, then, is the modern seeking after system upon system, as though help was to be found there . . ."[10] But he refuses because he was not able to continue one. His disparagement of systems, not systematic or logical reflection, is repeatedly expressed but seldom with the succinctness one finds in the following journal entry:

> The majority of men in every generation, even those who, as it is described, devote themselves to thinking, (dons and the

9. The remark is Professor Swenson's and is used to point up the contrast between Plato and Kierkegaard. See *Philosophical Fragments*, "Introduction," xvi. Note the illuminating remarks on "Comparing Søren Kierkegaard and Plato," in Brandes, *Søren Kierkegaard*, 50–61, 117–29.

10. Dru, *Journals of Søren Kierkegaard*, entry 590 (*Papirer* VII A, 102).

like), live and die under the impression that life is simply a matter of understanding more and more, and that if it were granted to them to live longer, that life would continue to be one long continuous growth in understanding. How many of them ever experience the maturity of discovering that there comes a critical moment when everything is reversed, after which the point becomes to understand more and more that there is something which cannot be understood. That is Socratic ignorance, and that is what the philosophy of our times requires as a corrective.[11]

Kierkegaard's Socratic ignorance was philosophically articulated. He discovered by intellectual analysis that a system of logic was possible, but that a system of existence was not possible. This meant not simply a repudiation of the ontological logic of idealism and particularly Hegel but also the repudiation of the attitude that assumes that philosophers are particularly commissioned to know the objects or referents for the great words like "good," "true," "beautiful," "God," "reality," etc. Discovering as he did that these words had passional significance and only to a limited degree cognitive significance, Kierkegaard was able to restate his own relation to philosophical inquiry in categories that for his time were indigenous and novel. The corrective he brought to philosophy was the reasoned case for the admission of ignorance. In more formal language, it was an analysis and argument concerning the limits of cognition and propositional truth. Perhaps it was not ignorance of the object that made the difficulty. Kierkegaard is bold enough to suggest both that there may be no objects for the cognitive intelligence and that, therefore, there is no wisdom to be had in such matters at all. What passes for philosophical wisdom might be something much less. But again the limits of cognition and philosophy on these matters are his interest. He does not exploit our ignorance by strongly asserting this suspicion.

In the common man's view of the matter, a philosopher is a man who has a set of beliefs on fundamental questions. Kierkegaard had beliefs and they were coherently related to one another. But this set of commitments he did not communicate to others as his "philosophy." He believed that an argument in a rational form concerning these or

11. Dru, *Journals of Søren Kierkegaard*, entry 962 (*Papirer* X1 A, 679). Suffice it to say that there are numerous entries in the papers for especially 1849 emphasizing this point.

An Introduction to the Problem 9

any other beliefs of ethical and existential import would bring persuasion only in virtue of the dialectician, the fashionableness of the view, the accidental fact of someone's cleverness—these and more, all of them essentially irrelevant to the argument at hand.

Instead of all this, one might invoke another and more limited conception of philosophy and the philosopher. Recent Anglo-American philosophy has perhaps prepared most readers in part at least for the kind of thing that Kierkegaard chooses to do in this respect. There is a technical-scientific conception of philosophy which has always existed and has been amply illustrated—especially in the history of Western philosophy. Because it has so frequently been written out within the compass of a more vernacular and vulgar conception of existence by the tough-minded, it has lost many readers. In the works of Spinoza, for example, it takes great patience and perspicuity to discover that he was a logician and epistemologist who, while he was summarizing beliefs on very important issues, was also concerning himself with the rules for articulating, for defining, and for conceptualizing many issues. The latter interests have only recently been separated sharply enough from the former to bring general awareness of this kind of inquiry. But the propriety of the complete separation as one sees it today among those who analyze without synthesizing, who make language the subject matter for philosophical scrutiny, is another and involved matter. The point is, however, that philosophers can and do provide a kind of knowledge, claiming to be true and therefore possibly false, about matters which are not directly of ethical or metaphysical significance. Much of modern philosophy, from Descartes to Hume and Kant and on to the contemporaries, is the criticism and analysis of knowledge and ethical claims and is for this reason called "critical" rather than "speculative." But even if there have been confusions created, perhaps by grammatical similarities which in turn have concealed logical and cognitive dissimilarities, this does not mean that the philosophers who discover these confusions do not speak the truth. It is in this sense that we shall discover Kierkegaard in fact to be a philosopher. In highly original and artistically pleasing ways, he did write about points of view that men might hold about nature, man, and God.

Kierkegaard is not an empiricist rather than a metaphysician, a critical philosopher rather than a speculative one. But like Socrates he found delight in sticking to a few elementary category questions. He found Pascal, Hume, Hamann, Kant, and Trendelenburg to his liking, especially to the extent that all of them were the critics of extravagant philosophy, the kind which offered God, immortality, and freedom within the system.[12]

Kierkegaard continues to write about the big issue of philosophy. But the mode in which he does it still puts enormous distance between himself and his readers. Kierkegaard secures his critical and detached vantage point by contriving pseudonymous authors to do the asserting for him. This very device both credits the passions as the source of the affirmations and philosophy as the formal study of such affirmations and their reasons and causes.

Earlier philosophers like Spinoza, Locke, Plato, and numerous others gave precedence to metaphysics as the body of doctrine about the ultimate nature of things. The principal interest was here because other disciplines, logic and dialectic for example, were instruments leading to metaphysical knowledge and ethics was the body of practical conclusions that could be drawn from it. In classical philosophy, except for the very few who were almost idiosyncratic in their detachment, there was no need to isolate the tools of intellectual construction, and therefore the critical analysis, although it takes place, seldom is given the status that it plays in modern philosophy, where under the rubrics of knowledge or the theory of knowledge, it is a separate discipline. Kierkegaard also conceals the latter kind of inquiry and therefore he is also so easily assumed to be another muddle-headed and somewhat eccentric philosopher. When there is no other way in which to describe a thinker's peculiarities, the history of philosophy always seems to offer antecedents. But that does not happen in this case. For Kierkegaard's concealment on these matters—or rather, his refusal to propound and elaborate his critical standpoint—was not

---

12. Søren Holm's *Historiefilosofi* is an able statement of Kierkegaard's relations (on a few points) to Kant and other philosophers. Note especially 7–20. Even though tangential to the issue talked about above, this book shows how much of traditional philosophy Kierkegaard got rid of. See also *Papirer*, especially vols. II–IV, and Dru's translations for the same year. The *Kierkegaard Commentary* by Croxall gives some clue to Kierkegaard's interest in Hamann. So too does James O'Flaherty's book on Hamann, *Unity and Langauge*.

the consequence of obtuseness. It was not the result either of the conviction that there were other domains of greater cognitive importance in comparison to which these latter were either derivative or trivial.

And on the other hand, if one attempts to turn Kierkegaard into a crypto-analyst, a philosopher of language, one also does him an injustice. He was much too complex to be described so easily. He was too many-sided to be the forerunner of any school or emphasis. Because he attacked the idea that the ends of thought (clarity, definiteness, precision) were, as such, the highest ends for human existence, he is at pains at once to oppose both the speculative and the metaphysical kind of reflection and on the other side what for him would have been among moderns an undue concern with the instruments rather than the substance. His own literature is a criticism of all objectivity, whatever its kind, that becomes of culminating importance, and with this he writes out a description in great detail of the subjectivity, the concerns, passions, interests, and enthusiasms which he believes are the essential expressions for personality. But at the same time he is not a romantic fulminating against reflection. In *Concluding Unscientific Postscript* his author Johannes Climacus writes:

> Only a very limited intelligence, or someone who cunningly wishes to guard himself against feeling impressed, could here assume that I am in this objection playing the role of a vandal, seeking to violate the sacred security of the precincts of science, and to have the cattle let loose; or that I am a lazarene, placing myself at the head of newspaper readers and balloting idlers, in order to rob the modest scholar of his lawful possessions, earned by the employment of his happy gifts in resigned toil. Verily, there are many, many, who possess more than I do in the realm of the mind; but there is no one who more proudly and gratefully believes that in this realm there prevails an eternal security of property rights, that the idlers remain outside. But when a generation *en masse* proposes to dabble in universal history; when demoralized by this, as one is by playing the lottery, it rejects the highest of human tasks; when speculative philosophy is no longer disinterested but creates a double confusion, first by overleaping the ethical, and then by proposing a world-historical something as the ethical task for the individuals—then it is due to science itself that something be said about it. No, all honor to the pursuits of science, and all honor to everyone who assists in driving

> the cattle away from the sacred precincts of scholarship. But the ethical is and remains the highest task for every human being. One may ask even of the devotee of science that he should acquire an ethical understanding of himself before he devotes himself to scholarship, and that he should continue to understand himself ethically while immersed in his labors. ... But when, on the other hand, a tumultuous scientist seeks to invade the sphere of the existential, and then proceeds to confuse the ethical, ... then he is as scientist no faithful lover, and science itself stands ready to deliver him up to a cosmic apprehension.[13]

While agreeing with most of the critics of metaphysical philosophy that the *a priori* cognitive certainties about matters of fact, and especially history, were quite impossible, Kierkegaard did not therewith leap to the other extreme of making philosophy scientific by limiting its subject matter to an analysis of cognitive form. As we shall indicate in later chapters, there is a high degree of competence displayed in incidental remarks, footnotes, and addenda to his other writings on these very issues but, nonetheless, his literature combines analytic powers with a synoptic grasp of fundamental beliefs. Philosophy is not therefore for Kierkegaard only the totaling of beliefs. Nor is it either the "truth," i.e., the true beliefs in contrast to the false ones. The conceptual and systematic language of reflection is used in his instance to state and analyze and complete the persuasive, the convictional, and the belief-ful languages describing the subjective and passional existing of persons. Thus, on the one side, he moves away from the attempted concreteness of traditional philosophy, a concreteness essayed through extending the powers of objectifying cognitive awareness to problems where cognition was not possible, to a formalistic and detached analysis.[14] But rather than staying there and gaining certainty by limiting the area and omitting all concreteness, Kierkegaard returns to the concrete again, this time to the life

---

13. *Postscript*, 135-36.

14. Already in 1835, as a young student, Kierkegaard had concluded that knowledge was not incremental and productive as other people said. Even if one possessed knowledge, one might not possess the idea for which one could live and die. Note here the letter addressed to P. W. Lund, June 1, 1835. This is included in *Breve og Aktstykker vedrørende Søren Kierkegaard*, I:32-36. Part of this letter is translated by Dru in *Journals*, entry 16.

of subjectivity. What contemporaries have only suggested by drawing distinctions, albeit insidiously between cognitive and emotive meaning, Kierkegaard long since has explored. One of his ablest philosophical critics has summarized his acuity on these matters thus:

> If I were to compress into a single word the intellectual significance of Kierkegaardian literature, I would say that it consisted in mapping out the sphere of the inner life, the subjective life of emotion, with constant reference to the ideal. And great as has been the energy devoted to reflection in the centuries past, wonderful as the productions of human thought have been, with reference to all the impersonal and objective problems—nature, logic, mathematics, metaphysics, history—it must be confessed that the inner life of the emotion has been comparatively unchartered sea. Herein lies Kierkegaard's originality, herein his permanent contribution to thought.[15]

III

Kierkegaard's chosen path in philosophical writing appears to be a kind of *via media*. He combines poetic and reflective talents. He refuses to exclude the passional components in order to achieve certainty. He was attracted by the scientists, the logicians, and mathematicians but still refused to submerge his poetic talents to the kind of extirpating discipline that their style of writing demanded. On the other hand, he decries making philosophy a declamation or a reading of tea leaves or the derivation of certainty from doubt.[16] He admits with his imagined critic that his literature is a combination of "a little irony, a little pathos, and a little dialectic." One need not, in his estimate, exclude one for the other if one has enough virtuosity. And furthermore he asks, "What else should anyone have who proposes to set forth the ethical?"[17]

Though Kierkegaard was a religious author from first to last as he repeatedly says, he refused to use his talents for a forthright apologetic for religious faith. To do so would have involved him in the same

---

15. Swenson, *Something about Kierkegaard*, 69.
16. *Postscript*, 137.
17. Ibid.

tissue of difficulties he had noted in the classical metaphysicians and theologians. His sympathies were stirred by David Hume whom he knew only cursorily and by Hamann whom he knew quite well. Both of these writers had encountered insuperable difficulties in the claims of theologians and the natural philosophers. God was not an object to be scrutinized nor did either theology or a natural philosophy provide proofs of his existence and/or a description of His nature. With a deftness that seems incommensurate with the conceptual tools at hand, Kierkegaard finds it necessary to completely rephrase the traditional problems too. Once this is done, and even though he writes a kind of religiously oriented literature, still what he says cannot be said to constitute a conceptual enrichment of anything metaphysical or transcendent. In fact he discovers both religious and logical reasons for delimiting cognitive claims and this is why he insists that his dialectic plays over "pathetic" (passional) matters. Kierkegaard again never flinches as he approaches the sharply defined limits he has set himself. Almost completely alone as he was in his day, he refused to adopt the conventional language and phrases, the adoptive formulae and circumlocutions, that would have given him an audience, but at the price of misunderstanding.[18]

The world is full of books about Kierkegaard and most of them report faithfully what he did and what he said. There is almost no end to the number of studies that tell you who said similar things and why and when. With the scholarly industry being what it is, one can expect more books in the same genre during the coming decade. Kierkegaard is still fair game in the world of scholarship. He wrote a great deal and he bears a lot of repeating. But, there is still the strange neutrality and dispassionateness about the man's writings that goes

---

18. Early in his life, Kierkegaard saw that the greater number of people were given what he calls their "categorical imperative" by their social context. Their propensities are directed, they are led by their surroundings, and they work in allotted paths. About these people Kierkegaard says that they "experience in life the real meaning of the Hegelian dialectic." The philosophers who document this story are metaphysicians—the historically oriented metaphysicians who see the dialectic moving in transempirical totalities, in time, and in history. Kierkegaard was like Johannes Climacus, for whom the dialectic (and logical rules) related one idea to another. He stood alone, trying not to be intimidated by the rhetoric and the grandeur of scope that others have commanded. Note Dru, *Journals*, entry 16 (*Papirer* I A, 72); see also *Breve*, I:32–36. See also the introduction to *Postscript*.

a-begging. Even with his profoundly religious and Christian writings, there is still a stylistic feature of them, and, in addition, a context of language and reflection that keeps the persuasiveness and propagandizing at a minimum. Kierkegaard supposes a nexus between his books, between himself as author and his books, and between his books and the reader, that he nowhere chooses to describe at great length. That he was aware of it, there can be no doubt. There is a dialectic governing his literature and the description of this dialectic is his formal philosophy.

Kierkegaard has no need of a public advocate. His own talent and abilities assure him his place. However, it must be said that many who praise him most misunderstand him.[19] He did not want readers who would become Christian in virtue of his authorship. In fact, the burden of the explanatory work, *The Point of View*, is just this, namely, that he cannot in virtue of his own understanding of himself, of the Christian faith, and of his authorship, constitute himself as a direct agent for the production of religiosity in another. The kind of publicity he gets nowadays, however, suggests that he failed. The public advocates are mistaken. Many of them, at worst, are fawning before a genius or, at best, are overly anxious to give honor where their debt is great. There is, though, another misunderstanding and this is rooted in the failure to read and to understand the man's authorship as the kind of work he wished it to be.

Kierkegaard believed in the validity of his writings and the correctness of his delineation. Furthermore, these can be discovered and understood apart from the acceptance or rejection of the Christian faith or, for that matter, anything else about which this author was mightily persuaded. There was and is an objective validity about the works that their author presupposed. That this was capable of refined description and minute structuralization also cannot be denied. Even the study and care that went into the various pseudonymous and aesthetic works (which often seem so logical, so rhapsodic as to be almost inspired and surely not argumentative or didactic) seems to indicate that the relations between each of them and their author were carefully considered. The papers again (especially section B of

---

19. Kierkegaard's repudiation of a disciple, Rasmus Nielsen, seems to me to be in consequence of the kind of misunderstanding evident in those who do not take seriously Kierkegaard's dialectical powers.

each volume) indicate the refinement of grasp and detailed dialectical considerations that went into the making of many books. We shall find that a structure is implicit in all of his writings and serves as a kind of wide context, albeit neutral and without passional importance, without which everything fits. Furthermore, such a context is directly described by the many remarks he makes about logical and epistemological matters, both in his public writings and his semi-private papers. And above all, if the literature is to have any consistency at all, such a referent for its various pieces is also necessary. More of this will be indicated in later chapters.

It is this set of philosophical components about which Kierkegaard said relatively little (for reasons that are explicit and will be noted again) that are most important to the interpretation of Kierkegaard's authorship. Few men have been motivated by such evangelical zeal as Kierkegaard. But being a reflective man and his medium being ideas, it would have been ridiculous for him to pen a literature, and a reflective literature, if all communication were "*Cor ad cor loquitur.*"[20] His literature was in one sense a direct communication from one person to another. The theory that describes the direct communication is a philosophical theory. This very theory enables the author to say that the direct communication is, however, not all there is to the matter at hand, for there is another kind of communication that Kierkegaard calls "indirect." Repeatedly in his authorship Kierkegaard draws attention to the fact that what his own literature communicates directly is not as significant as what it communicates indirectly. The Danish philosopher, for surely we ought to be prepared by now to call him that, knew that direct communication did in fact take place with the help of words, sentences, and obedience to reflective rules. He was interested in theories that told one how this came about.

But the irony of the Kierkegaardian literature is that it concerns all kinds of human interests, the passions and modes of subjectivity, none of which as subjective states are communicated by the language about them, even if that language is true. At this point Kierkegaard suggests a theory of indirect communication, which describes his own authorship and which is posited upon knowing the limits of

---

20. This expression gained its currency from John Henry Newman's wide use of it.

communication, the necessary logical structures upon speech, and in a broad sense, the rules of intellectual play.

This is the way then to indicate something of Kierkegaard's intellectual mastery. Without noting the care taken, both to describe his writings and to orient them, one might assume that they are nothing but extended rhapsodies or ingenious homilies. By noting this care and precision of reflection within which they are measured, one can see what is valid and hence really philosophical in Kierkegaard's authorship.

CHAPTER 2

A Glance at a Contemporary Effort in Danish Philosophy

THE TITLE OF THIS chapter is taken from an appendix in the middle of Kierkegaard's *Concluding Unscientific Postscript*. The first two hundred pages of that book are a discursive argument about a subject familiar to all kinds of intelligent people: "the objective problem concerning the truth of Christianity." The purported author, the pseudonymous Johannes Climacus, is a thirty-year-old student of philosophy. He is bristling with the latest learning. He is not a Christian, but he has an interest in the question of what it means to say that there is an "objective problem" concerning its truth. So, he writes, trying to isolate all the logical properties of "objective," "subjective," "truth," "logical system," "reality," anything in fact which will help him get at the issue to see whether the problem can be solved. But he meets up with all kinds of snags. Therefore, in the middle of the book, he concludes that the issues are altogether different than they have been posed.

The name "Johannes Climacus" comes from a Greek monk of the seventh century, author of *Scala Paradisi*.[1] Kierkegaard uses his name for his specifically philosophical works, suggesting the temptation to make a ladder of syllogisms by which to climb into heaven.[2] Some months before Kierkegaard wrote the *Philosophical Fragments* and the *Postscript* he had conceived a work to be called *Logical Problems* by this same Johannes. His papers also include a lengthy

---

1. Translated into English with the title, *The Ladder of Divine Ascent*.
2. Note the *Papirer*, especially II A, 335 and ff.

analysis of doubt by this author called *De Omnibus Dubitandum Est*.[3] This strange author is used to make the strongest case for an intellectualist interpretation of Christianity. But his construction falters. By considering the various arguments offered for saying that certain propositions of Christian literature are objectively true, the author sees several things: one, that the arguments are not compelling; two, that the problem is not one of evidence or of argument; and finally that the concept of truth at work here is the utterly wrong one. But to conclude this much, is to shake the foundations of the intellectual culture of his day. Johannes Climacus, being an underling and only thirty, hardly dares to face the consequences.

> What happens? Just as I sit there, out comes *Either/Or*. Here was realized precisely what I had proposed to myself to do. It made me feel quite unhappy to think of my solemn resolution, but then again I thought: you have at any rate not promised anyone anything, and, long as the work is done, all is well. But things went from bad to worse; for step by step, just as I was about to realize my resolve in action, out came a pseudonymous book which accomplished what I had intended.[4]

This is the contrived way that Kierkegaard sums up the inter-connections of his literature. When he glances at this literature, sprawling as it already is, he finds that it fits the purposes of a man interested in logical problems. In effect, the *Postscript* is an analytic piece, "dialectical" he calls it, on matters that are full of pathos. The literature which is already in hand is the subject matter within which his wrench from the grasp of the "objective problem," by which he gains freedom to see the issues differently, is finally perpetrated.

But now, before we get to some of the philosophical differences that are proposed, we, too, have to take a long glance at that literature. What is it? What is it about?

---

3. Translated by T. H. Croxall under the title, *Johannes Climacus, or, De Omnibus Dubitandum Est*. Note the discussion of these matters on 17–19.

4. *Postscript*, 225.

I

The tale stretches one's credulity. Beginning with *Either/Or* in two parts (published as two volumes in the English translation) in February, 1843, Kierkegaard published fifteen books within the ensuing three years. Some are very long, some very short; all are odd indeed. On February 27, 1846, the massive *Concluding Unscientific Postscript* was issued and this, the fifteenth, marks the completion of a phase of his literary productivity. After an interim piece, *The Literary Review* (March, 1846), the flow begins again. In March of 1847 comes *The Edifying Discourses in Various Spirits* (translated in English in two volumes as *Purity of Heart* and *The Gospel of Suffering*), and this is the first of another spate of fifteen volumes. Two of these, *The Point of View* and *Judge for Yourself*, were printed posthumously by a brother, Peder Kierkegaard, in 1859 and 1876 respectively. Besides the formal books, a voluminous journal was accumulating these very days, several other works were projected and even outlined, and one, a long book, *The Book about Adler*, was several times recast, then never published.[5]

If we cast this account in chronological terms, we discover that this literature is published from his thirtieth year (he was born in 1813) through his thirty-eighth year. When we remember that his desultory university education began in 1830, that his now notorious engagement to Regine was terminated in October, 1841, that his dissertation *On the Concept of Irony* was submitted in September of the same year and marks the end of his university life, then we can very readily understand how single-minded and concentrated his literary effort was. From the '40s and on, Kierkegaard's authorship is the story of his life, and it is little wonder that he conjectured about what more there was for him to do after it was completed.[6] The interesting aspect of this productivity is that it had a beginning and an end. A goal was anticipated and every effort was made to fulfill it. The details were not anticipated, this Kierkegaard himself admits; and sometimes the complexities were perhaps a little too great for the readers; this too the author admits. Nevertheless, the authorship was completed be-

---

5. It was edited from several versions and published in English translation by Walter Lowrie as *On Authority and Revelation*.

6. *Papirer* VII 1 A, 4 (*JP* 5, 5873), after the first surge was over, and again in 1850 in the many reflections. See also "Concerning Myself," *Papirer* X A.

fore his life was, and this alone distinguishes Kierkegaard from most authors. Furthermore, when the works were completed, he stopped writing and not because of senility or a cessation of creative energies. He resolved to stop, and did.

Therefore, it seems plausible that his volumes do not describe a fundamental development in the thought of their author; instead, they can be best understood as a single work in many chapters. Like most books, not every detail was anticipated, but the main drift certainly was. There are some changes of emphasis here and there, but taken in the light of the argument from first to last, they are relatively minor. Even the attack upon the established church of Denmark in 1855, coming as it did after a literary pause of many months, is not as detached from the rest of the literature as is commonly held. Except for its extravagant style and intentional re-iteration of small points, these pamphlets and articles are an application and use of concepts and arguments developed in earlier writings. These writings, now published conveniently in several languages in a single volume, are sharply polemical. They were published originally from December, 1854, to November, 1855, and addressed the illusions Kierkegaard believed fostered by the popularization of Christianity by the national church of Denmark. They are the addenda to the previous authorship, and are addressed to a more popular audience than are the earlier pieces.

II

There are several themes binding this literature together. A delicate plot in all of it begins to emerge as one examines carefully its content. Admitting "the ambiguity or duplicity in the whole authorship,"[7] Kierkegaard several times made a kind of public attestation to orient his readers.[8] His *Point of View for My Work as an Author* is neither a defense nor an apology. "This is not an instance of the common case," he says, "where the assumed duplicity is discovered by some one else and the person concerned is obliged to prove that it 'does not exist.'"[9]

---

7. *Point of View*, 10.

8. Ibid., 6. See also *Papirer*, entries for 1845–1846. Some of these are translated in Dru, *Journals*, 536, 600, 621, 644, etc.

9. Ibid., 10.

The ambiguity is intentional and overarches the several works and is something the author knows more about than anybody else. Why does he say there is a duplicity at all?

For one thing, it is not apparent, to some astute readers like Ernst Cassirer, that, for example, the author was actually a religious man.[10] The early books are aesthetic and eudaemonistic and rhapsodic. Even where they concern Christianity, as in the *Philosophical Fragments* and the *Postscript*, it is quite clear that one need not be a Christian or even religious either to write or read such volumes. The tone is a little ironic and the author is detached and a little casual. The shifting moods and vacillation of emphasis between points of view seem too explanatory and casual for religious commitment. Besides, the "Diary of the Seducer" in *Either/Or*, and the passion narrative, "Guilty or Not Guilty," in the *Stages on Life's Way* plus numerous other sections seem terribly this-worldly.

One can easily surmise that Kierkegaard was disappointed that the reading public grasped, as he said, with their left hand what he held in his right hand, and with their right what he held in his left.[11] For, it is actually the case that he was the author of two sets of writings, one in each hand. One was the brilliant and highly contrived "aesthetic productivity," which includes *Either/Or, Fear and Trembling, Stages on Life's Way*, and several more and, the other, a set of twenty-one "edifying" discourses published in seven short volumes. The first group was published pseudonymously, the second was acknowledged on each

---

10. Ernst Cassirer insisted that Kierkegaard was an unbeliever and that the early non-religious writings revealed the true man. The later Christian writings, he believed, were in consequence of a failure of nerve and a sense of filial duty. Walter Rehm argues that Kierkegaard was a seducer and, further, that he was not a believer, but was self-seduced. His literature is contrived, according to Rehm, but to the end that he dupes himself and others. Note his *Kierkegaard und der Verführer*, especially "Die Moglichkeit der Selbstverführung," 452–512. For critical comments on the same, see the reviews by the author in *Philosophy and Phenomenological Research* 12 (1951–52), 307–11, and *Philosophical Review* 61 (1952), 270–73. Note also the responses of Kierkegaard to the periodical literature about his books. These unfortunately can be read only in Danish: *Papirer* VII 1 A, 4 (*JP* 5, 5873; *KJN* 2, JJ: 415) and VII 1 B, 135 (*JP* 5, 5869) and several articles in periodicals of 1845–46 (note details in "Tidstavle," *Papirer* X, ix–xxv). Another author, Giovanni Papini, once said: "Kierkegaard was a terrible man. He attacked Christianity and all Christian and civil virtues." Papini is quoted to this effect by Walter Lowrie, who reported a conversation with him in a letter to Professor David F. Swenson.

11. *Point of View*, 20.

A Glance at a Contemporary Effort in Danish Philosophy

of the title pages to be by Kierkegaard. The public, buying neither group very eagerly (from 1843 to 1846), still paid the pseudonymous writings more serious attention than the "Edifying Discourses" and hence Kierkegaard's charge that they had been fooled in ways even he had not intended.

> Although *Either/Or* attracted all the attention, and nobody noticed the *Two Edifying Discourses*, this book betokened, nevertheless, that the edifying was precisely what must come to the fore, that the author was a religious author, who for this reason has never written anything aesthetic, but has employed pseudonyms for all the aesthetic works, whereas the *Two EdifyingDiscourses* were by Magister Kierkegaard.[12]

He offered the discourses with his left hand, hoping they would be taken by the public with the right hand, i.e., with enthusiasm, but this the public did not do. Therefore Kierkegaard wrote out an explanation of sorts which gives the author's point of view on the authorship. The literature has a religious orientation even where this is not apparent—"the religious is present from the beginning," he says, and cites as evidence the small discourses published under the author's name.[13] Furthermore, the religious does not succeed the aesthetic as old age succeeds youth. For that view (plausible only if one forgets the rapidity of composition) could only be inferred if the later, exclusively religious writings, from 1847 to 1851, were in consequence of an author having changed and become a religious author. But, this is false; almost to defy his interpreters and right in the middle of his most severely religious writing, he wrote another aesthetic article, "The Crisis and a Crisis in the Life of an Actress." Therefore, he argues, the early works hid the religious orientation and the later exclusively religious works hid the aesthetic and eudaemonistic factors. The author admits to this complexity and says repeatedly that, despite the appearances,

---

12. Ibid., 12.

13. Ibid. One cannot help remarking here on the very full evidence the incidental literature about and by Kierkegaard provides for this thesis. The *Papirer*, vols. I–II are most eloquent about Kierkegaard's early religious interests, and vols. IV–V show us how he conceived the religious and aesthetic works as parallel aspects of his work as they were being written.

he was a religious author from the beginning and was aesthetically productive to the last.[14]

But is this to say that the aim of the literature is only to gain religious allegiance? Is he trying to persuade? Actually he is not. His point is much more subtle. He writes his words about his religious aim with full candor and no apology. But some people might conclude from either of two thoughts about an author that he is not worth reading any further. If a man says that he is writing with religious purpose, one might assume that the outcome is predictable and cease reading; if a man says he is writing a literature for a laugh, for fun, for its own sake, one might decline another frivolity. Kierkegaard's point in saying these things about himself was, indeed, to admit both; but in saying that, his attack was directed upon other matters. Why the simple view—if not this, then that? If not objective truth, then subjective rantings; if not religious seriousness, then only enjoyment; if enjoyment, then no seriousness?

He is attacking the ground-plan of the current discussion. By changing the terms of discussion, his whole business looks odd. The pseudonyms and their purple passages made some wonder if this were not more romantic effusions. The inclusion of religious themes looked like an afterthought or a sign of psychological decay. When a radical move is made like that of Kierkegaard's a lot of explaining is in order. And he began it himself, rather than leaving it to the critics.

III

But, does all this say anything about Kierkegaard, the thinker? Might it not be, as Hirsch, Rehm, Lowrie and others have suggested, exclusively a feature of the writer's psychological quirks and a gratuitous style? I think not. What has here been said suggests also that there are a number of convictions, arguments and intentions, disposing this diffuse appearing literature. There were reasons for this literature which were not stylistic reasons. To say it in another fashion, there were conclusions about the limits of argument, how to communicate, how to understand certain things that were the reasons for his stylistic novelties and the very shape of his authorship which was so strik-

---

14. *Point of View*, 13.

ingly original. In deploying his reflection on all kinds of philosophical issues, Kierkegaard very early decided that he could not be "rational" and "objective" as the rest were. He quarrels with the paradigms here. For to be "rational" meant in his day to perceive the universal order of things, an intelligible plan of all existence. To fathom the regularities of the world plan and know one's place in it seemed the only philosophical and "objective" thing to do. Kierkegaard decided to protest and a literature with multiple themes, with co-existing dynamic factors within it, became a fitting blast to the systematic pretensions.

His miscellaneous appearing literature is not promiscuous and wanton. On the other hand, it is not, therefore, precise either. What is happening is that the literature in a variety of ways presents cases that make one doubt that the concept "objective truth," for example, is a particularly useful expression with which to handle ethical and religious difficulties. But no doctrinal deliverance will do this for the author; instead he cajoles the reader into doing this as he reads along. The literature involves one more and more. It starts rather wide and narrows the range of issues until one gets to the *Fragments* and *Postscript* where the philosophic pseudonym takes over. By then, the distinction between "objective" and "subjective," drawn Kierkegaard believed initially in logical and epistemological discourse, begins to seem inappropriate when invoked in the context of religious and moral discourse. What happens in the literature is that Johannes Climacus, who is feeling uneasy about many philosophic matters anyway, looks around for some literature by which to state his case; and it is already there in the early literature. The trouble seems to be that "objective" and "subjective," when used to distinguish across all kinds of literature, all kinds of problems, concerns and issues, are misleading. Then "objective" belongs with "true," "correct," and "real," and "subjective" belongs with "false," "invalid," "unreal," and the "passions."

Kierkegaard shakes up these constellations. For by providing a literature that contains literary criticism, lyrical effusions, a diary of a seducer, some austere moralizing about marriage, and a host of religious discourses, it becomes quite clear that there are very few common canons. There are many common words, but few common concepts, common distinctions, common "major words." Kierkegaard, therefore, uses the literature to show that "subjective" and "subjectivity" are linked with "truth" (not in logic or contexts where we talk science) in expressions like "I am the truth" or "the truth shall make you free," where nothing scholarly or intellectual is being proposed at all. He puts "true" together with "passion," and even says that there are times and social contexts where "objective" and "being objective" simply ought not to have any status at all. Instead of being unequivocally recommended, he shows that there are places where "being objective" is a fault. But this means that the ways of thinking and talking about "objective" and "subjective" have to be loosened up considerably.

This is what he means by "another movement of reflection" in his literature. Perhaps he has overstressed the decisiveness of this just a little and perhaps, too, he has underestimated the overtness and clarity of this "deeper reason," as he calls it. As one begins to read *Either/Or* and *Fear and Trembling* and *Repetition*, all published in 1843, one discovers several points of view. Instead of the picture of one's thought moving from the disparate facts to a generalization, and from one generalization to a still higher one which explains the first, and so on until the ultimate explanatory generalization, Kierkegaard pictures the life of reason as various ways to be "reasonable," all kinds of options or alternatives, not hierarchically ordered, but co-equally arraigned. Instead of "reasoning" one to find his place on the moving stair that human history is supposed to be, several other kinds of orientation are depicted. *Either/Or*, as the title suggests, presents two strikingly different attitudes toward the problem of existing. The first volume discloses the variety and richness of enjoyment views of life. If immediate and proximate satisfactions are the "*telos*," then luck, health, talent, opportunity, and one's environment will be the big terms, all expressions related to the conditions for achieving the maximal amount of pleasure.[15] Kierkegaard's depiction of the eudaemonistic lives—and they are many in style, intensity, and quality—corrects the chaste and over-systematic understanding of it that one finds in the utilitarian-hedonistic ethical literature. It is a favorite sport of undergraduates to criticize John Stuart Mill's inconsistencies, especially his identification of pleasure with happiness, and then pleasure with the good. Kierkegaard's pseudonyms know well that "duty"

---

15. Prof. Reidar Thomte's *Kierkegaard's Psychology of Religion* is excellent on the "aesthetic stage." See 16–38.

is incommensurate with immediate satisfactions, for it brings a reflective non-mediated concept and judgment to bear and thus shifts the whole argument to another area; so they will have nothing of obligation. Likewise, they decline to legislate between the pleasures. Thus, one of them is sensual, while another is an intellectual who loves the idea of a girl rather than the girl; some aesthetes practice an insinuating irony and secure advantages over others by invoking their talents to the other man's disadvantage. Some rejoice in moods, some in their health, some in their freedom. If one can be so bold as to speak for Kierkegaard, it would seem to be true that the aesthetic mode of life is variegated, is casual, is an expression of wish and will and feeling, untrammeled by a sense of duty by obligation, or by anything mediated by others. The concepts involved here are rather loose and ill-fitting. "Duty" and "obligation" are not important, and, if they are used, seem to be borrowed from another medium.

But the second half of *Either/Or* presents a contrasting view. This is written out ostensibly by a judge who stands, self-consciously in view of his legal profession, in a great social and historical continuity. Also, in virtue of what he calls his ethical view of life, he is most earnest about defining all of his concerns with the help of homogenous concepts. In two long letters, somewhat prolix, and a sermon by a country pastor which he encloses with one of the letters, he addresses an unnamed aesthete, apparently one of those whose attitudes and deeds are disclosed in volume one. Here again Kierkegaard's acuity as a philosophical thinker is most marked. He writes out an ethical view somewhat similar to Kant's. The judge is duty-conscious. Duty is defined in non-personal, yet inter-subjective terms. But unlike Kant's account, this volume does not develop a conception of a metaphysical and universalized reason which obligates each human being in turn. The matter is described instead from the point of view of a learned man, not a professional philosopher, who by resolution and reflection formulates a concept of duty so that it construes daily tasks in communicable and universal terms. By definition and resolve, the duty becomes universal. Part of the romance of the judge's ethical view of life lies in improving the thought and the deed so that they do in fact become describable by these homogenous *entre nous* concepts. Kants' metaphysical formalism thus stands corrected.

Another interesting correction of Kant's views is proposed by the Judge-ethicist who writes the second volume of *Either/Or*. Ruminating about the disastrous attitude now evident toward "duty," as if it were always a heavy burden, invariably contrary to inclination and a damper upon the common joys, he says:

> In opposition to an aesthetic view of life which seeks to enjoy it, one often hears of another view which places the significance of life in living for the fulfillment of its duties. With this a man wishes to designate an ethical view of life. But, the expression is very imperfect, and one might almost think that it were invented to discredit the ethical. In any case, in our time one sees it so used that one is prone to smile, when, for example, Scribe permits this sentence to be expressed with a low-comedy seriousness, contrasting very unfavorably with the gladness and merriment of pleasure. The fault is that the individual is placed in an external relation to duty. The ethical is defined as duty, and duty is defined as a manifold of particular sentences; but the individual and duty are independent of one another.[16]

Against this, Kierkegaard's judge proposes another way of getting at "duty" altogether. For here there is an attack upon the view that there are concepts or universals that can be looked at with some kind of philosophical vision. Congruent with the whole literature, there is no attempt to say that the meaning of duty is laid up in the evolution of the concept, almost as if it were an object open only to thought that is other-worldly and visionary. Instead, Kierkegaard's authors are dialectical in another way. They unscramble their concepts in the welter of language and behavior. And the judge contends that Kant's notion of duty is artificial and contrived, and hence that it does not possess the authority and power that it should have. It is alien to the kind of life where he wanted to use it. Again and again, Kierkegaard has noted how Kant invests words with meanings out of logical and other more purely intellectual interests and then misapplies them to ethical matters.

---

16. *Enten-Eller, Samlede Vaerker*, vol. II, 228, translation my own. See *Either/Or*, vol. II, 212–13.

Is the philosopher then only an inductive thinker? Is this what the materials, the examples, are for? Apparently not. Kierkegaard's authors try to show the incongruities in an example. So here with "duty."

> It is odd, indeed, that a man with the word "duty" can come to think about a relation outward, for the very derivation of that word ["*pligt*"] indicates a relation inward; for that which is incumbent upon me . . . surely stands in the most inward relation to myself. Duty is, thus, not an imposition ["*paalaeg*," i.e., "laid upon"], but something which is incumbent ["*paarligger*," i.e., "lying within"].[17]

Therefore, the word "duty" is misused when it is related to eternal things like laws, "a manifold of particular definitions," metaphysical realities, and even a transcendent God. The point seems to be not to psychologize the meaning of "duty" either, but rather to bring it into a different company. It is homogenous with pleasures and pains, wishes and inclinations, and it grows up, is incumbent, in the life-history of serious people. Kierkegaard is much inclined to take the pathos and mystique out of "duty" by showing how it, in fact, arises. It emerges in certain kinds of experiences that people have had over and over. It does not call for an array of external things like hidden imperatives always categorical, a law for all natural things, or the will of God.

Therefore, Kant's analysis which linked "duty" with "rationality" and meant by that a kind of formal rule is seriously disputed. Kierkegaard discovers that the concept of duty has no antecedent rational structure, no intelligible world, of which it is an expression. Kierkegaard is very far from worrying about the general question— and the emphasis here is upon the general question, not specific instances—whether concepts had "objective reality." This concern of Kant's, which pervades the *Critique of Pure Reason*, also extends to his second critique on ethics. Instead of worrying whether the significance of the concept of duty could be maintained without positing the objective existence of either an intelligible world or some fictional *entia rationalis*, Kierkegaard boldly evinces what the concept of duty is and does. He finds the concept of duty a necessary one for ethical reflection and behavior, but he does not go on to insist that there is, therefore, a state of affairs which it names or signifies.

17. *Samlede Vaerker*, vol. II, 228. *Either/Or*, vol. II, 213.

However, the major point here is the clue this content gives to the literature and its structure. Two views of life, we have said, are thus presented in the first pseudonymous work. *Fear and Trembling* and *Repetition* bring us to a third, the religious. The former is one of the most ingenious and thoughtful books that Kierkegaard ever wrote. He commented about it often later. One entry in his journal reads:

> Oh, once I am dead—*Fear and Trembling* alone will be enough to immortalize my name. It will be read, and translated into foreign languages. People will shudder at the terrible pathos which the book contains. But when it was written, when the man who was looked upon as the author went about incognito, as a *flaneur* and appeared to be lively and frivolous, wit itself: nobody could grasp its true seriousness. Oh, you fools, never was a book more serious than at that moment.[18]

But the religious position here was again described from the outside. Another pseudonym, Johannes de Silentio, is the author. The description it offers of the faith of Abraham cites aspects of both Jewish and Christian faith almost invariably neglected by other commentators. The possibility of a conflict between duty and the religious command is explored, and the fact that the ethical is in the nature of a commanding and disciplining principle over the raw material of human nature is designated as more typically an issue to be encountered within an ethical consciousness rather than the religious. Already, Kierkegaard's literature defines the religious more loftily, and it presupposes more pathos and earnestness of believers than most of the popular religion of the land does.

Philosophical Fragments (1844), *The Concept of Dread* (1844), and *Concluding Unscientific Postscript* (1846) all push the analyses of the ethical and religious ways of life even further. *Stages on Life's Way* (1845) is a lengthy recapitulation of the earlier points of view, albeit from somewhat different angles. All of these are again pseudonymous. The *Fragments* and *Postscript* and *The Concept of Dread* are all written disinterestedly too. Here the authors are not themselves religious though they write easily about religious issues. More detail shall be noted later, but at this point it is important to mark that the pseud-

---

18. Dru, *Journals*, 965 (*Papirer* X2 A, 15).

onymous literature begins at a point furthest from Kierkegaard's own and moves toward one which is his own This is why he pointed out that "the *Concluding Postscript* is not an aesthetic work, but neither is it in the strictest sense religious. Hence it is by a pseudonym, though I add my name as editor—a thing I did not do in the case of any purely aesthetic work."[19]

In summary, then, we must remember that there are seven major volumes in the pseudonymic series: *Either/Or, Fear and Trembling, Repetition, The Concept of Dread, Philosophical Fragments, Concluding Unscientific Postscript*, and *Stages on Life's Way*. There is a movement from the aesthetic, through the ethical (and tragic-comic, and ironic) and into the religious views of life. But simultaneously, the reader has had no issues resolved for him. No one view of life is said to be more plausible than any other. If one's thought moves, it moves through the literature's phases and this is the movement Kierkegaard called teleological; however, one's thought does not move from premises to conclusions, for there are no conclusions.

If one asks why there are no conclusions, the answer is simply that ethical and religious issues are not the kind of issues which permit premises and conclusions, or that according to Kierkegaard's understanding of the matter, it is a serious mistake to treat these matters in this manner. There is, indeed, plenty to think about, but the model of thought is not the sciences, neither is it history or logic. The appropriate way to reflect here, and indeed the only rational and fitting way, is to follow the "movement" of reflection which he proposes. This is how, then, he disparages the issue of "the objective truth" of religion and ethics. His point is that the logic of the discussion is wrong.

Kierkegaard is certainly not far at this point from certain philosophers of the twentieth century. But what distinguishes him so decidedly is the acuity and thoroughness with which he does his job on the particular issues of religion and ethics. Furthermore, there is a depth of psychological insight and originality which marks him off not as a follower but as an original genius.

Kierkegaard is certainly a child of his time. He was thoroughly immersed in that kind of philosophical literature called idealism. But he was also engaged in fighting his way out, step by step. He

---

19. *Point of View*, 13.

did not succeed on every count either, but his effort is perfectible if not perfect. If we cast up the account of the literature thus far, we can see why he said he was a poet-dialectician. For he was a poet in so far as he invented this enormous range of figures, views, and attitudes. Almost like a novel of Dostoevsky or Thomas Mann these pseudonyms espouse, analyze, expostulate, and express in emotional terms the major options open to a man. Unlike Hegel who also had an interest in views of life but construed them "dialectically" (and "dialectically" here meant seeing them in a relation of thesis, antithesis, and synthesis, a gradual unfolding, a kind of cultural evolving, etc.), Kierkegaard simply presented the alternatives. And then he develops a smaller more circumspect understanding of what it means to be "dialectical." For what he does *qua* philosopher is show that the concepts are all tangled up together and that they need to be separated. When separated, they can be more closely identified, compared, and contrasted. Furthermore their authority and power in our discourse can be ascertained and stated. This is what being dialectical means to him. But he is dialectical upon the material his literature provides. This is why the glance at the contemporary effort which he makes in the *Postscript* is so long. If we forget for the moment the pseudonymic apparatus and remember that Kierkegaard wrote all of it, we can see how important the range of materials is to him as a philosopher. No proofs or axioms, no conclusions are presented in all of it, but there is an incessant creativity that keeps turning up piece after piece, plus an insinuating doubt that penetrates into all of the logical values everywhere involved.

That there is an argument presented by the literature as a whole is also true. But it is an argument against something in a typically philosophical manner. For Kierkegaard thought that there was a distinctive philosophical way to argue, but this way was not modeled after logical patterns, science, history, or mathematics. But how the argument emerges will be discussed in our next chapter.

Right now, it will be appropriate to look at the other groups of literature.

IV

For our purposes, it would be helpful to consider all of the distinctively religious literature here in contrast to the kind that was called aesthetic, ethical and philosophical. For the picture thus far, presented by *Either/Or*, *Fear and Trembling*, *Repetition*, *Stages on Life's Way*, *The Concept of Dread*, *Philosophical Fragments*, and then *The Postscript*, is of a variety of expressive literatures all brought together by rambling disquisition interlaced with exacting analyses. The tragic hero is studied over against Abraham, to show that they are too different to be described together by any of Hegel's concepts of faith or belief. "Don Juan" in Byron's literature is not another example of the same thing in Mozart's opera; the common name fools people into a premature aesthetic wisdom, as if there are large similitudes gradually disclosing themselves in the creative writers.

Socrates' "teaching" is not the same as Christ's "teaching," as everyone knows; but the *Fragments* makes the point that "disciple," "passion," "truth," "occasion," and "learning," when used in these two contexts only fool a person into thinking that the same words have the same meanings. Here his dialectical talent, of which he was justly proud, causes him to distinguish where others have put things together.

Religious matters are dealt with thus far, but always from without. The concepts and events, feelings and behavior, are talked about in comparison to, and in contrast with, other phenomena. Kierkegaard's religious literature, all of it (with small exceptions to be noted later) written in his own name, remedies this situation. For in order to do justice to religion and its intellectual components, he thought that it was necessary to draw out something of the intellectual shape from within. Contrary to the spirit of his day, Kierkegaard did not believe that religion, or for that matter, the ethical and the aesthetical views which he had described, developed according to a necessary process. Neither was there a common logic or frame for all of them.

But there was a difficulty. As soon as Kierkegaard began to piece out the intrinsic fabric of religion, the net of concepts that one can call a logic, he discovered that religion divided into two large constellations. On the one side was a milder religion, he called it "immanental," in which the concepts were ethical-like, where the meanings seemed rooted in a way of life not explicitly dependent upon the figure of Jesus or other related extraordinary phenomena, God, miracles, or providence. Here everything necessary, everything edifying, was already at hand. This kind of religion Kierkegaard explores in his seven brief volumes of edifying discourses, which we have already noted for the years 1843–1846.[20] Here the same tenacious analysis goes on, not so much for the philosopher's curiosity and to resolve philosophical problems as it was for purposes of clearing up the confusions for the religious individual and stirring up his lagging enthusiasm. Granted the kind of reader that Kierkegaard had in mind, the former loomed large as the condition for the latter; for he was writing again for "his reader," a person who, because he was intelligent, was also likely, if confused, to be confused intellectually.

This literature, non-pseudonymic, was in his right hand. But the public was more interested in *Either/Or*. It was so popular that a second edition of it was needed by late 1846.[21] This was before Kierkegaard had had a chance to declare how things stood with his literature. Perhaps it was this unexpected response that made Kierkegaard see that the literature was a little too contrived to make clear all that he wanted it to do. In any case, he, thereafter, began writing a kind of guide to the literature, and his journal entries are particularly full for this period on "the plan" for the authorship.

These early discourses are mild in tone, non-authoritative, exploratory rather than declaratory and they delineate a religiosity that seems implicit in a lot of people. Strictly speaking, they are not as much exegetical of Biblical texts as they are of tender human beings, prone to a natural religion.[22] The intellectual side of this, taxing for

---

20. Published, except for the last three, as *Edifying Discourses*.

21. Note the letters about *Either/Or* by Kierkegaard to his good friend, Emil Boesen, January and February, 1842. Both suggest philosophical significance to it but also give reasons for considering religious factors too. Later, Kierkegaard believed that the total literature, religious and otherwise, had to be considered together. Note the letter to his brother, Peder (March 19, 1846). Meanwhile, negotiations for the second edition of *Either/Or* went on in 1847. Details can be read in Brandt and Rammel, *Søren Kierkegaard og pengene*, 41ff., and in *Breve og Aktstykker*, vol. I, 93–98, 104–7, 175–77 for letters, and vol. II for commentary on the same, by Niels Thulstrup.

22. Note the interesting comments upon these matters in the *Postscript*, 241ff., and also in the last pages, 520–44.

the philosophical wit of Johannes Climacus, is also exploited in the pages of the *Postscript*.

There an analysis is done upon Religion A and Religion B, immanental mild religion (something like Kant's religion within the "limits" of reason and also expressed in the *Edifying Discourses* already alluded to) and transcendental Christianity. The upshot in the *Postscript* is a neutral description of the differing concepts indigenous to each.

But Kierkegaard was not done. He wanted, principally in order to serve his task of reintroducing Christianity into Christendom, also to expound Christianity in a first-person manner, just as he had done the first-person declaring of several other views. Thus his later religious works have a decidedly different character. They include *Edifying Discourses in Various Spirits*, *Works of Love*, and *Christian Discourses*. Here all the vigor and demand of a highly developed Christian mind, fully aware of the otherworldly categories of the New Testament, are brought to bear upon sundry topics. It is well to remember that a deft study of the problems of being an actress, a purely aesthetic piece again, was also written during this period. Kierkegaard thought that the public would be a little shocked that so mundane a piece could come forth amid such religiosity. But his readers actually had not gotten very much of it straight as yet. Even the Queen of Denmark, after surprising Kierkegaard and the King at a meeting in Sorgenfri Castle, embarrassed both of them by trying to make an impression and repeating an error of the day, saying that she had read "*Either and Or*" (*Enten og Eller*). She was reportedly excused from the conversation with a wave of the hand.

The careful reader of these later writings does not need this interim piece on the actress anyway to convince him that Kierkegaard still commanded the same aesthetic capacities as earlier. The various moods in which he writes, for example, the *Edifying Discourses in Various Spirits*, are ample indication that the aesthetic and the ethical and the religious were still components within the author and surely not completely absent from the literature either.

The last group of writings, *The Sickness Unto Death*, *Training in Christianity*, *For Self-Examination*, and *Judge for Yourselves* (1849–1851), were written a little later and were not accounted for by their author in his most lengthy explanation, *The Point of View*. These were also published pseudonymously but for a different purpose: "All the earlier pseudonyms are lower than the 'edifying author'; the new pseudonym represents a higher pseudonymity."[23] Kierkegaard does not wish to impute as much religious perfection to himself as the lofty ideality of these works presupposes. He says specifically that his "anti-Climacus" pseudonym is so high that "he" stands condemned by his own creation "because my life does not correspond to so lofty a claim."[24] This somewhat histrionic way of speaking about the literature perhaps blurs a bit the plain fact that these writings make explicit, more explicit even than the writings of 1847–1848, the ethical and pragmatic significance of the Christian faith. These writings are among the most discerning discussions of the relations between Christianity and a host of ethical matters.[25] These books, though more hortatory in parts, lack nothing of the finesse and the sheer virtuosity of the earlier literature. But, throughout they are concentrated upon Christianity and all that being a Christian involves.

The rich diversity of mood, feeling, judgment and evaluation are again laid out in this later literature. Another fifteen books, long and short, are written during this four-year period. Countless analyses of relevant arguments and notions are to be found in each, thus showing what the subject matter is for logical problems. Again the aim is to help clear up the conceptual confusions that have accrued, not to further formalize them. In later chapters, some of these will be isolated for special attention. But now it is time to suggest that the purpose served by the entire literature, seeing it as a movement from the aesthetic, through the ethical and into the religious must also be assessed. This is the task of the next chapter.

---

23. "On My Work as an Author," in *Point of View*, 146.

24. Ibid.

25. Note the discussion by the author of special ethical matters and a selection of the appropriate texts in "Søren Kierkegaard," in Beach and Niebuhr, *Christian Ethics*, 414–44.

CHAPTER 3

A New Way of Philosophizing

THIS CHAPTER IS NOT just one more introduction to the life and writings of Kierkegaard. Though a little will have to be said about these, our interest here will be focused primarily upon the authorship as it stands. We want to know something about the logical geography of the literature, and therefore a kind of mapping of it will be attempted. There are at least two ways to do this. One can understand what the literature covers and what literature it aims to replace. Here one must know what the books are and what they do in the literature (for they were written almost as thirty-odd chapters of a very long book). But the other way is to map it by seeing how adequate the descriptions and the prescriptions are to the things and tasks. This we will do subsequently.

An odd feature of Kierkegaard's work already noted is the somewhat miscellaneous character of it. It includes a lot of things, including a couple of diaries, odd analyses of the Abraham and Isaac story, "fragments," "stages," and an "either-or," plus serious logical analyses, irony, pathos, wit, and humor. Is it a jumble? Is it symptomatic of a disordered mind? When one adds pseudonyms to all the other literary devices, it looks like anything but serious philosophy or even ponderous theology. Yet about all of it, Kierkegaard said that it was "his literature," and he said that it fulfilled a plan, advanced an argument, and made a very serious case for a radical restoration of our thinking.

Our aim in this chapter is to see the subtle ways in which Kierkegaard uses what he calls "his literature," stretching from *Either/Or* through the later religious writings of 1850, to correct major faults in the reflection of his day. For Kierkegaard found in his day a certain homogeneity of concepts and words, at least among the educated classes, that was intellectually impressive but also falsifying of the issues involved. The technical philosophers were largely German in origin and were replete with the vocabulary of Kant, Hegel, and other idealistic thinkers. Philosophy was bold, speculative, powerful, and a major force in the cultural life. Even popular education reflected the effect of Hegel's well-organized system. More than this, popular aesthetics and literary criticism traded upon the philosophical rubrics, and so did the moralists, both popular and technical. Kierkegaard's cultural circle was philosophically saturated.

When one sketches in the details about the theology of that day, the homogeneity becomes almost overpowering. For theologians could scarcely resist making Christianity into something exquisitely metaphysical, especially when historical studies and dispositions well fed on the natural sciences were beginning to make light of miracles, of divine causes and providential orderings. Besides, the reign of philosophy extended so far as to provide the frame of concepts within which empirical science was done, in addition to being understood and subsequently taught. Most of the cultural energies seemed to be not only documented but also forecast by a philosophical scheme. General as it was and tolerant of all kinds of opposition, that philosophy became the climate of opinion within which programs were projected, political policies evaluated, education measured and perpetrated. Even religion was so prefigured.

When Kierkegaard began to be troubled about a number of typical youthful problems—is orthodox theology true? ought he to be a teacher, priest, or writer and why? what ought he to live for? what is good and what is evil?—it became clear to him almost immediately that these several problems blurred into one another. They became then as they are now to most people "philosophical." For obscure reasons, they all seemed to involve each other. And why not, if reality were a system and if philosophy where also the system of reality? For this is what he imbibed as a sensitive young man struggling with his peers through the curriculum of the University of Copenhagen. Even the literary circles he frequented, the pastors he heard, and the popular literature of the day strengthened this outlook.

But as the early years went by, young Kierkegaard, probably in his early twenties, began to have misgivings about this way of conceiving of all kinds of issues. It was not simply that the questions were not answered, but it was the way of posing the questions that became so troublesome. All the issues looked as if they needed a kind of knowledge, a very subtle, to be sure, philosophical knowledge. As Kierkegaard matured, he also became aware of how decisive his own proclivities and energies were. He came to understand that moral character and a religious life were not functions of concepts open peculiarly to a philosophical understanding. Moral resolution plus a decisive need for the Christian faith strengthened some misgivings that he had in more neutral intellectual grounds; together these made him aware of how disparate the role of concepts actually was and how difficult it was to describe them within the large philosophical matrix available.

So it was very difficult for this extremely talented man to know what to do with himself, if he should decide to be a writer. The temptation was to complete the system, to go on in the context of concepts, questions and research that was mutually delimited already. These as the kind of radical misgivings he entertains—necessarily almost inchoate at first until he forges for himself the way of tackling them. Furthermore, he knows he cannot take the generation with him. Propelled always by his own religious enthusiasm and pervasive moral needs, he nonetheless succeeds in designing a literature that is, he believes, a better mirror, a conceptual one to be sure, whereby a man can understand himself and a range of aesthetic, ethico-religious, and also purely logical problems. But this major shift could only be effected by a large-scale literary productivity. So Kierkegaard begins at the beginning with *Either/Or* (1843). In the earlier chapter something was said about the successive books. Right now our interest will be best served by saying a few general things about the literature as a totality. In succeeding sections we will treat the theme that the literature is not the resolution of Kierkegaard's problems and should not be interpreted simply autobiographically; second, we will consider how the literature makes light of those philosophies which give room only for collectivities and large abstractions by portraying problems as articulated by individuals. It thus gives status to a concept of "individuality" but by a sly and indirect manner. Third, the thrust of the literature is a kind of *reductio ad absurdum* of a whole group of traditional philosophical problems like "truth," "reality," "the good," "objective," and others. The result is an entirely new notion of what philosophy is and does. As we shall see later this will combine at once an outlook, something like a new philosophical way to look at our ethical, religious, aesthetic and even cognitive problems, with all kinds of minute and separable inquiries concerning concepts in this or that kind of context.

I

Kierkegaard's life story is interesting because it is singular. It is a story of authorship from first to last. There are only forty-two years, from 1813–1855; a desultory university career, from 1830 to 1840; a major dissertation; an engagement and then the breaking of engagement; then a seven- or eight-year period of writing—over thirty books, a massive daily log of his plans and thoughts, a trip or two to Berlin, an attack upon him by a newspaper, and then his life became quiet for a few years only to be ended with a blazing attack upon the Christian Church. With that it is all over. A tender love for his Regina persisted throughout it all, but so did a deep melancholia and a triumphant religious faith. Put it all together and it is a story of a most remarkable devotion and intensity.

There is, of course, the miscellany of influences, travel, friends and events, but they are not many or efficacious. What looms up is the intensity with which his concerns are pursued. Looking at his earlier life from the vantage point of a strikingly successful authorship, both Kierkegaard and his biographers cannot help but note how all things extraneous to the life of an author are early cut away. Even the formative years, from 1835 through 1841 (i.e., before his authorship really begins), at a later glance seem almost tailored to intense authorship. But this story cannot be told here in any detail; furthermore, it is already well done.[1]

---

1. Besides works already noted there are numerous bibliographies published that list and in some cases provide evaluations of the vast scholarship on Kierkegaard's life and literature. For example, Kabell's *Kierkegaard-Studiet i Norden* is an account of research in Scandinavia; so too with Henriksen's *Methods and Results of Kierkegaard Studies in Scandinavia*; the pages of *Kierkegaardiana* (1955 ff.) carry current information about secondary literature. There is almost no end of biograph-

A New Way of Philosophizing

Suffice it to say for our purposes that his life story indicates how deeply concerned he was, and for a considerable portion of his time, with very abstract philosophical problems. Here too it is as if coming to rather negative conclusions about Hegelianism, about Fichte, and about Karl Daub and the latter's efforts to identify Christian orthodoxy and German rationalism were the prolegomena to his own authorship and the somewhat more limited view of philosophy that it suggests. But this too is a separate story and is drawn to the attention of those who are curious about the historical genesis and context of Kierkegaard's views.[2] And there seems to be little reason for assuming that his literature, again conceiving it as a totality, gives any kind of profile of Kierkegaard's personal life. Of course, there are allusions here and there to his own struggles, and the subject matter is, after all, drawn in large part from his own life. But the literature in the large is not a perverse way of disclosing something about himself. As with

---

ical and religious studies, but there are very few exhibiting Kierkegaard's kind of philosophizing. The volumes of Emanuel Hirsch, *Kierkegaard-Studien*, are decisive, especially the first volume. The works of Eduard Geismar, *Søren Kierkegaard*, especially the first two volumes of his six are relevant; Lowrie's *Kierkegaard* and Croxall's *Kierkegaard Studies* and *Kierkegaard Commentary* are appropriate, even though the latter are somewhat gossipy.

2. These matters have not been evaluated as often as they have been noted. The detailed researches of Niels Thulstrup on much of Kierkegaard's early preoccupation with "isms," names, and books are certainly exhausting, if not exhaustive. He has identified Kierkegaard's reading in order to explain the allusions in the *Philosophical Fragments, Concluding Unscientific Postscript*, and all of his letters. Besides he has done more of this meticulous work for a number of the German translations of Kierkegaard's writings. The only portion of this thus far translated into English is the set of pages by Thulstrup now included in the translation of the *Philosophical Fragments*, xlv–xcvii; 143–260. The appropriate Danish literature is *Breve og Aktstykker vedrørende Søren Kierkegaard*, vols. I–II, edited by Niels Thulstrup and *Fortegnelse over Dr. S. A. Kierkegaards efterladte Bogsamling,* edited by Thulstrup with notes. Also Emanuel Hirsch's notes to his translation, *Philosophische Brocken*, 165–90, are extremely useful. But, the most complete and intellectually impressive job on this aspect of Kierkegaard's life is to be found in Emanuel Hirsch, *Kierkegaard-Studien*. See especially vol. II, "*Der Denker.*" His discussion, comprising the entire volume, is divided into three sections: "The Seeking Thinker" (relevant especially to the years 1835–41); "The Work of a Thinker": part one, 1841–1846; part two: 1847–1855. Another account of a different sort is Frithiof Brandt's long book *Den Unge Søren Kierkegaard*, which tries to give historical antecedents and examples (relevant to Kierkegaard's early years), who were in turn the models for his pseudonymous authors. But Brandt omits the philosophy and forgets about the argument "in" the literature in favor of his argument "about" the literature.

most great philosophers very little is learned from his biography that pertains directly to the argument. Despite Kierkegaard's "existentialism" and the reputation that that kind of philosophy has for a kind of personal caterwauling, Kierkegaard never used his literature for personal confessions. Though he had all the respect in the world for a thinker reduplicating in actuality his thought (he found it difficult to imagine thinking the good life without seeking it, except at the loss of integrity), it did not follow from this that all thinking was simply a personal expression.

On this point we also have Kierkegaard's own judgment. He wrote a book called *The Point of View* which makes clear that there is a duplicity in the work. But the concept "duplicity" here only means that the literature is deceptive if one assumes that the author's life is being documented thereby. His second chapter, "The Difference in My Personal Mode of Existence Corresponding to the Essential Difference in the Works,"[3] makes this point very specifically. And these are borne out by his lengthy analyses of his motives found in his diaries. Together these accounts make quite clear that Kierkegaard never used his literature to tell the story of his own life or even an indirect and histrionic confession.

From this it follows, I believe, that Kierkegaard's literature can only be understood when it is analyzed in its own terms. Most of that literature consists of various kinds of conceptual analyses and arguments using these concepts. It is a mistake to place them always in a biographical and historical context and assume that that is the way to understand them. This does not deny that the Danish thinker was precipitated to reflection by external events. The correctness of his judgment about some of these events, especially the democratic revolutions of 1848, can certainly be questioned. It is, obviously, important to know about such events if one wishes to evaluate his claims. But the study of concepts and arguments has its own rules, and, as a philosopher, Kierkegaard knew and appreciated the freedom and the restraints of such study. Here the events of a life do not serve as the test for the validity of the ideas, and the objective expression can often be judged independently of the exhaustive knowledge of the matrix from which it springs. This is why Kierkegaard joked about students

---

3. *Point of View*, xx–39.

A New Way of Philosophizing

who were more interested in the biography of the thinker than his thoughts.

Granted this, there is still something to be learned from Kierkegaard's way of composing his literature that does bear upon what he came to think correct philosophizing entailed. Though Kierkegaard was a polemical thinker, he did not directly respond to every criticism leveled against him. Neither was he engaged by the latest literature that came his way.[4] Owing a great deal to Denmark, to the religion of the State, to Hegel, to romanticism, to Plato and Socrates, to his teachers, and to several contemporaries, it is, nonetheless, a mistake to construe him as a follower, a disciple of the leading views, or even, for that matter, a writer more negative than constructive. Because he reacted strongly to the way of conceiving and seeing intellectual problems and because he refused to write out explicitly one more way to do that, it does not follow that his real views are hid from view, buried in his intellectual history or melancholic spirit. These characteristics have caused some scholars to assume that there is a secret philosophy somewhere, an unwritten point of view only to be inferred from his enigmatic and single-minded career.

Here it will be insisted, on the contrary, that the things he found worth saying were said. But what has troubled the readers of Kierkegaard's literature is precisely the paradigm of understanding that that literature was seeking to dispel. Therefore, the temptation to assume that it all means something sinister, almost private, looms ever large. If Kierkegaard's reflections on his own life have any weight here at all, they show how long it took him to get clear on these very issues. He was so thoroughly taken up with the way of construing issues in the way that he termed "speculative," "abstract," and "philosophical," that he even came to rue his earlier writings. In his earliest extended work, his dissertation, *The Concept of Irony*, he criticized Socrates because:

> Influenced as I was by Hegel and the whole modern spirit, without sufficient maturity really to apprehend the great, I somewhere in my dissertation have not been able to refrain from showing that it was an imperfection in Socrates not to have an eye for the totality, but merely to look upon the individual numerically. Oh, Hegelian fool that I was—precisely

4. Ibid., 51–52.

this is the outstanding proof that shows how great an ethicist Socrates was.[5]

But this remark, testimony to be sure that his mind had changed, is not enough to credit the notion that every other view he held was also subject to subtle and indiscernible change during his career as author. We will have reason to show that Kierkegaard had great difficulty shaking off the effects of this early training. Some bleak passages in his literature, notably in *The Sickness unto Death* and a few other places, show that he could not quite get rid of the conventional rubrics and major concepts. This has caused some commentators, notably the brilliant Swedish scholar Torsten Bohlin, to assume that the older intellectualism was latent all the while. This again seems preposterous in the light of the shape and content of the literature he pens. It seems better to assume that such a radical reorientation was not perfectly consummated, for this is what the literature and the diaries indicate.

As we shall indicate, the highly contrived way of writing, with its authors within authors, is puzzling. But it does not need biographical documentation as much as it does a philosophical assessment. Kierkegaard believed that it was the right way to handle a certain spectrum of philosophical problems. We will find, therefore, the literature to be a totality giving the occasion for becoming clear on some general concepts, such as those of ordinary logic and epistemology, and to some extent of a kind of generic metaphysics. The specific books, on the other hand, supply the matrix within which special concepts (by "special" here is meant those of limited scope) are explored. These include "dread," "sin," "despair," "authority," "duty," etc. We shall explore more of this later. Right now, it is appropriate to turn to one kind of attack that the literature, in all its parts, helps to engineer.

---

5. Quoted from *Papirer* by Prof. David Swenson, *Something About Kierkegaard*, 13 n. 15. Another interesting example of this kind of reflection is to be found in a long letter by Kierkegaard addressed to a reflective friend. Therein, Kierkegaard explains that Socrates, even though over-run by his age, still had to be that kind of individual, conceiving himself and his task as he did. See *Breve*, I:205–6.

II

As one reads Kierkegaard, it becomes patent that he is polemicizing against the tendencies in society that give the totalities, the impersonal groupings, the hypothetical entities—the "idea of the good," "objective truth," and the "public"—greater significance than the individual. More than this, Kierkegaard moves steadily away from generalities, from abstractions, and from inflated concepts. Partly as a reaction, he repudiates the philosophies of his day because they are not descriptive enough. He wants to isolate concepts rather than to lump them.

Kierkegaard was indeed polemical, but in his polemicizing he does not always mention individuals and/or specific doctrines. As closely related as he is to Hegel and Hegelian teachers, as indebted as he admits to being to other scholars and men of letters, still he does not always specify them as his targets. His charge is a broadside, one must admit, but it is a broadside engendered by a large abuse. He is attacking a practice of bright people everywhere. The issue is simply that much of the sophisticated talk, scholarly and otherwise, which comes his way is not true to the way people are. In his words, men have forgotten what it means to exist. Philosophical and theological concepts, artificial and falsifying, have distorted the grasp of everyday occurrences. Philosophical people see the issues with concepts and categories quite inappropriate to our common life, and hence many of their "problems" are created in virtue of the tools of their reflection. Kierkegaard's plea is to look at ordinary existing once again and at the language which is appropriate thereunto. In the absence of that language he proposes to create it via his pseudonyms.

Kierkegaard was fighting too the cluster of views according to which explanation in terms of motives and human intentions was a mixture of ignorance and, at best, some very proximate philosophical reasoning. That the behavior of men was in fact made by factors largely beyond the control and responsibility of individuals was almost axiomatic among the learned in nineteenth century Denmark. The growth, "natural" it was assumed, of large units, of race, of nation, of church and "spiritual organisms," of religion, of civilization, and of the Hegelian World Spirit, by which the career of individual persons is to be explained, this growth and evolution was the subject of both quasi-empirical end metaphysical studies of his day. Even a theologian like Grundtvig came to speak in such large terms. Of course, all kinds of denials were made in Kierkegaard's day as in ours by the theorists meeting the objections of empiricists, but most of them consisted of footnotes that institutions, after all, do consist of individual men and women. The historically minded and the metaphysicians (Fichte, Daub, Hegel, Grundtvig and others in Kierkegaard's day) were inclined to treat nations, civilizations, and cultures as much more than convenient collective terms for individuals with something in common. Kierkegaard insisted that much of the learned talk, as well as the more technical philosophizing of his day, was vitiated by the fact that individuals were conceived to be less "real," less "concrete," and somehow more "abstract," somewhat artificial and lacking historical being apart from the wholes of which they are a part.[6]

It is Kierkegaard's merit as a thinker to be the critic of philosophers, theologians, and men-of-letters whose reflection was playing host to vast interrelationships between all men, nature, God, past, present, and future. "Being," the most embracing concept of all was typically attractive, and to invoke it as more "real" and more important than the existence of a single man was fantasy to Kierkegaard. Also, he resisted the temptation of identifying God's purposes with that of the great society of the living and the dead, of our ancestors and of generations yet unborn, as if somehow individual purposes and lives were but a tiny fragment of the larger purposes and lives belonging to collectivist totalities. As will be noted later, all kinds of epistemological problems can be raised here, and Kierkegaard raises most of them. But he goes further; he protests, too, on behalf of ethical and religious concerns. Both kinds of protests are heard in his pages—those engendered by logical-epistemological considerations about the concepts, terms, and logical values, and those fomented by his own ethical-religious passion. Often they are intertwined.

Throughout his pages, Kierkegaard wants to separate where others have united. He, therefore, had very small use for large collectivist terms of philosophers of his day. On the contrary, he never tires of separating. So, the concept of evil, which looms so large in Hegel,

---

6. These are themes developed in some detail in the *Postscript*. Note the following: "Happy nineteenth century . . . to let the ethical become something which it needs a prophet to discover, a man with a world historical outlook upon world-history . . ." (129); "The Quantitative Process" (128); "The Speculative Point of View" (50–55).

seems according to Kierkegaard to be made almost nonsensical. The large concept is supposedly illustrated as the "negative" in logic, as matter resisting mind in the physical world, as the opposite of good in an ethical economy, and as sin in the Christian vocabulary. Instead of contriving a master concept, a concept that totals all the smaller concepts and even undergoes a change from one to another, Kierkegaard chooses to separate each small concept from the other. There are many concepts and not one. "Evil" means these many things and he is quite content to leave the meanings that way, eschewing altogether the invention of an ideal inclusive concept. "By thus failing to let the scientific call to order be heard, by not being vigilant . . . ," Kierkegaard says, "one may indeed attain sometimes an appearance of brilliance, may give sometimes the impression of having already comprehended, when in fact one is far from it, may sometimes by the use of vague words strike up all agreement between things that differ."[7]

To polemicize against the immensities meant more than combating Hegel or launching a new movement in philosophy. Therefore Kierkegaard conceived the idea of creating a literature of vivid examples, highly idealized, but in which the characteristics of being an individual, ordinarily omitted from philosophical treatises, would be fully depicted. More than this, Kierkegaard contrived his literature to make it possible only for individuals to respond to it. It is almost as if it individuates the mass of readers, it isolates "him," makes "him" reflect about himself and not world history, "being," or massive collectivities. The "him" is "my reader," to whom so many prefaces to his books allude.[8] Being free of the necessity of having to please either the professors or the public—he was a man of independent means—Kierkegaard bent all of his energies and talents to this task. Though this was also his way of introducing Christianity to those who were already Christians—those subsumed by baptism in another immensity, the State Lutheran Church of Denmark—it is a mistake to see him

---

7. See the introduction to *Concept of Dread*, 9. The rest of the introduction makes a point for separations of other kinds of discourse too and for not assuming that the same words in various contexts are tokens of an overlapping meaning.

8. What Kierkegaard says in the preface to *Two Edifying Discourses* (May, 1843) can be said of his entire authorship: "I let my eye follow it (the published books) for a short while . . . it finally met that individual whom with joy and thankfulness I call my reader, that individual whom it seeks . . ." (Translation my own.) *Samlede Vaerker*, III:11. Also, *Edifying Discourses*, vol. I (Minneapolis: Augsburg, 1943) 5.

exclusively as a conventionally religious author. The major intellectual diatribe, which the entire literature is, must, therefore, not be omitted; it is indeed an attack from "behind," an attack upon the metaphysical dispositions of the day, in the interest of ethical and religious individuality, but it is also a shaking up of the conventional conceptual apparatus of the philosophers and their followers.[9]

All of this can be put another way. Coming to the judgment that the interests and concerns alluded to in much of ethics and religion were eminently his, Kierkegaard began looking for ways in which to delineate and to describe them. When he turned to the philosophical and theological treatises of his day, he concluded that the entire scheme of concepts of the philosophers and theologians was fundamentally wrong. As he plotted his own authorship, he also concluded that even the style of such writing, the solemn pedagogical manner, the lecturing style, was a betrayal of the subject matter. This is why it is so ridiculous to suggest, as some readers of his pages have, that he did not read enough of Hegel, or of Aristotle, or of Kant, really to get the point. True, Kierkegaard was not an historical scholar, and his historical judgments may well be faulty, but his philosophical point is not dependent upon extensive scholarship. He is a radical kind of philosopher, who sniffs out the mistaken way of handling issues after what may seem to be rather brief exposure to authors and their literature.

The interesting and often overlooked feature of his authorship is his very radical reorientation of categories. His religious enthusiasm, which is certainly constant and which gives him his goals, cannot be denied, but it is a mistake to dwell upon that enthusiasm without remembering how completely stultifying and falsifying he found the technical language of his time to be. His philosophy consists negatively in the repudiation of the categories, language, and style that were incongruent with familiar human things, and positively in the creation of a new literature within which those familiar human things could be portrayed and then analyzed.

---

9. Note the remarks to this effect in the *Postscript*, 225ff.; *Stages on Life's Way*, last sections. Kierkegaard's judgments about his own literature are important here, especially in reference to *Either/Or*, his first pseudonymous book: *Papirer* III B, 60, 179–80; II A, 454 (*JP* 2: 1578; *KJN* 2, EE: 93). Also note Dru, *Journals*, 286.

A New Way of Philosophizing

One of the incredible facts about Kierkegaard's literature is the fact that so many pieces of literature, about thirty-five, were written out as parts of a single plan. The entire literature, rather than the individual books, gives a reader the context in which some concepts of ethics and religion, plus numerous others of logic, including odd ones like "reality," and "truth," can be seen at their appropriate work. Unlike many authors who write out books as it pleases them, Kierkegaard's came forth almost as a single extended work. One must remember that they were written, except for corrections and revisions, within a seven-year period. Gradually that literature took in area after area, not in order to refute point by point the grand philosophy of the time, but to show by a *reductio ad absurdum* that the concepts proposed simply were inappropriate. Correlatively, a whole series of new ones began gradually to emerge. Their adequacy is not argued as much as it is shown to the reader in a leisurely way.

III

Two features of Kierkegaard as a philosopher can be noted herewith. The total literature of some thirty-odd volumes has a kind of appropriateness to human existing. But it is a mistake simply to conclude that it is a generic sort of description, so loose that it will fit all people. For in one sense it does not "describe" in the way that a newspaper reporter "describes" nor in the way that, e.g., Rousseau "describes" how he feels about daily life. Rather the author invents a large array of examples. These are highly idealized to be sure. But the total range of such examples, from a perverse seducer to a staid judge, and from a ladies' tailor to a literary dandy, fairly well cover the kinds of people that we are and know.

Kierkegaard puts this feature of his authorship to very good use indeed. For much of what he writes here allows him to bring out some very ordinary concepts, the kind that do not ordinarily engender any philosophical puzzles at all. By showing them in their original contexts, he also takes a lot of the "mystique" away from them. There is nothing particularly profound or puzzling about concepts which one learns in daily life and which grow up very easily after noticing rhythms and similarities in the real world. Concepts are not puzzling because they are concepts; he is at pains to show how naturally they grow up and how plainly they can be used. So, when he says: "One cannot think an individual man but only the concept man,"[10] he is not only making a subtle point about the interweaving of language, concepts, and the capacity to recognize, but he is also helping us get accustomed to the ordinariness of most concepts. He refuses to make as Hegel did a problem of the concept "man."

No, the literature that evokes all these examples (and more about them subsequently) takes all kinds of concepts and ideas out of the arena of the philosophically puzzling. Therefore, Kierkegaard provides the literary occasion for flatly asserting that only some concepts need philosophical explanations and elaborate elucidations. As we shall subsequently note in detail, Kierkegaard was particularly antagonistic to the Hegelian philosophy that made it seem that every idea, no matter where it arose or what it said, was a philosophical conundrum. Therefore, the contention of Hegel that every concept has to be philosophically unpacked is relevant: "every concept is a unity of opposite moments, which could therefore be asserted in the shape of an antinomy."[11] And when one of Kierkegaard's authors comments on his own little book he says:

> The concept all the while like an acrobatic clown in the current circus season, every moment performing these everlasting dog tricks of flopping over and over, until it flops over the man himself. May a kind Heaven preserve me and my piece from such a fate![12]

Hegel had said very extravagant things indeed about concepts. He hypostasized concepts so that they always included oppositions or contradictions within themselves, thereby suggesting that every ordinary concept, even those like "dog," "man," and "umbrella" (which we have learned by noting similarities in the world) were exemplifications of richer concepts. So rich were they that they were unities of dynamic contrasts, burgeoning with becoming. They were like living tendencies in existence.[13]

10. *Sickness Unto Death*, 195.
11. Hegel, *Science of Logic*, I:205.
12. Preface to *Philosophical Fragments*, 2.
13. This expression is used by Niels Thulstrup in his "Commentary" to the *Fragments*, 159.

A New Way of Philosophizing

For the moment, the detail is not the issue. Kierkegaard's literature with all of its variety and dramatic content is not a direct attack upon such views. If it had been so contrived, it would, of course, have had most properly another and more pedagogical style. Instead he chooses a more difficult way. He wants his reader not to learn another set of philosophical doctrines, for then he would play directly into the hands of the commodious interpreters of the history of philosophy. His position would then be conceived to be one more phase in the evolution of concepts, another example illustrating the very outlook he was intent upon combating. Instead, he forces the reader to see the ridiculousness of such a conception for himself. The literature, with its aesthetic, ethical, and religious spheres, gives instances of the same words, "good," "evil," "man," "truth," "pleasure," "duty," "God," "wrong," "real," and many more being used in different "*stadier*" ("stages" or more properly "ways of life" or "games of life"), with meanings that are not parts of a whole, opposites blending into one another, or stages in the evolution or unfolding of a vast notion. As a pedagogue, Kierkegaard is intent upon his reader coming to see that for himself. The literature that he writes is an array of examples, contrived to be sure but contrived only to maximize the opportunities for seeing the absurdity of such talk about concepts.

This, then, is his way of clearing the ground. The irony is magnificent and constant. So the *Postscript*, one of the pieces in that literature, says:

> Poor Jacob! Whether anyone visits your grave I do not know, but I know that the paragraph-machine plows all your eloquence, all your inwardness under, while a few scant words are registered in the System as your significance. It is said of him that he represents feeling with enthusiasm; such a reference makes game of both feeling and enthusiasm, whose secret precisely is that they cannot be reported at second-hand, and therefore cannot in so comfortable a manner, as a result through a "*satisfactio vicaria*," yield bliss to a prater.[14]

Instead of giving out philosophy as a batch of results, Kierkegaard's pathos, humor, irony as well as what he calls his poetic talent are expended "to exhibit the existential relationship between the aesthetic

---

14. *Postscript*, 224.

and the ethical within an existing individual." Lest one thinks this means murky German metaphysics, let it be added here that "existential" here means something like "that which actually obtains." Here his aim is descriptive.

This is to note one feature then of pervasive significance to philosophy. Kierkegaard was discontent with the abstract propositions of much of idealistic philosophy. He showed, but he did not demonstrate or prove in any conventional sense, that such propositions neither described the everyday world nor any other level of reality or more ideal world. He was not therefore opposed to abstract expression or to the conviction that they might apply in a multitude of ways, but invariably indirectly, to the real world. But his initial thrust is to invent a more adequate skein of language which is fit for the kind of purposes he has in mind. Once this is done the whole fabric of analogies against which classical philosophies had generated perennial questions begins subtly to change. And the effect of this plowing up of the field of language is to make many time-honored problems of philosophy disappear.

But there is the affirmative side too. For the literature is also the occasion for philosophizing, but in a smaller manner. For Kierkegaard is as intent as any philosopher has been upon the concepts. But he chooses to make the reader work hard. Because the purpose governing his literature is finally to provide the reader with the opportunity of seeing what Christianity is, Kierkegaard does not think that concepts are worth very much in themselves. His point is that the conceptual apparatus already available will not permit an adequate delineation of either ethical or religious seriousness—it falsifies both. Therefore, he is anxious to make clear the appropriate concepts only to show their use in certain ways that are congruent with his purposes. But his way has to be indirect. Here he comments upon Socrates in this same regard:

> Thus I see that Socrates, who otherwise holds so strictly to the method of question and answer (which is an indirect method), because the long speech, the dogmatizing lecture, the recitation by rote, only causes confusion, sometimes himself speaks more at length, and cites as a reason for this that his interlocutor needs some item of information before the conversation can get going. This he does for example in the

> *Gorgias*. But this procedure seems to me to be an inconsistency, an impatience that fears it will take too long before a mutual understanding can be reached. The indirect method would reach the same goal, only more slowly.[15]

It is Kierkegaard's theme, sounded clearly, that concepts that fit everywhere really fit nowhere.[16] "Truth" is one such concept, and much of the burden of the *Concluding Unscientific Postscript* is to show how unscientific and non-systematic that concept is if it is made to fit all kinds of discourse at once. One of the reasons his book is "unscientific" (or as the Danish word "*uvidenskabelig*" suggests, "not cognitive-like") is that the word "truth," while used in religious discourse and in moral judgments, also achieves therein quite a different conceptual content. The book, actually the most philosophical of his works, precipitates this different meaning out of his previous literature (as was noted in the last chapter) and its many examples. Here his literature is called "A Contemporary Effort," and he so contrives the intrigue of his pages that his pseudonymous author, Johannes Climacus, reads that earlier literature and finds his philosophizing limned in those other pages.

So, too, with "reality," another all-inclusive concept which the *Postscript* deflates considerably. The aim there too is to show that there are several discriminable uses for "real" and its cognates, and that the use in ethico-religious contexts is considerably different from the use in scientific and other scholarly discourse. And, there is no distinctively philosophical use. So, while it is true that Kierkegaard provides no substitute for the large all-inclusive concepts that he ridicules, it is also his argument that there are none to be substituted. Philosophy becomes more a matter of discriminating the meanings rather than inventing another one. On the other hand, he does not eschew altogether philosophy as also discriminating various views of life, for concepts do indeed have their vitality within ways of life. Kierkegaard has created several of these ways, the aesthetic, the ethical, the mildly religious, along with the strenuously Christian, in order to show that concepts relevant to how to live and to die cannot be assessed "*sub specie aeternitatis*."

---

15. *Postscript*, 247.
16. *Concept of Dread*, note especially the argument of the introduction.

By the same token, these "stages" can be further discriminated. Part of the function of philosophizing is to do just that in a rich variety of ways. Isolating the concepts is only one of them. Philosophy is not, however, itself a view of life. Kierkegaard is more inclined always to suggest that philosophy is more like disinterested analysis rather than interested preoccupation. Views of life grow up in the tangle of concepts, behavior, and language that are properly ethical or religious, Christian or humanist, as the case might be. Kierkegaard is at pains to show how these things interlock, so that even a concept is like a knot in a net. Still, there is, strictly speaking, no such thing as a philosophical view of life. Philosophy is not that provident. It is more "about" them than it is one of them.

This is why Kierkegaard's "existentialism" is not itself a view of life. His existentialism is only a concerted effort to bring a larger range of concepts under intellectual and discriminating analysis. He does not want to stop short with the cluster of issues that are logical and epistemological. He is here overtly a champion of Socrates' style rather than what he thinks is Plato's. His endeavor is to bring what he thinks are the universal and repeatable features of our subjective lives into philosophical purview. Unlike most philosophically talented people, he found the passions, moods, fantasies and emotions, everything we have come to think of as subjective and hence private, also replete with regularities and order.[17] These are what he finds to be terribly important to our everyday life. Here, too, there are conundrums, puzzles, confusions, and a need for clarification, and, even more than that, for discrimination. So, his stages are like *loci* for them, where in a literary context that is descriptive and also expressive (for remember, each is written by an author-advocate, in persuasive fashion), the occasion for isolating the concepts is created.

This is a good part of Kierkegaard's affirmative philosophical task. In the previous chapter, we took a closer look at Kierkegaard's successive books, and the themes of this chapter can be confirmed

17. Kierkegaard's pages are full of examples of what he notes as "a linkage" of incorrect mood with incorrect concept. (See *Concept of Dread*, 33). His journals, especially for the years 1841–45, are crammed with reflections like that. He came to believe that there were instances of incongruities that were not strictly like those of contrary terms or concepts, but still were noticeable and were a source of our disquietude. These were only mistakenly "philosophical" problems.

therein. Kierkegaard's existentialism is only a name for the willingness to philosophize about a number of matters very close to our everyday problems of existing. Because it turns out that the nest of such problems is not itself peculiarly to be resolved by a philosopher does not mean that those problems are not subject to kinds of philosophical study. In fact, even getting the relevant concepts straight is one admirable way to see them to be moral, scientific, aesthetic, religious or what have you.

CHAPTER 4

The Bible and Christianity

Nothing that Kierkegaard ever wrote is so apparently tangential to the history of philosophy and theology as the chapter "The Subjective Truth, Inwardness; The Truth Is Subjectivity." Scarcely anything within his own literature is so important and has the same bearing and logical authority as does the pregnant thesis of that chapter. Being the crucial chapter in Kierkegaard's most philosophical work, *Concluding Unscientific Postscript,* and being the theme of the most philosophical of pseudonyms, Johannes Climacus, this chapter (and its thesis about truth) has almost an empty formal character. But its abstract neutrality allows it to point to something important about the earlier aesthetic and ethical works as well as the early and late religious discourses. In addition, this thesis draws attention to the concreteness that Kierkegaard finds religious and ethical truth, essential truth as he calls it, to possess. Also, it states part of the logic of the ethico-religious discourses in contrast to the logic of much of scholarly discourse.

I

Kierkegaard's early literature is characterized by an almost hectic eloquence. The verve is almost satanic. Readers of Kierkegaard's Danish know well the uniqueness of his style, the fullness and richness of mood that underlies his phrasing, the depth of passion that constitutes the stream on which these moods are borne. Besides, there is a subtlety of allusion and a wealth of imaginative coloring in the material. Some of these qualities carry over into the other extreme nuance of Kierkegaard's varied style. The last literature, the polemical pieces, translated happily under the title *Attack upon Christendom*, are in the powerfully stirring style of a master agitator, addressing himself to a popular audience, chiseling his scorn into linguistic form, and as Georg Brandes put it, ". . . hammering the word until it forms itself into the greatest possible, the bloodiest injury—without for a moment letting it cease bearing an idea."[1]

These two extremes seem to exemplify the old adage that extremes meet. But the meeting point, as we have already argued, is really in the calmer and more leisurely styles of the philosophical works, by which Kierkegaard more surely belongs to the future of the world. For it is in these (especially in *Fragments* and *Postscript*[2]) that all of the features of Kierkegaard's style already noted are combined with rigorous exactness of thought and precision of terminology. The definition of truth, truth as subjectivity, is proposed neutrally and abstractly in *Postscript*, with, however, the understanding that the concreteness to which it refers is every person's individuality.

Almost all of Kierkegaard's writings are both an occasion for, as well as an illustration and kind of defense of the thesis that "truth is subjectivity." Initially Kierkegaard conceived the doctrine as a characteristically Socratic view and used it, in his early literature, as a tool to attack aestheticism and worldliness. Later, Kierkegaard even dares to use this same thesis to attack Christendom and especially the Church. For the Church had become, in his estimate, one of the chief demoralizing agents in society, precisely because it too failed to recognize the peculiar shape that moral endeavor and the religious life really have. Thus, early and late, the same concept served as his philosophical springboard. The pretensions of philosophers and aesthetes, on the one hand, and the ineptness and religious grossness of the Church, on the other, were both a reflection of a forgetfulness of what human life really is, and consequently also a misuse of concepts and propositions about religious and ethical matters.

---

1. Brandes, *Søren Kierkegaard*, 256.

2. Stylistically there are the two extremes noted; then there is also an intermediate style, seen best in those books named above and in *Works of Love* and *Christian Discourses*.

Clearly the thesis is itself objective in Kierkegaard's sense, for it is stated in propositions, and, secondly, believing the thesis is not an instance of the subjectivity that he describes. For the "believing" here is "objective" too, in Kierkegaard's sense of the term. Thus Kierkegaard is at once proposing an objectively true view, a piece of philosophical knowledge about what ethico-religious truth is, but he is not saying that the truth of that view is an instance of the truth therein described. The concreteness of personal life and the richness of subjectivity demanded by such a view were richly acknowledged in the rest of the literature, within which this concept functions. For if "religious and moral subjectivity is the truth" is a significant sentence (and more will be said about this later), then that sentence is a proposal for one's belief. This sentence must be true or false. Kierkegaard, of course, believed the sentence to be true, and hence argued for its objective truth on appropriate grounds.

But here a little caution is in order. The sentence "truth is subjectivity" is really a sentence about the concept "truth." Kierkegaard is claiming for that concept some specific differences. His literature gives the occasion for our seeing that there is no one definition of truth, applicable to all the circumstances where the word is used. Kierkegaard's quarrel is with those writers and popularizers who have extended the use of the word "truth" in cognitive matters to ethical and religious areas. Therefore, he shows that ethico-religious "truth" has a different role altogether than does "truth" in the context of historical research or in logic or, for that matter, in metaphysics. Furthermore, it is the role in the ethico-religious literature (which he has penned) that clues one into the meaning, i.e., the concept. He is not arguing for any relation or event, mental or metaphysical, for which "truth" is supposed to stand. "Truth" as a concept, here is seen in the subjectivity of the depicted subjects—it draws together the significance of the seeking and striving of subjects. Learning the meaning of "truth" in this context is more like finding the words for a practice than it is like discovering a heretofore undiscovered object.

The thesis that truth is subjectivity (in ethico-religious matters) is a piece of philosophy. It is a true description of what concept is operated within ethico-religious contexts. His grounds are commonsensical and ordinary aesthetic and religious living, the actual existence of man. His transcriptions and idealizations of such existence are only so perpetrated as to serve his own philosophical interests. If they in turn are falsifications, his case would fall.

There is something reminiscent here of Immanuel Kant, who, though he said that he was destroying knowledge in order to make room for faith, was actually only showing how the concepts and categories of one were not the concepts and categories of the other. Kant showed that theoretic knowledge about matters of fact did nothing to generate the sense of obligation; Kierkegaard shows that knowledge about ethics and religion really have little to do with ethical passion and religious belief and the concepts involved therein.

Kierkegaard's literature, both aesthetic and religious, makes very embarrassing the juxtaposition of "objective truth" and moral and religious concerns. If the passional and conative factors are as relevant to moral and religious decision as his pseudonymous literature portrays, if the enthusiasm and content of Christian faith must be described in their subjective locus, then another concept of truth is, in fact, already at work. The movement of the dialectic of the pseudonymous literature is, as the author of *Postscript* tells us when he quixotically edits those books that have appeared just before his own, "a polemic against the truth as knowledge."[3] Furthermore, these earlier books provide through the labors of others what the author himself needed to show, the claim that truth is subjectivity.[4] The actual relationships between aesthetic and ethical factors within existing individuals is the subject matter of the pseudonymous literature, and it is these, rather than world history (beginning with China and Persia as does Hegel's philosophy of history) which begs the definition that the *Postscript* provides. So again, Kierkegaard provides the literary accounts and then a formal definition and analysis which illuminates it. The concept of truth is the turning point in the whole argument.

Once again we can note Kierkegaard writing on two levels—he provides a convictional and poetic literature and then a kind of literature about it which is its analysis. Reflecting upon this himself, he believed that it was necessary for pedagogical reasons to begin by writing the "poetical" works, the convictional works, in order to get the issues into their proper *loci*. Kierkegaard found moralistic and

3. *Postscript*, 226.
4. Ibid., 224.

religious literature, even persuasive and sermonic homilies, so informed by the notion that religious and moral truth was analogous to ordinary kinds of cognitive truth that whatever the moral and religious problems were, they were not only not resolved, but, besides, were wrongly stated. Therefore, his own early works state them in a form in which it becomes clear that the issue is not cognitive at all, that the lack is not of truth as knowledge. Then, too, he is saved from the ignominious responsibility of penning a philosophical work which will solve religious and moral problems by providing knowledge. Kierkegaard's thesis about truth is couched in language that must itself be true. For reasons that will be noted, neither he nor any of his readers can assume that this philosophical language, even if true, will resolve a religious or moral problem. That the moral and religious issues are not a matter of discovering knowledge is made clear in the pseudonymous literature: that these can be reflected about to the extent of knowing that the concept "truth" here is subjectivity is a major burden of his philosophical analysis.

In what follows it will be instructive to follow Kierkegaard as he controverts several positions, then to note his analysis of the cause of misunderstandings, and finally to re-read his insistent claim that ethico-religious truth is subjectivity.

II

Kierkegaard was convinced that all quantitative approaches to faith, all amassing of evidence in the hope of verifying faith, were misunderstandings. Furthermore, any apparent success, however efficacious in immediate result, was, he thought, an illusion.[5] The difficulty in this matter is always felt by the man who is a scholar, the one who has a willingness to learn. For a scholar, especially one with any kind of ethical enthusiasm or religious passion, wants to use his gifts and training to make his convictions a little more certain and, perhaps above all, commensurate with the stringent requirements of the learned community. Putting this in more abstract forms, it means that scholars and scientists are easily motivated to turn ethical and religious convictions into hypotheses or generalizations and thus seek their

---

5. Ibid., 15.

The Bible and Christianity

certification in the public domain. The very requirement of looking for evidence is to take the problem out of its subjective locus, where the relationship is properly between a conviction, a persuasion, and an individual, and translate it into an objective problem concerning the relation between the conviction and evidence. Everything in the life of learning and scholarship is on the side of getting every problem stated so that it is no longer idiosyncratic in bearing, in reference, and in meaning.[6] It is no wonder, therefore, that religious and ethical questions have also been treated with the same concepts that make other issues scientific and ostensibly universal.

If the translation is to succeed, if convictional matters are to be dealt with evidentially, then Kierkegaard contends that it is only done by transforming faith and morality into something else. For then such a transformation has all the advantages of being decked out in proofs, of being scientific and modern. The Danish thinker was an acute enough observer of his fellow humans to know that soon the accompanying rhetoric and bombast would be quite enough to convince most readers and listeners that here indeed was the latest and the best, even though the initial ethical and religious quest had been subverted.

Some Kierkegaard scholars cannot resist the suggestion that a good dose of French and English empiricism would have been a worthy antidote for this supposedly speculative tendency of Kierkegaard's mind, fostered as it was initially by the "bloodless abstractions" of German metaphysics.[7] Aside from the fact that the romantic tendency in German philosophy was not exactly "bloodless," whatever other faults it may have had, it seems doubtful whether this so-called empiricism would have had any message for Kierkegaard. We must not forget that Kierkegaard was in reality a much more concrete thinker than Mill, Comte, or Marx ever dreamed of being, in the same sense that Socrates was a more concrete thinker than the so-called naturalists who preceded him. As early as 1835, when only twenty-two, Kierkegaard saw that empiricism, with its absorption in the explana-

---

6. Ibid., especially the introduction, 14–29. Here the problem is defined to show that an objective formulation is mistaken.

7. See Hollander, Brandes, Collins, and numerous others. Note as an example Hollander, *Selections from the Writings of Søren Kierkegaard*, translator's introduction.

tion and description of natural facts, was as incorrigibly abstract and remote from ethico-religious issues as was any speculative idealism. Furthermore, the logic of empirical thought and the categories and concepts thereof were as irrelevant to moral and religious discourse as were those conceived by speculative idealist philosophers. And the reading of the empiricists of the eighteenth and nineteenth centuries does not have to be very detailed or lengthy before one discovers that most of them were misled by their scientific attitudes into the formulation of shallow, half-popular, compromising philosophies of life of exceedingly doubtful intellectual and moral value.

From all of this Kierkegaard was saved. His sincerity and interest in personal assimilation, his non-sentimental and rigoristic Christianity, his poetic endowment, and above all his exacting logical insights were his antidote against speculative aloofness and against the immodesty of the scientist who wants to claim too much for his kind of learning and its concepts.

But one form of study which was becoming empirical already did in fact engage young Kierkegaard. This was the field of Biblical studies. As most students of the intellectual history of the eighteenth and nineteenth centuries know, there was a great upsurge of interest in historical and textual analyses of ancient, including Biblical, texts. Kierkegaard read some of the studies of the day.[8] The major issue that concerned him was not the truth or falsity of specific claims by biblical scholars, but rather the attempt of theologians to use historical evidence as a point of departure for theological statements and positions. While John Henry Newman these very days was discovering in historical studies the ostensible reasons for making important religious decisions, Kierkegaard was finding that historical and Biblical studies (of an empirical sort) were not the means of proving faith or enhancing religious certitude. He concludes that their logic is altogether different.

His author, Climacus, says ironically:

---

8. The catalogue of Kierkegaard's books, already alluded to, gives a clue and so do numerous references in his works. For example, he read Feuerbach, Bruno Bauer (and *Zeitschrift für Spekulative Theologie*), Hamann, Schleiermacher, and D. F. Strauss. The "Author Index" by A. Ibsen in Kierkegaard, *Samlede Vaerker*, XV:483–507, should be noted.

> How much time, what great industry, what splendid talents, what distinguished scholarship have been requisitioned from generation to generation in order to bring this miracle to pass.[9]
>
> As far as the Bible theory is concerned, the present author, even if he became even more convinced of the dialectical misdirection that lurks within it, will never be able to remember otherwise than with gratitude and admiration its distinguished achievements within the presupposition, the rare and thorough scholarship exhibited in its writings . . .[10]

Here again, however, Kierkegaard is aware of category mistakes. Scholarship within its narrow limits does not lack validity, but when this same scholarship is so defined that the labor of criticism is suddenly supposed to yield a harvest of faith, then there is an apparent difficulty. Historical statements and religious statements are in two different logical genres. Scholarship, even on the Bible, yields knowledge, but to say that that knowledge, in turn, should be evidence for faith is an indication that the orders of knowledge and of religious and ethical conviction have been confused.

Neither does Kierkegaard believe that Christians are bound to the view that the language of Scripture is therefore only probable.[11] His point is not to suggest a fundamental religious dogma as to how one should consider Scripture. Neither is he prone to deny Scripture's authority or truth, nor does he dispute its place in devotion or worship. His question is a more exacting one. He is concerned with the logical issues. He is contending that the sources of religious beliefs, whether these beliefs are about Scripture, the figure of Jesus, or God, do not lie in the discernment of the facts as defined by historical study. He never says that a Christian should not say that the Scriptures are the absolute truth. But the concept of truth is the issue. His point is that the fundamentalist-like belief in the truth of Scripture is also a confusion, however strong it seems religiously. Assertions of this

---

9. *Postscript*, 26.

10. Ibid., 44. On this issue the remarks of Torsten Bohlin, *Søren Kierkegaard*, concerning his use of the Bible are most instructive.

11. From a scholar's point of view, Kierkegaard admits that every sentence of Scripture must be tested like any other sentence that bears inquiry. It might well be that the sentences are then only probable.

variety do not grow out of proofs, out of research, or out of revealed facts. Religious belief, even if it includes a belief about Scripture, is not a truth-function of some elementary, more factual, plainer, or more historical assertions.

Once the learning game is played, doubt enters in; for the Scriptures are from the vantage point of a learned inquirer probably true or probably false. To assume that a religious belief will follow from the learned inquiry is a flagrant assumption, contrary both to the faith and belief described in Scripture and also to the proprieties of learning and logic. The attempt to introduce a dogmatic guaranty, the doctrine of inspiration, is then another mistaken effort, because it still assumes that learning and faith are in a kind of continuity, albeit needing this slight addition to get from one to the other.

Kierkegaard objects not to scholarship but to this use of Biblical scholarship on several different grounds. First there is an epistemological ground. All knowledge, even if gained by the most strenuous learning and the most astute of critics, is hypothetical, or in the words of *Postscript*, approximative.[12] One of the guiding maxims proposed within the Kierkegaardian literature is: ". . . the greatest attainable certainty with respect to anything historical is merely an approximation."[13] This means that the sentences of Scripture, when considered by an historical scholar, insofar as they are about events of the past are hypothetical in the same way as those in other history books. It means, also, that the scientific scholarship done upon the Bible and its documentary sources does not change this fundamental hypothetical character of the sentences into something less hypothetical. There might be a change, of course, from less probable to more probable or *vice versa*. If the scholarship stays within its limits, the material does not change into something of religious consequence.

At this juncture, Kierkegaard sees a major flaw in a certain pattern of theological argument. He says, ". . . a dogmatic guaranty is posited: Inspiration."[14] The flaw inheres in the following. Under the

---

12. *Postscript*, 26. See also 169. Just how Kierkegaard came to the view that all empirical research led only to "approximative" conclusions is a little difficult to say. He seemingly holds this only for research-like knowledge, not for matters of common sense.

13. Ibid., 25.

14. Ibid., 26.

mistaken impression that the truth of Scripture must be conceived as invariant and absolutely certain, on the one side, and measurable by the same paradigm or standard as the critical scholar otherwise uses, the concept "inspiration" is the only way to effect the two at once. Kierkegaard has no objection to the religious use of inspiration, as a way to declare that the Scriptures are, for example, the word of God or that they ought, in certain contexts, to be treated differently from other books. His objection is again logical. From the scholarly standpoint, the Scriptures are not certain and the facts that they assert can never be said to be completely described. Therefore scholarship must go on and on, for completeness is not conceivable. But for those who are not conceptually clear, this suggests that the Scriptures are not usable for religious purposes. It postpones the day until research is complete. But then a principle is cited that puts a stop to the demand for evidence and explanations: inspiration. Kierkegaard believed that such a dogmatic guaranty, asserting closure, was simply a mistake, confusing both the empirical inquiry, which ought not to be closed, and the religious, which ought to be closed but not respecting erstwhile factual matters.

There are several smaller points involved here. As will be noted at greater length later, Kierkegaard distinguished between necessary tautological truths and probable hypothetical truths about matters of fact. If both, as the philosophical culture of the day had it, were truths about being, it became clear that ambiguity lay in the word "being." The approximative character of empirical truths is a function of two facts: the empirical object is "unfinished," contingent, in space and time; moreover, the empirical subject, "the existing cognitive spirit is itself in process of becoming."[15] Therefore, there is always incompleteness. "Being," in the instances of tautological truths, is however non-contingent, and precisely to the extent that it is non-contingent it is only "the abstract reflection of, or the abstract prototype for, what being is as concrete empirical being."[16] Tautological truths are certain because contingency on the sides of both the subject and the object are abstracted from, and thus intentionally excluded. Completeness is assured by definition. Empirical subjects and objects, in contrast, are

15. Ibid., 169.
16. Ibid., 170.

both in process. Kierkegaard contends, almost like a Humean, that the logic of empirical research confirms the thesis that all such claims are only probable. They cannot be otherwise. This he also says about the hypotheses formulated in Biblical studies.[17]

But the issue in respect to Scripture has been to show that its sentences are logically peculiar and as sharply differentiated as are the God and the people to whom they refer. Therefore, if one argues that Scriptural sentences are also only probable, then one is apparently jeopardizing the confidence in an unchanging God by admitting that the sentences about Him are neither inviolate, nor unchanging, nor certain. Whatever the reasons, the Scriptural sentences have been at once claimed to be factual in reference and yet certain. Because no empirical investigation can even begin to verify a sentence which is both certain and existential (and here the word is used in the logician's sense), it is necessary to posit a dogmatic guaranty. Both in Kierkegaard's day and in our own a number of other topics are then studied—canonicity, the trustworthiness of the authors, the relationships between the books—all on the ground that the inspiration of the books will be made evident on these counts. Whatever the results dug up by the scholar's industry, Kierkegaard is convinced that an able dialectician would not be put off by this subterfuge but would see that inspiration and critical inquiry are logically incommensurate. One does not substantiate the other, nor can the Scriptures be considered within the same net of concepts to be both incontrovertibly certain and also verifiable.

As Kierkegaard repeatedly says, such an argument, instead of making the religiousness of the truth claim of the sentences most specific, betrays the whole effort. For once inspiration or any other dogmatic guaranty for the sentences is introduced, then the interest is shifted from the subject matter they describe to inspiration. Inspiration is not a matter of knowledge—it can neither be proved nor disproved; it is something toward which one must either have belief or credulity. Furthermore it is a discussion-stopper. Scientific investigation ought not to be stopped, and religious doubts ought not to be stopped by such a principle. Inspiration becomes a pseudo-religious

---

17. Ibid., 25–35. Early in his life Kierkegaard discovered that theological studies are not conclusive, at least not conclusive if one was seeking decisiveness and faith. See *Breve*, I:36–37.

The Bible and Christianity

belief in itself; instead of substantiating belief in sentences about God, the inspiration doctrine itself must be believed. Kierkegaard argues that inspiration, by trying to declare empirical sentences to be qualitatively distinct, i.e., empirical and yet indubitable and divine, must break with what he calls the quantitative dialectic of verification and proof. The introduction of inspiration in such discussions is like introducing a new quality, namely, that the text is divine. This then functions as a premise, maybe an inference-ticket, which is then utilized and ostensibly even discovered by Biblical and theological research much later. But such a principle is neither true nor false by the logic of critical studies. This is why Kierkegaard finds that any argument using it has introduced an incommensurability into the knowledge system. All of this is to show in different ways that the inspiration principle does not make Scriptural claims about God true. Instead, it introduces another and alien consideration, namely, whether there is such a thing as inspiration that finally becomes more fundamental than the truth of what is said about God.

Closely related is another logical consideration. In both the *Fragments* and the *Postscript* the limitations of a strict kind of logical deduction are explored again and again. The inspiration principle is actually being used in a sophisticated tautology to provide truths about God. By assuming an inspiration, it then becomes possible to deduce, by elaborate redefinitions, subtle methods, and careful exegesis all kinds of claims about Deity. But Kierkegaard assumes here, as he does in respect to the argument from design, that all the arguments then do is draw out the consequences of what was assumed.[18] Inspiration, even though it is not itself an hypothesis about the facts, only predisposes, almost by definition, what other empirical things really are. But it slips in the content non-empirically, and it comes out looking like an honest judgment about the facts. This again is to point to the fact that much theological argument using Biblical research, when informed by such principles as inerrancy or inspiration, proliferates a confusion of categories. Insofar as conclusions of research are offered in this manner, they are deductive truths, true really in respect to the premises with which one begins, and the empirical flourishes

---

18. *Fragments*, 74ff. One of the objections that Kierkegaard has to the Protestant orthodoxies, which were also Biblical, rests on this kind of misgiving. It is the logical shape that is wrong.

are actually rhetorical. Insofar as Biblical sentences are known to be true in virtue of research, then they very likely lack the kind of certainty about matters of fact that would seem to distinguish them from other factual claims. Without inspiration, in other words, they would be true (or false) in virtue of evidence and not God's inspiration, and this would give them a cognitive-like character but not a religious character.

Let us summarize thus far. By tugging and pulling at the terms involved, Kierkegaard is doing what he calls his "dialectical" study. This involves establishing a grasp of the territory to be covered by the terms, and also something of the power and authority these terms have in argument. Kierkegaard found it to be a logical offense to introduce a non-arguable and unquestionable principle into intellectual inquiries about the truth or falsity of what was written. For, if one is certain of that kind of guaranty, there is no point to the inquiry (say Biblical research), and if one is not certain of the guaranty, there is no certainty attaching to any conclusions presupposing it.

III

But then there is one of Kierkegaard's *reductio ad absurdum* arguments to consider. It begins with granting that every word in the Bible is inspired and therefore true. Furthermore, the reader of Scripture is granted all abilities to know and understand every sentence. Of course there is a question whether it makes any sense to say this about Scripture and to propose such a knowing subject. In any case, Kierkegaard makes his point by allowing us to think of a man for whom there were no doubts, no questions, and everything he wanted to know about the God of the Scriptures was so certified for him.

Once the picture is sketched in, Kierkegaard asks: Is a Christian one who has all kinds of certainties, i.e., certainties that count for something in scholarly research, in historical studies, in learned philological and other analytical inquiries respecting the Bible? Kierkegaard's point is: how absurd! For a religious man does have his certainties but they are not the sort that count for anything, except indirectly, in this kind of learned inquiry.[19] If they do, there is again a confusion somewhere.

19. See *Works of Love*, 302–10.

But there is more that is wrong too. For if we had a language that represented God and His relations to the world by analogy with other scientific accounts, say of the fauna of Brazil, Kierkegaard contends, such an account would again put God into the wrong kind of discourse. The very concept "God" would thereby be changed. It is Kierkegaard's theme, through his entire literature, that the Scriptures do not need to be translated out of their many kinds of literary style into something more precise, objective, and factual. So that the inspiration principle, granting its applicability, would only make it seem that every sentence in Scripture was ideally, if not as it stood, a true claim about a state of fact. Kierkegaard has all kinds of discomfitures about that. He is not saying that there is no fact or no object, for that would admit the justice of this way of construing the texts. His point is a more serious one. He is claiming that in the religious context, when a man is undertaking a role on the Christian stage, there is not much point to saying that God is an object and then construing the Scripture as though it were some true sentences about that object.

Again the logic is wrong. "God," the very concept, does not correlate in the Scriptures with "objects" or "facts." Therefore Kierkegaard says that there is a serious fault in construing the Scriptures in that way. Further, God is not an object to be described. Besides, the logic of "belief" is also at stake.

The very point of descriptive language that purports to be true is that it is true providing that there is no obstacle to representation given by the knowing subject. That supposes that the existing subjectivity of a person is not involved. Being religious is, however, being involved, being concerned, being a qualitatively different person. If a language claim, even about God, is believed to be true, there is nothing in that kind of assent to its claim that is productive of religiousness.[20]

Then there are those who would say that believing that the Bible is inspired is a religious act of belief, even of faith.[21] This Kierkegaard finds to be a superstition, arising out of an honest misunderstanding. Anything offered as a belief, even if religious, which keeps the dialectical away, which stops doubt and inquiry, which causes the uncertain

---

20. *Postscript*, 29 and 112.

21. Claims about the Church, the papacy, the sacraments, etc., are treated in *Postscript*, 35–47, with the same intent.

to appear certain, is a superstition, be it offered with religious purpose or not.[22]

The assumption that God, the Holy Spirit, and other distinctively religious themes can be treated in an objective manner and that all we lack is sufficient knowledge of them in this manner, is a sustaining hope of much of religious scholarship in our day as well as Kierkegaard's. Kierkegaard was quick to see that if one takes away this interest in the "objective truth," or what we are here calling the cognitive view of religion, religion is dissipated for many people. For the tantalizing edge of a kind of scientific religious research was and is that certainly religious results will follow. Kierkegaard's irony is at its fullest on this point.

> The years pass, but the situation remains unchanged. One generation after another departs from the scene, new difficulties arise and are overcome, and new difficulties again arise. Each generation inherits from its predecessor the illusion that the method is quite impeccable, but the learned scholars have not yet succeeded ... and so forth ... With the assistance of the clergy, who occasionally display learning, the laity get an inkling of how the land lies ... for the laity become objective merely by looking at the clergy, and expect a tremendously significant result, and so on. Now a hostile critic rushes forward to attack Christianity. He is precisely as well oriented as the scholarly critics and the dilettante laity. He attacks a book of the Bible, or a suite of books. Instantly the learned rescue corps rushes in to defend; and so it goes on indefinitely.[23]

To the extent that an actual learning goes on, Kierkegaard finds that everyone concerned must avoid making decisions; in fact, he must postpone all personal decisions until the learned inquiry is at an end. But the learned inquiry never ends and so no conclusive result follows. The logic of this learning only allows an approximative result anyway. This Kierkegaard does not deplore nor does he suggest any other recourse. Neither revelation nor inspiration ought to be used as a shortcut to certainty. These are the conditions of the intellectual inquiry. What Kierkegaard does disparage is the confusion that learn-

---

22. Especially, ibid., 29. Several of these category errors are noted in Fr. Heinrich Roos' *Søren Kierkegaard og Katolicismen*. See pp. 37–51. This book is published by Newman Press of Westminster, Maryland (1954) in an English translation.

23. *Postscript*, 28–30.

The Bible and Christianity 71

ing has introduced into the consideration of religious discourse. The proper scientific and scholarly air is, he insists, one of detachment and objectivity. Objectivity, psychologically at least, means precisely to eschew one's personal interestedness in deciding and thus to suspend judgment until the inquiry is complete.[24]

But religion and morality suppose that one has an "infinite personal interestedness," a masterful passion, that is the defining condition of a human subject's life.

So, granting even the most extravagant successes in respect to the truth of Scripture—what follows? He observes, "Faith does not result simply from a learned inquiry; it does not come directly at all."[25] Even if one produced countless objective truths, these truths would, if they were perfect realizations of the meaning of the evidence, still be approximations, still hypotheses, and they would warrant only the objectivity that is incommensurate with faith or a sense of ethical duty and obedience.

By the same token, supposing that the opponents have succeeded in proving what they desire—what then?[26] Neither will they succeed in destroying faith. For granted that the books are not authentic, that many of the sentences are false, etc., that many historical views claimed by believers are not true, still religious faith is not really touched. But, of course, in the objective sense, "there are indeed . . . results everywhere, a superfluity of results. But there is no decisive result anywhere."[27] That is to say, there is no knowledge, and knowledge is true or it would not be knowledge, but the decisiveness that religion is inheres in subjectivity alone, essentially in its passion.[28]

At this point Kierkegaard must be carefully followed, for he is not saying that empirical truths about matters of fact discussed and even disclosed in the Bible are impossible, nor is he denying that Biblical scholarship has a subject matter. His point is rather that a religious or an anti-religious use of knowledge to establish or disestablish faith is

24. Ibid., 30, 67, 169–70, and numerous other places in his published books and papers.

25. Ibid., 30.

26. Ibid., 31.

27. Ibid., 34–35. Note the masterful discussion of this issue in *On Authority and Revelation*, 57–64.

28. *Postscript*, 112.

a misunderstanding, a confusion of a logical sort, on both the side of knowing and of faith. For it is an unwarranted assumption, namely, that a scholar's truths either relieve or command the responsibility of being a believer. All of this he argues, never denying that there is a God or that Christ died for others. But even those beliefs are not finally the kind that function in any kind of scientific discourse.

Kierkegaard is however assuming that belief in Jesus Christ, for example, is not seriously affected one way or the other by Biblical and historical research. But this is so for him because the existence of even Jesus is not believed to be a predication like other predications, made on the basis of evidence or discredited by it. What evidence did credit was the character, the qualifications, of whatever one believed to exist, not existence itself.[29]

Kierkegaard is here stressing a distinction, or better perhaps drawing one, where there is otherwise a very learned kind of ambiguity. Kierkegaard is not denying that even the religious and moral life can be scientifically described. Though it is pushing the analysis a little far, it is relevant to point out that Kierkegaard admits that morality and religion have as part of their stuff, their raw material, ordinary human experience, about which one can also have scientific hypotheses. With sense data, motives, purposes, emotions, wishes, thoughts, we can also exercise our curiosity and spend our energies describing them. Or, we can use them for other ends and purposes. Religion and morals use emotions and purposes and are not simply their description. A point to remember here is that the Danish Socrates is not putting the empirical sciences, history, philosophy, ethics, and theology, etc., in a continuum with the sciences as foundational and more basic. Instead he argues that the difference between scientific truths and what he calls "essential truth," ethico-religious truth, lies not in data, but in the way we use what we have. Moral passion, the sense of guilt, a sense of duty, an interest in one's existence—these are not extraordinary and mere phenomena given by heredity or the gods. But, in respect to them, one can cognize them, draw conclusions from them, consider them as data, work them into laws, conceive theories from which one can deduce other laws, etc., and this would be one mode of

---

29. This matter will be dealt with in other chapters, especially chapter 8. The *Fragments, passim,* makes this point very succinctly.

The Bible and Christianity

interpretation. Otherwise, we can also practice life with each of these, maximize them and make them rule our lives, and we can concern ourselves with being good, being responsible, being obedient, and being kind. The difference between these two modes Kierkegaard called a leap. This is not the familiar inductive leap from "some to all"; it is rather the leap from one mode to another, with no warrants predisposing it, and no implications demanding it.

The same distinction obtains in respect to the religiousness of the Scriptures. Wherein does the faith lie? In more sentences? In sentences which prove the first sentences? In some basic facts? Kierkegaard contends that once we are entangled in the quest for proof, we must keep within one mode of discourse. It is only by shifting the mode, shall we say even the mood, and the attitude (the subject's weight?), that the religious may begin to appear. But when it appears, everything is again subject to the new mode of interpretation. This brings us around again to the significance of philosophical reflection. For it is precisely philosophy and Kierkegaard's kind of dialectic that reminds us of kinds of discourse and which enables us to see the importance of subjectivity, i.e., entertaining interestedly rather than describing disinterestedly our passions, emotions, and feelings. So, the language of love about one's beloved uses the passion of love to describe the world and everything else one pleases. This is not to say that the language is only expressive or only subjective. It may well be about otherwise familiar things. But its concepts everywhere are achieved by the use of the passion, and not simply by the description of the passion.

IV

What has here been noted concerning Kierkegaard and the Bible is remarkable for several reasons. Clearly Kierkegaard was stating, on both logical and religious grounds, reasons for repudiating the relatively sophisticated fundamentalist position. However, he was doing this, not because of a tissue of general philosophical or religious beliefs, not because he too was riding the anti-orthodox wave of the hour, but rather because he knew, on the one side, religiousness and ethical earnestness with such firsthand vividness and intensity, and, on the other side, epistemic and logical matters with such clarity and exactness. The upshot is the beginning of a new way to philosophize about religious matters.

Secondly Kierkegaard is here very suggestive on the uses of ethical and religious discourse. Though these matters can be discussed from many points of view, and though Kierkegaard variously conceived them (another example of this variety is considered later) too, still he is indicating how ethical and theological discourse actually becomes meaningful. According to his analysis, there are various kinds of discourse: scientific, religious, moral, and specifically Christian, plus several more. It is tempting to say that these are interpretations. But there is a misgiving about that expression "interpretation." For Kierkegaard did not deny that there was a world, a God, and all kinds of events. But there is no purely factual descriptive account of this world more basic than the rest. Therefore, there is no factual language, no non-interpreted facts, known to be so. So the force of the word "interpretation" is considerably blunted. It is not as though we can know the facts as facts and also then have various interpretations of the facts.

Therefore the point that we have been making heretofore can be seen again in this connection. The attempt to describe God and other erstwhile religious facts and phenomena in a scientific language as if here was the court of appeal, the final analysis for theology or for any other supposed interpretation, he categorically rejects. He denies that science or scholarship is to facts as theology or morals is to the meaning of the facts. Kierkegaard's diatribe against speculative philosophy is pertinent at this point, for he does not admit that there is any way to penetrate more deeply into these language differences and rate them by reference to a philosophical standard of veracity, of rationality, or facticity.

Therefore the account of Jesus in the Gospel of John is considerably different from the account of a scientifically trained historical critic. But the difference is not necessarily that one is more factual than the other, for this supposes that "fact" and "factual" are somehow irreducible terms and that we can see and know a fact *qua* fact when we see one. Kierkegaard supposed, of course, the distinction between "fact" and the account thereof. This dualism, as will later be argued in great detail, he finds inescapable. But this dualism is made usually in all universes of discourse, so that theologians, as well as jurists, moralists, aesthetes and scientists talk about the facts. Kierkegaard denies that one can distinguish between degrees of "factuality." His pseudonym Climacus writes, "Factual existence is wholly indifferent to any and all variations in essence, and everything that exists participates without petty jealousy in being and participates in the same degree."[30] So Kierkegaard decries all schemes of degrees of being or degrees of facticity. But this is to say surely that the concept "fact" is not the same in theology as in the scientific-historical accounts. There are then "facts" within theological contexts and within scientific contexts.

In sum, there is a logic of religious discourse that emerges as one begins to penetrate into the differences between scientific study of the Scriptures as over against theological uses thereof. For this "logic" is simply the string of conceptual differences that one must mark in order to think correctly about those matters. And "fact" is one knot on this string. Theology is not then an "interpretation" of a non-religious fact, as if that "were to be discovered as the kernel beneath the husks." Neither is the Bible, then, a contrived rendering of something that ought properly to be treated otherwise.

Thirdly, Kierkegaard's disparagement of an ultimate objective fact means that he must have another way of discriminating between, say, the Scriptures themselves and the scientific studies of the Scriptural materials. This is part of what is done by his emphasis upon subjectivity. He is not using subjectivity as a principle to declare that some kinds of discourse are without rules or therefore beyond criticism. But he is bringing forth reasons to show that the attempt to make a kind of critical science to adjudicate differences between theology, morals, history, and the natural sciences by reference to "fact" is a mistake. Nonetheless, there is still a way to distinguish them. This is by way of reference to the extent and how the passions, moods, feelings, and interests—in truth the panoply covered by "subjectivity"—became also ingredient in the string of concepts that make up the logic of all kinds of concepts. "To the concept of sin," he says, "corresponds the mood of seriousness."[31]

---

30. *Philosophical Fragments*, 33, footnote.
31. *Concept of Dread*, 15.

More will be said on this subject in subsequent chapters. But right here it is clear that Kierkegaard is not arguing that all of the non-scientific discourse is, therefore, expressive only as over against denotative and referential discourse as is allegedly the case in the instance of the scientific language. Neither does he share the vulgar prejudice that the phenomena of feelings and moods, passions, and emotions are private in any ordinary sense.[32] His point is rather that all thinking and speaking takes place within contexts where meanings are not simply a function of facts. Meanings of concepts, up and down the string of them, are a subtle consequence of how a person, a subject, addresses the things around him. When he does it with maximal interest and passion in saving his life and future, Kierkegaard's argument is that every concept in such discourse also expresses that "how." When he does it with a temper that is more antiseptic, more objective as we commonly say, the concepts are accordingly different. "Fact" in one instance might be the "Our Lord and Savior, Jesus Christ"; "fact" in a more critical description might be "one Jesus of Nazareth." Neither is minimal or more basic to the other. Each is basic within its own kind of discourse. These distinctions are drawn by Kierkegaard not to disparage one against the other, but rather to lessen the confusions and temptations to confusions.

Fourthly, it seems rather striking to have an author so dedicated to the Bible as Kierkegaard delimit so sharply, and so early, the scientific objective approach from the religious and ethical appropriation.[33] Most authors, scholars, or homileticians seem to have a vested interest in blurring this distinction altogether.

---

32. Note here those passages in volume VIII of the *Papirer* where a range of this kind of issue is discussed, especially those under the heading "A," which have to do with *Sickness Unto Death*.

33. All kinds of studies have been done on Kierkegaard and the Bible. P. G. Hansen in his *Søren Kierkegaard og Bibelen* very tiresomely excerpts the papers on Biblical topics. This gives a clue to the extent of Kierkegaard's interest over a large number of years. Anders Gemmer's *Sören Kierkegaard und Karl Barth* shows how Barth was influenced by Kierkegaard's Biblicism, but Gemmer does it so poorly that it is a discredit to both his heroes. A comparable theme is treated by Pelikan, *From Luther to Kierkegaard*, which book is a spirited, but brief, account of how Kierkegaard can be conceived to be repudiating Lutheran "objective" orthodoxies and reconstituting a Christ-centered Biblicism, full of the rich devotional interest of Martin Luther. But few studies do as effective a job of indicating Kierkegaard's indebtedness to the Bible as does *Kierkegaard and the Bible: An Index* by Paul Minear

The Bible and Christianity

But, in addition to being an able dialectician, it ought to be remarked, Kierkegaard was a remarkable student of Scripture. Most of his literature shows how at home he was in both ancient literature and the Bible. Allusions come easily to him and they are invariably apt, penetrating in unsuspected ways, and indicative of the most careful reading and understanding. The many entries in the papers on Scriptural themes are examples too of a pervading enthusiasm and long preoccupation, albeit without involving him in any pseudo-magical view of Biblical literature. His concern is devotional, but in addition he is always concerned with the root questions of how the misunderstandings arise.

With every reference to the Bible it is made clear "How the Subjectivity of the Individual Must be Qualified in Order that the Problem may Exist for Him."[34] Kierkegaard points out that "Christianity assumes that there inheres in the subjectivity of the individual, as being the potentiality of the appropriation of the good, the possibility of its acceptance . . ."[35] But there are persons who are ethically immature or half-awake; others are willfully perverse. The point is that religion requires interior experiences, in other words, passions and emotions, which are available to all and to which all have access if the subjectivity is properly qualified. "For in fact," says the author of *Either/Or*, vol. II, "the universal exists nowhere as such, and it depends upon me, upon my energy of consciousness, whether in the particular I will see the universal or merely the particular."[36] The religious reading and understanding of the Bible presupposes an ethically qualified subjectivity in the reader. Otherwise the scientific study alone is in order, and this consists invariably in widening the cognitive base, trying to find the principles correlating the variety of data. The religious outlook that the Bible itself everywhere evinces asks for an intensive treatment of the datum, so intensive that passion is brought to a maximum. One's own existence is at stake and that single instance, myself, is enough to establish the religious signifi-

---

and Paul Morimoto. This gives a sizeable testimony to Kierkegaard's scholarship as well as evidence of how clearly he kept himself within the limits noted.

34. This is the title of Part Two, Book Two, *Postscript*.

35. Ibid., 116.

36. *Either/Or*, II: 275. Note too the discussion about knowing sin "*in abstraction*" and "*in concreto*," ibid., 46.

cance of the Scriptures.[37] This is obviously a rich anthropomorphic view of the Scriptures, though not lacking, therefore, an intersubjective meaning. We shall note features of this Kierkegaardian anthropomorphism later.

In the succeeding chapter, several additional questions will be canvassed with the hope that the issue here discussed can be more richly enjoined.

---

37. The meditation "What Is Required in Order to Look at Oneself with True Blessing in the Mirror of God?" is appropriate, as the title already suggests. *For Self-Examination*, 7–62.

CHAPTER 5

History and the Sciences

SEVERAL OF KIERKEGAARD'S RESTRAINING views concerning the limits of knowledge have already been noted. Kierkegaard was not a devotee of general learning for its own sake. He does not easily read the scientists and the technical scholars, unless their concerns overlap his own. Kierkegaard was not like Kant, who reputedly read every item, whatever the topic, from his publisher in Königsberg. On the other hand, Kierkegaard is not therefore anti-science, nor is he poorly read. On the contrary, he had a large library and read most of it. He is not convinced, however, that philosophical and theological concepts grow out of scientific ones or that metaphysical philosophy is a higher level of generalization over the same subject matter. Neither is he persuaded that the reading of nature, any more than the scientific reading of Scripture, is the way to ethical maturity and the Kingdom of God. For even a century ago, while practicing much of what twentieth-century philosophers call analytic philosophy, he also refused to make philosophy only a syntactical science or a study of the logic of the sciences.[1]

Kierkegaard's tentativeness about metaphysical philosophy has several roots. Certainly he was skeptical of philosophers' abilities to discern in empirical assertions, whether of natural scientists or historians, new kinds and levels of meanings which they did not know

---

1. As did Rudolf Carnap, *Logical Syntax of Language*, 277–333. Kierkegaard's empathy for the variety of ways of speaking and for the variety of views of life kept him from even linguistic kinds of reductionisms. In fact, his criticisms of metaphysics were so stringent and exact that they kept him also from asserting the finality and irreducibility of facts too.

were there. So what he calls this "reading of tea-leaves" he thinks is often the play of charlatans. He dislikes, too, the linking of knowledge, whatever its kind, with "transcendent reality." Whatever the reason, Kierkegaard is not prone to large generalizations, to multiplying entities and to conjecture about the unknown. Whether these are symptoms of being tough-minded rather than tender-minded is difficult to say.

The reason for addressing here questions about the natural sciences is simply historical. It is true that much of the metaphysics and large-scale theological writing of Kierkegaard's day looked like a gloss upon these sciences. It was as if a certain kind of understanding, let us call it a kind of metaphysics, could give a new appearance to historical and scientific facts. There seemed to be a new point of departure. But Kierkegaard is critical. He thinks the philosophical concepts are insertions, and spurious ones at that, onto the account of the way things truly are.

He has no objection at all to metaphysics as an interested interpretation. He makes a rather strong case for considering metaphysics in just this way.[2] But he does object to saying that it is a maximally disinterested science—as if there is no interpolation and as if all the concepts of realty, of the good, and of goals for the totality were already implicit and had only to be shaken out of something given to us. Metaphysics, especially the new grand kind of the Hegelians and their theological followers, emerged as an innocent study of what was already present. This sort of subterfuge Kierkegaard is anxious to exhibit. He shows us, for example, what historical concepts are and how and why they cannot be theological concepts.[3]

But there is a complication in Kierkegaard's analysis. For it was not the overt and explicit metaphysical arguments that Kierkegaard belittled as much as it was the strange and almost "natural" metaphysics, that which seemed almost indigenous to minds as minds. The metaphysical arguments of Descartes, Leibniz, and others were often intrinsically noteworthy. Besides, Kierkegaard thought that he could detect the interests that they served and, at least, could argue the mat-

2. Note his remarks in *Repetition*, 33–35. See also vol. II of *Papirer*, especially, 280ff. Some pages of these sections are translated by Walter Lowrie and are included in the "Editor's Introduction" to *Repetition*, xvi ff.

3. This is a major point in *Philosophical Fragments*.

History and the Sciences

ter. They made sense at least. Though he most often concluded negatively respecting many metaphysical arguments, it was not all or any metaphysics that he was flailing. He seems to think that metaphysics does many different things and that there is no single logical pattern by which one can conceive of all metaphysics. Nonetheless there is another kind of argument, a kind of metaphysics of the mind that was his *bête-noir*. In short, it was the inchoate metaphysics of the mind of "the professor in each man."[4] For the professor in us, he says ironically, makes us believe that to have a mind meant knowing something, both as a condition for doing, for feeling, for being faithful, if not just about anything else, and as a concomitant to these things. Everything gets turned into knowledge. Therefore, a kind of knowing was believed to be characteristic of being a man. And it was this kind of metaphysics of the mind, this generalized and predisposing belief (which we will discuss more fully in chapter 6) that all of the new knowledge of the age was feeding and, unfortunately, said to be illustrating.[5]

The results include technical mistakes too. For the philosophers and theologians, insofar as they did specialized epistemological study, pretended to find all kinds of cognitive concepts involved in even non-cognitive matters. Furthermore, the philosophical theologians, those with practiced dialectical skills, looked at the new sciences and at history and claimed to discern in their concepts the concepts also of theology and metaphysics. This is why Kierkegaard finds that the enthusiasm for "reflection and understanding" is so difficult to address. It rests finally upon a mistaken myth-like view of how people think and behave.

Here we only approach the major difficulty. For his procedure was to start at the circumference and work inward. The correction of the metaphysical view of who and what the subject was is the upshot of his whole authorship, not any one book or argument. We will, therefore, only approach it slowly. Here we turn to the epistemological issues of history and science as these bear upon the confusion Kierkegaard is anxious to undo.

---

4. This expression is quoted from Kierkegaard by David Swenson, *Something about Kierkegaard*, 93.

5. Dru, *Journals*, no. 652 (*Papirer* VIII A, 92). He writes, "The misfortune of the age is understanding and reflection."

I

Perhaps unexpectedly, Kierkegaard gives repeated accolades to the sciences and scholarship. Like most continental thinkers, he did not always distinguish sharply between natural science and humanistic scholarship. He was content to lump these as instances of "*videnskab*" or knowledge. But his diatribe is nonetheless specific. He is concerned to show that the concepts of knowledge do not transmute into qualitative moral concepts. He disparages attempts to relate concepts of differing contexts "internally" as though they evinced the same meanings. Furthermore, in respect to religion and morality, he is at pains to show again that though religious faith and the moral life are learned, the kind of learning is not the same as academic and scholarly learning, nor is it directly dependent on it. It is not only scientific Scriptural inquiries that are irrelevant in this respect (however relevant these interests may be in other respects), but almost all kinds of learning that issue in scholarly results.

It is tempting to assume that Kierkegaard is simply drawing a now familiar distinction between a factual judgment and a value judgment or, as Herbert Butterfield has, the distinction between knowledge about an event and moral judgments about an event. Though it complicates our story considerably, it must be insisted that Kierkegaard's distinction is not so neat or so simpleminded. In accord with the view noted in the previous chapter, he denies that there is any single minimal factual judgment or proposition possible. Therefore, in regard to events he does not say that there are at first purely factual descriptions, that are simply statements of what is what, and then secondly some evaluative judgments about these facts or events. In fact, Kierkegaard's analysis undercuts this perspective altogether.

His contrasting depiction is of alternative ways of construing, i.e., of building up and setting in order one's life and the world around one. For reasons that we will later note in some detail, Kierkegaard considers most scholarship under his rubric "aesthetic," implying only a kind of passivity and indifference on the part of the subject. Historical knowledge is, of course, about events, but so are moral judgments, religious language, and the pages of most poets. He rejects the notion that the language of any one of these forms of life is of one logical type.

Therefore, he does not argue that moral language is only imperative or evaluative whereas scientific language is exclusively descriptive. He shows us by his pseudonyms that those accounts are falsifying. And he does not insist either that there is any one language in which word and event singularly meet. There is no language for the event simply as an event, subsequently to be overlaid with evaluative or more elaborated descriptions. His rebuke about the claim of metaphysics being disinterested reminds us that there has been an almost continuous effort to show that metaphysics is the science of reality as it is, without distortions or falsifications, and altogether independent of observers. The problem with this is the metaphysical concept of reality. Kierkegaard is at pains to show instead that history is also objective and has a legitimate use for a concept of "fact" and even "reality" within the context of historical description. So too do moral language and theology. The concepts of "fact" and perhaps "reality" are not the same in these special kinds of discourse. In a later chapter on Kierkegaard's metaphysics more attention will be paid to some of these matters. Our point thus far is only to insist that for Kierkegaard moral discourse is neither reference-less nor less objective than historical discourse; correlatively, he argues that these kinds of discourse cannot be scaled invidiously.

Nonetheless there are differences, otherwise one would not be called historical and the other moral. An example illustrating differences might be judgments about Napoleon. If an historian describes Napoleon's abilities as a military commander or as an administrator, Kierkegaard contends that the judgment is "quantitative." In contrast, judgments about the morals of Napoleon or about his greatness, including such questions as whether Napoleon's career was for the ultimate good of France or Europe, are "qualitative."

Herbert Butterfield has noted in some detail the distinction between technical historical judgments which are factual and descriptive, and moral judgments about the same event, person, or policy. According to him, the sweep of events technically described finds its most accurate objective account in the disinterested technical language of the historian. Therefore, questions of truth or falsity are resolved here. On the contrary, Butterfield urges, "It is the nature of Christianity to transform history for those who have faith—to transform the meaning of the story and the mode of experiencing it even though the course of the world's events remains the same as before."[6] It seems suspiciously to be the case that the historian's judgments have "a certain minimum significance"[7] whereas other judgments, whether of a moralist or a religious person, fill the story with significance not already provided.

Many historians are strongly inclined to separate historical judgments from moral evaluations as facts are separated from interpretations. Butterfield is an illustration once again:

> Nothing can exceed the feeling of satisfaction that many people have when they meet some such system which helps them through the jungle of historical happenings and gives them an interpretation of the story seen as a whole. In such cases our interpretation is a thing which we bring to our history and superimpose on it, however. We cannot say that we obtained it as technical historians by inescapable inferences from the purely historical evidence.[8]

In some such way a sharp distinction is drawn between two kinds of judgments. Historical judgments are described as if only evidence constituted them. Moral judgments made ostensibly about the same events are thus more often than not an expression of the subjectivity of the viewer. It is out of such considerations that the invidious distinction has grown between judgments that are really pseudo-judgments, even though they purport to refer to the world but are only expressions of a person's passions and feelings, and real judgments, those that are not expressions of anything but are only records of the way things are. Whatever Kierkegaard's merits as a logician, while certainly quick to reject Hegel's blurring of sharp logical distinctions, he was also reluctant to draw another distinction like that of "fact" and "interpretation" or "fact" and "value."[9]

---

6. Butterfield, *Christianity in European History*, 45.

7. Butterfield, *Christianity and History*, 19. See also note, 23.

8. Ibid., 23.

9. More of Butterfield's remarks on these issues are to be found in *The Englishman and his History*, 118–39; *Man on his Past*, especially the sections on Lord Acton; *Christianity and History*, particularly "Judgment in History," 48–68. Kierkegaard's remarks are to be found principally in *Postscript*, 25–48; *Either/Or*, II: 108–117 and passim; *On Authority and the Individual*, 130ff.; and numerous places in the *Papirer* III A, 1 and 103 (JP 2, 1587 and JP 5, 5494); IV A, 103 and 164 (JP 3, 3077, and JP

Kierkegaard makes his case in several different ways. First, he draws a distinction between quantitative and qualitative judgments in the context of Hegel's philosophy of history; second, he develops a kind of *reductio ad absurdum* argument again; third, he provides a reflection or two about being moral. In these several ways Kierkegaard begins, via his philosopher-pseudonym, to draw a map of those concepts that will give us a place for the most unusual concept, the concept of truth as subjectivity. But it is very important to watch him at work on these misuses of history first.

II

According to one scholar, "Kierkegaard's polemic against Hegel is the classic philosophical and spiritual polemic in the nineteenth century."[10] Such a judgment is plausible to anyone who has taken the trouble to follow the argument that Kierkegaard wages against the new historical metaphysics. However, it is worth noting that Kierkegaard is not scornful of Hegel's historical scholarship, for this remains for him an awesome and almost frightening accomplishment. The difficulty lies rather in the metaphysical theory that Hegel proposes, which is a theory that serves as a kind of high-level and unifying generalization within which both ethical judgments and historical hypotheses can at least be understood even if they cannot ostensibly be deduced. Again Kierkegaard is very subtle. He is not opposed to the metaphysical view as much as he is to the way in which it is claimed to relate to history and to morality. More precisely, he denies that metaphysical

---

1, 1030); VI B, 45 and 57; VIII A, 11 (*JP* 3, 3089); IX 2A, 9; X 1 A, 510–48; X 2 A, 195 (*JP* 6, 6532). Also note Søren Holm's *Søren Kierkegaards Historiefilosofi*, which is a very learned study of Kierkegaard's views about history. But Professor Holm has slight regard for a bare conceptual analysis, so he says in his Foreword (translation my own):

> Of history Kierkegaard surely had little conception, neither methodological nor cultural-social. But his special debt to Christianity caused him to formulate a philosophy of history, which was at the same time a polemic against Hegel and constitutive of the substance of Christianity.

10. Bense, *Hegel und Kierkegaard*, 7. (The translation is my own.) Though this book is written in a strange aphoristic style, it is very suggestive on technical points.

concepts are so rich that they include the concepts of history and historical writing and, in turn, of ethical judgments.

Hegel was specific on one point, namely, that the justification for his historical metaphysics lay in a process of verification, quasi-empirical verification, in respect to historical facts. Furthermore, he suggests that his metaphysical view, not least his philosophy of history, grew in an inductive manner from the particulars to the hypotheses, and then to the philosophical-historical principles.[11] In ways like these empirical concepts and metaphysical concepts overlap. The historical fabric, i.e., historical events and not simply the knowledge of history, commits every person to a kind of self-abnegation. Then empirical concepts get involved, subtly but firmly. To know the magnificent sweep of temporal events is to know "the great principle of living in the Spirit (*Geist*) of one's people," and all other circumstances, not least the individual's, are subordinate.[12] As Hegel tells the human story, the entire past of the race is like a pre-condition for the individual's moral life. Therefore, by a maximal historical awareness, the most complete objectivity, a given individual begins to realize his role and ethical task. So, too, do the metaphysical-historical concepts include the ethical, admittedly in an odd and confusing way.

Kierkegaard found this very amusing and promised ironically to do nothing whatsoever to augment his "*Weltgeist*." His own books were only pieces, certainly not additions to this system. He refused also to "go farther" by pushing Hegel's ideas to new arenas. One of his authors says that he already had quite enough for his weak head in the very thought of what a prodigious head every shareholder in the historical system must have—with such prodigious thoughts.[13] One issue is very sticky: just how is the transition made from historical knowledge to becoming a moral man? But one need not press that. How do historical concepts become ethical concepts? How does that happen even in the systematic view? The transition is not clear in Hegel's writings, and Kierkegaard made the most of the ambiguity.

---

11. See Hegel's *Lectures on the Philosophy of History*, 8–9. Also note Findlay's recent work on Hegel, *Hegel: A Re-examination*.

12. Haldane, *Wit and Wisdom of a German Philosopher*, 9. The quotation is from Hegel's *History of Philosophy*, vol. I.

13. *Fear and Trembling*, 6.

But first let us hear him in the *Postscript*. The learned are now united, he says, in a singular conclusion:

> ... that the objective tendency in the direction of intellectual contemplation, is, in the newest linguistic-usage, the *ethical* answer to the question of what I *ethically* have to do; and the task assigned to the contemplative nineteenth century is world history.[14]

So, in brief, the situation is something like this. Kierkegaard has already shown us in his earlier literature a variety of aesthetic views, an ethical view, plus religious outlooks too. Each of them is given to us as a language "of" a respective view but also and simultaneously with a language "about" many familiar things of the everyday world. Kierkegaard has developed these with care and earnestness. But Hegel's philosophy purported to explain these as permutations of the world-spirit. The concepts, in turn, were supposedly to be understood as in some way dependent upon the large matrix of history. What happens to an ordinary person in such a world as that? Kierkegaard's quixotic author, the independent philosopher Johannes Climacus, treats this question by developing several considerations that would be forced upon the moralist (and the ethical theorist) if such a sweeping and inclusive awareness were the highest task, especially in the ethical sense.[15]

But now to his criticisms. Kierkegaard points out that one consequence must be that ethical concepts would be neutralized by being handled in the language of "the great and significant."[16] This means that the terms, categories, and words of historical description would have to replace or redefine these most distinctive of ethical judgments. But this violates a moral person's use of ethical terms and demands a concession that a moral person would certainly refuse to make. Suppose that we experiment from the other side and invest everything significant and historically great, the heroes and notables, with ethical qualities because of the quantitative facts. Then the ab-

---

14. *Postscript*, 119.

15. Ibid., 119ff. The question is also put negatively: "What conclusion would inevitably force itself upon ethics, if becoming a subject were not the highest task confronting a human being?"

16. Ibid., 120. See also *Either/Or*, II: 112.

surdity becomes manifest. For then an incommensurateness is apparent. The concepts are different and cannot be blended together. The author asserts: ". . . neither by willing the good with all his strength, nor by satanic obduracy in willing what is evil, can a human being be assured of historical significance."[17]

From either point of view, either an historian's or moralist's, the attempt to derive goodness or badness from quantity, or historical and quantitative significance from goodness or badness, is equally implausible. "If I know that Caesar was a great man," Kierkegaard says, "I know what greatness is, and it is on this knowledge that I base my judgment of Caesar; otherwise I do not know that Caesar was great."[18] This is to argue, therefore, that arguments about greatness, about moral stature, are not "to be had gratis when buying in large quantities," or by recounting the number of things for which he was the moving agent. Questions of moral stature suppose that one knows something besides the historical details, what Kierkegaard calls "the ideality." This is why the strange statement is made: ". . . access to the realm of the historical is subject to a quantitative dialectic, so that whatever has historical significance has passed through this dialectic."[19] Kierkegaard never denies, it must be insisted again, that ethical factors are present in the historical process. The ambiguity of ethical factors in society was something of which he was well aware. But he denies that a man learns these to his own ethical advantage within even the most complete knowledge of historical and natural events. Climacus writes:

> For God, the apprehension of the historical is interpenetrated by His knowledge of the inmost secrets of the conscience, alike in the greatest and in the humblest. If a human being seeks to occupy this standpoint he is a fool . . . it must be reckoned a piece of presumption to attempt to see it there, a reckless venture which may readily end by the observer losing the ethical himself.[20]

---

17. *Postscript*, 120. See also *Either/Or*, II: 112ff., and *Concept of Dread*, 26.
18. *Postscript*, 289.
19. Ibid., 126. Note another use of this distinction in a rejoinder in the *Attack*, 159–61.
20. Ibid., 126–27.

Kierkegaard laments the mixing up of concepts that certain kinds of popular philosophizing produced. So he says via Climacus:

> Philosophy has answered every question; but no adequate consideration has been given to the question concerning what sphere it is within which each question finds its answer. This creates a greater confusion in the world of the spirit than when in the civic life an ecclesiastical question, let us say, is handled by the bridge commission.[21]

Not least of the achievements of a philosopher is, therefore, simply the matter of learning which sphere is which. Kierkegaard was convinced that scholars of a philosophical sort were misled by the notion of history including everything human to thinking that the concepts of history included (in an odd logical way) all the other concepts used in the human scene. It is to his merit then to have distinguished historical questions, answers, knowledge, and concepts from those of the moral sphere.

But, on the side of morals, this adds up to a view something like the following: that ethical language is *sui generis* and not reducible to other kinds of categories. Furthermore, ethical speech about events is not an instance of historical speech about events. It is almost as if Kierkegaard is accusing philosophers of his day of an historicistic fallacy rather than the naturalistic fallacy. The later fallacy was noted by G. E. Moore in an effort to keep clear the "*principia ethica*" against those who ostensibly saw ethical qualities as if they were qualities of nature, attributable to natural phenomena and men as was their color, their size, or their mass. But Moore's context was late nineteenth-century British idealism and evolutionism, which made metaphysical views out of the natural sciences and the suggestive hypotheses therein. Kierkegaard's context was early nineteenth-century philosophy, German principally, which conceived its metaphysics as a temporalizing, as Arthur Lovejoy noted, of the chain-of-being. The arguments of both Kierkegaard and Moore are, on the positive side, an attempt to keep ethical categories ethical; on the negative side, they are both fighting the reductionists of the day who find dualities and pluralities, even of ethical principles and factual accounts, to be reprehensible.

---

21. *Postscript*, 288.

Kierkegaard impugns the view that everything moral is also visible to the historian. His suggestion is that there are two histories, one external, and the other internal. One cannot be reduced to the other. The internal history is the locus of interest to the poet, to the ethicist, and to the religious man. Moreover, the internal history is the story of a person coming to possess his own stature, or "coming into his own," as the popular expression has it. This is the kind of history that is relevant to every person.[22] And the external history that is the quantitative history, subject to the scholar's accounting, does well in eliminating altogether the ethical and internal from its scope. The fault in the metaphysical histories, as Kierkegaard sees them, is the attempt to put these two together in another kind of synthesis, as though both could be understood in a third medium.[23] Kierkegaard's insistence upon an internal history does not involve him in anything like the recent distinction between the "inside" and the "outside" of an event. On the contrary, he uses "internal history" as a concept to refer to each person's "learning to strive with time." His examples are numerous, but one might suffice:

> If I would imagine a hero who stakes his life, it can very well be concentrated in the moment, but not the business of dying daily, for here the principle point is that it occurs every day. Courage can very well be concentrated in the moment, but not patience, precisely for the reason that patience strives with time.[24]

Otherwise, Kierkegaard has no objection to "external" histories, to ordinary historical studies; he even allows one of his pseudonyms to suggest that deterministically conceived studies of this "whole of existence" are in order, if students think that they have the leisure for it.[25] Kierkegaard does not insist that "internal history" is private in any internal epistemological sense. His point is only that, granted the most complete historical account of behavior, this still does not permit us to say that moral categories are done away. They belong to

---

22. *Either/Or*, II: 112–14, 146–50.
23. Holm, *Søren Kierkegaards Historiefilosofi*, chapter 2.
24. *Either/Or*, II: 114.
25. Ibid., 147.

History and the Sciences

one's "internal history," and when applied to "external history" they are done so only by an individual with courage so to use them.

III

But there is another kind of consideration. Again the reflection applies to endeavors to construe both ethical and religious judgments within the widest empirical knowledge. Suppose, then, that the science of history will also provide true ethical judgments. Then, it is argued, one must admit that ethical truth is somehow abstracted from world-historical experience and is a kind of refined and derived truth. This supposes that the ethical is something quite different when it has to do with millions rather than with simply a single individual. This is a learned disparagement of the primitive, the "*Oprindelige*," within each person in favor of the contemplated. "We contemplate universal history," he says, "and seem to see that every age has its own moral substance."[26] Kierkegaard finds this to be a consequence of an analogy which is false. Because passion and knowledge are inimical to one another, it is assumed that passion and ethical assurance are also. Kierkegaard denies the latter, but not the former. To do away with passion altogether is to do away with the ethical altogether. To accept the notion that world history is the only knowledge of "moral substance" is also to disparage that ethical individuality which is the source of ethical awareness.[27] In other words, morality and religiosity demand the intensification of passion, and if passion is a kind of subjectivity (again, this is not privacy), then the emphasis upon objectivity and upon disinterested knowledge is inimical to the existence of moral and religious passion.[28]

Once more a kind of "*reductio ad absurdum*" argument carries the reader along. Ethical enthusiasm would properly have to be ex-

---

26 *Samlede Vaerker*, VII 1 17–18, and *Postscript*, 129.

27. *Postscript*, 136; and *Either/Or*, vol. II: 146, where "objective time" and a kind of lived time are contrasted.

28. *Postscript*, 117. See also *Papirer* III A, 2 (*JP* 3, 3723). In an entry of 1840 young Kierkegaard noted that the Reformation started "a movement to study world history. We note this in the way that everyone now feels it necessary to study the world's past and the scholarship which produces a massive running comment on every sort of dogma." The translation is my own.

pended upon the contemplation of others, and upon world history, and this would mean a distraction from oneself. Climacus writes:

> The true ethical enthusiasm consists in willing to the utmost limits of one's own powers, but at the same time being so uplifted in divine jest as never to think about the accomplishments. As soon as the will begins to look right and left for results, the individual begins to become immoral.[29]

The controlled and disciplined spirit of objective detachment, essential to scholarship, excludes the passion, the moral kind of reflection from the primitiveness of the moral and religious life. The detached attitude is only one model of how to be rational, and Kierkegaard says the following about it:

> But the more complicated the externality in which the ethical inwardness is reflected, the more difficult becomes the problem of observation, until it finally loses its way in something quite different, namely, the aesthetic. The apprehension of the historical process therefore readily becomes a half poetic contemplative astonishment, rather than a sober ethical perspicuity.[30]

Therefore there may be said to be several mistakes involved: the error of assuming that the good or the ethical has not been found but is yet to be discovered—in short, that it is an object or even a truth, and that the inadequacy of our words about it will be remedied when knowledge is fuller; another error, closely related perhaps, is that the ethical objectivity, the good, will be found in history with the millions rather than in one's individual life. Added to these is the dubious notion that if such "moral substance" can be found, then an individual will become ethical upon awareness of such a substance.[31]

But the major thrust of this argument is still to make it clear that there is a confusion, of a gentle and yet plausible sort, awaiting us in metaphysical history. Kierkegaard is anxious to show us the absurdity of losing touch with our ordinary aspirations, wishes, hopes, and

---

29. *Postscript*, 120.

30. Ibid., 127. He also uses the phrase "spoiled by the habit of contemplation," 120–21.

31. Ibid., 115–17. Note again *Either/Or*, vol. II: passim, where the whole volume is a gentle evocation of another use of "good" than that proposed by assuming that it is a name of something.

loves. Few of the young intelligentsia were as tempted as he was to let an air of intellectual detachment sweep away all these more ordinary components of personal life and concepts which go with them. Who can deny that the whole of history seems, on the face of it, a more fitting subject for consideration than one's own miserable personal life? Furthermore, however important ethical issues seem to be, how plausible it appears to be to assume that they too must be resolved in the large—world history, rather than in the small—one's own life. But, Kierkegaard's discernment here is again very keen. He charges that to yield to this view means both intellectual confusion and, finally, an actual moral deprivation. There will be no ethics at all.

Closely related to this detail is an issue concerning teleological and causal judgments. Once again it seemed plain that much of the ethical language is teleological. This means only that purposes, goals, and intentions are said to be realized and that behavior is so construed. It is a familiar matter since Kant (whether justified is another question) that descriptions of natural phenomena issue in causal judgments whereas descriptions of historical phenomena issue in teleological judgments. But the issue for Kierkegaard is not quite this. Once again it is the temptation, and literally that, to assume that the teleological judgments of the historian, who ostensibly sees great purposes being realized in history, are only more comprehensive instances of the teleological judgments of an ethical subject. The logic of these two kinds of teleological judgments, he insists, is different. That they are both teleological is not saying enough to treat them as though the comprehensive judgment somehow includes the particular judgment that a man must make for himself. Therefore, though he doubts the thesis that historical judgments are necessarily teleological, Kierkegaard denies in particular the claim that moral judgments, because they are teleological, must necessarily be apprehended within a larger teleological (preferably historical) context. Again it is the logic of this kind of argument that he sniffs out.

Again Hegel is the target. For Hegel does not allow that historians add the *telos* by the dispositions they bring to the facts, but rather that both the factual judgments about actual events and the events themselves are already and intrinsically teleological. Events are teleological and, therefore, the judgments are. It is this that Kierkegaard especially traverses. He argues, instead, the pedestrian notion that judgments are only approximate and hypothetical. Hegel's kind of language suggested something else, namely, that historical judgments were certain, something like logical deductions, and furthermore that they disclosed the ideality and ethical component, the teleological factor, within the real and actual. This was the meaning of saying that historical judgments were teleological; for using the vast expanse of history, beginning with China and Persia as Kierkegaard never tires of repeating, the Hegelians proposed that one discovered the "*telos*" of everything at once.

Instead of being convinced by this account, Kierkegaard is stung to the most exacting criticisms. Using the language offered, he notes again that historical assertions are probable, and then says that they are subject to "a dialectic" that Hegel does not understand. By "dialectic" here he means only the rules and limits that tell us what the concepts involved actually are. Hegel had argued in the *Encyclopedia* that there was a logico-historical dialectic, a kind of intellectual activity in events, that made it possible to use logical categories to describe everything occurring in history, all of religion, art, thinking, and even wars and catastrophes. The overlap of concepts is so large that a single logic, a single set of rules, can discern the totality. All sentences about ethics, aesthetics, and matters of fact are related to one another in a logical fashion. However, Hegel is not novel on this point, at least in the nineteenth century, and it is well to realize how formidable the view was in Kierkegaard's day.[32]

But, in addition, Hegel proposed a very strong view about logic, namely, that there was a logic of facts and events, not simply of language and sentences, but of historical events in their real and ontological relations. Thus the Hegelian dialectic closed the gap between the two poles, the ideal and the real. Actual events are also dynamically related, one to another, in logical relations. Philosophical historical judgments are logical and teleological at once, in virtue of the character of actuality itself.[33] Against this Kierkegaard suggests that

32. See Holm, *Søren Kierkegaards Historiefilosofi*, 16–20. Also see the discerning pages of Isaiah Berlin in *Historical Inevitability*. The latter, a single lecture, is a criticism of the notion that history is a tissue of "... those vast impersonal forces ..." (T. S. Eliot) and is especially appropriate to Hegel's views.

33. See Jean Hyppolite, *Logique et Existence*, especially "Introduction" and

human beings and consequently historical knowledge are involved in another dialectic. There are, in fact, several sets of rules and several congeries of concepts, quite distinct from one another. Climacus proposes that there is:

> ... a conflict between the ideal and the empirical, a dialectic which threatens every moment to prevent a beginning, and after a beginning has been made threatens every moment a revolt against this beginning.[34]

In consequence, Kierkegaard does not admit that an ideal goal or *telos* can be apprehended in the same way as historical events. Again he neither affirms nor denies that teleology and goals may exist in history. Perhaps there is a far-off divine event, perhaps there is a pillar, an end, towards which everything is conspiring, but Kierkegaard denies that Hegel knows this as he knows other facts. Hegel and some other philosophers profess to command so wide an arena of happenings that they can discern both facts and values, the real and the ideal, "what is" and "what ought to be," within a single comprehensive kind of seeing.

Kierkegaard's criticisms of all this again revolve around a few elemental but well-developed considerations. Like Socrates he has few ideas, but he has them seemingly always. Philosophy is a matter of intense exploitation of rudimentary distinctions, those already given to us, rather than an exploitation of extensive hypotheses. A kind of secular, and if the theologians were to be taken seriously, even a Christian piety, attached to the view that every event in life was but an episode in the large pattern of human history. Kierkegaard deplored this misplaced piety, but, more than this, he criticized the theoretic and logical case for saying that all events, or at least the fabric of history, described an objective and teleological pattern. If a man were speaking ethically or religiously, it would be a different matter. But the historical-teleological view, he believes, involves a logical mistake or two. Hegel's philosophy became an historical cosmology in which

---

"Conclusion," 1–6, 231–47. See also McTaggart, *Studies in the Hegelian Dialectic*, which makes this thesis very explicit too.

34. *Postscript*, 134. Note the discerning treatment of Kierkegaard's criticisms of Hegel in "*La Lutte Contra le Hegelianisme*," in Jean Wahl's *Études Kierkegaardiennes*, 86–172.

every object, nation, person, and idea was ostensibly explained. Explanation in this teleological compass means attributing to each element within the totality the proper and objective place that it has in the universal pattern.[35] Though Hegel admitted that there were limits on what we can know of the good in this direction, still this is the only direction in which to look.[36] "*Die Weltgestalten*," this teleological world-pattern, was also the means to a contemplative knowledge of God.[37] Without saying that the ideal factor is simply a myth or an interpretation growing out of a loose use of language, Kierkegaard is more modest and content to say only that the ideal cannot be known historically or scientifically. The "grammar" and the "logic" of the terms simply do not permit it. The conflict of which he speaks is, therefore, between the *telos* considered as the work and expression of pathos and passion, and the vast array of facts. The attempt to write teleological history is a relatively dangerous matter if the choice of events illustrating the *telos*, i.e., the choice of empirical facts, is determined by the passion of the writer. This means that the truth claims of teleological history perhaps reflect not simply empirical facts but also the subjectivity of the historian. Again, Kierkegaard is not opposed to teleological historical writing, but if one wishes to do it he is critical of the pretensions of objectivity that go with it. Furthermore, he is not a subjectivist in the invidious sense of that term.

Kierkegaard recognized a problem in writing history without a teleological and limiting interest. On the other hand, he saw equally well that endeavors to read teleology "out of" history and to show that historical statements were already teleological meant inclusion of non-cognitive factors, inimical to the claim of objectivity and disinterested truth. A pseudonym writes:

---

35. Note, for example, Hegel's *Encyclopädie der Philosophischen Wissenschaft*, especially Part III, 332ff. Stace's *The Philosophy of Hegel*, especially 438, and Part IV tells this story.

36. This point is, I believe, sometimes forgotten by Hegel's critics. It is well stated by McTaggart, *Studies in Hegelian Cosmology*, 95–128.

37. World history is a kind of theodicy, the justification of ethical and religious faith and the arena in which God turns the bad to good. Note Iwan Iljin's *Die Philosophie Hegels*. His point is well stated and to the effect that the whole philosophy is a *"contemplative Gotteslehre,"* 340ff.

> Philosophy turns toward the past, toward the whole enacted history of the world. It shows how the discrete factors are fused in a higher unity, it mediates and mediates . . . In the first place, there is no answer to my question what I ought to do; for if I were the most gifted philosophic mind that has ever lived in the world, there must be one thing more I have to do besides sitting and contemplating the past . . . What philosophy maintains, however, is that there is an absolute mediation . . . That in this way of regarding history much foolish and inept talk is mingled is at least my opinion; that especially the young wizards who wish to conjure up the spirits of history seem to me ridiculous, I do not deny, but I also incline with profound reverence before the grand achievements which our age has to show.[38]

Kierkegaard suggests that this view of history involves an error as simple as believing that what individual persons in a poem said or did were the poet's opinions and deeds. Hegel was mistaken in assuming that "what happens receives God's approbation simply by happening," that the teleological is what has in fact occurred.[39] But this is not to dismiss the teleological altogether. For Kierkegaard almost like Kant seems to suggest that teleological principles are regulative of historical knowledge and certainly of historical existing. The Judge in *Either/Or* says that as a married man he is absolutely dependent upon purposing from day to day. He must resolve and must make choices. And so too must the historian who chooses to write, to limit his subject matter, to believe in the existence of past events, etc. But these antedate his writing and account for the stance of the historian, not for the truth or falsity of his judgments about historical events.

If an historian chooses to write history in virtue of teleological judgments, he probably writes something humanly significant. But to write such a history without admitting "the inward work," the disposition by which one construes the material, is to fail both morally and

---

38. Those remarks are attributed to the Judge, *Either/Or*, II: 144–48, and can be noted in less developed form in the *Papirer*. Note especially the latter sections of vol. III.

39. Dru, *Journals*, 1377 (*Af Søren Kierkegaards Efterladte Papirer*, edited by H. Barfod and H. Gottsched, ix, 271).

intellectually,[40] for it neglects the role of passion in the very concepts that make up the teleological history.

The issue might be put in still another way. Suppose that one does write a teleological historical account, showing that history progresses for example in the direction of increasing freedom. This was the theme of grandiose histories in Kierkegaard's day. Kierkegaard finds this kind of *telos* still devoid of any immediate ethical interest for any given individual. He distinguishes rather sharply between the metaphysical "*telos*" which serves to connect truths to one another and an ethical "*telos*" which an individual purposes with enthusiasm. The first is an invented and contrived *telos* which serves its purpose when individuals grasp it cognitively and use it knowingly. Kierkegaard, it is fair to say, did not believe that such a *telos* was as cognitively significant as some enthusiasts said, but his point is a different one. An ethical *telos* does not exist to be known but as something to be done.[41] About the spectator apprehending the historical world he writes:

> Whether he is able to glimpse a *telos* for the race I shall not attempt to say; but this *telos* is not the ethical *telos* that exists for the individual, but a metaphysical *telos*. In so far as the individuals participate in the history of the race through their deeds, the dispassionate spectator does not view these deeds as reflected back into the individual and the eternal, but he views them as connected with the totality. What makes the deed ethically the property of the individual is the purpose; but this purpose is precisely something that never gets included in the world historical . . . World historically I see the effect, ethically I see the purpose; but when I apprehend the purpose ethically and understand the ethical, I see also that every effect is infinitely indifferent, that it is indifferent what the effect was; but in that case I do not see the world historical."[42]

Confusing cause and effect categories by investing them with the colors of guilt and punishment is an indication, too, that the historian has not divested himself, for the purposes of his knowledge, of ethical passions. There is no intellectual merit in this. To try to write history

---

40. *Either/Or*, vol. II: 148.
41. *Postscript*, 121.
42. Ibid., 138–39. Note the similarities to *Either/Or*, II: 144 ff.

in order to enhance apprehension of the good and of God is a mistake, for neither the good nor God are the scholar's subject matter *qua* scholar. Kierkegaard does not deny that one can evaluate the world as did the Apostle Paul. But then the aim is not disinterested scholarship in the manner of critical history, but it is conversion. Kierkegaard's point is not to compare these ways of writing, as if "truth" belonged to one while "propaganda" belonged to the other; rather, he is only trying to keep the categories straight. The concepts change as the aims and purposes do. And his point is that one cannot do all things, ethical and religious, aesthetic and scientific, in a single context.

So closely related are passions with the knower, and so closely related are guilt and evil in the objective order of history, that they correspond almost in the relation of one to one. Kierkegaard is convinced that only ethical passion discovers ethical values and that without the first in the observer the second will never be found in the objective order. Contrariwise, the judicious objectivity of the knower guarantees that he will never see the guilt of any individual. The consequences of the deed might be there for description, but they would be ethically neutral, just as the spectator is himself. It would be assumed "that the well-meant, quite as often as the ill-meant, deed brings the same consequence in its train; the best of kings and a tyrant bring about the same misfortune."[43] Attempts to provide discernment of God in history are no different, for from an intellectual standpoint God does not appear in history any more than does the ethical. Where He does have a function ascribed by the historians it is again only as a regulative idea, a kind of defined point, and the use that is made of the God-idea does not actually furnish knowledge of God's activity in human history. Thus Kierkegaard tells us that:

> In the world-historical process the dead are not recalled to life, but only summoned to a fantastic objective life, and God becomes in a fantastic sense the soul in the process. In the world-historical process God is metaphysically imprisoned in a conventional straight-jacket, half metaphysical and half aesthetic-dramatic, that is, the immanental system. It must be the very devil to be God in that manner.[44]

---

43. *Postscript*, 139.
44. Ibid., 140.

Instead of metaphysical knowledge of God and ethical values, Kierkegaard is suggesting what Kant had suggested, that historians and scholars who use such notions are only using them as regulative ideas, and are not making, and cannot make, substantive disclosures.

IV

Perhaps only slightly disguised by the polemic against Hegel and his followers is Kierkegaard's conviction that is certainly pervasive, though only occasionally evident, that all of this is beside the point anyway, for knowledge of another person's ethicality is, as we will note in another chapter, only the possibility of ethicality for myself. All that can be said of historical and even statistical studies of human behavior is that they describe the way of life of other persons, in this or another period of history. Supposing that such were truly described, Kierkegaard fails to find anything in true accounts alone that motivate him to realize their ethical actuality for himself.[45] But it is not only the issue of motivation that is important but also the realization of the plain fact that another person's moral and religious life is only the possibility of the same for oneself. Knowledge multiplies the possibilities and these are not themselves ethical or religious. Instead of saying that there is no passage from the "ought" to the "is," Kierkegaard says that there is no necessary transition from the possible to the actual. This is a complicated way of reminding the reader that that there is no necessary relation between saying "that is true" and doing it oneself. Though all of knowledge, he says, is a translation of actuals into possibles it is through passion and interest that possibles become translated into the actuality of one's own existence.[46]

But what does it mean to say that knowledge about another person's ethicality is only a possibility? Nothing very obscure is at stake. The point can be seen by considering only the language used to describe, for example, another person's sacrificial life of service to alcoholics in a slum district. Kierkegaard's point is not that a description will deceive one simply because it is in words or in concepts, for

---

45. Ibid., 282ff. Note his remark that "... because of the great increase of knowledge, we had forgotten what it means to exist ...," 223.

46. Ibid., 288.

there is no "necessary" deception if the account is trustworthy. His point is rather that the very character of describing will convert the moral purposing of another—his very source of passion and enthusiasm—into concepts quite lacking moral vitality. That is, unless the reader "wants" or "cares," and "purposes to" or "has decided to be" a person so possessed of himself, the description is only an account of the moral life, not the moral life itself. Again, the differing contexts for the words makes the same words sometimes deeply moral, and at other times only descriptive. The context provides the "how" and makes for differences in meaning.

Kierkegaard's practice as a philosophical writer invariably is to insist that words which we use to transact moral behavior, judgments, evaluations, and the rest get their logical powers and their meaning only in such transactions. Therefore, the description of another man's life, even with its moral proportions accurately limned, does not involve a kind of moral transaction in the describer. On the other hand, a responsible moral use does. A dialectician is, according to Kierkegaard, precisely that person who notes these differences and helps make them explicit. A dialectician in his literature is the kind of thinker who extracts out of the moral life on the one side, and, for example, history, on the other, those ways by which the words do their work. His Judge, the pseudonymous author of the second volume of *Either/Or*, is a case in point, for that judge uses the moral words for moral uses. Furthermore, he detects them in a dialectical way, teasing out their logical properties with deftness and great sensitivities to the differences that moral use brings to them.[47]

Hegel's dialectic was something altogether different. It required putting together various differing uses of a word and deriving a common conceptual meaning, ostensibly rich enough to cover all the instances. Where Hegel synthesized, Kierkegaard invariably separates. "Dialectic" is his word for describing in detail the rules and practices and therefore the concepts that are in fact already operative.

Therefore it is the opinion of the author of the *Postscript* that though dialectical skills (the talents to identify and to untangle the

---

47. In the section called "Equilibrium" of *Either/Or*, vol. II, there is an illuminating illustration of his kind of dialectical analysis, in this case respecting "faith." Note especially, 168–69. Also note this point in *On Authority and Revelation*, 103–4, 163, and in the preface, xv–xix.

relevant concepts) are indeed necessary to discuss even ethics, irony and pathos are even more essential.[48] Unless one has a "passion" to link with the possibility, the moral concepts do not stand forth. Furthermore, one will never experience the purpose and motives that are needed to realize a possibility in the manner that another probably already has. Ethical concepts are operative only where there are passionate interests at work. Otherwise, they become something else.

Teleological behavior, whether it issues in living a purposeful life or in his moral judgments about the course of human affairs, is part of the moral dignity of man.[49] Kierkegaard insists upon a duality here. Relative to the individual himself, a view of life is ingredient with an ethical and pervading enthusiasm; enthusiasms and drives are not acquired, like information, as a direct and immediate result of a course of study. Neither are they communicated as results, nor gained simply by the reading of moral treatises, for finally, relative to the individual again, a view of existence is not only objective knowledge, but is also a subjective conviction. This is why it is not an article of commerce and why Kierkegaard like Socrates always scoffed at the Sophists who talked as if virtue could be acquired in a few inexpensive sessions. All this has to be said remembering that morality is nonetheless taught. But clearly, it is not taught as are the sciences or history.

A duality exists for reflective human beings, those for whom Kierkegaard wrote, because there are "stages" or alternatives open to choice. What is taught is a moral possibility among other possibilities. Another person's moral existence, whether that of the tragic hero of ancient Greece or the Knight of Faith, may be presented as a moral possibility, as an envisioned goal for one's own self-development. But such goals invariably are multiple, whereas the need in one's own life is always for the singular. Reflection, on the one side then, opens the alternatives to view; moral passion requires making the choice. Intellectually there are options; morally there must be choice and the will's decisive commitment. Already the differences between entertaining moral possibilities and choosing one begin to make clear why the concepts also become different.

---

48. *Postscript*, 137.
49. *Either/Or*, II:148.

Kierkegaard therefore expresses repeatedly his moral indignation with those theorists who are content to say that morality comes more fully to those later in time and that ". . . the infinite host of individuals one generation after another," those of the past, must have lived with less moral opportunity.[50] The aristocracy of the view that rests content with the conviction that the whole world-process was set going only to make it possible for the last man in time to know more of the good is contrary to Kierkegaard's pervading moral conviction that attributes equal moral significance to each human life. But also it shows how easily one can get confused, for the evolution of the race is not the same thing as moral betterment. Here two contexts, the "world-historical" and the ethical are lumped together and their differences forgotten.[51]

All of this makes ethical values a little too much like the glinting play of colors coming from a shoal of herring in the sea, but here there are no herring, only men. An ethical passion that wishes to unite the simple man and the wise man, if not in knowledge then in the difficult process of becoming ethical and good, is violated by all notions that invest the differences in intellectual abilities with ethical value. In contrast there is the deeply moved ethicist who feels himself gripped by a profound humanity:

> . . . which reconciles him with the whole of life: that the difference between the wise man and the simplest human being is merely this vanishing little distinction, that *the simple man knows the essential*, while the wise man little by little learns *to know that he knows it*, or learns *to know that he does not know it*. But what they both know is the same.[52]

If the passions are ingredient in ethical and religious behavior, if the attempt to achieve scientific and scholarly truth as the means to ethical maturity is in vain, then indeed men are united by the essentials, the passions. The difference is that it sometimes takes the man of learning longer to discover this fact because of his time-consuming discursive efforts. He must reflect his way out of the intellectualizing

---

50. *Postscript*, 141.

51. See *Fragments*, and also the title page and notes in *Papirer*, vol. V, especially B, sections 1, 2, 3, ff.

52. *Postscript*, 143.

and back into his passions, out of the interesting and back into the simple.[53]

More could be said about Kierkegaard's understanding of the attempt to use other sciences for ethical and even religious ends. But in the main it would be but a repetition of the same epistemological argument already noted. Kierkegaard does not denigrate in any way the search for the truth about whatever one chooses. Neither does he deny that knowledge can be an instrument to be put to all kinds of services. In this latter respect he thinks that knowledge is neutral and that it can be used this way and that, for good or for evil. But always he draws the same line between saying this and saying that there is an objective and disinterested grasp of the good or of God, for in such a claim a philosophical mistake is beginning to take shape. Nowhere does Kierkegaard deny the possibility of a kind of ethical theory. But again an ethical theory is knowledge only of how human passions motivate behavior, of how people conceive of themselves and their values, and of what the possibilities are and how they are constituted. An important point to remember is that such an ethical theory is again a bit of knowledge and its concepts do not reflect the transactions of the moral life where passions and feelings are the very stuff.

Kierkegaard does not deny that philosophers can speak truly nor does he negate the possibility of a limited kind of existential philosophy.[54] He notes his own views repeatedly on these matters and says typically:

> While the Hegelian system goes and becomes an existential philosophy in sheer distraction of mind, and what is more, is finished—without having an ethics (where existence properly belongs), the more simple philosophy which is propounded by an existing individual for existing individuals, will more especially emphasize the ethical.[55]

In an earlier work, a pseudonymous author chides a young admirer of the philosophers in these words:

---

53. *Point of View*, 97.

54. Note the very penetrating essays by Louis Mackey, "Kierkegaard and the Problem of Existential Philosophy," two parts, *Review of Metaphysics* 9, nos. 3 and 4, 404–19, 569–88.

55. *Postscript*, 110. Also see 274.

> Hence, in our age as the order of the day we have the disgusting sight of young men who are able to mediate Christianity and paganism, are able to play with the titanic forces of history, and are unable to tell a plain man what he has to do in life, and who do not know any better what they themselves have to do.[56]

The difficulty with the philosophers lies not in their intent to be wise. But the unfortunate side of the matter and what has been forgotten is that turning philosophy into a matter of results, into objective knowledge, omits the subjectivity altogether, and here is the locus of the ethical and religious need, as well as the secret of the meaning of ethical and religious concepts. Men become wise and become philosophers when they remember the objectivities, conceive them how they will, and express them in a rich variety of ways, but in addition (and the qualification is all-important) they so formulate the communication that the recipient will not read about its objective content alone, but will let it reflect back upon his own existence and let it also involve his own emotions, feelings, pathos, and interest. This is double reflection, first in the direction of systematic ideation, and secondly in the direction of so calculating the objects of reflection that they cannot be appropriated as results, but rather stir the inwardness of a man and demand an increase of his self-understanding and self-concern. This double reflection qualifies the results, whatever they may be, historical, scientific, or philosophical.[57] The point is simply that philosophy is not a matter of results at all. It is more a practice and a way, an activity, which uses scholarship but is not scholarship. A philosopher is a man who conforms to the way things are after his dialectical analyses have made clear his role and his place. The ordinary man might well do this without all the fuss and bother.

Kierkegaard loved to satirize the philosopher who could by incorporating "the toilsome labor of some genuine scientist" and submitting it to his own "*ein, zwei, drei,*" come up with an incalculable

---

56. *Either/Or*, II: 145. In the *Papirer* IV B, 16 one finds this sardonic comment by Johannes Climacus: "[the young philosopher] is in despair. His life is spoiled. His youth has disappeared with his deliberations, and life has not acquired its full significance for him. This is the fault of philosophy."

57. *Postscript*, 282–307. See also, 122–25 and 165–67.

treasure.[58] Ah, all glory to the reader of the tea-leaves, he says, but all of it with the slight qualification that everything cannot yet be said because the System is not quite finished!

Philosophy undoubtedly lives as Kierkegaard suggested by the pretense that it will someday supply these objective truths that will make a decisive difference to the common passions of humanity. Few authors have said as harsh things as he about the pretense of the philosophers. In one way or another, even the debunkers of the old philosophy manage to make the new kinds also intimate definers of human living, if not metaphysically, then scientifically or analytically. Kierkegaard was intent upon separating out these admixtures of hope and knowledge within philosophical discourse and also within the meta-discourse about philosophical discourse. He discovered that the speculative point of view was, instead of the most comprehensive and full, actually the most empty and abstract. Furthermore, if philosophy is only objective results, it too is wholly indifferent, he says, to everyone's human happiness.[59] Giving it all the honor that it deserves, Kierkegaard suggests, still does not mean that one must confuse philosophy by making it directly incremental to the common good. Of course there is a kind of happiness of thought itself, a genuinely aesthetic experience, not to be denied.[60] But there is nothing in such a moment that can be made to bear any great weight or constitute a large promise for the rest of mankind.

If philosophy is to be adequate, it must conform to the actual existence of human beings. This is why the analysis of concepts is important. For by analyzing carefully the concepts of history and putting them to whatever use is appropriate, we see that such concepts are only the means for knowing the truth about others. In consequence, we can see that these concepts are not the sort that can be put directly to a use in the moral life. Furthermore, moral concepts are also distinct, being the ruled ways that we judge, evaluate, and handle ourselves in our moral proceedings. So there we have two kinds of concepts. Where Hegel had extorted a new concept inclusive of both and had made philosophy a matter of extorting concepts at once

---

58. Ibid., 134.
59. Ibid., 53.
60. Ibid., 54.

ethical and historical, Kierkegaard makes philosophy an eliciting of concepts within each domain. (Of course, we shall see in later pages how he does this for several other domains too.) But is this all there is to philosophy?

Not quite, for as we have noted a philosopher is the one who cannot convert this kind of analysis into any very worthwhile results. Unlike modern analytic philosophers, who have quite forgotten that philosophy was an activity to Wittgenstein and not a matter of holding analytic doctrines, so too with Kierkegaard. He thought that a philosopher would be a man who would use what he knew ("conceptually" let us say) to stay appropriate to the human task. A man's life is a synthesis of status and task, and the task requires a never-ending striving. So to the striving! Here is the end, then, of vast systematic philosophic syntheses and final facts and other fancies of invention. There will be no system and no finality because human life is an unfinished business.

It is as if philosophy is then like the practice of the most scrupulous honesty. It should never let us forget what is plain, the fact that our life is unfinished. This is why it is so important to say that assenting to the truth of a sentence, whatever its referent might be, is not itself a religious or an ethical achievement. This is to presuppose, too, a sharp distinction between belief as an act in the contexts of knowing and belief (or faith) as it is understood ethically and religiously. Kierkegaard's argument is to the effect that sentences about facts, about values, and also about metaphysical entities, would not, even if they had sense and were true, produce a corresponding moral transformation in the subject.[61] It is proper that anyone interested in scholarship and history should omit himself. The lie of the world of scholarship and perhaps most poignantly of speculative philosophy is to insist that the use of truth follows as a matter of course upon its being brought to light, and, further, that this use is supposed to require the transformation of the subject.[62] But there are no results about God and the good except in a fantastic medium of speculative metaphysics. Even if there were, there are no invariant connections between knowing about the good and God and being moral and pi-

---

61. Ibid., 38.
62. Ibid., 24.

ous. When there are connections it is because of a powerful passion. Any philosophy that disregards the latter loses what it has aimed to be: a teaching dignifying our common humanity.

In all that has been said thus far it must be clear that Kierkegaard's philosophizing hinges upon relatively few and simple distinctions. None of them is quite as important as that drawn between objective truth and truth as subjectivity. It is to the latter that we now turn.

CHAPTER 6

Truth Is Subjectivity
Some Radical Criticisms

Kierkegaard is surely one of the greatest of dialecticians of all times. Yet, his expression, "truth is subjectivity," seems to be an absolute denial of all dialectical powers and values. In fact, the very expression is offensive. It smacks of romanticism, of relativism, of self-assertion. Martin Heinecken has noted very perceptively that:

> "Truth is subjectivity" are fighting words. It is better to say them with a smile. They must be clarified quickly—before the pistols are drawn. This sounds on the face of it like what Roman Catholics regard as "the" Protestant Error, namely that each isolated individual makes himself the sole judge of the truth. It sounds like the return of sophistry which relativizes all truth and all values . . .[1]

It almost seems that Kierkegaard is returning to a Protagorean doctrine or some kind of unbridled and primitive individualism, the very opposite of everything objective and ordered which Plato's dialectic and Hegel's, too, for that matter, claimed to discern. This is what Kierkegaard has his philosophical observer say in *Training of Christianity* too—"perishableness being the very essence of subjectivity."[2]

However nothing could really be farther from the truth. It is true that Kierkegaard breaks with much of philosophic tradition and he is

---

1. *The Moment Before God*, 225. The entire chapter 8, "Truth is Subjectivity," is an extremely valuable treatment of Kierkegaard's views.
2. *Training in Christianity*, 52.

proposing in effect a different course from that of Greco-European philosophy. By and large, he is a Christian philosopher, contending that the Scriptures picture human existence and the world differently than do most European philosophers, not least, Hegel. He believes the scriptural account and he does not believe the grand systematic philosophical accounts. However, he is not so naive as to assume that this is all that can be said or that the authority of Scripture forbids further discussion or reflection. Kierkegaard, it was noted in the last chapter, finds the comprehensive philosophic systems, whether Hegel's or Spinoza's, to caricature the ordinary world that every one of us already knows. Accordingly, he acknowledges no responsibility to fill out any one system or to follow out the age-old development of classical philosophies, as those were being described by the new histories of philosophy of the early nineteenth century. Instead he wishes to call a halt and to bring up short the whole business.

The theme, "truth is subjectivity," is a major one in that endeavor. For here he begins to draw his strands of argument a little more taut. The multifariousness of the literature begins to focus rather sharply. But now, we must look at his criticisms, for it is in these that we see what work the theme actually does. In this chapter, we will note respectively: why it is not enough to consider only the "what," but also why the "how" of a subject's life must be taken into consideration; the role of a kind of misunderstanding, which is more pervasive than a philosophical view and keeps us from intellectual clarity and seeing that the truth is sometimes subjectivity; and, finally, a glance at the misunderstanding of the concept of immortality, whereby it is made into something it is not.

I

Already we have remarked upon aspects of Kierkegaard's rebuke of traditional philosophy. On the one side, he is proposing that philosophers take on a much more retiring role as dialecticians. For Kierkegaard conceived a dialectician as one who traces meanings, who did it by considering what can be said, denied, commanded, etc., but who did not propose them. This accounts for his demand for a dialectician to work in "the language of the Christian concepts."[3] Also it takes a careful and sensitive dialectician to trace out the concepts in the *patois* and careless conversational language of everyday life. A dialectician must not be taken in by the appearances; he must be patient and penetrate very slowly the context of behavior and language before he concludes anything.[4] His task is the separation of the concepts from their environment, and that can require the capacities to hear the telling emphasis as well as the phrase, to see the arched look as well as the benign smile, to watch all that accompanies the words as well as hearing what is said. Kierkegaard's point is that the "how" is sometimes as significant as the "what"; therefore, the dialectician must be very skillful as a listener, observer, and spy. The difference that the Danish thinker introduces here is, of course, the emphasis upon the "how." But this difference cannot be abridged in a theory of the "how"; instead the "how" requires something of the observer—it requires him to be qualified by the appropriate emotional and psychological development, and it requires, too, a variety of concepts, subtle and declined to fit the panoply of human behavior.

So, Kierkegaard says:

> It depends then, not only on what a man sees, but what a man sees depends upon how he sees it. For observing is not only a receiving or a discovery for it is also a matter of bringing something forward; and in so far as it is that, the crucial matter becomes what the observer himself is. Thus, if one man sees one thing and the second something else in the same thing, one discloses what remains hidden to the other. In so far as the object of observation belongs to the eternal world, the "how" of the observer is a matter of indifference, or more properly what is necessary to observing is something his deeper nature is unconscious of. On the contrary, the more the object to be observed belongs to the world of the spirit, the more important becomes the issue of what the observer is in his deepest being.[5]

---

3. *On Authority and Revelation*, 166.

4. *Stages on Life's Way*. Note the various uses of "dialectic," all congruent with the kind of detecting work that goes on. See 277, 363, 404, ff.

5. From *Samlede Vaerker*, vol. III, 277. The translation is my own. Compare Mrs. Swenson's translation, *Edifying Discourses*, vol. I, 67, where she makes several rather serious mistakes.

On this account, we can note that Kierkegaard certainly takes seriously the outlook of the Christian tradition as part of a "how" and counterpoises that against the panoply of views indigenous to much philosophical literature, e.g., Stoicism, Epicureanism, materialist views, objective ideals, the rationalisms of Spinoza, Hegel, and Christian Wolff. But he is a critic in an altogether different manner too, for he is proposing a technical reform in philosophy. Dialectical analysis must also take into account the "how," the personality of the thinker, for even the concepts and the language can only be understood when they are put into a context that includes both a "what" and a "how." Without denying objectivity in the least, Kierkegaard is making a point, subsequently familiar to readers of the later Wittgenstein, that even the form of life is something to be considered when puzzling what it is that men say and see.

"One assumes," says Kierkegaard in 1844, "that personal concern not only does not make a man biased, but that it is precisely this which makes him capable of reflection."[6] Accordingly, "What is in a man, then, decides what he discovers and what remains hidden for him."[7] So, then, objective things are not things-in-themselves, brute facts, there only to be discerned, but things also are constituted for us by "how" we use them, by the "way" that we conceive them, and by the form of life and the kind of language that requires us to see them, name them, and eventually to describe them. Without exaggeration, it can be said, then, that Kierkegaard is making a radical proposal for even technical philosophy. Granted, he is a Christian thinker, but his telling contribution as a reflective genius does not depend solely upon his avowal of Christianity (for he thought Christianity anyway to be a gift and not something one proved or apologizes for) as much as it does his conceptual skills. Here he is radical, proposing that there is a kind of analysis of concepts which cannot be justified if they are abstracted from personality and subjectivity but can only be justified if done within the context of the subject's concerns and interests.[8] Unlike, then, some language analysts, who study the language without the user, Kierkegaard does the analysis but with the user. The

---

6. *Edifying Discourses*, III:98.
7. *Edifying Discourses*, I:67.
8. *Edifying Discourses*, III:114–15.

numerous differences this makes to the concepts themselves is the burden of much of his literature.

Kierkegaard's notion of dialectic—and of philosophy—is that it ought not to give new information or even a new theory about religion, ethics, or aesthetics, for we already posses an ample supply of information about each of these, plus a host of practices, rites, habits, and appropriate dispositions, most of which are neither derived from, nor dependant upon, the contentions of philosophers. For Kierkegaard's dialectical analyses, his philosophizing, does not increase what we know of Christianity and other familiar human activities as much as it rectifies "the logical geography," to use a phrase of Gilbert Ryle, of the relevant practices and knowledge that we already have. But there is novelty in Kierkegaard's insistence that subjectivity is not a chaos, nor is it simply a morass, quite without regularities and order. On the contrary, because subjectivity—the emotions, passions, feelings—are not private there are rules and practices; consequently there are also concepts. It is these that Kierkegaard is bringing into purview. He is denying then that subjectivity is private so that it escapes all conceptual analysis. But to study such concepts requires that the "how" of a person's life also be considered.

Even Hume and Kant, startling as they were, were tame and moderate revolutionaries compared to Kierkegaard. The break that Kierkegaard introduces into philosophic history is, therefore, a wide one. It is more impressive when one remembers how strong the forces were that he was combating and how solitary and alone he was in his day. For whatever extraneous factors have subsequently aided his cause, and these are today altogether too many, still the plain fact is that his reversal of philosophic trends is based upon a detailed and commonsensical acknowledgement of the peculiarities of human personality. How these get entangled in language and argument is a good part of his story.[9] The cardinal distinctions between ethics, aesthetics, metaphysics, reason, and faith, dear as they are to systematic philosophers, simply fail to do justice to existing people and our

---

9. Again the volume *Authority and Revelation* ought to be consulted. For its argument, against Magister Adler, who had "revelations" and was deposed, is that Adler is confused conceptually. He makes up meanings as if they could be originated and also be Christian. Kierkegaard finds this to be a complete misunderstanding, not only of Christianity but of what concepts are and what they do.

working concepts. For Kierkegaard the fact, long overlooked and to be reckoned with above all others, was the significance of differently oriented individuals and the "stages" or "forms of life" which they exemplified. For this reason he depicts by his pseudonyms the ironist, not irony, the humorist, not humor, the aesthetes, not aesthetics, ethical people, not ethics. His argument is to the effect that an acknowledgement of "how" such persons are involved shows that the very logic and form of systematic philosophies, especially on matters of aesthetics, ethics, and religion, are ill-fitting and absurd. The present conceptual schemes misrepresent rather than clarify.

Naturally enough Kierkegaard could not break with everything in the systematic traditions. He plainly has respect for objectivity as a logical ideal and for the rigorous conception of science developed in European life. More than this, he acknowledges the place and role of logical criteria. For Plato, logic becomes linked with dialectic, and dialectic is described as a driving passion which pushes men step by step, from the human to the superhuman, ultimately unto possession of the divine. Hegel professed to find logical properties in things themselves. His thought was dialectical when it was commanded by the intelligible lineaments in history and nature, the totality of existence. Philosophy, then, became an elaborate joining of the reason in things to the reason of the thinker. Although Kierkegaard uses the same word, the place and promise of dialectic is both more modest, and in his way of judging, more important. He makes dialectic a kind of everyday tool, the way to become clear on ordinary matters.[10]

For Kierkegaard the point of juxtaposition, the nexus between dialectic and things, again is personality. He rehearses very well indeed how philosophy came to be made up of the rules of dialectic; how dialectic, according to Hegel, springs from contradiction; how dialectic issues in dialogue, argument, and language. He wrestled gladly with those tenacious and hardheaded technical thinkers who had to make their thoughts transparent to themselves; he is quite at peace with Descartes' program of thought, but not its resolution, with all those thinkers who want to make things clear for themselves with what is called dialectic. This much of the temper of classical philosophy he does not reject.

---

10. Note the discussion in the *Postscript*, 498ff.

But the issue at stake for Kierkegaard was precisely to use philosophy to dissipate misunderstandings and to state a kind of philosophy appropriate to the person, a philosophy which would include the widest kind of dialectical practice. Kierkegaard rejects any escape from detailed analysis. As far as he was concerned, it was necessary to yield to the intellectual taskmaster. He saw no escape from argumentation, no respite from doubt, no easy surcease from confronting contradictions and endless distinctions. There was no escaping the tentativeness, the everlasting pursuit, that dialectic was. For all we had, we had on the basis of evidence, discussion, careful attention to detail; these were the very condition for being dialectical. For there are no ultimate facts to stop the questing, no ultimate system to dry up research, no way to see that which would overrule all other vistas. Philosophy could not be stopped by revelations or faith, visions, or hunches. But this is because philosophy is dialectic, only a kind of elucidation of what is already there. All of its problems turn out to be rather small. The big matters are settled otherwise anyway. But the task of philosophy is precisely to show us how to philosophize our way out of big problems and make us honest men once more, able and willing to resolve big issues the way the ordinary man must do.

Thus, Kierkegaard's thesis, "truth is subjectivity," is finally itself dialectical. It does not settle big issues for people. It is also an elucidation, not a new and major doctrine. It is not a matter of perception; it does not represent an aesthetic intuition or a poetic surmise; it is neither an undialectical intuition nor a revelation from God. Neither is it an immediately apparent or self-evident truth. It concludes a kind of inquiry. It presupposes objective warrantability. Furthermore, the claim, namely, that "truth is subjectivity," is subject to logical criteria and other intellectual requirements. Thus, the question with which we began this chapter, namely, whether this contention does not violate all notions of intellectual standards, can plainly be answered in the negative. The very definition supposes some common intellectual rules and uses some familiar notions to state the case. Bur there are also grounds for asking if the peculiarity of the view that ethico-religious truth is subjectivity also requires some of the peculiarities of Kierkegaard's intellectual style. There is already a consensus of behavior anterior to Kierkegaard's analysis, and it is out of this consensus that he draws in his dialectical way something to teach his reader, not the least of which is this thesis.

II

However, a contemporary reader of Kierkegaard's literature might well be troubled by all of this. Someone accustomed to the protocol of cultivated people of our day might say: "Tell me, does this mean that ethical and religious language is not true? Are there no ethical and religious truths?" Certainly one can understand both the temper of this remark as well as the remark. It is born of rather long-standing convictions, now almost standardized, of trying to specify the truth and the meanings that belong to different kinds of grammatical expressions. But Kierkegaard's answers are not always satisfying, for he refuses the question and seems finally to evade it altogether.

Why does he evade such questions? Here we come to a major difficulty in understanding Kierkegaard's writings. For the exercise of dialectic, which we alluded to earlier in this chapter, as well as questions about truth and meaning, do not require strictly a new philosophy, a new scheme of reality. And this makes Kierkegaard's writings seem incomplete. It is as if he were criticizing others but not making explicit his own position. Also, this tentative kind of writing suggests that he really has a position all along and that, for various reasons, maybe fear of attack, a deceptive streak of character, or an inability to reason constructively, he failed to declare himself. There have been no end to the scholars who have wanted to supply the lack; and so he is a scholastic, an arch-idealist, a realist, and any number of other kinds of philosopher, including an existentialist, if one is to trust the scholarly literature about him.

But another kind of issue is at stake altogether. Kierkegaard is always occupied with the "how," for how a man states Christian doctrines also will modify what he believes and says. How a man addresses the tasks, how he pays attention, how he cares, how he interests himself—these determine even reality questions, let alone entire ranges of concepts, ethical, religious, and even everyday ones.[11]

---

11. *Postcript*, 280. "*Hvad*" and "*hvorledes*" are his words, *Samlede Vaerker*, vol. III, 169.

But as Kierkegaard began to address the confusions of his day he saw quickly enough that it was not one philosophy versus another that was the difficulty. No philosophy could correct what he thought was wrong. The philosophies shared the difficulty, even exemplified it, but strictly speaking, they did not create it. What then is the difficulty to which the definition of truth as subjectivity is addressed? Is it simply that "truth is objective"? Actually this is not it; and here is another reason why the literature is as circuitous as it is. Instead there is a kind of myth at work—a very generalized and inchoate conviction, operative in the literate people of Kierkegaard's day. And perhaps it is not dispelled even today. It must be attacked in a variety of ways. "But above all," his author says:

> . . . it must not be done in a dogmatizing manner, for then the misunderstanding would instantly make the explanatory effort itself into a new misunderstanding . . . if communicated in the form of knowledge the recipient is led to adopt the misunderstanding that it is knowledge he is to receive and then we are again in the sphere of knowledge.[12]

What Kierkegaard here calls a "misunderstanding" may also be called a myth. It engenders a certain kind of question and creates an expectation of an answer. In brief, it is a misunderstanding that is not so much found among the ignorant as among the sophisticated. Accordingly, it is not dissipated by information. It is not always a matter of being misinformed as much as it is a habit and a tendency, a disposition and a "how," a feature of the thinker and not a "what."

For Kierkegaard is addressing a long-standing myth. And this myth is partly philosophical because it has taken technical shape out of the efforts of master dialecticians. However, it is powerful even in less formidable ways too. In brief it is the representation of behavior and concepts from several familiar human contexts in the idiom and style appropriate to only one of them. The manner in which this has been done, however, has made it seem as though the myth were simply the standard and only way to be rational. No one man ever makes up a myth and myths are not lies, fairy stories, or deliberate concoctions. Therefore, a myth is more like a climate of opinion than an explicit doctrine, more like a general distortion than a specific

---

12. Ibid., 223.

mistake. This myth is not learned because it is taught; it is learned by being imbibed, assimilated without effort.

Furthermore, a myth is often not clearly or completely stated. It is fair to say that the intellectualist-myth which Kierkegaard was fighting was also one which tempted him personally. But it was not, therefore always clear to him. He found his own reflection disordered, and his lengthy journal and his writings for the public were, he insisted, again and again, his own education. He became clearer as time went by, not always before he wrote but often "as" and "because" he wrote.[13] With his remarkable intellectual abilities, he knew well the temptation of the intellectualist-myth, and the vehemence of his criticisms is most often the severest for those aspects which had already victimized him.

The intellectualist-myth grows up very slowly. Kierkegaard had slight interest in tracing its history, but his pages were studded with references to authors he holds responsible.[14] Most of these references are casual and no attempt is made to coordinate them into an historical account. But it is important to remember that Kierkegaard is more concerned with the intellectualist-myth, and what he calls "*misforsteaelsen*," than he is any one kind of philosophy. It is a mistake to construe his writings, therefore, as only a diatribe against "idealism" or speculative philosophy or metaphysics, although, indeed, each of these in turn is his target. Likewise it is wrong to read him as though he must be a realist because he is not an idealist; or a skeptic because he is not a metaphysician; or a critical thinker because he is not speculative, though again, he might well be some of these things too. His target is both more elusive and yet also much more powerful. The intellectualist-myth is not the prerogative of technical philosophers alone. It is found among all kinds of bright people and, therefore, its origins cannot be traced to this or that source. It is as much a feature of critics of idealist philosophers as it is of Hegel himself. It is not

13. "... I came to understand myself by my writing," he says in 1848. *Papirer* IX A, 213 (JP 6, 6227).

14. E.g., St. Augustine for confusing "faith" by using Plato's *Republic* to define it; *Papirer* XI 2 A, 380 (JP 2, 1154). Also, note, *The Last Years: Journals 1853–55*, 336. Even in *Journals*, 2838, e.g., he began to insist upon a "paradox" in order to emphasize that concepts were radically different. Cf., II A, 755 (JP 3, 3070; *KJN* 2, FF:152). Also see the references to Leibniz, and "understanding": IV C, 29 (JP 3, 3073), V C, 1 (JP 3, 2345).

less manifest in romantic literature than in science or more obvious in Plato and Aristotle than in some Christian writers. He finds it in post-Reformation theology as well as Catholic tradition.

Of course, there are differences. Hegel's philosophy is a more technical rendition than H. L. Martensen's *Dogmatics*, so Kierkegaard chooses the more technical account for dissection. In previous chapters we have described several contexts within which Kierkegaard's philosophizing can be traced. However, the story about "truth is subjectivity" is relevant to these several contexts and more. But it is also the case that what he is combating is no single theory and no one philosophical view. For this reason, we note here in the intellectualist-myth a richly inclusive kind of standard view that rests upon a whole group of smaller confusions. And Hegel's philosophy was only the contemporary technical rendition of that myth. But the myth has a firm hold on the minds of the literate and is as pre-Hegelian as it is post. Kierkegaard was fearful that the intellectualist-myth would spread with the popularization of learning and it is certainly the case that whatever social significance his thought has derives from his intent to combat this myth rather than simply to combat the technical philosophers.

But now, just what is the misunderstanding, this myth? We have already said that a myth in this context means only the representation of behavior and concepts of several areas of human endeavor in terms of the model of one such area. A myth is "intellectualist" when the style and idiom of distinctively cognitive activities are made to represent the range of religious activities, of ethical life, and of the host of transactions that Kierkegaard covers by the expression, "aesthetic." The words of the intellectual life, e.g., science and logic, are, typically, "objective," "objectively true," "necessary," "evidence," "probable," "scientific," "belief," "prove," and a host more. When these words are transposed into other contexts so that we get "the objective truth of Christianity," "an objective ethics," "the truth of art," such that the concepts used in our cognitive endeavors are thought to be exemplified in other endeavors, then the myth begins to take shape. Of course, Kierkegaard is not denying any facts nor is he denigrating ethics or Christianity. But he is clearly relocating their concepts on the conceptual map.

His attack upon the philosophical myth may be described here then as a matter of talking sensibly and truly about concepts and behavior in these various areas. To this extent, Kierkegaard is attacking the technical philosophy, most particularly Hegel's, that compounds the myth by stating it all in technical language and with the help of erstwhile dialectical and logical tools. But Kierkegaard did not suppose that a correction of the philosophical scheme would aid materially in the use of concepts or aesthetic creativity, except negatively. On the other hand, there is a non-philosophical and more common form of the intellectualist-myth. This is found everywhere and it may be that this is sometimes taught by philosophical views, but most often it seems to be a confusion almost indigenous to the intelligentsia. The bright man is tempted to think that there is an intellectual core to every human activity, that all the concepts are intrinsically cognitive, and that in all kinds of activities, ethical, religious, aesthetic, even ordinary, there is an unexpressed set of beliefs, a secret set of convictions, some presuppositions, assumptions, or mental content that is also being entertained. The intellectualist-myth makes the sensitive man think that all language somehow tells you something about the way things are even when the user of the language is doing something else with the language.[15]

In a succeeding chapter, we will have more to say about Kierkegaard's revamping of technical philosophy, and the correction that he brings to this intellectualist-myth and its formulation in philosophical systems. But right now our interest is his attack upon this misunderstanding as it shapes itself in the very general conviction that every distinctive mode of human activity involves an underlying theory or bit of knowledge that somehow unifies and states the aims of that activity. For the "objective truth" of Christianity, the issue with which Climacus is concerned, is a concern with the supposed implicit theory in being a Christian. First one must have the theory and then the practice. To have the practice without the theory seems to be a major fault. Furthermore one must know that the theory is true, or to put it in even more semantical terms, the truth of the theory must be established before one can put into practice what it enjoins.

---

15. Note examples in *Training in Christianity*, 43ff.

Kierkegaard's literature is an attack upon this in several ways. For one thing there is the abstract conceptual analysis that declares baldly that the concept "truth" in ethico-religious areas belongs with subjectivity, not with objectivity. Here the company the word "truth" keeps is said to be different; and, in consequence, the concept of truth is not in an intellectualist cognitive domain at all. Here is Kierkegaard's dialectic at work, ferreting out the morphology of the concept. But there is another attack upon the myth too. For he helps his reader to remember what it means to exist. Once one recalls the features of our dynamic daily life and begins to use the vocabulary of daily life for right and wrong, obeying God, and even mundane things, the intellectualist misunderstanding loses its grip. This seems to be the aim of his literature, namely, to help one out of the thralldom the myth makes.

Our earlier theme still holds too. The proposal about subjectivity as truth appears as a kind of clarifying stroke that brings some sense and shape to Kierkegaard's literature. It follows chronologically the somewhat miscellaneous literature in which kinds of pathos and subjectivity have been opulently displayed. In a rather precise way, this conceptual analysis even seems to explain what has been going on in an otherwise obscure but interesting batch of books. But this is only to say that the concepts that these authors were operating with are now made the subject of description. All of the early literature is, therefore, an indirect attack upon the intellectualist-myth, whereas the special analysis of truth is a correction of a technical rubric within that tissue of confusion.

But another context for discussion, though necessarily rather general and perhaps demanding more elucidation than Kierkegaard gave it, is blocked out by the argument that no objective ethical reality exists.[16] He is not denying the existence of ethical theories which, of course, are objective and cognitive simply because they can be written out and discussed, judged, and the rest; nor is he denying that all

---

16. "The pseudonymous authors are subjective" he writes in *Papirer* VI B, 54–55. There is no science of ethics, because ethics is not a science at all. But Kierkegaard does not deny that one can write philosophically about ethics; however, that would mean doing a dialectical study and describing the concepts of ethics. An ethical man, like his Judge (*Either/Or*, vol. II), talks sense with them. But he also is philosophical and talks well about them.

kinds of ethical concerns and interests are objectified in another sense of the term "objective," in the life of institutions and individuals. He was as conscious as contemporary anthropologists and social scientists seem to be of the omnipresence of value components wherever one looks, and he did not deny the possibility of making them a subject of scientific study. But he did not confuse such study, philosophical, anthropological or sociological with the use of ethical concepts or ethical purposes. In such a context, there are, obviously, ethical facts to be talked about. But this is not Kierkegaard's point or his topic. Once again, his correction of the pervasive myth is to be gained by thinking about what it means to be a dynamically oriented person— one with purposes, enthusiasms, goals, and tasks. Here is where the concepts of ethics and faith have to be discerned. And Kierkegaard denies that ethical men are always "seeing" the good before they do it. He is against the "objective" ethics because it tries to state what ethical men "believe," "while" or "before" they behave.

To be a human subject is precisely to be dynamically oriented, to have goals and drives, to become something and not necessarily to contemplate something. With the help of both light nuances and heavy broadsides, every pseudonymous author helps make clear that being ethical and being religious are not matters of simultaneously cognizing corresponding objectives. Hence, to confuse "moral" or "ethical" by linking them with a quality of a sentence, or to mix up religious achievements with prepositional matters means the nadir of both knowledge and the spiritual life. This is why it is apposite to point out that the pseudonymic literature is an argument against misplaced cognition. The intellectualist-myth confuses passions and concepts by juxtaposing them as opposites. In turn, the pseudonymic literature gives grounds for seeing dispassionate knowledge to be fully compatible with a passionate ethicality. Further, each has its own distinctive concepts. Dispassionate ethicality and passionate knowledge are, on the contrary, mystifications and confusions by which the popular concern for philosophy probably thrives, and Kierkegaard does not propose answering any problems raised by this muddle. By making the distinction between passionate ethicality, or the dynamically oriented person, on the one side, and the dispassionate knower on the other, Kierkegaard reminds his reader of where important differences lie. To remember this much is also to be a philosopher, responsible to the way human existence is, and to be able to stay clear about the relevant concepts. It does not mean necessarily that one is a good man.

There is, clearly enough, still a function for the intelligence in ethical and religious matters. However, it is not that of providing objective truths, always preparatory to believing or to ethical behavior. Kierkegaard trims the myth by insisting that believing sentences is not always necessary to moral action, or to all aspects of what Christianity calls faith. But getting clear on such matters might reduce the power of the confusion that is otherwise so determinative and this might not be a slight matter.

III

Kierkegaard would by no means ascribe all the intellectual snarls of the history of philosophy and theology to the abuse of language. It was characteristic of the Danish philosopher not to invoke any single general principle by which to diagnose intellectual difficulties. Although he was as severe a critic as anyone of construing truths as if they were intrinsic to all ethical behavior and religious believing, he did not leap to the other extreme of denying cognitive worth to every ethical and religious assertion. He saw too many issues to permit a single resolution. Insistent though he is that ethico-religious truth is subjectivity he also makes clear that ethico-religious expressions are not, therefore, exclusively admonitory and quickening. They do many things, including "telling" us the way things are. In this section, therefore, we shall briefly explore the entanglements and, as it were, the foreign relations of at least one concept that invites both a religious interest and concern with objective truth.

The example is from the *Postscript*.[17] The particular belief concerns immortality. Most persons who entertain the matter will immediately ask whether it is in fact true that there is an immortality or whether it is plausible to believe in immortality.[18] Then comes

---

17. *Postscript*, especially, 152–58 and 180ff. But I have drawn on numerous passages in the *Papirer*, too, and discourses, e.g., "The Expectation of an External Happiness" in *Edifying Discourses*, III:95–121, and *Christian Discourses*, 210–21.

18. *Christian Discourses*, 210.

perhaps a lifetime of research and scholarship, a long listing of proofs and counterproofs, definitions and re-definitions. In one sense this is perfectly proper, but only if the learner has no anxiety whatever engendered by his possible death and future. Obviously, this is what the learned community means by becoming disinterested or becoming objective. But it is another question whether such detachment is not at the expense of forgetting one's daily life.

The counter tendency to forego evidence and leap to a conclusion without considering any of the relevant questions is also characteristic of thoughtless people. No one can deny, therefore, that the quest for proof has a certain kind of importance, and this is all the more reason for paying strict attention to relevant methodological procedures and the canons of evidence. Men look serious when they inquire for evidence. Such an inquiry is better than not looking for evidence, or so we are inclined to think most of the time.

The learned approach to the issue is to start by becoming clear on the meaning of the word, and, therefore, one begins the study of the word "immortality." One must ask whether anything corresponds to it as its object.[19] Then the responsibility is to relate the words to immortality (whatever that is!) in such a wise that the words will be true of their referent. Whatever the proofs, the thinker, says Kierkegaard, enters upon "a never-ending approximation," a quest in which all the evidence will, at most, give a degree of probability to the truth claim. Of course, this is to suppose that the quest for proofs is in principle even possible. Kierkegaard for the sake of the argument supposes that proofs in this instance will have a cognitive content. Actually, however, resident in the very attempt itself and the question the inquiry seeks to resolve, is the difficulty. The difficulty is conceptual, for the question is whether the concept "immortality," in religious discourse, is actually linked with a state of affairs. Does it refer to something as people say "beyond space and time"? Kierkegaard finds this question ridiculous, but the absurdity is, nonetheless, a cultural phenomenon. For the linkage of "immortality" is not such that it permits proofs and that kind of vindication objectively. Instead it "asks thee whether thou dost reckon thyself among the just or the unjust."[20]

---

19. *Postscript*, 177. Again, note *Christian Discourses*, 210–11.
20. Ibid., 210.

> Modern philosophy has tried anything and everything in the effort to help the individual to transcend himself objectively, which is a wholly impossible feat; existence exercises its restraining influence, and if philosophers nowadays had not become mere scribblers in the service of fantastic thinking and its preoccupation, they would long ago have perceived that suicide was the only tolerable practical interpretation of its striving.[21]

But what if the proofs are offered—suppose the impossible if you can—what then? The presence of three proofs to the genuine scholar and intellectual means that you look for four and, furthermore, that you test and re-test the proofs, re-formulate and re-examine. If you do not die before all this is done, then you are perhaps ready to assent to the hypothesis that there is some probability for the view about immortality.

> But those who have the three proofs do not at all determine their lives in conformity therewith . . . the three proofs . . . do not profit them at all because they are dead to spirit and enthusiasm, and their three proofs, in lieu of proving anything else, prove just this.[22]

But now what are the intellectual issues involved? Several separable issues can be seen in Kierkegaard's several discussions. First the concept of immortality in religious contexts is not at all like our intellectualist-myth causes us to conclude. It is not, first and most importantly, a picture about an everlasting state nor a hypothesis about everybody's future nor a thesis that denies that men die. For the moment, though, we must dawdle a bit with the issues, for it certainly is true that in some way or another "immortality" veritably is linked with death, the future, and eternity. But "in some way or another" is the point, and it is Kierkegaard's contention that that connection is indirect, not direct and not immediate. In other words, to be concerned with immortality in religious contexts does not necessarily entail believing an elaborate theory embracing deathless life and a changeless future. His point is, rather, that the religious concept is linked with expectation and hope, not verification and proof—at least so he declares in his edifying addresses. But more, it belong to people who

21. *Postscript*, 176.
22. Ibid., 180.

have suffered deeply in this life and yet who say, as the Apostle Paul, "... our light affliction, which is but for a moment."²³ So, immortality is more like consolation, a prize in the middle of what looks like a losing race, than it is a truth about a state of affairs. "Immortality" works where people need consolation, have courage, are striving, seek a way out. He writes, "When he [Paul] is sitting in prison, when error grows and flourishes while he can do nothing; when the goal of his activity is foolishness to experience, because it goes backward, then is heaven his goal."²⁴

Therefore, the interest to prove is not congruent with such a concept; in fact, the very quest for proof changes the concept altogether. It makes it like a picture of a state of affairs and it transfers enthusiasm from the resolution of "being immortal" or "putting on immortality" to whether or not the picture is true of a state of affairs.

> What has given occasion to all this error about immortality is the fact that people have completely confused the statement of the case, have made a question, out of a task for action, a question for thought. . . . we can speak rightly about immortality only when we speak of the judgment; and naturally when we speak of the judgment we speak of immortality.²⁵

Kierkegaard's point is that the religious concept, then, has been almost destroyed. It is feasible to say, that the cunning of the human race, which he notes is "slyer than the cunningness of shrewd politicians," is another way to mark the intellectualist-myth we have already noted. In this respect, it has been a cunning which has invested the concept altogether by treating it as a problem.²⁶

Then there is a second matter. It is not only the concepts which have to be considered, it is also the school or way of life in which the terms are employed. In accord with his views about how to detect concepts it is quite apparent that "immortality" belongs to one rather definitive and requiring religious context. He is at considerable pains to show how peculiar this form of life is, in fact, this is the burden

---

23. Note, cit., 105ff. In other places, e.g., *Stages*, he notes that the concept of immortality is ethical, 426ff.

24. Ibid., 107.

25. *Christian Discourses*, 213.

26. Ibid., 220.

of several addresses already alluded to, as well as almost numberless entries in his journals. So, in the *Postscript*, his philosophic author contends that the question is not addressed to the learned world in general but rather is put to a single subject. Thus, the question cannot be put in social terms nor answered in social terms. The manner in which Christianity handles the matter clearly pinpoints the expression, forcing an individual not to an answer or to seeing it as a problem, but rather as an obligation and task. Therefore, there is a peculiar context in which the concept gets it expert treatment and where it can be properly understood. In fact, the concept is this way of behavior in this context.

In contrast, once "immortality" becomes a more general concept, then the philosophers take over. Precisely because most of them do not practice anything expertly except abstract thinking, the concept means everything and nothing. There are, consequently, no rules at all to determine how to deploy the expression "immortality." The man becomes objective and even chooses to handle the question of immortality "objectively." Kierkegaard notes that then a disagreement arises as to whether there is such a concept and, in addition, dozens of proposals as to what the concept is supposed to be. Nothing shows so clearly Kierkegaard's distain for abstract thought as this kind of issue. But, of course, he is not criticizing in the least a certain kind of objective reflection, even abstract reflection, at all. The study which he does himself of the Christian use of the expression is an objective and abstract study of a subjective use. His point is that there is a locus in which to find that concept, and he proposes that the concept can indeed be studied, objectively if one chooses. But then one must take into account the way of life and the qualities of subjectivity to which it is linked, for without these, there is no concept at all.

Contrariwise, the notion that the concept has a meaning independent of any context is the mistake. It is absurd, therefore, to examine the concept *qua* concept, as if it were a pure mental content, bracketed from the world, men, and use and entertained mentally while one were, perhaps, trying to become immortal. All of this is wrong and Kierkegaard labors mightily to destroy the power of such intellectualism. There simply is, then, no philosophical concept of immortality of a pure and unalloyed kind, supposedly implicit in all the rest of the everyday concepts of heaven, immortality, eternity, and everlasting joy. Kierkegaard takes savage delight in showing how meaningless the learned talk is here, for without a precise and restraining task to which the expression is addressed, almost anything goes. About the learned discussion, he says:

> ... it does not occur to me therefore to want to combat them, for such an undertaking is so dialectically difficult that I should need a year and a day before it could become dialectically clear to me whether there is any reality in such a contest ... Moreover, I know that some have found immortality in Hegel, others have not; I know that I have not found it in the System where indeed it is also unreasonable to seek it. . . .[27]

Kierkegaard had traversed the road from general philosophical thoughts about immortality to a more precise locating of the concept within ways of life in a few brief years. So, one can find him, early in his career, arguing with Plato, Kant, and others on the topic. Occasionally he concludes something to the effect that "the real question will certainly be the nature of immortality," and then he discourses bravely about levels and kinds of consciousness; but those are youthful interests which he subsequently gives up.[28] Ten years later, with most of his books behind him, such inquiries appear vain to him. Learned inquiries by which one settles questions of the "nature of immortality" remind him of a story.

> That is just as though a man were to raise a stick to strike one and say: now you will get a good thrashing—if this is a stick that I hold in my hand—and then, instead of hitting—gave three reasons in order to prove that it was a stick and concluded with an Amen, i.e., forgot to hit. O frightful folly. . . .[29]

But the summary line, however archaic it may sound philosophically, is found in the discussion in the *Postscript*. There Kierkegaard's aim is to describe what it means to be a subject and the learning

---

27. *Postscript*, 152–53.

28. *Papirer* II A, 387 (JP 2, 1946; *KJN* 2, EE:39). The entry dates from 1839.

29. Dru, *Journals*, no. 911, 308. In *Either/Or*, vol. I, the author says that at the age of fifteen he wrote an essay proving the immortality of the soul. It won a prize. Now at the age of twenty-five the author cannot produce a single one. Therefore he concludes that in Denmark, parents ought not to destroy the themes of their fifteen year olds. "To give this advice is the only contribution I can make to the welfare of the human race."

Truth Is Subjectivity: Some Radical Criticisms   129

"how" that is required. Then comes the line: "Objectively the question cannot be answered, because objectively it cannot be put, since immortality precisely is the potentiating and highest development of the developed subjectivity."[30] So we are back at the dynamisms of the person once again. The requisite, says a character in "In Vino Veritas," for immortality is that life be "*uno tenore*."[31] A man's life must be one breath, one kind and quality, with a character and continuity that needs no change. Thus, the interest is ethical, not metaphysical, a quality of one's life, not of truth or falsity; and the concept of immortality is accordingly so differentiated.

In a fashion like this, then, Kierkegaard brings the concept "immortality" to heel. Instead of it being a part of a general conceptual scheme, illustrated in this place or that, Kierkegaard denies it all such generality. He is quite specific; there is one concept in the Greeks and another in the Apostle Paul. But, once Paul is considered, it becomes clear that immortality was not something to prove at all. The point is not that he "failed" to prove it or could not do so, but rather that the very logic of the term was bound up with putting on immortality and living in a new dynamic way. Paul did not put irrelevant questions to matters like that.

Socrates was another who posed the issues correctly, principally because he did not share the intellectualist-myth on any religious and ethical issue either. Socrates, as Kierkegaard understood him, treated the matter properly. Accepting and developing the view that there was a sharp difference between Socrates and Plato (the first was tentative, an ethicist, a non-metaphysician, the second a metaphysician who tried to ground all of Socrates' convictions in the cognition of reality),[32] Kierkegaard finds that Socrates puts the issue "objectively," but also ironically and problematically. By this Kierkegaard means that Socrates locates the concept, and a proper one too, in order to have something to think about; but he prefaces his remarks with an "if": "if" there is an immortality.[33] There is an admission of objective

    30. *Postscript*, 154. Also, *Either/Or*, II: 226.

    31. *Stages*, 28.

    32. "Here the way swings off; Socrates concentrates essentially upon accentuating existence, while Plato forgets this and loses himself in speculation." *Postscript*, 184. *Papirer*, especially vols. I–IV.

    33. *Postscript*, 180. Note again the reflections in the *Papirer* relevant to this same book: vol. VI B, 13–99.

uncertainty to the effect that when the word is used to refer to an objective state of affairs there is uncertainty; but when used to order his life, it is his hope, and it gives him confidence, courage, and a great willingness to die.

So then the word "immortality" for Socrates can be employed in two ways. On the one hand, one can use it as a descriptive word. Then all the language of the intellectualist family of words comes into play. But Kierkegaard thinks Socrates cuts that out with his "if." For Kierkegaard this is a clue to a logical feature of such words. When the concepts of another domain are introduced, they are objectively uncertain. But on the other hand, "immortality" works otherwise for Socrates as we have already noted, and here the working of the word excludes those activities of asking for proofs and seeking the objective referent.[34]

But Kierkegaard does not deny that immortality is a concept. He is not one to think that every analysis falsifies that concept. The point is that there is a concept and that it is rigorous. But one must look for the concept where something is being done with it. Of course, there are numerous concepts, but Kierkegaard contends that there is not any concept of immortality that is not within a context. And the intellectualist context—which we have been calling a mythical context—is a falsifying one. For it changes the concept by making it a descriptive word, as if a man who uses it must be sure, with the use, of an objective state of affairs or otherwise he could not properly use it. This charge does not say that there is no valid objective study "of" the concept. Kierkegaard's own literature could not have been written unless there were. His study has shown us that the only locus for the proper employment of the concept is where passions, feelings, emotions, and all kinds of other subjective phenomena abound.

It is the quality of the subject that becomes the burning issue to the man who uses the concept properly. But to say this much indicates that the concept, indeed, can be studied, albeit in relation to the dynamism of everyday living.

---

34. Note the remarks in *Sickness Unto Death* about Socratic ignorance and why and how it is relevant to such instances. Cf. 160ff.

IV

In these pages we have noted that Kierkegaard paid attention to kinds of persons, their behavior, their questions, goals, wishes, and their language. It is only fair to him to remember that he thought this was a necessary condition for tackling the intellectual confusions of his day. His point is simply that a large range of concepts, particularly those of ethics and religion, can only be found when subjects who care, love, hate, do their duty, and exercise their passions and emotions, are considered. The point is that even "truth" in ethical and religious contexts has to be relocated here. This does not say, of course, that these concepts are only psychological concepts or that there is one concept for every person and his idiosyncrasies. The latter point, which supposes that subjectivity implies privacy or utter individuality, as if each concept is also private and individual, obviously makes nonsense of the very notion of a concept.

Kierkegaard did not argue any such insanity. He believed that subjectivity also had its rules and, therefore, its concepts. This is his point, namely, to show that subjectivity is not private and random. There are knowledgable practices and transactions which make our concepts here. Kierkegaard is pointing them out, not creating them, and drawing the lines by which to delineate one from the other.

Then we have also argued that Kierkegaard's pages are an attack upon a misunderstanding. But this is not a local mistake or one which happens upon occasion. We termed it a myth, because it has a kind of status. It is an intellectualist legend, for it proposes a kind of fabulous cognitive content for almost the entire range of human activities. Kierkegaard charges that art, ethics, and religion have been expounded in accord with notions of there being invariably this intellectualist content. This entails the misuse of words like "objective" and "truth," as though other enterprises could be parlayed by these concepts without difference, and the mistaken view that while doing whatever one does in the pursuit of these other activities, one was synchronously "knowing" something too. The proposal that "truth is subjectivity" breaks the spell of the invariable association of "truth" and "objective."

But, last, there is the consideration of what it means to be immortal. Again the aim of Kierkegaard's pages is certainly to show that the concept of immortality does not make sense if it is treated as though it involved a major truth claim; instead he relocates it by showing that it requires attention to what we are, not about a state of affairs except indirectly and thereafter. Once again, the case against discussing "the objective truth of the belief in immortality" disappears as the absurdity of so doing becomes manifest. And the concept "truth" in ethico-religious contexts, then, demands an altogether different elucidation, one, we might add, not suggested at all by the intellectualist-myth to which we otherwise succumb. This further elucidation will be attempted in the next chapter.

CHAPTER 7

Truth Is Subjectivity
Some Logical Considerations

"THE MODE OF THE apprehension of the truth is precisely the truth. It is, therefore, untrue to answer a question in a medium in which the question cannot arise. So, for example, to explain reality within the medium of the possible, or to distinguish between possibility and reality within possibility."[1] This is a crucial passage from Kierkegaard's pages on the issue of subjectivity. Shortly thereafter come the dicta:

> The esthetic and intellectual principle is that no reality is thought or understood until its "*esse*" has been resolved into its "*posse*." The ethical principle is that no possibility is understood until each "*posse*" has really become an "*esse*." An esthetic and intellectual scrutiny protests every "*esse*" which is not a "*posse*"; the ethical scrutiny results in the condemnation of every "*posse*" which is not an "*esse*" . . . Is the real then the same as the external? By no means.[2]

Clearly, we have some general concepts working here, like "possible" and "actual" and "possibility" and "reality." Our problem in this chapter will be to use these significantly for the themes noted in the earlier chapters, not least, for the distinction between "how" and "what," and Kierkegaard's repudiation of the pervasive intellectualist myth.

For here we will be concerned, in addition, and in some detail, with what we might call Kierkegaard's logic. For him there was a kind of logic embedded in various kinds of discourse. We shall indicate

1. *Postscript,* 287.
2. Ibid., 288.

something about his logical theory (insofar as he had any) later. But in this chapter we shall be concerned with the working logic of his notion that truth is subjectivity. It turns out that the abstract terms already noted in the quotation are nowhere nearly as important to that working logic as are a number of other topics. So, successively, we will look at his conviction that philosophy is an activity, not a doctrine, and the concept of the responsible subject, the "I," who engages in such activity; secondly, the distinction between essential and non-essential knowledge will be invoked, again linking both terms of the distinction with the activity of a subject; thirdly, again the recognition of "objective uncertainty" will be seen in another way; fourthly, why the "how" and the "what" engender the role, along with the rest of the above, for the concept of subjectivity. All of these together will also give significance to Kierkegaard's language about *posse* and *esse*.

I

To reiterate a general point, Kierkegaard is not, strictly speaking, writing out another philosophy. Indeed he is philosophizing but he is not replacing the philosophies he criticizes with another one. What he is doing is something much more modest and also much more difficult, namely, practicing another kind of intellectual activity. He tells us:

> In Greece, philosophizing was a mode of action, and the philosopher was therefore an existing individual. He may not have possessed a great amount of knowledge, but what he did know he knew to some profit, because he busied himself early and late with the same thing. But nowadays, just what is it to philosophize, and what does a philosopher really know? For, of course, I do not deny that he knows everything.[3]

Therefore, in the *Postscript*, where the explanation of subjectivity goes on, we get examples, in a succession of four thinkers, whose activity is their philosophizing, who do not enunciate results or state philosophical truths. On the other hand, they are not wildly subjective or ruleless either. They are responsible, philosophical, clear, and are ob-

---

3. Ibid., 295. Also he says, "The Greek philosopher was an existing individual, and did not permit himself to forget that fact . . . It is necessary only to have the courage to be human, and to refuse to be terrified or tricked into becoming a phantom merely to save embarrassment," 274.

viously articulating something. They are not baldly inventive or rhapsodic. They make distinctions, elucidate a host of matters, and isolate concepts. In this way, they also philosophize and they see something they had not seen before and become straight where they previously were confused. So, too, it goes with their readers.

Besides that, his subjective thinkers are existing individuals. On the face of it, the claim to be an existing individual sounds like one more philosophical conundrum. "An existing individual" has the ring of a typically philosophical concept, one coined to do whatever a philosopher wants it to do and quite without the restraints and qualifications it would have if it were a concept used in law, say, or in medicine, or by a census official, or, for that matter, by a tax collector. But here one must be very careful indeed. For Kierkegaard's use of "an existing individual" is not a specialist's use; it is not a special concept needing a whole gamut of philosophic rubrics to get its meaning clear. He uses it to call attention to the man (not the "average man") that each of us is when we love and hate, think and rusticate, argue and dream, and talk and imagine. He is not, thereby, proposing a new philosophical doctrine of the "ego," nor deducing a new transcendental category, nor advancing a subtle anthropology under the disguise of plain talk.

Someone might say: "The existing individual—why should I take him seriously? I am a man, indeed an existing individual, ignorant, often ill, a mixture of feelings, tormented by doubts and notions of insufficiency; I am afraid of what others will think of me, willing to think big but prone to live small; I am jealous, stupid, mean, fitfully happy, full of plans, and loathe to die; I am often uncertain about what I ought to be doing or whether what I do is the right thing to do. Certainly I will admit all that, but what does that have to do with philosophy?"

But this is precisely Kierkegaard's philosophical point. "The realm of pure thought is a sphere in which the existing individual finds himself only by virtue of a mistaken beginning," he says, and then continues: "and this error revenges itself by making the existence of the individual insignificant, and giving his language a flavor of lunacy."[4] Here the aim is not a correct description of an existing individual at all. There is no question here of Freud's theory of the ego versus Fichte's or an existentialist theory instead of an Hegelian

---

4. Ibid., 277.

one. Kierkegaard's intent is to awaken all of us to the fact that there is already a correct use of "I" at our behest. Anterior to our abstract doctrines there is a consensus, and the expression "the existing individual" only reminds us of what we have had all along. Therefore, those philosophical systems that substitute notions of the pure ego as if they were the logical essence, the pure conceptual translation of what we had in more ordinary circumstances where we used "I" or "I think," are wrong. But what makes them wrong? Again it is not a mistake in the ordinary empirical sense (misinformation or the wrong facts or no facts but only opinion), nor is it quite a matter of saying that a theory is wrong or inconsistent (to be replaced by a more adequate one); rather, it is a kind of forgetfulness of what must be normative.

Kierkegaard's analysis is analogous to certain philosophers who have invoked common sense or ordinary language as a norm for certain kinds (not all) of extravagant beliefs and extraordinary uses of language. So, if two people disagreed whether a piece of music was a tone poem or a symphony, we might propose that they should know the music equally well and also that they should agree upon the canons, such as they are, for a tone poem and for a symphony. But if one said, "Though it would ordinarily be called a symphony, I think of it as a tone poem," then we have a case where the ordinary use of the term is normative. The man talks nonsense when he departs from the established use of the terms. Profundities in his defense would very likely be pseudo too. Kierkegaard has the profoundest regard for the power and authority of language, but he is not quite an ordinary language philosopher. Whether his views are compatible or not is a moot point.[5]

---

5. In his papers from 1840 there is a remarkable passage about philosophers and language. It reads in part (translation my own):

> If the claim of philosophers to be without presuppositions were correct, it would be necessary to consider language and its entire meaning and relation to speculation, for there speculative philosophy has a medium which it did not give to itself. And what the eternal mystery of consciousness is for speculative philosophy as the unity of natural and free determinations, so is language, part of it being given and part being freely developed. Similarly the individual, however freely he develops, can never reach the point of being absolutely independent; because being truly free, contrariwise, consists in bringing into oneself what is given and through one's

But there is certainly an analogy; for his rebuke of the abstract philosophers does not inhere in disdain of technical concepts nor in the dismay that technical language is not widely understood, but rather in the awareness that it is necessary to philosophize from the consensus and back to the consensus.[6] There is already something present, concepts included, by which to bring philosophizing back to a standard. And the standard is not the correct philosophy of man; it is not in philosophy at all. One has simply forgotten what being a subject is, and the philosophical schemes about the "I" are a mirage.[7] The ordinary self or "I" is neglected.

Therefore, part of the restraint being imposed by Kierkegaard's philosophy is not that of another philosophy but is the restraint of what we already know, but have forgotten. Philosophy brings this to mind again. It is the familiar "I," the subject or subjectivity that we already have, that one must acknowledge and concern oneself with. Part of Kierkegaard's *reductio ad absurdum* argument is to show how ridiculous it is to forsake the familiar and to contrive specialized concepts, philosophical ones, to replace the familiar. He shows, instead, that there is an "I," an "existing individual" (when he refers in the third person) which is not a philosophical invention at all. All of us are existing individuals and knew full well how to refer to ourselves and others long before we developed specialized vocabularies or thought abstractly. Kierkegaard is engrossed in showing us that philosophical concepts need not replace these in every context. Philosophy may distract us from what we already have in non-philosophical ways. Furthermore, by redefining the "ego," substituting an abstract "ego" for the "I" that I already am, the issues of religion and ethics become altogether unreal too. The plain man has a task, and to this task reli-

---

freedom being absolutely dependent. So it is with language, and we meet here the mistaken disposition not to accept language as the freely appropriated given but to suppose that one gives it to oneself, whether this shows itself in the highest regions where it ends as the negation of language, in silence, or in the personal isolation of complete silence . . . (*Papirer* III A, 11; *JP* 3, 3281)

6. Even *Fear and Trembling* (translated by Lowrie) identifies "the universal," not by epistemic concepts but by a kind of consensus. Note 98ff.

7. The real subject is the ethically existing subject, not the "cognitive" subject, the "I" which is the subject of the "*cogito*." This is the argument again in the *Postscript*, 281.

gion and ethics already make their proposals. The use of special concepts for the subject makes all the issues highly abstract and, besides, causes a man to think that the real issues are too high for him—they are philosophical and abstract.

What then of philosophy as a mode of action or an activity? For this is where we began a few pages ago. Kierkegaard clearly wants his reader to think with him, but philosophizing does not require another "what" as much as it does the "how." Part of that "how" is simply remembering that one is an existing individual, and that requires that one think with the customary "I," not as an universalized "ego" or a general disembodied spirit, and not *sub specie aeternitatis* either. What, he asks rhetorically, is this same subject? He is referring to Hegel's repudiation of the tripartite division of man into spirit, soul, and body and his substitution of the notion of three developmental stages within "the same developing subject." Kierkegaard writes:

> Surely not an individual existing human being, but rather the abstract concept of man in general. There is nothing else for science to deal with, and in dealing with it science is, of course, fully within its rights; but here, too, we are often put off with a mere game of words... Everywhere it is decisively concluded that thought is the highest stage of human development; philosophy moves farther and farther away from primitive existential impressions, and there is nothing left to explore, nothing to experience. Everything has been finished, and speculative thought has now to rubricate, classify, and methodically arrange the various concepts. One does not live anymore, one does not act, one does not believe; but one knows what love and faith are, and it only remains to determine their place in the system.[8]

But to Kierkegaard there is no correct philosophical view to propose, not even a view about the subject. Instead there is a correct way to proceed, a primitive and plain way, already available. Philosophy is one of the means to getting us back to where we are.

Kierkegaard is convinced that the life of a person has as much structure as the law-governed inorganic universe. And he has very conscientiously worked out a detailed map of the subjective life of

---

8. Ibid., 307. I have put together the first two sentences of the footnote with the text from this single page.

the emotions and will, feeling, and passion. He has also conceptualized these matters at great length. Nonetheless, with all that we have said about his ability to provide such conceptual analyses, he was not content to give only the objective recipe. This is the place where most thinkers would have stopped; he, however, gives also a poetic visualization of the subject's life in character and context, creating figures who talk, think, feel themselves out with drastic consistency. His philosophizing both isolates the concepts and then puts them back to their appropriate work. This, too, is part of Kierkegaard's non-dogmatic and indirect way of philosophizing, once again commensurate with his criticism of the intellectualist-myth to which we earlier referred. For his philosophizing is not only as sharply refined as that of the rarest of reflective geniuses, but he makes one present in the situations, so that one does not think about the concepts but one learns to use them, concretely and in the situation where they are disclosed. One uses them as the subject, not simply as the objective spectator or analytic student of the other's use. This is why his claim to distinctiveness is so sure.

For while his purpose was to explain and to resolve riddles of human life and reason, he chose not to do it in such a way that would increase the store of knowledge.[9] Having diagnosed the evil of his day as a confusion of knowledge with life, he saw all kinds of illustrations. To be aware of the concepts of faith and love is not the same as the ability to use them; to be an expert on "love" is not the same as being a great lover, and to be an expert on "faith" is not the same as being faithful. But it would have been a mistake for Kierkegaard only to contribute a few more paragraphs to compound the confusion. Therefore, he again breaks with the pattern altogether. He chooses to teach, by a kind of indirection, what it means to be a responsible person, and, thereby, he also hopes to provide the clue even to the ordering of one's concepts. His pseudonyms are living subjects who show us the uses of the "I" with which we are already familiar.

Once more we are obliquely approaching the topic of this chapter. For now it may be possible to see what Kierkegaard means by "subjectivity." Every man has to synthesize his hopes, his plans, his expectations, and his projects with actual situations. Therefore, being

---

9. Dru, *Journals*, 16:7 (*Papirer* I A, 72).

a subject is a matter of effecting a synthesis. This is what Kierkegaard means by reality. And there are two extremes. A so-called practical man might give up thoughts and aims, become insensitive to all ideals and altogether forgetful of his moral tasks. He and his life would be unreal and he would lose all subjectivity, however preoccupied he might be with this and that which pass as the realities of the everyday objective world. Another man, perhaps a thinker or a poet, might luxuriate in the contemplation of the grand ideals and the reconstruction of the whole social order, but never bring his own life into conformity therewith. To this very degree, he, too, would be unreal and quite lacking in subjectivity. Therefore Kierkegaard says, "Subjectivity is truth, subjectivity is reality."[10]

When a man puts ideals together with realities, not in cognitive endeavors but in his daily life, he becomes the subject of his own endeavor. This is the kind of synthesis and simultaneity of factors that he is describing in his essays about subjectivity. But this takes us to other themes concerning subjectivity. Note, however, before we turn to these that a concept in the context of the intellectual pursuits is often simply the aim. But in ethics and religion the concept is there to effect another kind of activity. In one case an "*esse*" becomes a concept, a "*posse*," a possibility; in the other a "*posse*" becomes an "*esse*."[11]

II

Here let us turn again to one of Kierkegaard's distinctions. He draws a sharp line between essential and non-essential knowledge (more often he says essential and accidental knowledge). What does this distinction mean? First, consider some of his lines:

> All essential knowledge relates to existence, or only such knowledge as has an essential relationship to existence is essential knowledge. All knowledge which does not . . . , is, essentially viewed, accidental knowledge; its degree and scope is essentially indifferent . . . But it means that knowledge has a relationship to the knower, who is essentially an existing

---

10. *Postscript*, 306.

11. Note in addition to the cited passages of the *Postscript*, the analysis of "possible" and "reality" in *Training in Christianity*, 66ff.

individual, and that for this reason all essential knowledge is essentially related to existence.[12]

Perhaps the distinction is the same as the one that Kierkegaard drew in an edifying discourse written in 1844. There he says:

> There is a truth whose greatness, whose sublimity, we are accustomed to extol by saying that it is an "indifferent" truth, that is, equally valid whether anyone accepts it or not; indifferent to the peculiar circumstances of the individual, whether young or old, happy or distressed; indifferent to its relationship to him . . . ; equally valid whether he subscribes to it with his whole heart or acknowledges it coolly and unemotionally . . . ; equally valid whether he has himself discovered it or only repeats what he has been taught. And only that man's understanding is adequate and admiration justified, who grasps that this justification is what chiefly matters . . .
>
> There is another kind of truths . . . which we may call "concerned" . . . they do not quite fit all general occasions, but only into special and individual occasions. They are not indifferent to the particular conditions of the individual, whether he is young or old, happy or distressed; for these determine for him whether they are to be truths for him . . . this kind of truth is not indifferent as to how the individual receives it . . .[13]

Suppose we look again at some sentences under the heading of "essential" knowledge. Is it correct to say that they are knowledge? The sentence "Jesus Christ is God" often connotes, depending upon the context of course, that "there was a man by the name of Jesus Christ." Along with numerous amplifying sentences describing the man, it looks like an historical sentence. Other readers might assume that the "is God" predicate is a metaphysical expression. Still others might treat the "is" as one of identity, and then the sentence "Christ is God" becomes a tautology.[14] Needless to say, the sentence, whether treated historically, metaphysically, or as a tautology, then is subject

---

12. *Postscript*, 176–77.

13. *Semlede Vaerker*, vol. IV 123–24. *Edifying Discourses*, III:71–72. The translation is my own.

14. Kierkegaard reflected much on these issues while in Berlin in 1846. Note *Papirer* VII A, 73–89, especially entry 139 (*JP* 2, 1347) in which the thesis is "Immanently (in the fantastic medium of abstraction) God does not exist . . ." Also note the first pages of *Training in Christianity*.

to doubt. It becomes difficult to believe, either because one cannot see how it is true or, in the instance that it is a tautology, because it is trivial. But this is Kierkegaard's point. In all these instances the "how" of the treatment, the way the sentence is construed, is wrong. The logic is askew. One must bring that sentence back into the right company. The knowing subject, the "I" who thinks it, must be made perspicuous in order to start the correction.

Kierkegaard therefore admits that a claim such as the one noted requires a peculiar treatment and use. It has its special occasion and use. Insofar as it is a sentence and treated with analogy with other statements which are deemed either true or false, it is not possible to verify its claim one way or the other. So it is with sentences about God, about providence, about the Trinity, and about immortality and hell. So it also is with sentences about duty, law, obedience, right, and wrong, for all of these can be treated by rules and devices which construe them as descriptive, factual, and even historical. "Essential knowledge" according to Kierkegaard often refers to the world and everyday things, yet it is not, strictly speaking, to be treated as one more claim about objective things. Furthermore, there is a heterogeneity about it, for the canons of logic that apply to "objective" sentences do not really apply to these ethico-religious claims. This is why he says that such teachings are objectively uncertain and remain so. The objective uncertainty is not a function of negative evidence, nor is it mitigated by the passage of time or by the presence or absence of talent in the knower. The uncertainty is, instead, a function of the very logic of the use of the sentence. This is why Kierkegaard insists that such sentences are misunderstood if construed by analogy with other knowledge claims.

On the other hand, it is not enough to say that ethico-religious language has only one function, helpful as it may be, and no claim upon our allegiance or belief. Is there nothing to believe, but only something to do? Kierkegaard saw the force of such reflective doubts quite clearly and never ceased wrestling with the involved logical and epistemological technicalities. However, he is not prone to resolve these matters by dogmatism, either religious or philosophical. He claims no divine revelation for his thoughts about these things and claims no new facts that reorient the entire philosophical apparatus.

His instruments are, in his language, "dialectical" and nothing else, except some *ad hominem* appeals. By "dialectical" here we mean only that he wants to untangle what are massive intellectual confusions and this he does by assessing the languages of faith and morals and comparing them in detail with the knowledge that we might have about these and other matters. By "*ad hominem*" we mean that he appeals to the panoply of uses that the ordinary person already knows about when thinking responsibly.

The intellectualist-myth of which we spoke in the last chapter is evinced in the conviction that a belief about God, Jesus, and the Good is essential. If one asks, "Essential for what?" the answer is: "Necessary in order to effect a moral and religious change in one's life." This relation Kierkegaard believes is wrong. His point is that if we begin the discussion about ethico-religious teachings by asking "Are the questions true?" then we must conclude that in such a context of question-asking there is only a general answer: "They are objectively uncertain." This does not say that there is nothing to believe, but only that what there is to believe cannot be made believable and tractable to such an inquirer. Instead one can show that there is a disparity between the question and the answers, a gulf in kind, which Kierkegaard fixes by the concept of "objective uncertainty."

Kierkegaard's analysis of ethico-religious language does not say that they are not knowledge-like claims. On the contrary, he uses the expression "essential knowledge" over and over again. Plainly, he does not deny the referential use of the claims or what moderns often call the ontological claim. His point is not to stress the attitudinal at the expense of the objective, the psychological at the expense of the truth claim, or the function at the expense of the disclosure. The notion that truth is subjectivity is not intended to give solace to anyone who says that religion is only a subjective matter or that ethico-religious language is only an index of the feelings of the user or that the sentences are only symbolic. Neither does his language simply limn a catalogue of duties or disguise imperatives in the form of indicatives. But he is intending to do something about the riddle and puzzlement into which the intelligentsia has fallen. Because this language cannot be shown to be objectively certain, they are inclined to give up on the ethico-religious quest. It all becomes absurd. Kierkegaard thinks that this way of proceeding is completely wrong. The philosophical scheme has created the conviction that either the word "true" applies in a certain way, or it does not apply at all. Or, the concept of certainty becomes the guarantor of seriousness, without which nothing can be pursued.

But is this to say that only an inference is mistaken? Not quite. By the logic of this situation we mean not simply the rules of inference but also more subtle matters, a kind of protocol by which we determine what questions apply, which do not, how we ought to construe ethics, logic, creeds, poems, history, and the rest. The philosophical convention which interprets each of these as though the same concepts were deeply embedded in each domain, only awaiting the elucidation of the philosopher, Kierkegaard believed to be erroneous. He considers, instead, each domain in turn, trying to isolate its concepts and relate the same to the appropriate behavior and use. In this wise, he also considers something about "essential knowledge," namely, that this requires first, chronologically, an interest in doing something with one's life and oneself.[15] If this concern is present, the logical matter of "objective uncertainty" no longer is the only canonical consideration. Then the sentence also becomes something to actualize, and increasingly the attention is drawn from the relation between the sentence and objective states of affairs to the relation between the sentence as a proposal for one's life and one's life. This difference is not, of course, to be marked in the sentence as much as it is in the use of the sentence. This kind of sentence "is not indifferent as to how the individual receives it."[16]

Furthermore, this is not a matter of having a doctrine about the sentences of religion and ethics as much as it is a matter of disposing oneself properly, being the proper "I" or subject; hence, it becomes a matter of deploying correctly the concepts involved. This correction calls for a re-ordering of one's dispositions respecting the sentences, the "how" again, and not a new set of sentences or a meta-explanation or translation of those teachings. Furthermore, once the task of using them as projective possibilities and possible ways of living one's

---

15. In a beautiful letter to his niece, Miss Lund, Kierkegaard makes the point that "the good" has to be wished by each person in turn, otherwise it cannot be possessed. *Breve og Aktstykker*, vol. I:183–84.

16. *Edifying Discourses*, III:72.

life begins, the entire issue respecting their objective truth or falsity begins to change too. The logic remains the same; i.e., relative to the canons of history, metaphysics, and other kinds of descriptive language they remain objectively uncertain. But a thinker no longer lets the objective uncertainty keep him from believing. A man begins to want to believe them, and his certitude about them grows with the passage of time and the strenuousness of his ethico-religious striving. But more of this later. It is clear now that the stress upon the necessity of the "how" is, of course, a measure of the concern with reality and also with the truth as subjectivity.

III

But the reason for Kierkegaard's analysis is the widespread phenomenon of literate people everywhere treating the language of morals and of religion quite differently. The admission of objective uncertainty is the grounds for either a forthright rejection and a disdainful indifference or a subtle process of transforming the literature into something more amenable. The intelligent man proposes "another understanding," or he searches out "the meaning," or he discerns another "reality" which will change the logical case rather more favorably.[17]

Kierkegaard contended that the newer philosophies and theologies of his day had effected translations that were downright deceptions. One such deception is to construe the religious and ethical teachings in the manner of erstwhile empirical statements. Something like the following seems to be at stake. The tissue of language is conceived to make truth claims about God and ethical qualities. The objective ethico-religious stuff is likened to facts or, at least, to a kind of reality other than and different from the language. This causes one to treat the claims in what Kierkegaard calls "the objective-appropriation Process," something akin to what recent writers might have called an empirical method or John Dewey might have referred to as a scientific method.

---

17. Kierkegaard likens such philosophical renditions to sophisticated comedies which do not become any less a misunderstanding because the actors happen to be "private-docents and speculative philosophers." *Postscript*, 189.

The other eminently respectable way, one seen frequently in highly abstract logical and epistemological philosophies (that are often called "idealistic"), is to say that God is a being who has no factual existence but only exists essentially—"whose being is identical with its existence."[18] Then the objective uncertainty disappears. Furthermore, there is no fundamental problem even conceivable about verification or meaning. The only issues are the adequacy of the sentences, the propriety of the words, issues to be settled by conceptual analysis and more adequate definitions. Such a translation has tempted philosophers of every generation and not least in Kierkegaard's day. He makes a point about tautologous reasoning that applies here:

> I merely develop the ideality I have presupposed, and because of my confidence in this, I make so bold as to defy all objections, even those which have not been made.[19]

The attractiveness of this way of treating troublesome religious propositions and, of course, certain ethical proposals, did not long escape young Kierkegaard. In his early twenties he felt the lure of the powerful rationalisms as a way to satisfy the sense of "the imperative of understanding" which he felt almost painfully.[20] Restless and distraught as he often was, uncertainty was almost an insufferable additional burden. The quest for certainty seemed to be absolutely ingredient in the quest for a way of life. And certainty is what the subtle idealistic schemes offered. For where the predicate of a sentence was understood really to be part of the subject, at least in the better logico-reality schemes, there could be no objective uncertainty. If there was uncertainty it was only psychological and could be removed by insight into the meanings of the terms. "For the only consistent position," he says when assessing the strengths of these philosophical reconstructions, "outside Christianity is that of pantheism, the taking of oneself out of existence by way of recollection into the eternal, whereby all existential decisions become a mere shadow

---

18. *Fragments*, "Foreword," 22–23.
19. Ibid., 33.
20. Note his early letters in *Breve og Aktstykker vedrørende Søren Kierkegaard*, edited by Niels Thulstrup. Some of these are translated and appear in Dru's selections from Kierkegaard's papers in *Journals*, especially that on 4ff. The quote is from the letter of August 1, 1835, from Gilleleje.

play beside what is eternally decided from behind."[21] Philosophies can be dangerous because they cause original and primitive sentences to lose all ethical and religious significance. By substituting logical relations for demands to obey and to follow, attention is diverted, and there is nothing in a logical transition from one sentence to another which produces a qualitative change in the knower. This "lure of immanence" of which Kierkegaard repeatedly spoke, often occasions a forgetfulness of the fact that the ethical and the religious are rooted in the important concern of trying to learn how to exist; it is a fantasy on the part of philosophers to resolve the latter question by translating the question into a medium where the quality of one's existence is no longer an element. Whatever logical validity there might be then is largely irrelevant to the interest that engendered the inquiry.[22] In the other instance, where religious and ethical views are treated as hypotheses, he asks how one can recognize God as an empirical object. The elaborate endeavor to treat sentences about God as empirical truths is vitiated logically by the fact that God gets into the empirical material only by being placed there by the thinker, by an act of interpolation. Kierkegaard's rhetorical question seems apt: ". . . what else is this but to presuppose that God exists, so that I really begin by confidence in him?"[23]

But somewhere between his youthful days and the time of writing his philosophical works, Kierkegaard concluded that being an ethical man and even a Christian was fully compatible with the admission of objective uncertainty. Manifestly this does not mean that Kierkegaard wanted to be uncertain or that he advocated insecurity and uncertainty. What happened was a kind of recognition of where the problem lay. The quest for certainty was serious enough in the young but was also ambiguous. Kierkegaard saw that certainty was no one thing. The conventional way of describing the human situation in terms of a general uncertainty (everything becomes uncertain in

---

21. *Postscript*, 203.

22. Ibid., 184–85, especially the footnote. See also *Fragments*, 29ff. Note a remark in *Papirer* about the ethical consequence of the identity-principle. Here the gist is that there are none except self-annihilation, for by definition identity is a logical and non-temporal matter. For a person to become non-temporal means that he must die! See entries from *Papirer* V A, 68.

23. *Fragments*, 33. Also see entries from *Papirer* V B, 5.

the same respects) and a general certainty (everything must become certain in the same respects) was an egregious howler. Therefore Kierkegaard began to attack what he called the "riddle of life." The riddle had been made deep and profound by thoughtful people, even by philosophers and theologians.

Another way to assess his pages, then, is to say that he begins to see that relative to one kind of quest, namely that which wants to treat all language as a picture or transcript of things and happenings, there can be no certainty for ethical and religious teachings. A man must be weaned from so questing. Not in such a way as to disparage historical research or critical textual studies, but only from considering that the quest for cognitive certainty is equally appropriate to ethics, logic, theology, and even the Bible. Kierkegaard's concern is with the conceptual confusions, not least those inhering in the concept "certainty." He wants to show that respecting God there simply cannot be that standpoint from which one can compare the statements about God and God and say that the statements are true. Such a standpoint does not exist. No man is such an abstract ego as to be able to exercise such detachment. Neither is God the kind of object who can be "seen" or "heard." Therefore, the upshot is obvious: one must watch the issues very carefully and see to it that one does not deceive oneself.

For self-deception is what happens altogether too easily. Either one forgets in the enthusiasm for objective certainty, which is supposedly generic, who it is that is seeking it, or one gets misled into thinking that there is only one kind of certainty. When despair couples with ingenuity, one disguises the issues in a more refined set of concepts and everything gets a subtle and rarified look. Self-deception can occur in simpleminded obtuseness or it can happen via those philosophies and theologies that deprive a person of all primitive originality.

All of this enters into the context of Kierkegaard's reflections upon statements that in fact already exist, and that, in virtue of being religious and ethical, are also called "essential." Two extremes have been noted: those words and sentences might just imply and mean other words and sentences, "ideal" objects or more "possibles" (a homogeneity of possibles, ideas about ideas, words about words, propositions about propositions), or they may even be about God, evil, and other facts within the world, but hypothetically so.

If the first, such sentences can never be existential in any factual sense nor could they effect ethical or religious passion and interest except in a peculiar pedagogical circumstance. They would very likely be similar to other factual sentences, quite without power to bring about anything other than an appreciative assent. But there is another possibility, which, before Kierkegaard's time is relatively unexplored. This is to show that this language about God and His relation to the world, even though it is not directly verifiably true or false in regard to God and the world, is nonetheless part of the depiction of a human being's possibilities. The point is that their ethico-religious meaning inheres principally in the latter, and in the former only tangentially.

To say this much is to put another emphasis upon apprehension and use. Instead of the sentence being clearly true or false about the world or whatever else it seems to refer to, the sentence is admittedly uncertain. The sentence is not logically meaningless; it makes minimal sense because it is free of logical contradictions. But the point that Kierkegaard notes is that they are so formulated that in the right context and with the right use they are not probable or improbable, yet are used as referring sentences about people, God, historical events, and natural phenomena. Thus, to say that "all things work together for those who love God" is to talk, after all, about historical and natural events too. The sentence "Jesus is God" is about a man. But if one is misled by the undisciplined desire for verification, if one asks for proof, all kinds of difficulties ensue. Is it the case that the sentence is only an extrapolation from one case to all? Is it the case that one extends one's certainty from a few things, which have worked for good, to the hopeful view that all do and will? And is not this subjectivity at its worst?

IV

But again Kierkegaard's stress is upon "how" the sentence is used, not the "what." Put in another way, the issue is something like this: there is no meaning to sentences once they are stripped of their contexts, psychological, linguistic, and otherwise. The same sentence, i.e., "same" in a grammatical sense, can be used in an aesthetic way of life, and it then can be used to please, to stimulate tears, smiles, or disdain, or even to cause admiration and awe. So it is with a sentence to the effect that "Jesus died on Good Friday for the sins of men." One might hear this sentence in such a way that sighs over the iniquities He suffered will be the only response or an aesthetic interest in the blood on his brow or the thorns hurting him the only noticeable consequence. Others might be fired with a picture of moral fervor, a good man dying at the hands of a mob, and they might well engender moral outrage at that picture. But most of us, Kierkegaard contends, have been led to conceive of the sentence, first, as though we must be sure whether it is true before we respond in any other way to it. The yen to verify seems fundamental and almost the sign of rationality and good sense.

To this extent there is a "how" already operative. This "how" is already general, and, Kierkegaard thought, a result of the popular intellectual culture of his day. Kierkegaard denies though that the statement means anything simply as it stands. He refuses all mechanical views of language, e.g., any which make words simply the mirrors of things, or any logical view that would declare that sentences have an inherent logical form that proposes the meaning of the sentence.[24] Therefore he refuses always to say that first one must verify the meaning that the sentence already has, and thereafter add to it other valuational and religious meanings. Long before the practice was criticized (or for that matter even very well formulated), Kierkegaard refuses the conventional outlook that makes factual meaning elemental and objective and evaluative meanings derivative and subjective.

But we must pause on this point. It seems natural to say about the sentence noted that questions of truth and falsity are merely a matter of ascertaining what the words actually denote or name. But this, unfortunately, is how we naturally think about words. First they denote or name, then they connote or mean something in addition. The intellectualist-myth of which we earlier spoke and against which Kierkegaard was ever contending occasions the notion that words do some things almost by themselves, such things as "naming," "denoting," and "stating." But other things are done with words by using them, namely, "evaluating," "relating," "judging," and "criticizing." The

---

24. Note his remarks about language in *De Omnibus Dubitandum Est*, where questions of attitude and meaning are proposed relative to Cartesian "doubt" of everything. Note especially 130ff.

Truth Is Subjectivity: Some Logical Considerations　　　　151

use of words for a variety of purposes seems to be dependent upon the veridical character of words; however, the veridical character does not seem to be as clearly a function of the use as it does of the words themselves and their relations to reality.

Without the technical apparatus of later philosophy, Kierkegaard is intent upon the criticism of such an outlook. The stages in life's way are all depictions of different "hows," different contexts in which words and sentences get different meanings. These are permutations of dissimilar ways of a subject behaving, thinking, describing, evaluating, meaning something or other, deciding, feeling, and even sensing. Therefore even the interest in the "what," often described as though it were objective and pre-subjective, logically anterior to anything subjective, is to Kierkegaard just one more way to get meaning and to describe and even to construe words, things and even oneself. Therefore the tendency of intellectuals to treat words first in this way is not, Kierkegaard believes, strictly a logical requisite. Nothing in the nature of words or of logic requires it, although this is what the intelligentsia mistakenly believes. This situation is precisely what Kierkegaard is struggling to dispel. In fact, he is trying to show that all the activities of the intelligence—description, evaluation, judgment, etc.—are matters of the "how" and that one never escapes a "how." Thus there is no non-subjective and completely objective "what" in knowledge and speech upon which the "how" is dependent. All the "whats" are in turn a function, in part of the "hows."

Correlatively, Kierkegaard does not say that because there is no language of existence *qua* existence, or of "being" *qua* "being," there is only a language of subjectivity. By the same token, there is no language that is altogether without objective reference either. Nonetheless, there is no basic objective language and there is none that is purely subjective. There is no pure description and no pure expression of a private subjectivity either. Kierkegaard's analysis is much more refined. When language of the ethicist such as his pseudonym in *Either/Or* is being used, it is being used referringly. So it is too with the authors of the New Testament. Therefore his argument leads one to see that in all the various stages (or what Wittgenstein might have included in his language games) language is also being used about objective things. The differences among them cannot be adjudicated by reference to an objective standard. The reason is simply that there is no standard, either within language or outside it, objective and independent of all the various uses. Once one raises the issue in this way there is only objective uncertainty.

Of course, there is such a thing as verification. But again, the concept "verification" plays its role and has its meaning in a context and not in all contexts. Kierkegaard thinks that it functions where objectivity, a kind of temper and a "how," has its sway. Science and scholarship require this "how" just in order to describe the "what."[25] Because this "how" is relatively easy to attain and to practice, Kierkegaard is not particularly concerned to analyze and to describe it. The quality of subjectivity is like one pole; the other extreme, he avers, is to be found in the context of Christianity. Again, though, the aim of ethico-religious language is not served if the verification question is thought to be primary.

It should be stated unequivocally that Kierkegaard is not suggesting that the fact that a "how" is more fundamental than a "what" means that there are no standards for judgment. On the contrary, there are standards for truth just as there are standards for right and wrong. Kierkegaard never denies these. His point is that the exclusion of the "how" from the philosophical account has produced a false and harmful tendency, one which erects an impossible and artificial view of the objectivity of science in contradistinction to the subjectivity of morals and religion and aesthetic judgments. His view is that there are various "hows," various qualities of intending and of subjectivity within which concepts can be defined and rules ascertained. By getting these straight and not allowing the overlap of language to deceive one into thinking that the concepts were identical, Kierkegaard thought that a large part of the task was done. This, at least, was the technical responsibility of philosophy and theology.

However, Kierkegaard did not believe that such an analysis as here summarized would mean an end to questions about objective truth. On the contrary, the very fact that the language of ethics and religion does refer when used in certain ways by the interested person sustains the concern for their truth. But Kierkegaard argues that the discovery of their objective uncertainty is a significant warning for the

---

25. Kierkegaard also describes "scholarly objectivity" as one permutation within the aesthetic stage. See, for example, Dru, *Journal,* entry 1054 (*Papirer* X 2 A, 439).

sophisticated reader, as to their religious and ethical use and meaning. For the continuing and gnawing awareness that there is genuine objective uncertainty and that the uncertainty is even a consequence of the cognitive virtues of detachment and disinterestedness and objectivity might confront the knowing subject with the likelihood that this interest in the truth of the sentence is the wrong interest.[26] At least, this is what Kierkegaard hopes for him.

The right question often cannot arise as long as there remains the possibility of mere cognition. But, if this "how" finally must stop because there is nothing more to be achieved, i.e., if the very logic and use of the sentence require the uncertainty, then objective uncertainty is placed in abeyance. In a variety of ways the uncertainty grows:

> I contemplate the order of nature in the hope of finding God, and I see omnipotence and wisdom; but I also see much else that disturbs my mind and excites anxiety. The sum of all this is an objective uncertainty.[27]

The religious sentences (and the ethical too but to a lesser degree and with less urgency) can be used to make drastic and sweeping claims. Religious people say something about all the world, all of history, and all of a person's life and qualities. Besides, they relate all of these to a deity who is as qualitatively distinct from everything human as righteousness is said to be from sin, and love is from duplicity. The question of the objective truth seems easy and plausible, but it is Kierkegaard's theme that there is no cognitive resolution to such a problem. For the problem is not a genuine one at all. To see that it is not cognitive is to have it transferred from the objective to the subjective; he writes that "it is this which precisely increases the tension of that infinite passion which constitutes his inwardness."[28] A math-

---

26. In one of his edifying discourses (*Edifying Discourses*, IV:15), Kierkegaard says that everyone must learn that the grace of God is "without external confirmation."

27. *Postscript*, 182. He continues, "Nature is, indeed, the handiwork of God, but only the handiwork is directly present, not God." *Postscript*, 218.

28. Ibid. Note especially 182. When Kierkegaard read in preparation for his book on Adler during 1846–1847 he underlined and marked with a double cross the remark "*At kunne er tro*" (to know is to believe). The entire fourth chapter of that book is about the lack of subjectivity in Adler and also in Hegelianism. See also Lowrie's translation, *On Authority and Revelation*, 172ff.

ematical proposition because it never refers to human existence—"its objectivity is given," Kierkegaard's author says[29]—also remains an indifferent proposition, whether true or false. But a religious and ethical proposition does reflect back on one's existence; it does apply and judge and predispose one's own existing life. This is not to say that it is true or false. But this is Kierkegaard's point. A cognitive interest in a religious-ethical proposition endeavors to resolve the question of truth or falsity, with the result that the proposition cannot be significantly verified. If the proposition is neither true nor false, then what is it?

Kierkegaard's answer seems to be that it both commands and defines a future possibility of any person's life. A technique is required to learn to use it religiously and/or ethically. Because it pertains to the actuality of one's life, one's own interests and subjectivity, it does have a peculiar and unsuspected reference. But this reference lies only in the user, not in the words. Furthermore, it must be used to stimulate an interest in the quality of a person's life, of a subject whose qualities are continually being lost and gained. Thus there is no finality. The existing individual, Kierkegaard's author claims, is

> In the temporal order, and the subjective "how" is transformed into a striving, a striving which receives indeed its impulse and a repeated renewal from the decisive passion of the infinite, but is nevertheless a striving.[30]

The cognitive interest—"the objective accent"—falls on WHAT is said, while the subjective accent falls on HOW it is said. Climacus writes:

> But this is not to be understood as referring to demeanor, expression, or the like. Rather it refers to the relationship sustained by the existing individual, in his own existence, to the content of his utterance. Objectively the interest is focused morally on the thought-content, subjectively on the inwardness.[31]

---

29. Ibid., 182.

30. Ibid. Löwith's *Von Hegel bis Nietzsche* is especially appropriate on the eternity-time issue, especially on Kierkegaard's use of these terms in ethical ways. See 125–30, 192ff.

31. Ibid., 181. Note also the comments on 115. Many remarks from the *Papirer*, 1844, are also relevant here. These relate the distinction between "how" and "what"

The common issue in religious sentences is not the cognitive truth of the sentences but rather the quality of the subject who encounters the sentences. The task is not the verification of the sentences, for such sentences are thus misunderstood, both epistemologically and religiously. As he says, "to seek objectivity is to be in error."[32] The task is to learn how to use the teachings to validate one's own life rather than using them to make truth claims.

Even the Scriptures can be understood this way. Every sentence can be scrutinized and treated in a variety of ways, and the entire upshot will be a kind of learned inconclusiveness. Kierkegaard does not say that evidence is unimportant or that matters of fact are not what they are regardless of what a given individual happens to think. Truth or falsity of the Scriptural sentences can be made a matter of an indifferent scholarship too, but Kierkegaard's argument is pointed to the fact that the Scriptures suppose another type of involvement, and another kind of use altogether. The Scriptures actually are an attack upon their reader; they ask for obedience and transformation; they command attention. The Scriptures talk about justification, not of sentences but of people. One must be lured away from assuming that their jobs are done via their truth. On the other hand, they are not therefore false, either.

The one remaining function of the proposition, again provided that an interest in one's own existence is present, is to let it reflect back upon oneself just because it cannot be cognitively judged. So it is with Scripture itself. If one permits this, then the problem shifts to the subjectivity of the human subject. The issue then is not to effect a transformation in the proposition or to find a meta-claim about it as much as it is to do something about oneself. Such teachings, then, are not properly the objects of disinterested and objective analysis, except to a philosopher or student who wants to study them for their own sake. But in order to use them religiously or ethically, such an analysis is not essential. Kierkegaard could not agree that even his own inquiry had any direct religious or ethical consequence. Of course, if one chose to study them as linguistic expressions, there is, obviously, the possibility of discovering truths about them. This, however, is

---

to both the philosophical tradition and also to the early pseudonymous literature (VI B).

32. Ibid., 181 and sections following.

something different from saying that the original propositions themselves can be seen to be "almost probable, or probable, or extremely and emphatically probable"[33] in respect to objective things. All that remains therefore after a learned inquiry is an ethical or religious interest and passion with which the inquiry was motivated initially. Instead of moving from those interests to a cognitive certainty one is left with those same interests and passions and a cognitive uncertainty. Religious and ethical truth is then

> an objective uncertainty held fast in an appropriation-process of the most passionate inwardness . . . the highest truth attainable for an existing individual . . . The truth is precisely the venture which chooses an objective uncertainty with the passion of the infinite.[34]

About one of his books, *Training in Christianity*, Kierkegaard ruminated at considerable length. He saw the work as an illustration of his tactics, including the artistry that he believed the topic required. However, he then reinforces the objective uncertainty theme by suggesting that even that book could legitimately be construed as "an idealistic support" for the church or as an attack upon it. Here, again, Kierkegaard insists that "all doubly reflected communication makes contrary interpretation equally possible, and the judge will be made manifest by his judgment."[35] So here we have it again. That book can be variously conceived. If someone looks at *Training in Christianity* as a set of true or false statements, he might well study them as a scholar, trying to see whether they stand or fall by the canons of evidence. Then the book is another essay in the unending stream of more or less trivial knowledge which people can have or not have as they choose.

On the other hand, the title suggests that it had another aim too. For Kierkegaard believed that the book came close to actually training a reader in the use of its concepts in an ethico-religious interest. To this extent, it was a bit of essential knowledge. Such books are, he

---

33. Ibid., 189.

34. Ibid., 182. The italicizing of the English translation is omitted.

35. In the supplement to *On My Work as an Author*, included in *The Point of View*, 159–64.

says, like mirrors, and the purpose served by the mirror is to enable you to see yourself and not the author.[36]

V

The wheel has come full circle. Kierkegaard's inquiries into the way that philosophies fit the human scene are rather negative. By examining both the shape of the philosophies and the way that human existence actually is, Kierkegaard concludes that the logic, including the form, the concepts, and the articulations, is simply wrong. So in this chapter we have seen how easy it is, in the course of the actual reflection upon ethical and religious topics, to slip from a self-concern which was personal, indigenous, and genuine to one which is general and artificial. This happens when the subject and subjectivity, the "I" where the concern is resident, is replaced by the generic "I" of the *cogito*. To make philosophy a responsible activity as it was for Socrates requires not doctrines but a kind of integrity.

Upon this depends the distinction between essential knowledge and accidental knowledge, the former being relevant to the tasks of the primitive subject, and the latter being a matter of indifference. Every time the essential issues are treated as cognitive issues, a kind of trivialization occurs. Essential matters become accidental and are objectively uncertain. However, we have seen that there is no doctrinal way to establish the importance of these essentials. For "how" one treats even essential knowledge determines whether one will profit from it. There are no automatic increments in the life of the spirit. So, we are back to the powers and authority of subjectivity. This does not deny objectivity nor does it mitigate the authority of the objective truth. We have been concerned here only to show the logical locus in which "truth is subjectivity" takes on its meanings.

---

36. This figure of the "mirror" is used by Kierkegaard in *For Self-Examination*, part I.

CHAPTER 8

Some Epistemological Questions

THE HISTORIES OF PHILOSOPHY and theology are full of attempts to ground all kinds of claims in metaphysical views. For example, it has been argued that metaphysical beliefs were inescapable and, hence, that every other kind of assertion, ethical, theological, or even logical, presupposed a metaphysical view. Part of the reasoning for this conviction has stemmed from the fact that metaphysical distinctions were couched in language that emerged exhaustive of the possibilities. Thus the idealist/realist distinction does not appear to leave any middle ground not already claimed. So, too, the materialist/idealist divergence and the later process/structure dichotomy do not appear to leave any middle ground. Therefore, it has been tempting for students of the non-systematic thinkers, like Nietzsche, Pascal, Kierkegaard and now Wittgenstein, to ask whether they were idealists, realists, materialists, scholastics or metaphysical skeptics.[1] The point is that a metaphysical position is deemed inescapable, and, therefore, every man illustrates, more or less perfectly, one of these.

However, Kierkegaard does not agree that every thinker must decide in one of these ways, or for that matter decide at all. In the next chapter, we shall note his views on metaphysical topics in some detail. Our negative interest in this chapter will be to display that (and why) he refuses to agree with another convention in the scholarly world

---

1. So it is with Kierkegaard. Note the eight brief studies of Albert Bärthold, beginning in 1876 and every so often until 1890, in which a kind of idealism is delineated (for example, *Noten zu Sören Kierkegaards Lebensgeschichte*); see also Torsten Bohlin's work and that of James Collins, *The Mind of Kierkegaard*, which are further illustrations of this kind of scholarship. Note the following page.

concerning epistemological matters. For with the passing of metaphysics from high favor, it was tempting to contend that philosophy was the science of how knowledge was possible. If philosophy had any subject matter, it must be, according to the critical tradition in contrast to the speculative, the knowledge of epistemological elements, of sense data, categories, concepts and theories, in short, the foundational stuff of the mind at work. Once again it has been tempting to argue that if there are such foundations, then any philosophical or theological writer can be assessed as to how he takes account of them, where he puts his weight and where he treats matters rather lightly. But Kierkegaard was as wary of the deduction of transcendentals as he was of Hegelian metaphysics.

Again the working supposition of many commentators is that major philosophers and theologians properly "take up" positions and consequently have philosophies in an extroverted and obvious sense; for they must, the argument goes, build a scheme of reality or spin a web of doctrine from the foundations, metaphysical or epistemological, and on up. Minor figures are, then, those who have their philosophies inadvertently and whose foundations have to be otherwise discerned, precisely because they are not overtly declared. In this regard, Kierkegaard is then a lesser figure, because he never did write out a metaphysical or an epistemological scheme. And he has had his doyen-like commentators who have declared his metaphysics and his epistemology for him.[2]

The argument of these pages will be that such attempts to construe Kierkegaard's pages are grossly mistaken. For Kierkegaard did not believe that the intellectual life was as complicated as these accounts make out. It was indeed complex, because one could argue in a variety of ways and live and think in various stages. But complexity

---

2. Walter Ruttenbeck, *Sören Kierkegaard: Der Christiche Denker und sein Werk* argues for the influence of Schelling, Böhme and Trendelenburg, all to the effect that reality is non-rational and mystical (note 68ff. and 82ff.). Torsten Bohlin in several lengthy works has argued that there is a very refined intellectualism in Kierkegaard's pages. He contends that Kierkegaard made up his mind but obtusely refused to defend these difficult abstract critical positions. Collins in *The Mind of Kierkegaard* finds traces of realism and a kind of Aristotelian sanity. Harald Høffding's several writings but especially his book on Kierkegaard, *Søren Kierkegaard som Filosof*, tries to make Kierkegaard rather a conventional realist, arguing philosophical views that no one wants to deny.

means only that a plurality of options is conceivable. What he denies is that being an intellectual or being a Christian, being an aesthete or a responsible moral citizen, necessarily involves taking up suppositions, or the having of presuppositions, or the use of foundations that only a philosopher can detect and properly state. In brief, this means that Kierkegaard did not think that there was very much that was distinctive to know as a metaphysician or as an epistemologist. There were no doctrines of this sort in his pages because there was little to have doctrines about. In effect, Kierkegaard wrote a kind of doctrine-less philosophy, even when he wrote about metaphysics and epistemology.

Most of his efforts in these regards, therefore, are spent in a kind of *reductio ad absurdum* argument, which in his case uses humor, irony, as well as conceptual analyses. On the other side, there is something that looks suspiciously like philosophical doctrines. There are numerous passages about reality and a comparable number on purely conceptual and epistemological matters. Thereby, however, hangs Kierkegaard's tale. These things are said not to disclose another level of existence or of being, nor do they mark off unexpected epistemic entities and essences; instead they show us the logic and the location of metaphysical and epistemological terms, at least some of them, within our rather ordinary discourse. Therefore, as will be noted in chapter 9, the words "real" and "unreal" do occur in a variety of ways. Kierkegaard will show why a special and technical meaning of the term "real" is nothing but a learned deceit. Furthermore, he will argue that there is no special level of being to which the term uniquely corresponds. Thus a conceptual study of the expression "real" is done only to make it clear that there are several differing meanings and that the ambiguity is deeply systematic, that is, there is no philosophical knowledge of reality, only philosophical knowledge about what and how people believe, think, and say that reality is. Philosophy is, at least, once removed if not twice.

So, too, it is with some familiar epistemological distinctions. Instead of these dualities marking the limits of thought for all time, Kierkegaard will show only that "ideal" and "real," "fact" and "interpretation," and others have no disclosure-like function. When read back into the actual usage of the thinker, they come to have a pragmatic scope that cannot be denied. But this part of the tale his ruminations on epistemological issues tell. He is, again, the philosophical student of these differences, but critical philosophy does not deduce these differences or establish them. Finally it describes them, and it dispels the aura of mystery from the doubt clustering around the issue: how is knowledge possible?

I

We have seen with Kierkegaard in the two previous chapters various kinds of uncertainty. But even "uncertainty" is a many-valued concept. More properly we ought to say that there are many concepts with the same name. Perchance we can say that there is a kind of overlap of meaning, but if so it is a kind that permits no further identification or summarization and no master concept.[3] In previous pages we tried to show that a concept of objective uncertainty arose in a certain circumstance where someone might try to treat ethical language as though it were true or false by some objective standards. Then that language is seen to be uncertain because incommensurables are being put together. There are other occasions for "uncertainty" as a concept arising too. Because every man's death is conceivable at any moment, all kinds of things are insecure in relation to any individual. Respecting death, Kierkegaard says that it is "the one thing certain, and the only thing, about which nothing is certain."[4] The sure knowledge that we have of the race, namely, that all will die, does not mitigate the uncertainty about when anyone, including oneself, will die. Therefore, knowledge mitigates uncertainty only in part and never dries up the occasion for insecurity in one's own case.

Not least of Kierkegaard's accomplishments as a writer is his ability both to state this truth in a somewhat detached manner but also to help his readers preserve the thought in the more pressing moments of everyday life. For here again it is not enough to have the concept evoked once and for all; it is necessary to let it arise over and

---

3. Note Ludwig Wittgenstein's remarks on this issue in *Philosophical Investigations*, paragraphs 67ff.

4. *Thoughts on Crucial Situations in Human Life*, 101. Note also the remark in his journal: "... because existence ... is so arranged that nobody knows whether he will live for another hour—and it is this very uncertainty which Christianity uses to bring about a decision for the eternal." *Papirer* XI 1 A, 529 (*JP* 1, 408).

over again where it occurs naturally. Therefore, his addresses and discourses try to make us hear the whisper that otherwise gets crowded out. It is well to remark, almost parenthetically, upon the two levels of his authorship once more, for as we will see, when he philosophizes he is telling us how the concepts of knowledge relate to the concepts of ethics, religion, and our everyday evaluations. "Certainty" in one is not productive of "certainty" in the other. Here the logics are different and Kierkegaard's pages are a kind of logical ordering, a specification of types. But his addresses are evocative and persuasive, causing us to remember our own uncertainties and failures.

But there are other occasions for uncertainty too. And Kierkegaard was inclined to say that this is singularly manifested in how knowledge and existence are related. Every body of knowledge is permeated by a kind of uncertainty. For reasons which are not altogether clear, Kierkegaard was inclined to believe that scholarly and scientific knowledge of matters of fact was only probable. The most certain truth would still be in his language "an approximation"; and any future verification would always be well within the logical limits of an absolutely certain proof.[5] It is fair to say that Kierkegaard did not reflect in great detail on why knowledge must be this way, nor did he discuss in detail what look like interesting exceptions to the rule. But there are cases where we are certain about matters of fact. I am certain, for example, of my name and my age. Also, I am certain that I exist. Kierkegaard knows full well that one of the reasons for being certain is that we do not ask for evidence, i.e., we do not bring objective standards to bear. But this is his point. Not all kinds of sentences, even those true "about" something or other, are subject to the same requisites. Furthermore, Kierkegaard is inclined to leave a rather large category for the kind of sentences which we have in virtue of commanding passions. Nonetheless, when we construe all of these claims in one given way, we can make them seem to be objectively uncertain. As we shall see, he is inclined to think that uncertainty is circumstantial in many instances and logical in others.

Another kind of uncertainty arises whenever a man faces the future. Whether one faces that future proposing to use the knowledge

---

5. "For it is true of all historical knowledge and learning that it is only approximation, even at its maximum." *Postscript*, 509.

Some Epistemological Questions 163

for the realization of an end or with no knowledge, the uncertainty is there.[6] This kind of uncertainty is not a direct consequence of the certainty or uncertainty internal to knowledge, for it arises in the attempts to apply it and is, therefore, of another order altogether. Kierkegaard thought that even though principles of logic, like mathematics, were highly certain, still they were not infallible when used in relation to anything in the real world.[7]

So, one might possess knowledge as almost a universal coin, insisting that it was the same everywhere, yet its use in a particular context, he thought, would always be somewhat precarious because of the conditions that were external to the knowledge itself.[8] The increase of knowledge finally does not reduce the precariousness materially, for as long as one draws the distinction between knowledge and its application or use, there is an admission of these external conditions. There is no way to reduce this hiatus, for it is self-contradictory to propose a theory that mediates between knowledge and its use or between theory and practice. Furthermore, there is no knowledge so concrete that it could make the use of knowledge as certain as the knowledge itself is certain. Even axioms become hypothetical when applied to everyday things, however certain they might seem within axiomatic systems. And all knowledge, certain and probable, becomes in Kierkegaard's view, something like a system of possibilities when projected against the real world.[9] Considering these matters, it is almost as if the larger the scope of a given man's knowledge, then the larger the range of possibilities for his choice. Every fact can be explained in a variety of ways and hence there are several hypotheses even within some sciences.

Kierkegaard was never even tempted to think that there were some elemental and brute facts, some simple and plain components, from which all the rest of knowledge could be constructed.[10] He

---

6. Note the discourse "The Expectation of Faith" in *Edifying Discourses*, I:17–33.

7. *Postscript*, 100. Note, too, the comments on logic and existence in Dru's *Journals*, 357–58.

8. Note the comments on the misuse of certainty and a superstitious use of science and scholarship, *Concept of Dread*, 124–26. This is also why it is absurd to judge thoughts without considering the thinker; see *Postscript*, 296.

9. "All knowledge about reality is possibility." *Postscript*, 280.

10. But there was an elemental learning more important than the rest. Note his pages in *Gospel of Suffering* where he says: "Alas, we may well say that instead of

refused all dogmatisms here—there was no plausible deduction of transcendental categories, valid for all experience, available to him; neither were there plain and uninterpreted facts. Consequently, he is not in the least tempted to think about philosophy as a unified science or a philosophy of necessary and universal categories. Both the Hegelian system and materialism and positivist schemes seemed to him to have arbitrarily excluded the equivocal and multiple features of both knowledge and the world.

Therefore, he insists that no increase in the power and scope of knowledge and no magnification of the precision of our conceptual tools will exclude alternatives from our future. On the contrary, every increase in the effectiveness of our tools of learning will mean a multiplication of the alternatives, and the more one knows, the more difficult it is to reach a decision or a conclusion.[11] "Ah, no," Kierkegaard says,

> if it is true that he is defrauded who gets only a little knowledge, I wonder if he is not also defrauded who acquires so much that he can assimilate nothing at all! Man progresses slowly, even the most glorious knowledge is merely a presupposition. If we increase the presuppositions more and more, we are like the miser who heaps up money for which he has no use... there is also another difficulty, that there is an illusory knowledge that beguiles the soul, a security in knowledge possessed which also deceives... it was terrible... most terrible of all that one should have known everything, and not have begun to do the least.[12]

Therefore, knowledge when it is not linked with the passions can be as devastating to the personality as unbridled passion. For reflection can also run wild in its own endless ramifications finally postponing all action and decision. This is how Kierkegaard uses the

---

learning something, every man needs first to 'learn' what is the principal thing to learn. And this first, most profound instruction underlying all other instruction, ... is the one which is least desired," 49.

11. But his point is not that the knowledge is faulty—rather is it the disposition to believe that in greater objectivity the answer will be found. But there is no decision possible this way. Note his remarks about wanting "to construct a plain transition from culture to Christianity," *Postscript*, 536. All of this leads not to decision and the use of knowledge, but "lukewarmness."

12. *Thoughts on Crucial Situations*, 17–18.

biblical proverb, that the increase of knowledge means the increase of sorrow, in his contemporary setting.[13] Knowledge can be a shield against the uncertainties in such a deceitful way that one will never have to dare, to exercise courage, to make a leap, in short, the passions will atrophy altogether.

This is why the popular slogan about intelligence being the problem-solving activity of the ordinary person has to be taken *cum grano salis*. Kierkegaard was quite certain that only a stubborn intellectualism warrants the view that knowledge and reflection determine unequivocally a line of action or a major decision.[14] But he is not advocating "will" at the expense of "thought" or emotion instead of judicious consideration. His point is a simple one, that even complete knowledge is quite powerless to resolve a fundamental problem, except such as are resolved already before reflection begins. Part of his analysis of the intertwining of emotions and our thought is to indicate how often a predilection for one conceived alternative is excluded by our despair whereas another is included because of our hope. Rather than press for the abnegation of all these factors from consciousness, Kierkegaard is showing that without them no decision at all is possible and that otherwise the whole intellectual life would be an effete tilting with abstract possibilities. Only an intellectualist mythology, the sluggishness of our self-understanding and the paltry awareness of our passional life can explain the fantastic exaltation of knowledge in the economy of daily life.[15] The uncertainty that confronts an ignorant man is obvious and absolutely undisguised, for he has usually few words by which to conceal it. On the other hand, intelligent people confront the uncertainties of life with all kinds of talents. Some of them complicate matters by seeing the uncertainties as temporary gaps in an otherwise seamless robe of complete truth, and one is intimidated by the gallantry of the vision. Or, the certainties and

---

13. *Edifying Discourses*, vol. I, 100–101.

14. The issue is put this way in the *Postscript*: The cognitive subject is not the same as the ethically existing subject. Therefore, what is certain to the scholarly man becomes uncertain as soon as he puts it to an ethical use. The knowledge is the same; but the uncertainty inheres in the context provided by the concerned subject. Note "The Subjective Thinker," 267ff.

15. So Kierkegaard urges for "the simultaneity of factors" in the ethical subject as over against the singularity of them in the cognitive subject. Doubt and uncertainty are related to these all. *Postscript*, 307–12.

the uncertainties are lumped together in a more refined and idealized scheme, logical and sublime, which seems to take the sting away and thus remove the occasion for a primitive and natural response.

It is important to see that the consciousness of the persistence of uncertainty both within knowledge and in its use is not a reason for disparaging it. Kierkegaard like Socrates was an enthusiast for knowledge, but Socrates found the wisdom that is peculiarly human in the consciousness of one's ignorance. For Kierkegaard, the uncertainties, for they are several, which persist after learning and reflection have done their maximum, are our disciplinarians. With them we begin to see that there is no resolution in the aggrandizement of more knowledge. We are driven back upon ourselves. The objective search leads us to evoke energies within the personality that are more profound in their meaning for us, more characteristic of what we are, than any degree of more or less adequate knowledge. Here we return to subjectivity and the realities of the subject. Where knowledge is the same for this man and that and hence is a kind of universal, the admission of uncertainties and the need to resolve them by something besides our common knowledge calls for a different move of the personality. What is decisive for the destiny of the man is not knowledge but whatever he is able to muster as a subject.

This is how Kierkegaard uses some general reflections about knowledge and its uses to show that there are many occasions for faith. But here, too, there is one word and many concepts. For the objective uncertainties of several different kinds require faiths of several kinds. And Kierkegaard is not prone to use the variety to credit Christian faith, even though it, too, feeds on the continuing uncertainties.

Kierkegaard's distinction between the possession of knowledge and its use, between its existence and its application, is, perhaps, not argued in sufficient detail. Apparently he thought it was confirmed by everyday language as well as technical reflection. Arithmetic is the same to the wasters and spenders and geography is the same to the attack and defense. Here knowledge is not identical with knowledge-in-use. Again Kierkegaard is not deciding whether knowledge is useless or useful, or whether useless knowledge can even exist. His point is that it has a kind of neutrality, that some knowledge is unused, and that to use it means taking a risk not anticipated in that knowledge.[16]

16. Note the remarks from the *Journals*, appended to *Stages on Life's Way*, by Lowrie, 448.

In the last chapter we noted how Kierkegaard found certain theoretical translations of the teachings of ethics and religion attractive.[17] For using logical and mathematical examples as models, certain thinkers, most notably to Kierkegaard, Spinoza, have tried to impose upon all knowledge the characteristics of certainty reserved for tautologous reasoning. Then the issues become resolvable by maximum clarity of thought. Error seems to be excluded providing that one understands the premises and their meanings. But Kierkegaard noted that the objects discoursed about exist only because they are thought, and ideal or intentional existence needs no other verification than is required to think them clearly again.[18] He says with misgivings: "Even if the consequences be conceived in a purely logical relation to their cause, and hence under the form of immanence, it still remains true that they can be conceived only as identical and homogenous with their cause; least of all will they have a transforming power."[19] This is why Kierkegaard begins to draw back. He sees that this is a kind of elaborate trick. The uncertainty concerns God's factual existence, but Spinoza proves, by logical demonstration and a most persuasive insight, God's ideal or intentional existence.

> What is lacking here is a distinction between factual being and ideal being. The terminology which permits us to speak of more or less of being, and consequently of degrees of reality or being, is in itself lacking in clearness, and becomes still more confusing when the above distinction is neglected; when in other words, Spinoza does indeed speak profoundly, but fails first to consider the difficulty.[20]

The interesting fact about Spinoza is that despite his stress upon axioms and an impeccable deductive method, there still are reasons for reproof. Descartes' clear and distinct ideas have not been clear to everyone else. Therefore, even intellectual clarity is not entirely free of illusion, for what is indubitable at one time is not so at another, and what is self-evidencing insight is subsequently revealed as a confusion

---

17. *Postscript*, 305.

18. "It is necessary to be thus careful in dealing with an abstract thinker who not only desires for himself to remain in the pure being of abstract thought, but insists that this is the highest goal for human life . . ." *Postscript*, 272.

19. *Fragments*, 79.

20. *Fragments*, 32.

of thought. Therefore, though it may be the case that some varieties of abstract knowledge are exonerated from the kind of verification one knows in strictly empirical disciplines, this is only one kind of verification. There remains the verification requiring the repetition of the insight and, subsequently, the creation of the insight in others in order to communicate with certainty. This sort of verification can never be conclusive either. Besides, it depends sooner or later upon memory and that needs to be verified upon its own account.[21]

This is by way of returning to the theme with which we began this section, for we spoke about the uncertainty both within knowledge and that respecting its application.[22] Today it is a truism to say that scientific results are tentative. Kierkegaard was unusual in putting this awareness to other uses, some of which have been already noted. Whether respecting the Bible, political authority, the Papacy, or science, Kierkegaard noted the dangers of claiming their infallibility.[23] Once one understands the probative force of evidence, one knows that any conclusion must be approximative. With the increase of knowledge, better tools, and different aims, another age will draw different conclusions.

We have here two concepts of uncertainty at work, both under the same word. Even if all knowledge were intrinsically certain, there would still be uncertainty in its use. So Kierkegaard has already made an interesting distinction. His argument is that one is not reducible to the terms of the other. Increasing the certainty of knowledge does not reduce the uncertainty respecting its use; admitting the uncertainty of knowledge does not argue that its use is equally uncertain. These distinctions are part of Kierkegaard's descriptive philosophy, but only a part. We move on to other issues.

---

21. Note the context for this thesis "All skepticism is a kind of idealism" (*Postscript*, 315), where the juxtaposition of thoughts and things is again explored.

22. Kierkegaard heard Schelling in Berlin in 1841–1842. In the Royal Library there is a transcript of his notes to one of these lectures called "Philosophy and Actuality." This is found in *Pakke* 4, group 4. This issue was the chief one of all of his subsequent philosophical authorship.

23. Invariably he distinguishes between claims about infallibility and concepts of authority. He believes that putting the two together, supposedly in order to justify the authority, is another confusion. See *Papirer* XI 1 A, 436 (*JP* 4, 4991) and *Revelation and Authority*.

II

"The difficulty that inheres in existence, with which the existing individual is confronted, is one that never really comes to expression in the language of abstract thought, much less receives an explanation."[24] This sentence begins Kierkegaard's lengthy analysis of the radical dualism in all reflection and its components—in sensations, in concepts, in knowledge, in wishes, in fact, this dualism could be said to root in all human experience. But again this is to make Kierkegaard sound like another philosopher proposing his own point of view, terminology, and concepts. "The abstract problem of reality . . . is not nearly so difficult a problem," he adds, "as it is to raise and to answer the question of what it means that this definite something is a reality." How does a philosophical problem arise?

Kierkegaard's answer is simply that one can abstract from a knowing situation—one can reflect about one's reflection. Very much like Wittgenstein who asserted that most philosophical problems arise when language goes on a holiday and does not do its customary work, so Kierkegaard says that philosophical problems arise when one arrests the language's working and examines it.

> When thought becomes self-reflexive and seeks to think itself, there arises a familiar form of scepticism. How may this scepticism be overcome rooted as it is in thought's refusal to pursue its proper task of thinking other things, and its selfish immersion in an attempt to think itself? When a horse bolts and runs away, we might simply say, if we disregard the damage he may do in the meanwhile, "Let him run, he will soon tire." But of this self-reflexive scepticism of thought this cannot be said, since it can continue indefinitely.[25]

A very abstract kind of philosophy, an epistemological variety, then arises. This is purportedly a kind of knowledge about knowledge. Furthermore as Kierkegaard read Descartes, Schelling, or Hegel, each of them proposed philosophical answers to the skeptical problems that they had raised. In brief the issue is: how can a thought think existence or reality? Can we be sure that thoughts are about the world?

---

24. *Postscript*, 267.

25. Ibid., 299. In his essay on doubt, *De Omnibus Dubitandum Est*, he notes that "wonder is an immediate quality, and has no reflection upon itself," 128.

Can we answer radical skepticism? Interestingly enough, Kierkegaard is convinced that there is no knowledge, philosophical or otherwise, by which to answer this kind of problem.

Kierkegaard notes the questionableness of Hegel's "method" of answering Kant's skepticism in these words:

> A skepticism which attacks thought itself cannot be vanquished by thinking it through, since the very instrument by which this would have to be done is in revolt. There is only one thing to do with such a scepticism, and that is to break with it.[26]

But he extends his criticisms to all philosophical attempts to answer this pervasive doubt. But he has no philosophical answer of his own. Of course, he canvases most of the familiar ones, e.g., "Is thinking identical with creation, with giving existence?" and the notion of the immediate or the given being certain.[27] Fichte and other subjective idealists, he notes, have examined a range of difficult abstract issues, but he finds them to be unconvincing because:

> The good, the beautiful, and other Ideas are in themselves so abstract that they are indifferent to existence, indifferent to any other than a conceptual existence. The reason why the principle of identity holds in this connection is because being means in this case the same thing as thought.[28]

So Kierkegaard contends, this kind of response does not answer the question it started with and is altogether an evasion. One after the other of the familiar philosophical attempts to prove that thought can think the existent are assayed: Kant, Lessing, Jacobi, Hegel, Spinoza, Descartes, Schelling, Zeno. With all of them he is convinced that though they spoke invariably about the world and admitted doubts of a philosophical sort about whether there was a world, none of them proved by their philosophical schemes that there were things to

---

26. Ibid., 292. Note his remarks about Fichte in *Papirer*, especially vol. I and Dru's *Journals*, 84, 31 (*Papirer* I A, 302).

27. Ibid., 293. About the "immediate" one must examine his numerous pages on Hegel. Perhaps the clearest is in the *Postscript*, respecting "the dialectic of the beginning," 101ff.

28. Ibid., 293. Note in this regard again the reflections about "whether logical thought is abstract after existence or abstract without any relation to existence," in "A Logical System Is Possible," ibid., 99ff.

talk about. Climacus says, "For that which is talked about is already presupposed."[29] (Kierkegaard is not, therefore, arguing a doctrine about presuppositions either, and one reason for saying this will be made clear subsequently.)

Kierkegaard's analyses of self-reflexive thinking are several: again and again in early ruminations now recorded in his papers; then in his lengthy analysis of doubt, *De Omnibus Dubitandum Est*; in the *Fragments* and the *Postscript*; and in scattered notes and asides in almost all of his other books. In all cases he is skeptical, in turn, of the philosophical resolutions, for it turns out, he insists, that there is no problem which can be resolved in the medium in which the question is raised. There is no knowledge by which to mediate between sense data and objects, or between thoughts and things. Again philosophy only deceives one into thinking that there is.[30]

But now we must turn to the Kierkegaardian delineation of why there is a philosophical problem at all. For it turns out that there is a kind of essence of thinking that Kierkegaard is sensitive to and which he has captured for his readers. But it is a kind of essence that is not so much a matter of finding philosophical entities and abstract relations lurking beneath the appearances as it is that kind of essence which he finds by studying the use of the distinction between the ideal and the real, for these two terms work as "that with which one thinks," the ideal, and "that about which one thinks," the real. Kierkegaard finds human consciousness is a synthesis of these factors. The interesting thing is that Kierkegaard does not try to delineate the distinction as if it were a metaphysical distinction between two ultimate kinds of things; he does, nonetheless, find the distinction to be *sui generis*, and irreducible. The point of our saying this is simply that there is no real *qua* real and no ideal *qua* ideal, for a sensation can be thought about, and then it is real relative to another ideality by which one thinks it. The very language we use here can, in turn, be thought about, and it becomes, then, a reality to be treated by other idealities. Again, the concepts "real" and "ideal" are ambiguous when isolated and treated detachedly and abstractly; on the other hand, these terms are precise

---

29. See *De Omnibus Dubitandum Est*, 148.

30. A cogent discussion of "immediacy," especially as this was used to make a case for kinds of certainty, is found in *Stages*; note particularly 434ff. and the footnote on 435–36.

only in particular contexts and are then irreplaceable. Therefore, to have philosophers give a general answer to the question of "how philosophy begins with doubt," and "doubt" here having to do with the relation between the ideal and the real, is bound to appear ludicrous, for there is no general problem.[31]

Kierkegaard's delineation really has more to do with how "ideal" and "real" function in various contexts. So "speech is ideality,"[32] and what is talked about is reality. A thought is ideal, while a thing is real; a sensation of a star is ideal whereas the star is real;[33] a concept is ideal whereas its reference is real;[34] an ethical possibility is an ideality, whereas its realization is reality.[35] Therefore, "real" is not a name, and there are no ultimate irreducible reals. Neither is "ideal" a name, and there are no spiritual and ultimately non-material entities of which it is the name.[36] The separation of the "real" and "ideal" only occurs when men philosophize or think "about," perhaps indeed when language is on a holiday from what otherwise is a working synthesis. Whenever one reflects upon that which one thinks, one delineates what is otherwise the logical factor, and whenever one studies (and isolates) that about which one thinks and behaves, one finds the existential component. This duality, according to Kierkegaard, is the way, the "how," our reflection and language works. To discuss the duality is to lay bare the rules of intellectual operation. Because the ideal and the real are incommensurable, uncertainty is an inescapable feature. All of this is part of the essence and rules of thinking.

Another way to describe this distinction is to say that "real" and "ideal" are ambiguous, but in a defensible and systematic way. For we have to locate the "real" in each context or each system of discourse in turn. So, too, it is with "ideal." When Kierkegaard invokes the ideal, as

---

31. Again the remarks in *De Omnibus Dubitandum Est* are relevant, especially 132. In the *Fragments* he argues that doubt can be overcome not by a philosophy but only by another kind of "free act" (67). In other places he makes a case for common sense.

32. *De Omnibus Dubitandum Est*, 148.

33. *Fragments*, 67.

34. Ibid., 32.

35. See *Concept of Dread*. Kierkegaard is not using this distinction to mark the difference between mind and matter.

36. See *Postscript* and several of his edifying discourses.

he does in several contexts, e.g., against ethically insensitive aesthetes (*Either/Or* and the *Stages*), or against a logical monism that abrogates all logical distinctions (*Postscript* and *The Concept of Dread*), he is not making a plea for an abstract substance as over against otherwise concrete things or for essence as over against existence. Instead he is laying bear a logical difference, and this logical difference is inherent in the way and the "how" of thinking, even when the ideal in one context is different from the ideal in the other. Ideal and real, then, acquire significance depending upon the context, the dispositions, and all kinds of other factors by which they are placed in use. What is real in one context, is an ideal in the other, but this is no cause for misunderstanding unless one has already been misled into thinking that philosophy can do anything more than describe the use of distinctions. Certainly Kierkegaard found no philosophical way to justify such distinctions. His point is not to generalize them into worldviews or to pretend to get behind them and show their warrant.

Though Kierkegaard often uses the expressions "time" and "space," he seldom thinks about them. He seems to accept them from Kant and Hegelian literature and almost without the qualifications that are the rule with him. Nonetheless, he says, time and space are separating—they discriminate a here from a there, a present plan from the future performance, a wish from its fulfillment.[37] But the idealities of consciousness help create a synthesis of these discrepant factors, in a way completing the incomplete and also causing an illusion, that things done in thought and in word are done in fact. Respecting the first, there is a perfection which yields the possibility of a kind of wholeness to life at any one moment and place; respecting the second, there is the danger that a man will complete in an intellectual synthesis what he ought to be completing in an ethical way.

Accordingly Kierkegaard contends that the tools of reflection, the idealities, are different from the realities one thinks about. But again, it must be insisted, no conventional metaphysical use of these terms is intended. It is not the case that reality is factual and idealities spiritual; nor is it the case that idealities are forms and realities the matter. Kierkegaard is, instead, giving one a kind of essence of knowledge, but this is an essence that is stated by the ways in which the terms must work. For if "reals" were all there were, no questions could

---

37. *Postscript, passim,* and several of his edifying discourses.

be raised and not even reals could be distinguished. Everything would simply be, and there could be no issues at all. For questions, issues, and problems about "how" things are can arise only when idealities refer to realities. Antithetically, Kierkegaard insists, if consciousness were only a "bloodless ballet of categories," everything again would be, but in another sense of the term. In that case, he says: "Thought and being mean one and the same thing, and the correspondence spoken of is merely an abstract self-identity."[38] In another context, one of his pseudonyms notes: "The eternal expression of logic is that which the Eleatic School transferred by mistake to existence: Nothing comes into existence, everything is."[39]

It is not my purpose to defend every turn of Kierkegaard's thought; but his emphasis upon this duality is, however odd appearing, quite crucial. As was earlier noted, he thought very long and hard about doubt, and he was singularly unhappy with philosophical schemes by which to answer doubt. In the last analysis, Kierkegaard is not prone to thinking that it is at all sensible to say that there is anything in epistemology which will validate the claim of a man to know something other than his ideas. When John Locke says that all knowledge is knowledge of ideas, Kierkegaard finds grounds for protest. He believes that we know cats and dogs, sticks and stones, "by" ideas, and if we have knowledge of ideas, we have that knowledge in turn by the help of other ideas. Is it, then, a matter of philosophy to show that we have an idea "of" a real? Can a doctrine of intentionality also justify the claim of an intention? Kierkegaard believed not. Whatever else philosophy was, it certainly could not validate or demonstrate the validity of knowledge.[40] Philosophy is not for Kierkegaard a super-science that makes authentic everyday language or, for that matter, even the ordinary use and understanding of the language of science.

---

38. The reference is to 170 of the *Postscript*. Other places where this is argued are several: *The Concept of Dread*, 9ff.; note the catena of relevant passages which Croxall includes in his *De Omnibus Dubitandum Est*, 177ff.; see also vol. IV of the *Papirer*.

39. *Concept of Dread*, 12.

40. "As soon as doubt is expressed as over against others, an envy lies therein, which finds satisfaction in depriving them of that which they regard as sure, *Either/Or*, I:171. Note the discussion in vol. II of the theme in "modern philosophy" about "speculation beginning with doubt," (177ff.).

Some Epistemological Questions

Accordingly, philosophy is not a kind of science showing all the doubters that there is, after all, something there to be talked about, a reality different in kind from the ideas by which we apprehend reality. Descartes' claim: "We cannot doubt our existence while we are doubting, and this is the first knowledge we acquire when we philosophize,"[41] Kierkegaard thinks is a bit of absurdity.[42] For what is talked about is not proved by a philosophy to be in existence; it is always presupposed.[43] Consequently, there is no philosophical way to establish reality. But there is a way to show how the problem arises, and this is what philosophy can do. Once one sees that, the problem is no longer philosophical.

Here we must hear his philosophical author, Johannes Climacus, who says:

> The possibility of doubt then lies in consciousness, whose very essence is an opposition, which is brought forth by, and brings forth itself, a duality. Such a duality necessarily has two expressions. The duality is the real and the ideal; and consciousness is the relation. I can either bring the real into relation with the ideal or the ideal into relation with the real. In the real above, there is no possibility of doubt; but if I describe it in language, then the opposition appears. For I cannot describe it without bringing forth something else. Insofar as speech can be an expression for the real, I have brought reality in relation to the ideal; insofar as speech is a personal expression, I have still brought the ideal into relation with the real.[44]

According to Kierkegaard, the enormous variety of relations between such factors makes epistemology quite a different kind of study than most critical philosophers have thought. He notes that once one begins a study of how doubts occur, what makes them possible in this

---

41. Descartes, *Principles of Philosophy*, 167.

42. *Papirer* IV C 11 (*JP* 3, 2338). Also note his remark that "I think, therefore I am" is only a play upon words because "... 'I am' logically means nothing more than 'I am thinking' or 'I am a thinker.'" *Efterladte Papirer*, II:67 (translation my own).

43. Again see *De Omnibus Dubitandum Est*, 148.

44 This is found in *Efterladte Papirer*, volume II, 121–22 (translation my own). Compare this with Croxall's translation in *De Omnibus Dubitandum Est*, 149. Another interesting passage to the same effect is *Papirer* IV B, 13, translated by Croxall, op. cit., 187.

case and that, the entire account must not be expected to yield "what a sailor has on his chart,... for in the world of the intellect one cannot mark the points so precisely. Instead, though it is often simple, it is sometimes as strange as when a bumpkin says: 'First to the right, then to the left, again left then to the right....'"[45] Nonetheless, he asserts that there is a kind of order, perhaps more uniform than meanderings suggest.

This order is a kind of logic of the terms "ideal" and "real." In the large variety of contexts in which doubts occur, it is clearly impossible to suggest that one can doubt everything at once. So he heard a philosopher say:

> To doubt everything is no easy matter. It is not doubt about this or that, of such a thing or other, of something here or there. No, it is a speculative doubt about everything, which is, by no means, an easy matter.[46]

According to his somewhat youthful and intemperate account, one must, therefore, say "goodbye to these philosophizers forever," for nothing is finally said by them. They are talking nonsense. But he has shown that a philosophy cannot claim to produce a knowledge of reals and then impart that certainty to the other knowledge claims. Furthermore what is euphemistically called "the problem of knowledge" is not a resolvable problem at all, for the way to become certain varies depending upon the context one is in. He denies that there is a single and general problem. Nonetheless, philosophy is a kind of knowledge, but it is not a unique knowledge of either the ideal or the real. Instead it is the knowledge of these concepts, their likenesses, differences, and peculiarities. Most of what Kierkegaard does in the name of philosophy is to separate the concepts, thereby getting rid of confusion and restoring some of the vitality to their users that had been sapped by too much self-consciousness.

---

45. *Efterladte Papirer*, 116–19. Translation my own. Note *De Omnibus Dubitandum Est*, 143–44.

46. Note the discussions of this in E. Geismar's *Søren Kierkegaard*, I:27, and *De Omnibus Dubitandum Est*, 145. The reference is probably to his philosophy tutor, Hans Martensen. Also, Victor Kuhr's pages on logic are useful, even though wrong about Kierkegaard. Note his *Modsigelsens Grundsaetning*, especially the first parts.

III

The duality of the ideal and the real is, Kierkegaard argues, the logical ground for both certainty and uncertainty. The elaborate attempts to get rid of this duality have seemed to some philosophers to be the only way to achieve certainty. But Kierkegaard thought that either the idealistic or realist monisms were bound to come to grief, if for no other cause, in virtue of the fact that this dualism was enshrined in our everyday, as well as scientific, speech. The effort to say that a fact was certain whereas the meaning of the fact was precarious and uncertain, he thought, showed a failure to analyze sufficiently the concept of uncertainty. Likewise, to say that the immediate was certain, while the mediate and reflective was uncertain, was another and analogous mistake with which he is concerned.[47] Kierkegaard contends, on the contrary, that both certainty and uncertainty get their meaning as concepts only within the wide variety of ways that our ordinary ways of speaking, evaluating, and describing invoke ideals and reals.

As a matter of course, it must be noted that truth and error, knowledge and its object, language and things, intent and verification and other categories also mark the ideal-real distinction. But Kierkegaard recognizes no philosophical task to explain away these dualisms, either by reducing one to the other or both to a third. Philosophy does not create the dualisms nor deduce them. A sign of humility, fitting a philosopher who was moved by Socrates, was to reason from these commonsense distinctions rather than to explain them away.

At this point it is well to mark Kierkegaard's criticisms of Plato. With Socrates, Plato recognized that logical forms made the concept of knowledge possible. But unlike Socrates, Plato goes on to assert that genuine knowledge is only of the eternal and unchanging ideas. According to Kierkegaard this was a mistake, for one does not have to hypostatize them into metaphysical entities and forms, and neither are they the reals about which we think. It is only a kind of logical and epistemological artificiality that we think about ideas or forms. On the other hand, both opinion and science involve ideals by which we think. This is only to say that they are the tools and instruments

---

47. Note his papers for early 1840 where Hegel and these issues are discussed. See *Papirer*, III:78 and Emanuel Hirsch, *Kierkegaard-Studien*, II:570ff.

by which we think about any number of other things. Socrates recognized this and thought about a large number of everyday matters; Plato, on the other hand, made philosophy speculative and a study of forms as if they were reality.[48]

Kierkegaard consequently had slight sympathy with epistemological philosophies, ancient or new, that made the ideals their principle subject matter. Earlier we have said that he argues that philosophy is among other things a study of concepts, and he certainly does not object to a technical kind of conceptual philosophy, which describes the cognitive and logical concepts. However, he denies that such a study ever breaks through to reality. A case in point is the concept of the idea. He argues that in actual use it is an instrument for the knowledge of reals. He believes it falsifying to describe it too simply, as a metaphysical form or a psychological reality (brain waves and the rest) plus a logical and intentional (ideal in his discourse) function. Without the latter, ideas are blind, and in Leibniz's way of speaking, "windowless." Then they would be only events. Therefore, it is in the interest of accuracy that ideas be described in their primitive and natural settings and contexts. Once again we find good reasons for his reluctance to adopt an artificial and abstractive style. Philosophers must describe; they cannot explain or speculate about matters like these. When they describe an idea it is essential to describe it so as to include its reference, its "of" and "about" character. Accuracy, not necessarily a philosophical doctrine, requires as much.

Again Kierkegaard is distinctly Socratic rather than Platonic. Ideas and their dialectic were in Socrates' hands instruments to sweep away illusions, errors of fact and also careless ways of life, to make room both for human ideals and the truth.[49] Therefore, reflecting was for Socrates a means of self-discipline and incidentally also a discipline for others; but for Plato ideas and dialectic were transformed, more or less clearly and consciously, into an end in itself, and the epistemological components developed in knowledge and ethics easily

---

48. *Postscript*, 85, 184–85, 295; Dru, *Journals*, 1054 (*Papirer* X2 A, 439) ; *Concept of Dread*, 72ff. Note the effusive remarks about Plato in *Begrebet Ironi*, 123ff. in *Samlede Vaerker*, vol. XIII.

49. Note Kierkegaard's long letter about Socrates to this effect, *Breve og Akstykker*, I:205–8. Even as a young man in 1840, he says that Socrates had to be negative. *Papirer* III A, 7 (*JP* 1, 745).

Some Epistemological Questions 179

became the supreme realities. In Kierkegaard's terminology Socrates was an existential thinker, because he remembered when he philosophized that the ideas were instrumental and that they did in fact enable one to apprehend things, but Plato was a speculative metaphysician. Socrates accordingly had no objective results, no system, no higher certainties of the subtle philosophical sort. Kierkegaard says:

> ... Wonderful Socrates! You perfected yourself in an art which will forever be equally difficult for every successor; you left behind you not one single loose string of a result that a Professor might be able to get hold of; no, you took everything with you into the grave ... And for this reason it is now being said, O Socrates ... depreciatingly, that you were only a personality, that you did not even have a system.[50]

But now we return to an argument of an earlier chapter. For Kierkegaard is not content either to describe abstract logical thought as simply instrumental but actually compels it to perform a pragmatic service.[51] And the reason for insisting upon the theme of objective uncertainty is that anyone who analyzes knowledge isolates the idea from the real, the thought from the thing. Philosophy has no means of synthesis superior to that already done in ordinary discourse in a miscellany of ways. Therefore, to a philosopher who, as Kierkegaard says of himself, "stands afar ... at this distance from the moment, tracing the thoughts in their interconnection, entertaining himself, luring from it the expressions required ... ,"[52] to such a disinterested thinker the ideal factor in knowledge is one thing, while the reality is something else. It is in this kind of abstracted consciousness that uncertainty grows up. Kierkegaard believes that philosophical doubts are bound to occur. This demeanor is what makes philosophical doubts possible. Another demeanor brings certainty.

We have seen the temptations. One kind of philosophy, idealism, makes the forms and ideas into the realities, and then the issue of synthesis cannot arise and there is no uncertainty about reality. Another kind of philosophy construes idealities, whether sensations, ideas, or logical values, simply as reals, and again there can be no objective

---

50. *Papirer* XII A, 344 and 449 (*JP* 3, 3178 and *JP* 4, 4303).

51. This is the argument of David Swenson in "A Danish Socrates," in *Something about Kierkegaard*.

52. *Samlede Vaerker*, XIV:104.

uncertainty. On the other hand, the man who uses ideas in everyday fashion at least owns to no metaphysical problem as to whether there is anything to know. He simply knows that. The temptation in philosophy is to assume that there is a philosophical answer to the problem. Kierkegaard insists that there is not. Instead he shows, but does not argue, and he invokes the rules of the ordinary use of ideas. A consciousness in which ideas function is a mediating consciousness. One real does not transform into another real, nor does an ideal mediate into an ideal. Cognition is not the discovery or invention of a peculiar class of cognitive objects, but it does suppose a mediation. Kierkegaard can only account for the mediation by the activity of a person. Reals and ideals, by themselves, do not know, and they do not mediate or transform into each other. Neither do they refer; only people refer. Therefore, epistemological analysis, which omits the interested user, can only find the discrete reals and ideals. So, too, he discovers respecting perception, that when sense data become the primary objects of cognition, perception is robbed altogether of its cognitive and revelatory quality.[53] Kierkegaard insists that knowledge is possible only when there is a synthesis in use. Consciousness for Kierkegaard is nothing very esoteric or metaphysical.[54] He uses the word to describe only the power and intent whereby an ideal functions and so works as to refer and identify things other than itself. This he contends is something that men do with idealities that neither idealities nor reals do by themselves.

But here again is the source of both uncertainty and certainty. "Doubt arises because there is a relationship between two things,"—so we are told in his analytic study of doubt.[55] Kierkegaard construed the history of modern philosophy, at least since Descartes, to be largely an attempt to establish, by philosophical means, the indubitability of reality, and he tends to condemn it wholesale when he concludes that this is not a philosophical problem. Here a quote from his papers of 1840 (July 5) is rather typical:

---

53. *Fragments*, 67–68.

54. *De Omnibus Dubitandum Est*, 147ff. Again, note the entry in his papers for July 18, 1840.

55. Ibid., 151.

> A person might say that the whole of modern philosophy, even its most grandiose representations, is really only an introduction to the possibility of philosophy. Hegel beyond question concludes, but he concludes only that development, which beginning with Kant, was directed toward cognition. With Hegel we have come in a profounder way to that result which earlier philosophy has taken immediately to be the beginning point, namely, that that there was a reality for thought. But, that kind of thinking, which moves from this point of departure (or what is hailed as a result) into a genuinely anthropological contemplation, that we haven't even begun.[56]

Neither certainty nor uncertainty of the real reference is strictly speaking a function of any kind of meta-philosophy about knowledge. Kierkegaard's youthful aspersions upon Hegel and others who achieved a kind of ontological assurance—that there are objects, there is a reality for thought—are engendered by his wry conviction that the ordinary man has known that all along.[57]

Kierkegaard was certain as a young man that most of these confounding philosophical problems were not genuinely intellectual. They were confusions, not simply of language as later students have said, but often of a very intricate passional-intellectual sort. His philosophical literature is in part a correction of the exclusively intellectualist treatment of religious, ethical, as well as metaphysical questions. Respecting all of these he proposes a critique of the passions as at least an aid to understanding what makes such problems possible. This is how he corrects Kant's critical work, and this is certainly what he means by the "anthropological" contemplation which would also be a kind of therapy, helping to free a man from illusory preoccupations.

Factual existence, Kierkegaard noted repeatedly, is never capable of demonstration, whether in relation to stars, stones, man, or God. Not even philosophers can get behind the ideal-real distinction. Proofs, he insists, operate by means of the logical "*quales*," essences

---

56. *Efterladte Papirer*, vol. I, 247 (my translation). Also note the remarks about Schelling's lecture: "... when he mentioned the word 'reality' in connection with the relation of philosophy to reality, the fruit of my thought leapt for joy within me as in Elizabeth." Dru, *Journals*, 392, 102 (*Papirer* III A, 179).

57. He says: "Hegel ought to have explained how one sets about doubting ..." Later he says: "... to doubt everything is to abstract from everything." Quoted in *De Omnibus Dubitandum Est*, 178.

or ideal entities. In every proof of existence, the reality or facticity is presupposed or given. One cannot demonstrate the existence of a stone, but only that an existing thing is a stone. Kierkegaard believes that it is a logical mistake to ask for the proof of actual existence, for this kind of proof would demand the abrogation of the very conditions that make possible the question in the first place.

The ideal and the real are homogenous in thought, so Kierkegaard contends. Here he is insisting like Kant that as far as the components of knowledge are concerned, there is no discernable difference between real and imagined dollars.[58] The heterogeneity of real and ideal is marked for all of us by the difference between knowing a thing (knowing "what" a thing is) and being that thing. Since this heterogeneity is *sui generis* and irreducible, knowledge is uncertain and stands in need of verification. But as we have already noted, no verification is so complete as to vanquish all uncertainty. The only kind of liquidation of uncertainty that we can have is by the philosopher's sleight of hand and that vanquishes the distinction between the real and the ideal.

Kierkegaard proposes instead a recognition of this heterogeneity and a recognition of how the subject's life, knowledge included, is dependent upon belief. It is to this we turn in the concluding section of this chapter.

IV

If Kierkegaard's analysis of the structure of experience in what Georg Brandes calls "the great superdreadnought," the *Concluding Unscientific Postscript*, is well grounded, then our common life (as well as our knowledge) cannot move forward without the constant and repeated help of what we might call a factor in the subjective life. In the *Fragments* he distinguishes between ordinary belief and extraordinary. We have noted the distinction in another connection earlier. But belief (or the word "faith" as preferred by most of the English translators) is certainly an example of a family resemblance

---

58. Note the lengthy entry in Dru, *Journals*, 1027, 357–58 (*Papirer* X2 A, 328), on Kant and "conceptual existence."

word.[59] Kierkegaard gets that concept extended through a considerable number of contexts "as in spinning a thread we twist fibre on fibre."[60] There are an enormous number of ways of discerning objective uncertainties, in this and that kind of logical, ethical, religious, and cognitive context. But what we have been particularly concerned with in this chapter is the philosophical doubt about whether any language can refer to real things. About this Kierkegaard's pages make it clear that we can indeed formulate the "what," but only belief or "ordinary faith" comes to rest in the "that."[61] The conviction that there is a "that" is not strictly a function of the description. It is brought about by the subject, not by the "*quales*" that make up the "what." Real existence, he insists, following Aristotle, cannot be reduced to a concept.

The universality of objective uncertainty in this sense requires the universal presence of a motivation in man that helps make up our "belief." This "belief" or faith is not what recent philosophers have meant by assenting to propositions or acknowledging truth claims. For Kierkegaard understands the kind of belief he is talking about to be, strictly speaking, a passional matter. It is never the immediate and necessary consequence of a purely objective state of affairs; neither does it issue in more objective truth claims. In truth, to formulate this faith by coining cognitive beliefs as its products is another source of a nonsensical kind of philosophy. This leads again to metaphysics, the kind in which reality claims are proposed.

Kierkegaard reflected at length about Descartes' philosophizing. He quotes his treatise, *De Affectionbus*, and notes that therein "wonder" is the only passion. Without an opposing passion he goes on:

---

59. Ludwig Wittgenstein says: "Don't say: 'there *must* be something common or they would not be called 'games,'"—but *look and see* whether there is anything common to all.—For if you look at them you will not see something that is common to *all*, but similarities, relationships, and a whole series of them at that . . . And the result of this examination is: we see a complicated network of similarities overlapping and criss-crossing; sometimes overall similarities, sometimes similarities of detail . . . I can think of no better expression to characterize these similarities than 'family resemblances' . . ." *Philosophical Investigations* (translated by G. E. M. Anscombe), 31–32.

60. Ibid., 32.

61. Dru, *Journals*, 1027, 358 (*Papirer* X2 A, 328).

His detailed demonstration is rather weak, but it interests me that he has made "wonder" an exception, since as everyone knows, following Plato's and Aristotle's use of the concept, wonder is the philosopher's passion, that passion with which philosophy begins.[62]

"Wonder" is a passion, and its opposite is not another passion (e.g., the way that hate is the opposite of love) but the absence of passion, indifference or apathy.[63] Without wonder, which is an interest, the idealities can never "refer to" or "mean" a real. Therefore, we might say that for Kierkegaard the function of wonder is to cause a man to use the sensations, the ideas, and anything else ideal, in order to illumine the real. With wonder, there is no doubt; without wonder, there is no certainty. Passion here is nothing more than the medium by which the synthesis is achieved. Therefore, profound skepticism is a matter of being bereft of the passion, not strictly a matter of argument. And what passes as a sense for the real and the ordinary convictions that we do know objects and things are not conclusions of arguments nor can they, strictly speaking, be said to be philosophically established. "Wonder" and "interest" do not justify the conviction; they do not allow skepticism or doubt any foothold at all, and therefore make justification irrelevant. "If anybody, therefore," writes Kierkegaard, "by any so-called objective thinking imagines that he can conquer doubt, he is mistaken."[64] The only way to conquer doubt is to recover the passion and interest. The issue has to do with one's mental climate and with dispositions, even with what one might call the will.[65]

But we must return to the main theme once again. Kierkegaard has analyzed belief in a variety of ways. His point is that without the passional component, wonder, possessing a man, it is unlikely that all that we have called idealities will seem anything but that. To believe that there are objects requires wonder, and in this way belief incorporates cognitive elements into a testimony about the real world. If these small responses to the world require a move of subjectivity, it

---

62. *Begrebet Angst*, in *Samlede Vaerker*, vol. IV, 411–12. Translation my own.

63. Note *Papirer* IV C, 100 (*JP* 1, 197), where there is a related discussion of the concepts "*Esse*" and "*Inter-esse*."

64. *De Omnibus Dubitandum Est*, 152.

65. Note the miscellany of notes lumped by the editors under the title "Interested Knowledge . . . ," all from 1842–1843, in *Papirer* IV C, 99 (*JP* 2, 2283).

is thoughtless to suppose that such fundamental responses which we call views of life would ever be discovered without subjectivity. It can be shown that the great views of life, aesthetic, ethical, religious and Christian, are not strictly speaking functions of facts or learning either. Just as the advantages of superior philosophical awareness are neutralized in small matters of certainty and uncertainty by common sense and wonder, where even the most learned cannot demonstrate that there are objective things, so in matters of deep and lifelong responsibility, superior philosophical and theological culture only states refinedly a problem without resolving it a whit. In an essay, "What It Means to Seek God,"[66] Kierkegaard points out how the results of theological and philosophical sophistication are never adequate to bring assurance of God to another person. Unless "the passion of wonder" takes hold of a person, he says, doubt will have as free play with the sophisticated as with the unsophisticated.[67]

As we have noted earlier, Kierkegaard has argued that the objective uncertainty is a goad and stimulus to passion. So what one man has in his ignorance, not knowing why or how, hence being full (naturally and naively) of wonder and concern, the learned man has in virtue of a reflectively gained uncertainty. Kierkegaard thought that the great philosophical systems were, however ingenious and interesting as hypothetical logical exercises, often simply dogmatic ways of distinguishing these elemental matters. Uncertainty threw the individual back upon his own resources, forcing him to unlock the energies and powers of his own spirit. Even epistemology, if it were detached and honest, completely without pretense and metaphysical dogma, ought to give a man, but only indirectly of course, the occasion for forming these resolutions of disposition and thought by which knowledge, as well as other capacities of human life, are realized. Struggle, doubt, anxiety, hope, fear and trembling, despair, faith, and courage are, in Kierkegaard's placing of them, the noble disciplinarians that fashion the personality. None of them could work at all if there were not uncertainties, and these uncertainties must be for all, not just for some, otherwise one could neither explain their

---

66. *Thoughts on Crucial Situations*, 14.
67. Note *De Omnibus Dubitandum Est*, 128.

generality nor the lifelong need for them, no matter how astute one's learning or how vast one's experience.

Already in his day, Kierkegaard knew that probability was said to be the guide to life. He says, ironically, "probability is a commercial paper which is not quoted in heaven."[68] He has thought at length about this concept, too, and found it to be a deceitful one, masquerading as a serve-all concept, equally relevant to all issues. He is quite explicit on the fact that any description about "what" objects and events are is subject to limitations of evidence, available tools of research, etc. Here is where he uses the words "*en objectiv approximerens vei*," the "objective approximation-process,"[69] and where the concept probability has its proper locus. But he resists the extension of this concept to all arenas where uncertainty is discoverable. So, the awareness that there is always some kind of evidence and that it rarely, if ever, happens that the weight of evidence is equally balanced, makes it plausible to think that one must only discover and obey the preponderance of evidence in order that even the most encompassing of issues will receive an objective resolution.[70] The effect is to make knowledge, even if it does not abolish uncertainty, still the means of univocally ordering the choice. But a concept of probability which covers all these instances of uncertainty, Kierkegaard believes is the learned man's (as well as the ordinary man's if he uses it) superstition.[71]

The generalized concept of probability misleads its user towards a greater and greater accumulation of knowledge or what Kierkegaard calls objectivity. Everything in the subject, feelings, passion, wish, and wonder are banished as if they were troublesome and negligible appendages to be eliminated in the serious business of deciding. But here Kierkegaard's contention is that intellectual confusion abounds. All the claims to intellectual honesty notwithstanding, he finds it an error to assume that beliefs in the existence of objects, in God, in

68. *Stages on Life's Way*, 114. See also *Judge for Yourselves*: ". . . the man who never let go of probability never committed himself to God," 116.

69. *Afsluttende Uvidenskabelig Efterskrift, Samlede Vaerker*, VIII:177. See *Postscript*, where the concept of probability is examined in detail.

70. One of the themes he strikes in *De Omnibus Dubitandum Est* is that it is impossible to resolve Descartes' kind of doubt by the help of "an objective and absolute beginning." Note to 133.

71. Dru, *Journals*, 1175, 424 (*Papirer* X3 A, 727).

a moral view, are ever a simple function of facts or intellect alone. Though he asserts that for a variety of reasons people wish to believe in the improbable, even the paradoxical, they also want to believe in virtue of a more refined understanding.[72] Therewith, probability makes it seem that there is a hidden certainty, a lurking guarantee, in virtue of which the belief will no longer be improbable but on the side of certainty.

Of course, Kierkegaard defends strongly the virtue of casting up in an acute way the intellectual accounts. Again we must be clear that there are contexts in which we must not believe contrary to what the evidence proposes. But he distinguishes as we have seen between "ordinary" and "extraordinary" believing. It seems clear from his pages that the conviction a man of learning might express about the conclusions of his scholarly and scientific research is not a belief in any particularly strong sense of the term. Here a belief requires only an insight into the evidence and an apt assessment of its probative force. Such a belief is a consequence of a purely objective insight. This kind of belief is qualitatively different from believing that there are objects as over against saying that there are none. In beliefs of this sweeping ethical sort, also the belief in the existence of God, the evidence is amenable to either side, the affirmation and the denial. Therefore, where all the facts count, none of them count; and probability here has to bring in other considerations, such as "fittingness," longevity of the view and others, most of which are vague, irrelevant and a poor kind of evidence at best. Such considerations are the only material whereby the concept of probability can work at all on ethico-religious themes.

Kierkegaard found that though the concepts of the possible, the actual, and the probable all had objective reference, they did not name powers in nature. Probability is not an objective force working in events. Therefore, he tries valiantly to make his reader see that it is a concept, not a name, that its misuse can blind him to what the moral history of the race as well as contemporary life, will make clear, namely, that most causes which needed to be served were usually thought to be improbable. On the other hand, those who served causes where the chances of success were assured by a calculation of

---

72. This is part of the point made in the *Fragments*.

the probabilities were essentially the time-servers. Therefore, a belief in the improbable is not always self-contradictory or arbitrary. To keep confidence in another's virtue even when appearances are against it is certainly a part of being ethical. We rather wisely understand this as evidence of goodness in the beholder.

Therefore, Kierkegaard grades the issues of human life in quite a different manner than most philosophers. The more trivial the matter at hand and the more mediocre the ends set before one, the stronger the relationship between one's decision and the calculation of probabilities. On the other hand, the more demanding and completely transforming the issues, such as one finds in ethics and the Christian faith, the less the commensurateness between one's decision and the probabilities. For one comes to the point where there is maximal improbability, even a negative veto, on the objective side and a decision which, nonetheless, affects a completely new qualification of the person. Therefore, Kierkegaard's scale of human decisions that is most carefully worked out in the *Postscript* proposes that there are beliefs to which men commit themselves that are not unequivocally an expression of anything objective and eternal, but are instead, though used to refer to something objective (e.g., the language that says Jesus is God) principally an expression of the quality of the person who decides.

The great faiths, ethical, religious, Christian and even aesthetic (to confine ourselves only to those in Kierkegaard's purview) are not transpositions of more confounding and exacting metaphysical realities, assessable to objective speculative philosophers. There is no epistemological way to get them objectively to be certain. On the contrary, the thesis that Jesus is God (note chapter 5) is about an historical figure, but it is not therefore a simple assertion of facts either.[73] At a certain point, sentences referring to Jesus become an expression also of the qualities of persons who have decided for him. Most of us begin our active intellectual life by submitting everything to an examination, ferreting out all the details for what we believe is our advantage. But then the tables are turned and we are no longer examin-

---

73. Early in his career Kierkegaard criticized learning that makes "Christ into a sort of natural son." His point is that there are no conceptual meanings linking the concepts "natural" and "God." See *Papirer* II A; the entries for the summer of 1838 are replete with such reflections. Also note his remarks about "probability" and a thing happening once, *Either/Or*, II:34.

ers—instead we are examined. Human life is an examination in which one cannot cheat. "Or can you think of anything more frightful than that it might end with your nature being resolved into a multiplicity . . . and you thus would have lost the inmost and holiest thing of all in a man, the unifying power of personality?"[74] Then, and then only, does a human subject become complete. The answers to this kind of examination require the synthesizing powers of a person, and these answers are the fundamental faiths. Therefore, these faiths also evince what has come to birth within us.

Therefore, Kierkegaard's gradation marks the fact that fundamental faiths and the claims made within them are less dependent upon knowledge, whereas the more indifferent the claim, as in logic, mathematics, and the most abstract sciences, the more dependent upon the degree of knowledge. Here Kierkegaard has undercut the logical positivists' criticism of religious and ethical language by describing its peculiar logic and rules. If what he has said is appropriate at all, then the sprawling view that said that there was a single epistemological model for any kind of discourse about the world has to be radically revised. Kierkegaard has made the case for saying that there are different groups of rules governing, not only the respective propositions of science, ethics, theology, metaphysics, and aesthetics, but also that there are differing factors, motives, needs, dispositions, governing the adoption of these that place the propositions in radically differing contexts.

But Kierkegaard does find some links between these. Perhaps an example will suffice. That kind of philosophy which is so aristocratic that it gives up thinking other things and thinks itself usually fails to warrant its own activity. There is a fundamental skepticism that says that we are imprisoned in the present and cannot think the past or future, that numerically different thought cannot identify the same things and therefore memory is invalid, that skepticism cannot be healed by probabilities. Such doubts can be sustained indefinitely because very intellectual and opposing considerations are doubted in their own terms. Here, too, all objective considerations are of no avail. The issue is no longer a matter of evidence. The only cure is a new

---

74. *Either/Or*, II:135.

point of departure for the man who thinks this way.[75] Kierkegaard was bold at this juncture. He contended that elementary needs for making thought a tool and the passionate desire for another way to live do in fact release men from such intellectual paralysis. The plain man uses thoughts naturally, almost instinctively, and the epistemological philosopher is in no position to demonstrate that it really is valid. On the contrary, he either believes or he perishes, and his only advantage is his more acute consciousness of his necessity for a passionate resolution through being afflicted with the disease of doubt. Therefore the ordinary man and the philosopher are united in yielding to a noble human impulse. As long as a thinker wants to keep his reflection pertinent to existence, the objective uncertainties that bind him in this common need and passions will help create the faith.

Again the uncertainties are common to all. They are to be seen very clearly in relation to the issue of the existence of God. Kierkegaard noted that this issue was not scientific, philosophical, or even theological. For the laws of nature and the entire system of scientific explanations, as well as religious scholarship, are neutral respecting the issue of God's existence. Furthermore, scientific research and the dialectical development of the relevant concepts do nothing to bring one to a fundamental resolution. Even the proofs for the existence of God only formulate the problem more acutely. So, in the face of all this Kierkegaard concludes that it is precisely the imperfections and the uncertainties in the world that awaken the passion to believe in God. The moral imperfections and the uncertainties whether right will conquer cause men to believe in a righteous God, and the intellectual and objective uncertainties that easily make one despair also can elicit confidence in a God of light and truth. Part of Kierkegaard's teaching is to help each man see that this is the upshot of philosophical wisdom—not to provide the proofs but really to energize the subject once again.

Faith in God is not a possession warranted by any intellectual scheme. This faith is not an inference from things that are certain or causes that are probable. It is instead a response to the uncertainties, the improbabilities if not the impossibilities. The great convictions

---

75. *Either/Or*, II:144. Also see 178ff. Also note the contrasts that he draws between "personal and scientific doubts" on 80.

Some Epistemological Questions

then are not insights into verities nor are they the necessary outcome of reflection on other factors.[76]

Kierkegaard's epistemological reflections do not give any ground whatsoever for the criticism of human beliefs. But this is not to say that he thought that beliefs were either beyond criticism or therefore of equal worth. His charge is that even the most vaunted of the convictions of reason, that it will give guidance to a man, or disclose the world, depends upon a beggarly article of faith. Critical philosophy does not deduce the foundations for beliefs any more than metaphysical philosophy does. On the other hand, a criticism of beliefs is certainly possible. For beliefs are of varying content and value. As we have indicated earlier, a criticism of beliefs is not, in the strictest sense, a logical-epistemological matter, nor a matter of knowledge. It is a criticism of passions. And a critique of the passions is a large part of Kierkegaard's literature.

Nonetheless, his epistemological reflections have provided a number of the boundaries within which one can profitably reflect. Even to know that the transcendence of thought ("transcendence" in the small sense of thought thinking something other than itself) is posited by passion is to know something important. That all of us are objectively uncertain might seem a counsel of despair, but to Kierkegaard this is a discovery altogether worthy of the most acute and disciplined intelligence. For it helps one energize his passions and correct one with a better one. Instead of trying to make passionless science productive of a faith, of trying to evoke from philosophy what it cannot provide, Kierkegaard is content to let them, science and philosophy, be what they are, by and large descriptive, leaving a man pretty much where he was before he learned them.

Epistemology is an indirect teacher as to where the issues finally are. For one then learns that the battles of health and disease, happiness and pain, of the human spirit have to be fought on the right ground. It has been said that only two kinds of people know anything about love: happy and unhappy lovers; spectators must remain outsiders. If Kierkegaard is right, then every passion is known in this way. Therefore, the criticisms of those encompassing beliefs that make us ethical and religious are not open to the epistemologists who study the

---

76. This is the theme of the later sections of the *Postscript*.

correspondences between thought and things. Fundamental beliefs are in consequence of the pathos of persons who face the concrete uncertainties of existence. In the realization of this fact, we recognize also the differing logic of beliefs, thereby connecting dogmatic views, while simultaneously being conscious of the essential democracy of our common life.

CHAPTER 9

Kierkegaard and Metaphysics

Kierkegaard's lengthy literature is frankly and unabashedly evangelical. It aims to bring his learned reader into discussion and concern about religious, and particularly Christian, matters. Therefore, it might seem jejune to suggest that such a literature could be a place for the kind of imperturbability that philosophy conventionally demands. But this is precisely the anomaly that Kierkegaard proposes. One of his motifs is that the best kind of philosophy is a neutral and utterly honest literature. Metaphysics ought to be, *qua* a philosophical disciple, the most abstract and disinterested of all disciplines. But this is not so because it is about Being, ostensibly the most abstract and emptiest of concepts, or reality, in and by itself, but rather because it is about concepts, not whatever those concepts ostensibly refer to. Metaphysics does not produce reality concepts; instead, it is, in large part, the study of such concepts as they occur in more primitive, even non-learned, circumstances.[1]

The odd thing is that Kierkegaard believed that the speculative philosophy of his day, which was metaphysical in a grand and encompassing way, was also a failure because it was not neutral and descriptive. Metaphysics of the speculative variety made reality claims. These often conflicted with what an ordinary man believed was real and what was not, and they conflicted with the ordinary language of real and unreal as these occurred in morals and religion. Clearly this would not occur if it could be shown that a metaphysician has no authority to legislate on such issues. With his religious ardor it is tempting to suggest that Kierkegaard is criticizing metaphysicians

1. Dru, *Journals*, 617, the long entry on 181–85 (*Papirer* VII A, 186).

simply out of his own desire to save the faith, but it is not quite that simple.

There are several constellations of Kierkegaard's discussion to consider. We will begin with the most amorphous. With everything else, Kierkegaard is also a kind of social critic. From his first public writings, somewhat casual journalistic pieces appearing in 1837–1838, he was intent upon the climate of opinion in Copenhagen. For a variety of reasons, metaphysical concepts were predominant in the most sophisticated circles. The romantic movement in literature, plus a State Church with a very easy accommodation to faith and morals, gave notions of "time," "progress," "good," and "true" a decidedly metaphysical ring. Philosophers and theologians were quick to latch upon a new way to make big and weighty words relevant to the Danish scene. To Kierkegaard, this synthesis of opinion was monstrous, amorphous, and utterly debilitating.[2] Therefore, we must look at a variety of ways he attacks his age and its use of metaphysics. Here his pages are satirical and his pen positively outraged. In succeeding sections of this chapter we will narrow the discussion, aiming to see with greater precision what he thought of the metaphysical concepts, the meanings of "real," "reality," "true," and others, along with his proposals about the proper and improper uses of "real."

I

The large story told by Kierkegaard's literature concerns the development of the human being. But his concern is with moral and religious maturation, and his "stages," linked only by "the leap," are the contexts in which one can see aesthetic, moral, and religious concepts at work. These stages or spheres are separable as groups, not as systems. His point is that they do not coalesce one into the other, nor do they stand in the dialectical relations claimed by Hegel. They are logically discrete. But his only concern is not this. The metaphysical scheme of the day, not always articulated but inchoately presented (a "climate," not always an argument), suggested a close analogy between the develop-

---

2. Note how he characterized Adler's four books as "a satire upon Hegelian philosophy and the present age," and also as a literary monstrosity, not because they did not fit the age but because they did. See *On Authority and Revelation*. Note the Danish text, *Efterladte Papirer*, II:583 and 696.

ment of the person and organic and historical developments.³ Most of the metaphysical concepts lumped together the differences between political aims and religious, and between literary movements and the processes of moral perfecting. Where metaphysical concepts increasingly blurred the distinctions, Kierkegaard wanted to distinguish most sharply.

In Kierkegaard's first pages, the attack started as a broadside. Because he quite lacked a reformer's zeal, his tools increasingly became the more delicate ones of poetic invention and refined argument. There was something else too. He was always capable of raging scorn and invective. Throughout his work one finds many scathing asides linked with exacting argument.

Some things that he was always intent upon were foibles and half-truths masquerading as profound wisdom. Metaphysics loomed up as the most impressive pastiche of all. And the romantics' cloudy effusions, partly metaphysical, were also his targets. N. F. S. Grundtvig, the romantic nationalist clergyman and Old Norse scholar, combined the major popular movements in a persuasive and plausible way for many religious and patriotic Danes; J. L. Heiberg, a philosophical critic, had a ready audience among the more sophisticated. Both of these made ideas powerful in the national life of Denmark. In contrast, Kierkegaard wrote for posterity and his poet yet to come. But it was not from pique that he attacked these authors. In fact, in both of the above cases, he wrote lengthy criticisms primarily to clarify his own thought, leaving these pieces unpublished.⁴

When he was very young and a neophyte author, he read the renowned Hans Christian Andersen's novel *Kun en Spillemand* and then wrote a slashing essay, "Andersen as Novelist." Among other things he criticizes the incongruity of saying:

---

3. Note the careful attention given this analogy in Harald Høffding's essay "Søren Kierkegaard" in *Mindre Arbejder*, vol. II; see especially 190. Also note *Samtaler med Harald Høffding*, by Erik Rindom for casual remarks about these matters by Høffding. Kierkegaard's papers are full of comments upon this mistaken analogy.

4. They can be found in his papers for the following years: about Heiberg, about fifty pages, 1844; about Grundtvig, about fifty pages, 1846; about Goldschmidt, another literary phenomenon, about a hundred pages, 1846; about Adler, a religious-philosophical writer, several hundred pages composed over several years beginning in 1846 (note *Papirer*, vols. VII-VIII). For a brief account of Grundtvig's relation to Kierkegaard, see G. Lindhart, *Grundtvig*, especially 47–48 and 121–22.

> Paris has for the moment no religion; they have forgotten the Madonna, yes almost the Father and the Son; the Spirit alone prevails. One sees no monks on the street, no religious processions...[5]

Needless to say, he shows such chaotic reflection no mercy. That anyone could use such criteria for determining the state of faith in Paris was quite beyond him. For writings like these, a literary historian like Georg Brandes sees him as one of the first stringent and responsible critics of romanticism in literature.[6] Against them Kierkegaard demands definition, exactness, less formless passion and more responsible discrimination and judgment. He sounds like a rationalist. But he is quickly led to other matters, particularly the way romantic tendencies in literature feed new enthusiasms for metaphysics. Among other things, the new historical appreciation, fed by German sources, fed, in turn, all kinds of vague propensities among the Danes. The upshot is a new kind of popular metaphysics, historical, ostensibly helpful and almost impossible to criticize. Its murkiness and ethical tone made it almost invulnerable.[7]

Metaphysics, despite its serious pretensions, seemed to him at times like a fantastic joke. However, one could not simply laugh it off. Whatever one said about it, it had a kind of power in the lives of the sophisticated. Unlike many critics, Kierkegaard thought, these popular constellations, be they myths, stories, or science, were powerful and, therefore, worth tackling. In his day, metaphysics was a kind of arbiter within the university and Dano-German intellectual circles. Everyone paid respects to this science of ultimates and there was general deference if something was said to be a metaphysical matter. All the more reason, then, for Kierkegaard's scorn, for he had tried the metaphysicians, including Schelling in Berlin, Hegel, Plato, Aristotle, Descartes and others in his reading, and, of course, numerous lectures, discussions, and tutors during his university ca-

---

5. *Af en endnu Levendes Papirer* (1838), *Vaerker*, XIII:85.

6. Georg Brandes, *Søren Kierkegaard*, especially the discussion about Andersen, Antigone, Don Juan, etc. Brandes admired Kierkegaard's savage attacks upon the romantics very much, although he thinks that Kierkegaard is a romantic in part.

7. Also note his remarks about the literary situation—about novels, about "enthusiasm" in literature, about morals and literature—and his plea for more category analysis and greater clarity. In *En Litterair Anmeldelse, Samlede Vaerker*, VII:1-106.

reer. The anomaly of metaphysics being so highly thought of by the clergy, by the literary critics, in fact, by most of the intelligensia, while the grounds for the discipline were severely questioned and at the very best poorly defended by its most skilled practioners, this did not escape Kierkegaard's critical glance. No wonder then the sardonic remarks in *Either/Or*:

> I prefer to talk with children, for it is still possible to hope that they may become rational beings. But those who have already become so—good Lord!

Then, too, his familiar quip:

> What the philosophers say about Reality is often as disappointing as a sign you see in a shop window which reads: Pressing Done Here. If you brought your clothes to be pressed, you would be fooled; for only the sign was for sale.[8]

Part of Kierkegaard's protest is simply against the exalted status of metaphysics. Kierkegaard believed that serious intellectual, moral, and aesthetic matters were invariably maligned when given popularity. In one of his slighter papers, written to amuse but nonetheless full of bite, he comments upon the fact that "to write a book in our time is the easiest of all, especially after examining and using ten earlier authors who treat of the same subject, one therefore writes an eleventh on the same material."[9] Most of the philosophical writing of his day, he says, is like that, metaphysical and secondhand, socially important yet intellectually trivial. Most amazing of all is the practice of everybody learning about reality and the "immediate" from books, which at best mediate what others have written.

The new metaphysics is done by scholars who eat, like cannibals, other people's ideas. Kierkegaard could never restrain his amusement over this. Furthermore, the scholarly metaphysicians have to know everything, science, all of history (not the least that of Persia

---

8. *Either/Or*, vol. I, 15 and 25.

9. This is from *Forord*, 1844, in *Samlede Vaerker*, V:39. Translation my own. This book is one of the few not translated into other languages. It is about Danish popular culture and its intellectual pretensions. The title means "Prefaces." The book is made up of prefaces because the author had read so many books in which the best part was the preface that he decided to do a whole volume of prefaces—all of them promissory notes!

and China), theology, and lately philology. And yet they get their raw material from books—other people's books. Besides, they must scan and then generalize, and who is to call them right or wrong? With the whole world and all of the learning they can manage as the material, who can determine the rightness or wrongness of metaphysical judgments? As long as the System is not finished, ordinary logical criticism is ineffective, for until the System is completed, one will not be able to apply criteria of consistency and order. Of course, he notes, scholarship is never at an end.

Kierkegaard is very close to saying that a metaphysical system like Hegel's, which purports to establish its case on both logical grounds, having to do with concepts and their development, and on broadly empirical grounds, all the while being systematic, is outright nonsense. Other metaphysical schemes, like Schopenhauer's and the Stoics, Kierkegaard could take with seriousness, for they were at least first-hand personal expressions. But the confusions introduced by these devilishly learned and quasi-logical efforts, these were both subtle and pompous. Besides they were footnoted and learned, which was one more way to make a dialectician timid.

There is something else too. Kierkegaard was painfully aware of the need to be sharply specific. He wanted to sharpen and to intensify all kinds of issues, including moral and religious issues. But he explains:

> It is perhaps not beside the point to remind people of this, for our age, the age of movement, tends to bring fundamental assumptions under discussion, so the consequence is that a marvellous number of men in the mass get on their feet and open their mouths all at once in the game of discussion, along with the public which understands absolutely nothing about it, whereas the prodigious size of the problem advantageously hides the ignorance of the discussers and the speakers respectively... A learned twaddler who at bottom knows nothing can seldom be got to deal with anything concrete; he does not talk of a particular dialogue of Plato, that is too little for him—also it might become apparent that he has not read it. No, he talks about Plato as a whole, but especially about the wisdom of the Indians and the Chinese... So also it is much easier to talk about an alteration in the form of government than to discuss a little concrete problem like sewing a pair of

> shoes . . . our Lord and his governance of the world is something so prodigiously great that in a certain giddy abstract sense the most foolish man takes part in gossiping about it as well as the wisest man, because none understands it.[10]

Metaphysics was one way to think in generalities, rather than in specifics. Metaphysics was also that discourse which put everything into suspense. "The appearance of being in suspense," Kierkegaard notes, "always results when one does not rest upon the foundation but the foundational itself is made dialectical."[11] Even the foundational issues, those we noted in the last chapter, were thought to be in doubt and, hopefully, yet to be made secure by metaphysics. Furthermore, the new zest for metaphysics, while cutting the taproot of what Kierkegaard thought was moral and religious seriousness, was also ingredient in a society where the tax-supported State Church had also very successfully domesticated religion and morals.

To mention the Church is perhaps to cloud the issues even more. Kierkegaard thought that there was a very remarkable fittingness between the popular metaphysical schemes and the languid role of the state-supported Lutheran Church of Denmark. Romanticism in literature, adaptability to the national interests on the part of the Church and a genial kind of scholarship that justified the way things were on both historical and metaphysical grounds—this was the mélange which Kierkegaard thought kept decisiveness at bay. Mediocrity was guaranteed in such a society. Besides being the critic in the large, he is also the critic in the small. His concern is primarily with what happens to an intelligent man who succumbs to this form of sophistry. This way of construing things falsifies the way a man's existence is— and we have noted this charge in an earlier chapter. Philosophy has become a rationalization and justification for doing what men would do otherwise. But there is more. A distortion of the concepts and categories also takes place. Kierkegaard is positively acerbic about the decay in specificity that he notes in the particular scene.

The Church, indebted as he admits to being to it, has sustained the belief that simply being born in Denmark was enough to qualify for Christian nobility. It becomes a powerful deterrent to incisive

---

10. *On Authority and Revelation*, 31–32.
11. Ibid., 30.

thinking, needing, as it does, to use all religious concepts as if they were also political. No wonder, then, that Kierkegaard insisted, "a schooling in Christian concepts"[12] was absolutely essential for anyone who wanted to understand the Christian life. He marshals every instrument he has to satirize the effect of the Church upon religious thinking and life. His finesse and unrelenting skill marks him as a satirist equal to Jonathan Swift and Voltaire, but always with greater acuity on the intellectual side. For the Church has an intellectual accompaniment adding the *de profundis* note—the metaphysics of the newer Danish philosophy! The finesse that Kierkegaard brings into his satire is stupefying in its effects. The professors, the literati, and the clergy, together professed a systematic outlook, within which their own endeavors could be "understood." And how Kierkegaard detests the promiscuous use of that word![13] Stemming principally from Hegel and other post-Kantian idealists, some local and some German, this systematic scheme gave a metaphysical context to all human endeavors, including ethics and religion. "Reality" was rationally and philosophically discernable and was germane to everything human. One of his pseudonyms remarks that the more costly the fluid with which a man intoxicates himself, the more difficult it is to cure him. Philosophy, especially the bewitching metaphysical sort, was the most costly and the most intoxicating.[14]

Therefore, as Kierkegaard assayed the social scene he found that by making religion a department of state, the government had made religious qualities into a social commodity, almost to be handled by legislation and budgets, and as he looked at his fellow intellectuals, he found that metaphysics had become the science of the totalities, State, Church, and Cosmos, and simply dwarfed the small efforts of the single individual. There seemed to be no function for metaphysics, save as a kind of documentary upon the impersonal forces that ground out one's destiny. All of this he thinks is wrong.

When Kierkegaard moves in upon this situation it is, of course, the metaphysical philosophy that must be dispatched. We have al-

12. This is what Kierkegaard recommends after reading Adler's four volumes of effusive metaphysical theology.

13. Note *The Last Years*, 353. Here he notes how "this interminable mass of learned historical drivel" is a way to keep understanding postponed.

14. *Either/Or*, II:164.

ready noted how carefully contrived his books are to meet this philosophical morass. His piecemeal analyses, his attack upon large and artificial philosophical concepts, his use of examples in which concepts are brought to birth, his attack upon the intellectualist-myth, and the attack upon the supposed "content neutrality" of concepts like "objectivity," "fact," and "truth" are all relevant. Once this case has been presented (and this takes most of his years), then and then only does he move to an attack upon the Church itself. This attack is mounted only in the last months of his life, while the former polemic is a constant theme of his reflection, from 1837 until the end of 1855. The metaphysics of the day also pretends to be loosely historical, a kind of transcript of the way that historical reality unfolds in time. It is Kierkegaard's intent to show not only that this metaphysical schematism excludes theology and religion,[15] but that it is not a transcript of the concrete historical existence of individuals. The concepts of the large and the small are not the same and are not even analogous. So, too, the Church is an attack upon the personal life and its passions. It seems to Kierkegaard that the new learning and the Church together sustain an illusory view of human life.

This complex situation is the setting, then, for Kierkegaard's attack upon systematic metaphysics. What has been neglected in most Kierkegaard research to date is the fact that amid the attack, the satire, and persuasion, there is a very penetrating analysis of metaphysical categories and concepts. His criticisms are never irresponsible. He writes not as an historian but as a dialectician, and he perhaps caricatures a little too broadly, but his criticisms are undergirded by a most painstaking analysis, and do not, despite the passion, lack precision. He is willing, furthermore, to do as perhaps many contemporary critics of metaphysics are not, namely, let his analysis speak without any strident counter-metaphysical dogmatism.

In succeeding sections we will assess his reflections on the province and role of metaphysics in several ways: (a) something about the aims of metaphysics; (b) his judgments about the success of metaphysics; (c) the case for metaphysics as a study of certain kinds of concepts. In a succeeding chapter a reconstruction of Kierkegaard's view of the role of philosophy and metaphysics will be attempted,

---

15. Note *Efterladte Papirer*, II:337.

with special attention to what he believes is the fundamental and inescapably human way to use the word "reality."[16]

II

Metaphysics, as Kierkegaard sees it, is primarily an endeavor to learn foundational truths, anterior to and the ground for, theology, ethics, politics, and other enterprises. That such learning should not simply be of contemplative worth but also practical import is a conviction as old as the history of philosophy. But there has always been a noticeable difference between those who believe that objective truths are instruments for the furtherance of human ends and those who insist that they are this and something more, namely, the disclosure of those ends.[17] Metaphysics was the disclosure of those ends. In his early years Kierkegaard discovered that the multitude of scientific hypotheses did nothing to resolve his personal problems. He records his dismay in a letter to his brother-in-law scientist where he summarizes attitudes toward the natural sciences:

> ... I naturally find along the road, as along all others ... examples of men who have made a name in literature as a result of their tremendous industry in collecting facts. They know a vast amount of detail and have discovered many new facts; but nothing more. They have simply supplied the material for the thought and work of others ... For insofar as there is a sort of unconscious life in the knowledge of such a man, it may be said that science demands his life; insofar as that is not the case, his activity is like that of the man whose contribution to the preservation of the world is the decaying of his body.[18]

Of course, the hypothetical knowledge about nature and history would never yield an imperative, and this was Kierkegaard's constant contention. He makes the same point in other forms against those who zealously endeavor to convert theology into a scientific and empirical discipline thus hoping that a new objective certainty might

---

16. Editors' note: see chapter 10, "Kierkegaard and the Nature of Philosophy."

17. Note Kierkegaard's discussion of this issue in *Either/Or*, II:188ff.

18. Dru, *Journals*, 16, 6–7 (*Papirer* I A, 72). This letter is printed, along with others to W. Lund, in *Breve og Aktstykker*, I:32–37.

replace the rubric "I believe."[19] Even as a very avid young dilettante, Kierkegaard soon learned that philosophy promised major answers to major problems. But he felt thwarted. F. C. Sibbern, a Nestorian figure in Danish philosophical history, reports that young Kierkegaard met him in the street one day and asked how philosophy related to living and reality.[20] The fact that he could never resolve this issue to his own satisfaction and hence remained skeptical marks his attitude also to metaphysics. Like most young intellectuals he restlessly explored all kinds of learning, but unlike most of them, he stumbled upon the limits again and again. Today it is popular to report upon the impossibility of moving from fact to value, from indicative to imperative language, from the "is" to the "ought." In Kierkegaard's day metaphysical philosophy made a certain appeal to anyone caught in these formidable quests. In one way or another it professed to get beneath or behind the uncertainties and to tell one what one needed to become good and wise.[21] Besides it proposed getting at these foundational matters without dogma, without any context being involved. Metaphysics looked promising for it suggested that one could begin "from nothing," or contrariwise, begin anywhere.[22]

Rightly or wrongly Kierkegaard contrues the metaphysical concepts of his day to be primarily an attempt to unite what should otherwise be separated. Thus the gap between a cognitive truth and a moral imperative could only be bridged if there were both a disinterested perspective and at least one common concept. Or, one might suggest a third concept including the meanings of both of these others. The modern philosophy, as he understood it, claimed to occupy such a disinterested standpoint, which would include both, but without abatement of the peculiarities of each. Kierkegaard therefore stressed

19. Dru, *Journals*, 22, 15 (*Papirer* I A, 75). Note too the excellent discussions of Kierkegaard as a twenty-one and twenty-two year old on the status of dogmatics in *Papirer* I A.

20. Reported in "*Filosofien og Livet*" by Høffding, *Mindre Arbejder*, II:1. Also noted in *Glimpses and Impressions of Kierkegaard*, edited and translated by T. Croxall.

21. *Efterladte Papirer*, I:405. Kierkegaard wonders here about the distinction between life-wisdom and religiosity. By 1843 he was criticizing Munster for presenting scholarly views as if they were the means to religiousness.

22. See Kierkegaard's papers from March, 1844, which include an interesting "Post-Scriptum" to *Either/Or* in which this metaphysical pose is discussed.

this erstwhile "disinterestedness" of the erstwhile metaphysical standpoint because without disinterestedness and objectivity there could be no cognition.[23]

But the interesting point here is that Kierkegaard acknowledges such a disinterested standpoint, but he denies that there is any new concept that engages and which includes the others. Such concepts as there are in imperative language and descriptive accounts remain as they are—they do not transmute.[24] But metaphysics tries to do more than a logic does; it invents some new concepts that supposedly refer to a level of reality not even adumbrated in other concepts. Kierkegaard is convinced that this reality is a hoax, an invention and not a discovery. But the trick is a subtle one, for it is done by claiming that the concepts of otherwise different domains themselves transmute into metaphysical concepts which refer to the whole, the absolute, the totality, and not, simply, to the parts (as other concepts clearly do). Kierkegaard thinks one can be a student of concepts, but he denies that the concepts "move" or that there is transition in logic.[25] The transmutation of concepts is not observed at all; instead, Kierkegaard thinks that the whole idea is a preposterous illogical mishmash. He eschews this view of "dialectical" altogether. Metaphysics proposes to disclose not only internal conceptual relations between differing bodies of discourse, but that these concepts point assumedly to "objective" and ontological relations. The metaphysicians ostensibly discover them and do not make them. Following Hegel, the metaphysicians of Kierkegaard's day professed to discover these in history itself. So they lauded the "eye for history," beginning with China and Persia.

In brief, Kierkegaard believes that there are ways to describe relations between concepts. But a concept is rooted in a kind of behavior and life, and there it, of course, changes continually. However, this is perhaps a confusing way to describe a concept, for it makes it look as though it were then a mental thing. Instead let us say that concepts are meaning-complexes which are identified and described in a

23. *Concept of Dread*, 14–17, and especially the note on 16–17. See also *Postscript*, 122.

24. Note the perceptive section on Hegel and the method associated with his philosophy in Kierkegaard's papers for 1842, *Efterladte Papirer*, vol. I, 329–33.

25. "... a sheer confusion of logical science," *Postscript*, 99. Also, 306. Kierkegaard is a formalist on logical questions, denying, therefore, an ontological logic.

Kierkegaard and Metaphysics

variety of ways in our common life. The point that must be remembered is that they can be isolated and studied in abstraction from the context in which they are first constituted. Kierkegaard thought that this study was typically logical, if not philosophical. But Hegel made concepts in this new context, the logician's context, also subject to transition, as if mutual confrontation of concepts produced another concept. Kierkegaard finds this to be a mistake in fact about concepts. Concepts in a logician's context are static. So, too, the reference of a concept is not given with the concept. Kierkegaard rightfully points out that there are qualitative differences between concepts in the logician's discourse and the concepts that are used when we encounter the problems of daily life. To have elided these differences is the bane of that kind of metaphysics which claims to rest upon an ontological logic.

III

But Kierkegaard has also something to say about the attempt to make metaphysics the science of existence. There is certainly nothing in his pages to suggest that he denigrates descriptive sciences or the commonsense view that the sciences are about the real world. Neither does he categorically deny the possibility of putting together the fruits of empirical research and inquiring about the generic characteristics of what is. He does have misgivings about the usefulness of such a study and also about the multiple ways of doing it in the first place; but his major misgivings are not these. He is concerned rather with attempts to construe existence under some concepts that will be peculiarly existential and metaphysical. Kierkegaard says flatly: "The only thing-in-itself which cannot be thought is existence, and this does not come within the province of thought to think."[26] Again, "the attempt to infer existence from thought is thus a contradiction. For thought takes existence away from the real and thinks it by abrogating its actuality, by translating it into the sphere of the possible."[27]

Just what does he mean? One more brief quotation might be a clue. He says:

26. *Postscript*, 292.
27. Ibid., 281.

> That the content of my thought exists in the conceptual sense needs no proof, or needs no argument to prove it, since it is proved by doing it. But as soon as I proceed to impose a teleology upon any thought, and bring it into relation with something else, interest begins to play a role in the matter.[28]

Therefore, we can say that the ideal exists for thought; it is in Kierkegaard's language "a possible." But the real also exists for thought, for our thinking can only address the real by translating reals into possibles. In more formidable language, the ideal and the real do not differ in any way that concepts can mark. They are, then, the same in essence. They do differ in existence, but this difference is marked by the presence of passion and interest. Kierkegaard argues that the difference between the essence, or the "what" of a thing, and its existence, or "that" it is, is not to be marked by metaphysical concepts.

Perhaps we can illustrate the issue this way. If someone says: "Moses did not exist," it is tempting to think that there is a single and crucial meaning intended. So philosophers might want to say that "exist" and "not exist" mark the difference (no matter who or what you are talking about) between "being" and "non-being," or "a fact" and "no fact." But this is Kierkegaard's point, namely, that existence is not finally something in and by itself to think. Instead the expression about Moses means various things:

> It may mean: the Israelites did not have a "single" leader when they withdrew from Egypt—or; their leader was not called Moses—or; there cannot have been anyone who accomplished all that the Bible relates of Moses—or; etc., etc. We may say, following Russell: the name "Moses" can be defined by means of various descriptions. For example, as "the man who led the Israelites through the wilderness," "the man who lived at that time and place and was then called 'Moses,'" . . . And according as we assume one definition or another the proposition "Moses did not exist" acquires a different sense, and so does every other proposition about Moses . . .[29]

And "exist" or "does not exist" means something different, too, depending upon what Moses means. Therefore, the seductive notion, productive of so much philosophical inquiry, that existence must

---

28. Ibid., 283. Also note the previous chapter.
29. Wittgenstein, *Philosophical Investigations*, 36–37.

be uniquely understood in metaphysical concepts, becomes rather empty. So, Kierkegaard quite empties the claim of metaphysics to be a science of existence by showing that there is nothing residual or fundamental once one has used other interest-laden language to say what one means. Here Wittgenstein and Kierkegaard are much alike.

Here his ruling is again a matter of seeing, but not a matter of seeing anything metaphysical or looking at reality instead of the concepts of reality. On the contrary, here it is a matter of watching closely how concepts work. It is his contention that existence has no concepts. Instead it is a category in philosophical and ordinary speech, for it tells us only what condition or state a thing is in. Otherwise, it is a word that conveys no information, and is often "ethically deceitful and metaphysically unclear."[30]

Another way to put this is simpler. Kierkegaard discovers that there is no bare existent to which thought comes. He denies altogether that there is an uninterpreted being, beneath and below, all the rest of our predicates or the subject of all predications. Neither is he convinced that there is the brute and bare fact which a metaphysical dialectic can discover by stripping away all the other predicative language. Kierkegaard's quarrel is with such concepts as "being" and "brute fact." Like "reality" and the "*ding-an-sich*," these terms suppose that there is a final and ultimate analysis. Kierkegaard finds these to be only empty concepts, without any reference or function whatsoever. Such words as "fact," "reality," and even "being" do mean something but only in respective contexts. In the sciences, it is often true that the real is the external, the objects and events.[31] Here a teleology (an interest in the thinker) has brought something into relation with the thought—and we have the concepts "ideal" and "real" already working. So it is, too, in ethical, religious, and aesthetic thinking. But any time a speculative interest comes into play and looks for the reality in all these reals, the existent in all uses of existence, the brute and uninterpreted fact within the facts, there is a contradiction.[32]

Why contradiction? The word seems too strong. Kierkegaard means a contradiction in the strong sense, for nothing whatever is

---

30. *Postscript*, 283.

31. Ibid., 288. Note too his remark that "the systematic idea is the identity of subject and object, the unity of thought and being," ibid., 112.

32. Ibid., 281.

said when reality *qua* reality is made a philosophical concept. His point is that thoughts and precepts (idealities) are used referringly. The referring is done by persons, not by thoughts.[33] The teleology or intentionality of thoughts is "imposed from without" and belongs to disposed thinkers. Therefore "real" means something to an astronomer who discovers a "real" star, to a mathematician arguing about "real" numbers, to a man who is worried whether he is hallucinating or hearing "real" voices, and to a man who is wrestling with the issue whether there is a "real" God or only an *idée fixe*. But in these cases, there is no problem, for the real is that upon which one affixes his interest and nothing more need be said. So, too, it is with existence in Wittgenstein's example. To attempt to say more, by inferring existence from the thought of reality, makes the real itself an ideality (a possible) for which a referent has to be found. This is a contradiction, for it involves shifting "real" from being an object of interest (that which one thinks about in this context or that) to being an ideality whose reference is in doubt.[34] Kierkegaard thinks that this is a serious logical breach, productive only of nonsense.

One always reasons from existence, from the fact, from the being of something, not toward existence, the facticity and being of something.[35] So, one does not prove that there is a man and that he did great deeds, but that an existing man, of a certain description, did great deeds. One does not prove that a stone exists, but that some existing thing is a stone.[36] Therefore it is a breach of logical proprieties to make a philosophical problem of reality except in the somewhat paltry sense of showing by analysis why there is no way of showing this.

The matter of philosophical doubt arises, as we argued in the previous chapter, only when one forgets the proper employment of

33. "... who is it again who strings them all together on the systematic thread? Is he a human being, or is he speculative philosophy in the abstract?" *Postscript*, 109.

34. Note the discussion of Schelling and intuitions. Kierkegaard thinks that Schelling only admits the severity of the problem and little more. Cf. Karl Jaspers' "Was Philosophie für Schelling Bedeutet" in *Schelling: Grösse und Verhängnis* in which he argues that psychological factors, such as "will," "leap," etc., are more important than intuition by which to resolve doubts.

35. *Fragments*, 31–33.

36. In addition to the *Fragments*, note the *Postscript*, 268 footnote. Also see *Stages on Life's Way*, 126.

"real" or "exists" in various kinds of discourse.[37] The small uses are quite sufficient. The cure, we have noted, is not more thought, for that is what is being doubted. To suggest that one must look at all of history is an invitation to vagueness. Kierkegaard proposes that a new kind of personal intensity is the answer, and yet, it is no answer. For the resolution is not effected on paper. Philosophical perplexities, according to Kierkegaard, are not simply noted in confusion generated by language. They are infinitely more complex, often being rooted in wayward dispositions as well as the misuse of language and concepts. Philosophical problems, especially metaphysical ones, are often due to a radical disorientation of a man. He has forgotten who he is and what the world is. Furthermore, there might well be a dislocation of passion. He is concerned, but about the wrong thing and in the wrong place. The person must act, must believe, must be a human person, acknowledging his fate with other persons and affirming the anthropomorphic uses of thinking. Many of these confounding intellectual issues are not intellectual at all. The point that Kierkegaard wishes to establish is the right of a person to reflect also within his passionate interests and concerns and not always in such a way as to escape them.[38] When he does escape them, he tries to make disinterested reflection do more than it can. Language and thought then break with the strain.

But there is still a third way in which Kierkegaard understands the contemporary metaphysics. He discovers metaphysicians who are looking for a unity of the special sciences. A common ground is sought, or common principles, or a common referent. Again he sees the confusions abounding:

> The notion that every scientific problem within the great field embraced by science has its definite place, its measure and its bounds ... is not merely a *pium desiderium* ... but it is also in the interests of every more highly specialized deliberation, which by forgetting where its home properly is, forgets at the

---

37. Note the interesting discussion of Schelling in Kierkegaard's pages: *Postscript*, 96 and 296. Also see his papers, especially for 1842. Another group of references that concerns Descartes and doubt were engendered by a lecture, heard in 1837. See *Papirer* II A, 35 (*JP* 5, 5208; *KJN* 1, AA:25). Also see ibid., IV C, 12–14, which is relevant too.

38. This is the point made about "Subjective Thinkers" in *Postscript*, *passim*. Note too *Concept of Dread*, 10.

same time itself, a thought which the very language I use with its striking ambiguity expresses; it becomes another thing, and attains a dubious perfectibility by being able to become anything at all.[39]

Here we note that the metaphysical unities invariably make one system out of all the branches of learning, including morals and theology. Everything is said to relate, maybe in diverse ways, to the world or the cosmos, and to reality. Metaphysics becomes the science of this common referent, dimly adumbrated in the special cases. In dozens of specific cases Kierkegaard has protested this notion of a common referent. His criticism is that the concepts which point to the reals do not point beyond themselves to something else. The concepts do not refer or mean each other. The view that all of them must be internally related or that they refer to, or at least imply, each other he finds to be an outright imposition upon them. Here his aim is to show that this is a dogma not sustained at all by detailed studies of the concepts within the respective fields.

Kierkegaard's particular example is the conceptual structure of theological dogmatics which he describes in *The Concept of Dread*. The endeavor has been made with the help of metaphysics to demonstrate an identity between the concept of sin in Christian dogmatics, and the "negative" in logic. Besides particular reservations regarding the latter, Kierkegaard takes pains with this supposed unity. He denies that the two concepts overlap or mean a third reality or concept. He denies, for example, that motion "described in physics is the same as the transition" from premise to conclusion. He describes such science as immanent, meaning that the language of a science, any science, is logically interdependent. To insist that a science also be the demonstration of a reality in which the overlap obtains or that it include the transcendent principles upon which the immanental description rests—these are the errors of metaphysics.

Ethical science does not produce the sense of obligation, it only describes it. By doing more than describing it, for example, seeking to show that it is an instance of something else, and then deducing it, is to make the concept ambiguous. As Kierkegaard read Hegel, the concept "movement" was necessary to logic, but then Hegel went on

---

39. *Concept of Dread*, 9. Note the confusion alluded to in the *Postscript* when a scientist confusedly handles the ethical with scientific concepts, 136.

to say that logical movement enabled one to construe physical motion (*kinesis*), the sense of sin, the concept of obligation, the concept of God as divine mover and creator, and even the relation between the ugly (the negative) and the beautiful. The mediation and reconciliation of these various concepts was more than logical and scientific. It was said to be ontological, trans-scientific, and trans-logical. The odd mediation in which this was done was quite beyond Kierkegaard's comprehension. He goes even further: all of such elaborate conceptual shifts were only done by philosophers and were a kind of elaborate legerdemain. It comes of pretending that one can think *sub specie eternitatis*, and, again, the only cure is to remember that one is not all-knowing; one is not God or the Absolute.[40]

IV

Kierkegaard's literature is highly aristocratic. It supposes a kind of sophistication in his reader. For one thing, he never bothers to instruct on the rudiments of metaphysics, logic, or any other technical subject. He supposes an acquaintance with Plato, Aristotle, Descartes, Kant, Hegel, the Biblical writers, and others too. But there is another kind of sophistication that he takes for granted that is a little more subtle. He invariably assumes that his reader also suffers from all kinds of large intellectual problems. Therefore, he never tells the reader what they are; instead, he starts from the issue, taking for granted that the reader already has it. Nowhere is this clearer than on metaphysical questions.

It is a commonplace among writers to take such sophistication to be testimony to the genuineness of the problem. If everyone has it, then it does not seem likely that one can explain away the problem. By rights, one must resolve the problem. If everyone is hungry, then we must have food; and if everybody is looking for reality, then we must surely find it. It seems absurd, then, to spend time analyzing the concepts or the language. But Kierkegaard admits at once that metaphysical problems are widespread and are not just a consequence of bad teaching and also that they do not admit of resolution. They are

---

40. Again see *Concept of Dread*, passim; Dru, *Journals*, 497 (*Papirer* V A 73), 582 (*Papirer* VII A 80), 1323 (*Papirer* XI1 A 180), 1377, etc; *Sickness Unto Death*, 68–69, 126ff.; *Repetition*, 125ff.; *Either/Or*, especially II:103ff. and 269ff.

rooted in a condition not simply of language but also involving the passions, along with language, conceptual confusions and illogicality.

There is a fundamental criticism of metaphysics to be made. But it is important to mark Kierkegaard's argument with great care. It is altogether too easy to bracket the Danish Socrates with earlier and later critics of metaphysics, with positivistic and linguistic analytic thinkers. Neither is he quite a fideist or a Kantian. There are striking agreements to be sure, e.g., the criticism of idealism, of the synthetic *a priori*, of the confusions in thinking that existence is a predicate, of hypostatization, of analogical reasoning and of an ontological logic. Kierkegaard remarks often upon the intentions of the metaphysicians and how serious they are. He responds to the pathos himself. He finds that interests in broadly what one might call the philosophy of life are what impel the metaphysicians too. He is reluctant to say that these issues are inherently absurd or childish. So, he does not quite move in the direction of logical positivism. Metaphysics does not have to be either the analysis of language or the science of reality. This for him is an illicit disjunction. As we shall indicate, the motives for metaphysics are terribly various. A man might be cured of metaphysical talk by a religious life or by a forthright ethical concern and the appropriate decision. Or he might see what science is and does and learn that there is way to use the word "real" in that context too. But often a roving and hovering pathos, not properly fed in this context or that, keeps the metaphysical urge alive. The notion that language analysis alone would resolve it for all he would think to be downright absurd.

Like many later philosophers who have reflected about these matters, Kierkegaard admits that absolutely disinterested thought would be thought about thought. It would ideally be a conceptual study, not quite a study of language alone.[41] The point is that disinterested reflection secures its disinterestedness by being about things that are not in existence. So against the metaphysicians he says that absolutely disinterested and pure thought is not about reality; it is, in fact, thought about other thoughts. Instead of the most disinterested reflection being most metaphysical, obviously and clearly a disclosure

---

41. But concepts for Kierkegaard are not necessarily about universals or *ens rationis*. He seems to have no single theory about what they are. But he discovers them in the Abraham story to be different than in certain Greek tragedies. Note *Fear and Trembling*.

of what is, and "is" in the sense of actuality, this kind of reflection is conceptual and about that which has intentional, not actual existence.[42] On the other hand, a concept seems to be an achievement in practices and ways of behaving, including the talking. Disinterested philosophy is the description of these concepts, not their use. That is a matter of passion and interest. Kierkegaard thinks that others, including poets, are sometimes disinterested too, but philosophers are students of the concepts. Here he seems similar to many moderns. Philosophical literature of the past does include category analysis too. In criticism of several abstract treatises by Adler, a Hegelian and a contemporary, Kierkegaard complains because he can find:

> . . . no new concept he has explained, no new categorical definition he has supplied, no old and established one he has refreshed by new dialectical sharpness.[43]

Thinkers can think and discuss the differences between imperatives and indicatives, essence and existence, and this science and that one. Most of what is defensible in metaphysics could be handled in less pretentious language. Granted all this, Kierkegaard is quick to say that no philosopher is absolved from formulating a theory of existence. But he also declares that when he formulates such a theory, his logical acumen is of negative significance only as it tells him what not to do; otherwise such a theory must also be an expression of interest.

Awareness of concepts offers no higher proofs, no wider synthetic truths, no ethical ultimates.[44] In respect to the reality issue, this kind of awareness remains abstract; it never bridges the gap between thought and existence. Kierkegaard's point is that metaphysicians speak as if conceptual analysis and even new concepts, e.g., a better logical scheme, will provide certainties for the way of life if the thought is arduous and persistent enough. Throughout he is skeptical of formal logical systems, but only when, effecting a transition into a more refined medium, they pretend to be saying the same thing. He delights in pointing out that while one thought implies another, no thought ever implies or entails an existent. This kind of abstract

---

42. See *De Omnibus Dubitandum Est*, passim.

43. *On Authority and the Individual*, 18.

44. E.g., note his reflections in response to his own question, "What is a category?" *Efterladte Papirer*, I:329.

knowledge, logic if one will, never produces the additional knowledge relating ideas to things. Even the negative certainty that one has no knowledge relating the contents of consciousness to existents does not overcome the "reality" doubt.[45]

All of this is by way of making one criticism. If a man proposes to argue that metaphysics achieves its unifying certainties by perfecting analytic techniques and new logical instruments, Kierkegaard is content to show that knowledge about knowledge is, in respect to the referents of knowledge, still skeptical. Whenever metaphysicians make claims, Kierkegaard finds that non-cognitive attitudes, emotions, wishes, desires, etc., have given reflection a new point of departure. He does not object to the latter but begs only to point out that this makes reality claims also an expression of the metaphysician and not simply a description of something objective.[46] "Reality" concepts occur then only where other than logical concerns prevail. This is why Kierkegaard argues that purely conceptual schemes ought properly to exclude all reality words and concepts.[47]

Most of the regnant metaphysical discourse is, consequently, a mixture of two kinds of language. Insofar as it proposes to speak about perennial issues of the philosophy of life, its language includes concepts molded also by human passion. If it speaks disinterestedly it becomes a descriptive discourse about concepts and not the use of them in the interest of feeding the need for a view and way of life. To make a system of reflection "metaphysical" and mean by "metaphysical" a disinterested study of sentences ". . . is all right, but it is not a system which embraces existence, for in that case the ethical must be included in it, and to abbreviate the ethical is to make a fool of it."[48] That would mean that most people would quickly lose interest. A single language that purports to be both "quantitative and qualitative" is logically impossible. This is so because what makes a concept or even a word descriptive or interest-laden, as the case might be, is often not simply the linguistic content, i.e., the other words by which it is surrounded, but "how" it is construed and used by the person.

45. Note the sections in the *Postscript* about Lessing, who is as negative as he is affirmative.

46. *Postscript*, 283-88.

47. Ibid., 99-107. Also, see *Either/Or*, II: 220-22. Cf., *Postscript*, 313.

48. *Stages*, 404.

Kierkegaard and Metaphysics

Therefore, Kierkegaard denies that words are tokens of concepts just because they are words. Metaphysics is difficult to analyze because it combines logical talents and terms with widely germane human concerns. After a while, a metaphysical treatise is neither poetry nor logic; instead it disguises the logical transitions in the concerns for reality, while the passional cares are diffused in what look like dialectical exercises. Criticism becomes almost pointless.[49]

In the papers for 1844, there is a lengthy "Polemic against Heiberg." Professor Heiberg, a leading metaphysician, had earlier reviewed Kierkegaard's *Repetition*, and Kierkegaard thought his review to be a major misunderstanding. So he writes a lengthy piece primarily to clarify his own mind, for despite the length and quality of his piece he never published it.[50] The issue is whether the concept of "repetition" is the same in the following instances: among the Greek philosophers who talked about cycles; in remembering as a form of knowledge; among natural phenomena where a law is discerned; in world history; and a host of other contexts as well. Kierkegaard has great sport with the issue, making it painfully clear that he finds the meanings to be quite different, even where a single word does service. There is repetition, but the point of his book is precisely to make clear how distinct the meaning is in the moral life where reintegration of a personality is the topic. And he charges that only confusion results when analogies are exploited. Thus, he quips about Heiberg's seeing in astronomical phenomena what others can only see in far more limited domains, but his intent is always the same, namely, to restore distinctions. So we read another entry among his papers that states his outlook quite well:

> The time of distinctions has passed. The system has overwhelmed that as well as so much else. Anyone who learnedly clings to a distinction in our time is deemed a fool . . . The time of distinctions is past, and the fruitless idea of the four

---

49. Kierkegaard criticizes Danish philosophy by saying that instead of beginning "without presuppositions," it begins "with this presupposition: that there are things in heaven and earth which no philosopher has explained." *Efterladte Papirer*, II:73.

50. The references in the text are all from *Efterladte Papirer*, II:17–61; the particular passages are: 21–22, 39–41, 47, 52, 58, etc.

world-historical monarchies has vanquished everything to a nothing...[51]

He even proposes a sketch about distinctions, their origin, history, and validity, which though formal, he contends is of persistent relevance; but his meditation on this theme ends with the dismal thought that one ought to begin with the young for the more sophisticated elders are misled by analogies. He concludes with a story of his barber whose free association makes his rambling conversation about as intelligible as the philosophers whose distinctions are always abrogating themselves and becoming something else. Responsible philosophy is only possible if one ends the gossipy generalizing and aims to make specific the meanings involved.

Therefore, Kierkegaard is not decrying metaphysics on quite the same grounds as most critics. For example, he is not, like Kant, invoking critical principles which permit a deduction of some categories but more for general metaphysics. On the other hand, he is not, despite his deep religious interests, comparing metaphysics invidiously with Christian dogmas or the Bible. He is not quite a fideist urging the adequacy of faith against rational inquiries about the structure of the world. Neither is he saying that all metaphysics is nonsense; for he admits to no single standard of meaning by which to be so declaratory. He does not have, like some positivists, a notion of "fact" that denigrates metaphysical assertions, nor does he invoke sense experience, a general notion of meaning, or a scheme of logical functions by which to adjudicate all truth claims.

What, then, do his criticisms involve? Two considerations tie together his reflections. One is his conviction that "reality" words and concepts are all achievement words. They are not names. They are instead concepts which are the ways in which interested and concerned men, concerned in a variety of discernible ways, have demarcated, described, referred to, handled, addressed, and even made their world. They are anthropomorphic words, but are not, therefore, casual, only subjective, or arbitrary. "Reality" words are "*inter-esse*." And interest means "to be between," and "to be a matter of concern." He notes, further, that the Greek skeptics perceived admirably "that they could

---

51. *Efterladte Papirer*, II:60–61. Compare a softened version of this entry in the preface to *Forord* (1844), 6–15.

annul doubt by changing interest into apathy."[52] Yet Kierkegaard's point about metaphysics is not made only in this context; for granted that interest produces both doubt and certainty, still metaphysics also founders upon interest.[53]

Kierkegaard's style complicates our research here considerably, for what he says about another bit of conceptual research could also be said about all of his concern with metaphysical categories and concepts. He says that his exposition is not . . .

> in a learned style, still less in a style so scientific that every cashier in our philosophical bank could say, "one, two, three." I choose to describe and illustrate psychologically and aesthetically. In the manner of the Greeks, I let the concept come forth in the individual, in the situation, wending its way out through a host of misunderstandings.[54]

Once this point is made, Kierkegaard draws the consequence, namely, that there is no disinterested metaphysics at all, unless one means by a disinterested metaphysics the inquiry into the most general and abstract categories. Then metaphysics is an expression both of an interest as well as an account of the way that the world is. Metaphysics then loses its scientific character and becomes as the title of the *Postscript* suggests, *uvidenskabelig*, unscientific.

Consequently, the concepts of truth, evidence, and meaning when construed relative to metaphysical views, also have a different logic. Metaphysical views are views of life and write in the large the dominant concerns of the individual. Metaphysics becomes an anthropomorphic discipline. The criticisms of metaphysics involve a criticism of the passions. Because these passional motivations have not been admitted by the metaphysicians whom Kierkegaard has read, he castigates them. They pretend to be doing it all disinterestedly.

The other gauge of metaphysical systems has to do with the adjudication of the chief terms. Here he adjudges most metaphysical terms to be artificial, not just abstract. Metaphysics lives by putting the meanings of several areas of discourse together and erecting ostensibly comprehensive and rich concepts which are then said to refer to reality. Already we have seen through several chapters the kinds of

---

52. *De Omnibus Dubitandum Est*, 153.
53. *Repetition*, 34.
54. *Efterladte Papirer* II 33.

criticisms that he proposes. Perhaps here Kierkegaard has some kinships with some existential philosophers. His technique is invariably to show how a concept works in ethics, in theology, in science, in psychological description, and then show how the absurdity of invoking comprehensive concepts, ostensibly gathering up all the rest of the meanings, becomes patent.

This, in philosophical terms, is what existentialism means for him. For the touchstone of all philosophical usage is the use of terms within a cosmos within which every man already has access. Here there are expressions already at work, for which there is specific warrant. Working from this base, Kierkegaard is prepared to propose that the term "real" already has a meaning, and that no elaborate bit of philosophizing is needed to credit the word. And the cure for bad abstract metaphysics is to get oneself oriented to a responsible use of "real" and "unreal" in a more limited context. This is not just a matter of words—it has to do with a way of life.

A kind of logic of terms is, then, at hand, once one begins to penetrate the actual practices and niceties of readily accessible languages, behavior, and judgments and their appropriate psychological dispositions. Before long, a whole series of spheres emerges, and these are not so much systems as they are congeries and groups of concepts and behavior. Here the "how" is as important as the "what," and therefore the logic of these terms is not determined by their reference alone but also by the interplay of aim and object, intention and world, and interest and events. Once these begin to emerge—and these are as we have already indicated the burden of his stages—the metaphysical terms are seen not to be higher and richer expressions, overarching all the rest, as is often claimed, but, by and large, confused amalgams, gratuitous and nonsensical.

Seeing that metaphysical terms are really empty is not always a matter of logical analysis. Kierkegaard knew that metaphysical concerns were pervasive and deep. He was certain that metaphysical systems were absurd, for the big words in metaphysical schemes do just about anything that the metaphysician wants them to do. Kierkegaard saw the oddness of competing systems of metaphysics and felt the incongruities very poignantly. But he never concluded that they were, therefore, simply a reflection of fallacious reasoning or a consequence of logical lapses. Metaphysical systems also get their importance from the fact that human beings are unwilling to take seriously their own lives. Reality becomes the evanescent goal, always evading them, because they are not oriented to the reality that they already have. Conceptually this means that the concept "real" already has a use, and one has to learn to give it greater play where it already has its proper function.

For this reason Kierkegaard points with justifiable pride to his *Either/Or* as a logical achievement. He might have said it equally for his entire literature. *Either/Or* describes a decisive qualitative disjunction, yet the book is the logical synthesis, not metaphysical, of the aesthetic and the ethical.

> My particular concern with the whole of *Either/Or* is: that it should be quite clear that the metaphysical significance at the bottom of the whole work leads everything back to the dilemma. The same thing is also at the bottom of the little philosophical essay: tautology is the highest form of thought; that is to say . . . if the principle of contradiction is true (and that is expressed in "either-or"), it is the scientific expression for mediation, and is the only unity in which it can be resolved, the only way in which the system is possible.[55]

As other notes make clear, though a philosopher can annul the principle of contradiction and transcend it by thinking the contradiction in "a higher unity which exists for thought,"[56] this unity is not metaphysical and has no moral consequence. It is only logical, i.e., a unity of concepts and not a unity of reals. The task for every man is more than logical. It involves making a unity out of one's life. When he does this, another use of "real" comes into one's working vocabulary. And this is what *Either/Or* proposes for the reader. This is when abstract concepts of "real" become truly ludicrous, and metaphysical systems no longer delude one into thinking that there is a high road to reality.

V

If it is remembered that Kierkegaard's authorship includes two levels, the passionate declarative literature, and the dispassionate analytic,

---

55. *Journal*, 405.
56. *Either/Or*, II:144.

admittedly fragmentary kind, we must still ask ourselves whether and how anything metaphysical can be written. Kierkegaard was not quick to jump to conclusions. He refused to say that every bit of metaphysics was simply nonsensical. Almost every one of his books shows him carefully gleaning from the great philosophers. Even though he was not an historical scholar, he still read a great deal, and besides, seemed to need rather less exposure than most before he understood an argument and another author.

One must note, therefore, almost in passing, that with his admissions of the clumsiness of metaphysics, the downright mistakes, and the conceptual blunders, there is still something to be said for metaphysics as an interest-laden discipline. That this can be done by the talented and also with the advantages of precise logical tools he never denied. He proposes a corrective, but it is not an easy one to effect. Metaphysics has to be written and understood, remembering the peculiarities of our common life. Some facts are too plain not to be taken seriously, and it is to these that Kierkegaard draws our attention.

It is a mistake to omit the peculiarities of dynamically oriented aesthetes when thinking about his aesthetic concepts. It is a serious error to entertain ethical matters under intellectual rubrics and omit altogether the dispositions of an ethical man; so, too, it is a peculiar kind of fault to forget the peculiarities of Jesus' life and character in writing about the concept of God that his teachings provide. And so it is, too, with one's own concepts and scheme of life. When metaphysics gets launched by omitting subjectivity altogether, it also omits what is absolutely crucial.

Accordingly, Kierkegaard conceives of metaphysical views fitting the needs of our common subjectivity. His multiform literature gives us at once several ways that subjects have of addressing their need for a view and plan for the future. Also, he has made his case in his literature for philosophy fitting peculiarly the propositions of subjectivity. It will be argued in the next chapter that Kierkegaard saw that the terms "real" and "reality" were not subjective and promiscuous, but that they were systematically ambiguous. This, however, is the burden of our continuing story.

CHAPTER 10

Kierkegaard and the Nature of Philosophy

A TWENTIETH-CENTURY READER of the Kierkegaardian literature might, all too quickly to be sure, assume that the numerous diatribes against philosophy, and especially metaphysics, mean a total disparagement of the philosophical enterprise and a denial of the cognitive worth of all metaphysical claims. This is not quite the case with Kierkegaard however. As was noted in the previous chapter, the metaphysical claims of Hegel as well as other objective idealists were examined by the Danish thinker and believed to be either essays in a logical vein, i.e., about the logical structure in other knowledge claims—this if these claims were as pure and objective as Hegel said—or, an expression of some kind of subjectivity and, hence, not quite as pure as Hegel said, at least not if these claims were about actual existence as their author said that they were.

This dichotomous arraignment of the contemporary philosophies, especially the systematic historical metaphysics, is not the final position Kierkegaard takes, however. With a remarkable catholicity and flexibility he turns to another set of considerations by which he propounds a kind of metaphysics and, also, proposes a distinctive view of philosophy and its function.

It must be said at this point though, that with some rather obvious exceptions, most of what is here to be argued is not so much a direct reconstruction of Kierkegaard's texts as it is an interpretation based, it is urged, on rather long exposure to Kierkegaard's texts and their argument.

I

Philosophy is for Kierkegaard neither logical analysis nor a system of actual existence, metaphysics.[1] He refuses, while criticizing the philosophers of the day for attempting the latter, to say that, therefore, they can and ought to do only the former. In principle, and in virtue of logical rules, Kierkegaard does not believe that actual existence can be logically abridged. All kinds of considerations enter into his discussion here. Most of them have been amply dealt with already in numerous secondary works.[2] But to say this much does not mean that there is no metaphysics or no philosophical knowledge. Even to refine the argument and to say that there is no logically validated and *a priori* awareness of matters of fact, no *a priori* synthetic knowledge, is not to say there may not still be the possibility of metaphysics.

In this respect, then, Kierkegaard is not quite the logical analyst, or positivist or skeptic that he has been described as being.[3] He is much too complex to be so easily labeled. Nor is he exclusively protesting, as Étienne Gilson insists, the rights of a lived existence to a greater authenticity than a described existence.[4] While he is certainly saying this much, he is making his philosophy a repetition of this claim. Contrary to what has been so often argued, Kierkegaard admits a significance to reflection about actual and lived existence. That it may be an indirect significance, not immediately and cumulatively adding reality to personality as the magician adds the rabbit to the empty hat—this, of course, Kierkegaard also says. This is not, nonetheless, to deny all relevance to reflection, nor to deny that abstract thought can be true.[5]

---

1. The guiding theme of all of his criticism of Hegel is that "a system of existence is not possible." *Postscript*, 107–13.

2. Swenson, op. cit.; Hirsch, op. cit., vol. II again; Diem, *Die Existenzdialektik von Sören Kierkegaard*, especially 13–47.

3. Note Swenson, "The Anti-Intellectualism of Søren Kierkegaard," op. cit., 146ff. Shestov, *Kierkegaard et la Philosophie Existentielle*, chapters 9, 13, 20; Wahl, *Études Kierkegaardiennes*, "La Lutte contre toute philosophie" and relevant notes; Gilson, *Being and Some Philosophers*, 142–53. Weiland in *Humanitas Christianitas* surveys a considerable literature on this question, cf. 11–34 and notes 34–44.

4. Gilson, *Being and Some Philosophers*.

5. Note the analyses of categories in the *Papirer* IV C, 63 (JP 2, 1595) and 97 (JP 5, 5601) and references to Aristotle and Trendelenburg, *passim*.

Kierkegaard and the Nature of Philosophy

No philosopher (and perhaps no reflective man) can be absolved *qua* philosopher from the responsibility of formulating a theory of existence. This seems to be Kierkegaard's axiom. His own stages, his elaborate pseudonymity-devices, his rich use of pathos and dialectic together, were endeavors in this direction. His negative point, as we have previously noted, was that some of the theories of existence already extant, such as Hegel's, Fichte's, Schelling's, and those of others, were intellectually distinguished, logically ordered, but were still like that sign in the shop window, reading: PRESSING DONE HERE. But when you bring your clothes to be pressed you discover that the sign is for sale. So too is it with what the philosophers say about reality.[6] Somehow, unless the use of reflection and language are carefully calculated, the very features of actual existence which beg the theory, are omitted from theoretical description. It is Kierkegaard's endeavor to calculate his literature, to stress its "how," the appropriate mode of reading and appropriation, so the "*inter-esse*" character of reality will not be missed in the reading. But it must not be forgotten that philosophical works do this, his philosophical works, and that those writings can correctly be said to be existential philosophy.

This is to assert that Kierkegaard, with Socrates, Trendelenburg, and perhaps Hamann, roots philosophy in the common sense of mankind.[7] Furthermore, the substantial content of philosophy is this same common sense. Kierkegaard believes that there are essential anthropomorphic attitudes incumbent upon every man, when he faces the limits and contingencies of actual existence. Death, a sense of guilt, concern about the future, love for another, what to do next, etc., are of universal concern and interest. To ask philosophy to abstract from these is to emasculate it of its wide humane concerns.

To do as modern philosophers have, namely, refuse to address themselves at all to reality-questions, is for Kierkegaard the consequent of the illicit disjunction which says that philosophy must be

---

6. *Either/Or*, I: 25–26.

7. When Kierkegaard's author, Johannes, says: "The only comfort I have is Socrates," this is very close to being Kierkegaard's confession of intellectual dependence. *Postscript*, 144. Note *Søren Kierkegaards Opfattelse af Sokrates* by J. Himmelstrup for a detailed discussion and Martin Thust's reconstruction of Kierkegaard's dependence upon Socrates in *Sören Kierkegaard, Der Dichter des Religiösen* which mistakenly claims to be part of the "Foundation of His System of Subjectivity," 150–71.

either the analysis of language or the grossest kind of subjectivity, or what philosophers now call metaphysics. Kierkegaard suggests, instead, that philosophers can both express common sense and analyze it. The great philosophies can be understood to be comprehensive representations or commonsense attitudes, of those anthromorphic aspects of behavior which are inescapable. If they are escapable, and they seem in a restricted sense to be so, the result is psychologically no concern about actual existence, a passionless existence that Kierkegaard believed to be the worst of living damnations or, logically and philosophically, no theory of existence at all. Or, what is worse, they may be theories of existence which actually omit under another and more elaborate pretext everything that is actual.[8]

Common sense is a kind of centripetal power in human life. It is the point of mediation between the centrifugal energies of a person's existence, his skills and talents and knowledge. It is also the meeting point between the centrifugal energies given expression by different individuals. Kierkegaard is not writing out a doctrine about common sense, showing its advantages over science or scholarship. But he is intent upon showing that the most fundamental questions of human existence are not solved by philosophy. Every man decides to believe, to become, to be, to live rather than die, not because he is well instructed—for who can teach him—but rather because of attitudes which somehow fit the actuality of existence and which are not produced by the theory but to which a theory of existence can only give expression.[9]

Common sense is that in virtue of which men accept or reject supposed existences. Although Kierkegaard too was aware of the powerful monistic motives inherent in all ambitious thinkers, he found few grounds for rejecting the rock of offense, the dualistic orientation, of common sense. Any system of reality which construes the world and men, and daily strife and woe, as the appearance of something else, even God, is inventing another distinction, that of reality and appearance, as a substitute for the commonsense distinc-

---

8. Geismar, *Die Philosophie Hegels*, passim.

9. All that Kierkegaard says, with Lessing, about "the leap" is another way of describing the "transcendence" of common sense. The leap is subject to a qualitative dialectic and, therefore, has nothing to do with induction. Cf. *Postscript*, 86–97. This is a relevant consideration also to what follows in this text.

tions.¹⁰ The humor of all this lies in the assumption that philosophy provides proofs for the learned where the ignorant can only believe.¹¹ But Kierkegaard finds a flaw in this, for there are no proofs of actual existence, no proofs, for that matter, about the actuality of any kind of existent.¹² Philosophy, adroitly pursued, then discloses the limits of reflection by a process of reflection and unites the learned man and ignorant man in the need of affirming actual existence in virtue of something they have in common, not in virtue of that which otherwise distinguishes them. Where the ordinary man believes, the philosopher, like Socrates, knows he must believe and then believes. There is no transition from reflection to an ethical decision except by a breach of continuity, by a leap, which is the same for all men.¹³

Furthermore, any body of discourse that gives a reflective embodiment to such beliefs, with due attention being paid to all the critical and systematic activities and rules incident to reflection, is metaphysics.¹⁴ Metaphysics is that reflection in virtue of which common sense becomes illumined. To use Kant's suggestion, without metaphysics, common sense is blind; without common sense, metaphysics is empty. It is in this somewhat limited sense, then, that Kierkegaard is a commonsense philosopher.

If one reads Kierkegaard's writings, the conclusion that they represent a powerful and full-bodied anthropomorphism is inescapable. But, instead of apologizing for this, Kierkegaard is proud to acknowledge the fact. He refuses to be apologetic for being human nor is he ashamed to admit the belief that what is deepest in human nature and human life is also the key to the mystery of the cosmos. His point is that philosophical corrections of anthropomorphism cannot omit

---

10. Iljin, op. cit., 181. And Hegel's *Encyclopedia* is replete with contempt for "*zufällige Existenz*," contingent existence.

11. *Philosophical Fragments*, chapter 4.

12. *Papirer* V A, 7 (JP 2, 1334) and V A, 42 (JP 2, 1336). *Fragments*, 31, and *Postscript*, 485. Again note the remarks about the leap, the transition, etc. Another passage about these matters is in *Either/Or*, I:195.

13. *Postscript*, 306, 92–93, 262—all entries being characterizations of the leap.

14. Note, *Papirer* IV B, 120. Part of this selection is translated by Lowrie and quoted in the introduction to his translation of *Repetition*, xxvii ff. Note too *Concept of Dread*, first chapter and notes.

everything anthropomorphic or nothing human will remain.[15] And if this is an admission of an objective uncertainty on fundamental matters, well this is to say what Kierkegaard everywhere admits.

Kierkegaard protests the special metaphysical results of the idealistic philosophies, he decries the invalidity of the specific forms of reasoning within some kinds of metaphysics, but nowhere is he repudiating either the expression of metaphysical belief or the analysis of those beliefs. Properly speaking, when men believe, they transcend the contents of their own consciousness; they avow the existent of objectivities, the world, laws, God, what have you. Some men might call these acts of belief, "metaphysical" acts. But Kierkegaard restricts the term somehow. It would seem that the science of metaphysics is not so much the expression of the belief, as it is the analysis and conceptualization and articulation of that belief.

II

A second consideration, relevant to Kierkegaard's view of philosophy, concerns a feature of common sense. Against the major philosophical traditions perhaps, Kierkegaard proposes that the universal man is rooted in human subjectivity, not in objectivity. It is by way of a richer exploration of the passional life, one's individuality and idiosyncratic self, that the universal man and attendant norms come into view.[16] Unlike Kant and Hegel, both of whom abstracted from the self of inclination and subjectivity in order to find the categorical imperative and the ordering features of the personality, Kierkegaard plunges more deeply into these. The essence of morality is the synthesis of inclination and obligation and the essence of rational reflection is the synthesis of belief and logicality. Common sense is a denominating term. It serves to focus attention upon the subjectivity essential to human existence and in virtue of which both thought and deeds become teleological.

---

15. This is why he says that it is in the attempt to have a disinterested theory of reality that the philosopher-metaphysician founders. See here also the account of Diogenes walking back and forth, thus refuting the Eleatics' denial of motion. *Repetition*, 3ff.

16. *Either/Or*, II:178ff.

No decisions are ever made in virtue of reflection but always in virtue of what reflection presupposes. The question has often been raised as to whether these personal attitudes thus presupposed are expressions of habits, of customs, or of superficial inclinations. Kierkegaard is not denying the possibility of the latter being true in some instances. But his authorship is built around the view that actual existence is like a theatre in which everyone is a subject and player. The give-and-take is a process that has its crises. It is an existential dialectic, an examination in which we cannot cheat, in which we do not talk and can only be what we are. This is the subject's self-critical process, wherein he can evoke for himself his commitment. To this teleological process there is a minimal intellective response. But it only appears meager because it seems so repetitive, so casual, so unstudied. Kierkegaard insists that the participation in this kind of earnest existing means the erasure of human differences and the discovery of one's eternal identity and true and ideal selfhood.[17]

Already it is clear that Kierkegaard's philosophy is a denial of the supposed meagerness of common sense and ordinary subjectivity. Ordinary human consciousness, or at least what older philosophies called consciousness, is here being restored to a place of dignity and worth. For, unlike Hegel and other nineteenth- and twentieth-century intellectuals, Kierkegaard finds common sense neither thoughtless nor objectively determined.

Briefly, I wish to sketch a kind of interpretation of Kierkegaard's views on the structure and function of common sense in cognitive matters. For against the empiricists and especially Hume, Kierkegaard presses an analysis of the minimal epistemic relations which always includes belief or doubt, and never excludes them. It is important, not simply to read what Kierkegaard said, but also to reflect upon what he did not say, what he omitted, and why he omits it. He does not describe human consciousness in terms of ideas. Instead, human consciousness is a teleological process in which ideas are not properly described by analogy with physical objects at all. Ideas are occurrences within an individual's life history; they are temporal existents and have a consequent particularity, but above all, they refer to, or mean,

---

17. The essay by Prof. Swenson, "Editor's Introduction," to Geismar, *Lectures* is an interpretation to which I am here indebted.

objects and relations, and do not mean themselves. This intentional and purposeful character is initially a part of any idea. Kierkegaard finds most philosophies inaccurate and too abstract on this point.

Ideas are not mechanical and mental reproductions of physical objects. Their "of-ness" and "about-ness" is not external and adventitious, or, at least, not exclusively so. The psychological idea, described in the language of common sense is "of" and "about," in virtue of the irreducible teleological trait of every man's conscious life. Kierkegaard argues that one can abstract the teleology out of the process if one wishes. If one does so, then one submits the idea to a logical analysis and then either doubt or belief is logically possible. The relation between the idea and thing is neither an idea nor a thing; the relation is only constituted when the teleological subject is brought back, only when the actual existence of the thinker is allowed.[18] This is the "ordinary" belief of which the author of the *Fragments* speaks. But this kind of belief is not an expression of learning. Although it may take learning, or at least logical acuity to isolate an idea from its intended object, it does not take learning to relate ideas to things.

But, even this mode of speech violates Kierkegaard's views of the matter. For Kierkegaard does not understand thinking and knowledge as something to be done between ideas, themselves mechanical reproductions of things, as perhaps John Locke does, but, rather, that the representative function and teleological characteristic of thought are immanent to the most simple of epistemic relations. Abstract thinking, which omits the subject processes of the thinker, thinks the idea as a logical object; but concrete thinking grasps the world *via* an idea.[19]

Kierkegaard's thesis is that no kind of science, epistemological or psychological, ever corrects this kind of commonsense assertion. Neither does logic. For all the laws and formulations of any kind of science are subject to this same kind of analysis. Whenever an idea, or for that matter a verbal utterance, is offered as explanation or knowledge of something, somewhere there is a conscious state, perhaps both in the speaker and in the listener, in virtue of which

---

18. *Fragments*, "Interlude," 58–73. Note remarks on "wonder" and the epistemological function that such a subjective response has; see 66.

19. Again, *Papirer* IV B, 120 and Lowrie's pages in *Repetition*, especially 29. *Either/Or*, I:148, makes the same point.

a thing is being intended which need not be, and rarely is, identical with the process or state which intends it. This conscious state cannot be certified in advance. On the other hand, to discover this feature of consciousness is to find an irreducible trait of human life, one which cannot be translated into non-teleological terms. This is the source of transcendence, of novelty, of creativity, and of human greatness.

Commonsense belief may well be a habit sustained by patterns of thought and language. But Kierkegaard's claim is that these patterns are not casual or fortuitous. They are testimony to the very structure of actual existence and of the relations, ontological if one so chooses, between thought and things. Commonsense beliefs are an accommodation to actual existence. This is why common sense is the test of philosophy rather than philosophy being the test of common sense.

Throughout the Kierkegaardian literature there runs a criticism of any philosophy that assumes a single explanatory principle of all that is. Against Hegel Kierkegaard protests the use of logical and teleological explanation of the entirety of history and the cosmos. Without elucidating the non-objective leap by which he had construed historical events as logical consequents, Hegel looked ridiculous. Claiming the objectivity of a teleological factor in history, Hegel assured his readers that it was the objectivity of his reflection which made the apprehension of this teleology possible. But the other extreme is surely as repellent too. Kierkegaard anticipates the day when everything will be statistics, and we may say for him, when no teleological explanation will be given for anything, including ethical behavior and acts of thought. His way is again the *via media*: on one side, he allows the possibility of mechanical and causal explanations, but he insists just as earnestly that teleological explanations are complementary and that they are not shorthand or metaphorical speech for non-teleological ideas. They are neither sentimental nor a matter of fancy. Both kinds of means and explanation are, in principle, objective and verifiable; both kinds are a response to subjective needs and desires.

Kierkegaard's philosophy is also a protest against any view of conscious life which uses non-teleological principles to account for mental activities. Like William James who said that objects were associated, not ideas, so Kierkegaard insists that inferential knowledge and all kinds of judgments are not a matter of the physical aggregation of things called ideas. Neither is he anxious to assert that ideas are characterized by their objective possession of logical relations. Instead, he so defines an idea that the association of the mental thing and objective thing, be it a physical object or another idea, is what we mean by the idea. The idea, common sense again being the court of appeal, is the experience of that association.

III

Once again Kierkegaard's position is carefully guarded. Typical of almost every turn of thought he took, this one, too, is well guarded and the implications precisely considered. Admitting a teleology within the thinker, a teleology which is of moral and reflective importance to the individual is one thing. With this teleology every man has a firsthand contact. But there is another kind of teleology which is sometimes proposed by reflective geniuses as the pattern of development for the race and for the cosmos. Kierkegaard was inclined to stick to the lesser and simpler strategy as more fitting the human responsibility.[20] The grand strategy was certainly not a man's to bother with, be it a progress view, a providence interpretation of history, or even an evolutionary hypothesis. If a metaphysics entailed the latter kind of view it is fair to say that Kierkegaard is also quick to point out that unless the latter is a systematic development of the former, such teleological views of history and nature are abstract and conjectural. Furthermore, no human being has a firsthand contact with such magnitude of fact.

From considerations like these Kierkegaard therefore says:

> Existence constitutes the highest interest of the existing individual and his interest in his existence constitutes his reality. What reality is, cannot be expressed in the language of abstraction.[21]

---

20. Thus the contrast which the Judge draws between himself and his aesthete-friend. He, the Judge, has an inner enthusiasm which engages him night and day; the aesthete has to circumnavigate the globe, not once but again and again. *Either/Or*, especially vol. II.

21. *Postscript*, 279. Note here the discussion of Reidar Thomte, *Kierkegaard's Psychology of Religion*, 109–20.

If we are to understand "interest" in the first sentence of the above quotation as a teleological concern in perpetuation of one's own existence, then it will be clear, I believe, why it can be argued that "reality" for Kierkegaard is an ethical issue. Even though he is a realist and admits the existence of an objective world, still that world, existing as it is, is not properly the primary interest for any existing man. For to become interested in the natural or historical world means that one must establish a cognitive and mediating relation to it. To do this demands that one become objective and disinterested and one then abstracts from his own subjectivity in order to realize the maximal objectivity.

> Abstract thought considers both possibility and reality, but its concept of reality is a false reflection, since the medium within which the concept is thought is not reality, but possibility. Abstract thought can get hold of reality only by nullifying it, and this nullification of reality consists in transforming it into possibility. All that is said about reality in the language of abstraction and within the sphere of abstract thought, is really said within the sphere of the possible.[22]

The point is that this is not a criticism of cognition or of any kind of causal or non-teleological explanation. It is not Kierkegaard's intent to cast doubt upon the intelligence or upon the noetic power of observation and inference. His point is much simpler. Instead of learning amassing the dimensions of the real and, therefore, making all of human interests captive to that real, Kierkegaard insists that the success of the venture demands the cessation of the interest engendering it. Furthermore, "To clutch an hypothesis is like embracing a cloud instead of Juno."[23] And the *cognosciendi* always promise a Juno. Any kind of reflective apprehension of reality, a conversion of "what is" into ideas, is only this. Nothing teleological follows. Yet this is precisely what most metaphysicians contend must follow. No enrichment of personal reality actually follows. One cannot ask knowledge to yield a moral harvest; objective truths do not have to be edifying, and unless the pursuit of knowledge is already governed by a teleological interest, nothing teleological or ethical can be deduced from it.

22. Ibid. "I had rather be a concretion which means something than an abstraction which means everything," *Stages*, 70.

23. *Stages*, 247.

Therefore, if a person has an ethical interest, the arena is one's own personality, not world history.

> All knowledge about reality is possibility. The only reality to which an existing individual may have a relation that is more than cognitive, is his own reality, the fact that he exists; this reality constitutes his absolute interest. Abstract thought requires him to become disinterested in order to acquire knowledge; the ethical demand is that he become infinitely interested in existing.[24]

Knowledge means the translation of reals into possibles.[25] And "the aesthetic and intellectual principle," he says very precisely, "is that no reality is thought or understood until its *esse* has been resolved into its *posse*.[26] Therefore, it is a misunderstanding to be concerned about reality from an intellectual point of view, unless one understands already the incommensurateness between intellection and reality and guards his thought accordingly.

Kierkegaard's insistence is always on saying that the reality question cannot be raised abstractly at all. To return to the two kinds of teleology mentioned earlier, this means that one does not raise the question about everything in general or everyone else but only of oneself and his own interest in his own existence.[27] The interest in one's own existence is, again, a commonsense concern. Kierkegaard is not suggesting that there are reasons for this interest or that philosophy somehow has to vindicate this concern. But rather, it is in virtue of this interest that reality impinges upon reflection. In a somewhat different context Kierkegaard's author says:

> But as soon as I proceed to impose a teleology upon my thought, and bring it into relation with something else, interest begins to play a role in the matter. The instant this happens the ethical is present, and absolves me from any further responsibility in proving my own existence. It forbids me to

---

24. Ibid., 280. Again *Either/Or*, II:229, where the author argues that the individual has his teleology in himself, etc.
25. Ibid. Cf. the plea for disinterestedness in *Works of Love*, 296.
26. Ibid. *Postscript*, 288.
27. Ibid. Also n. 287.

draw a conclusion that is ethically deceitful and metaphysically unclear, by imposing upon me the duty of existing.[28]

Proofs for the actual existence of God, of the world, and of oneself are a misunderstanding. The convictions which men have here are teleologically achieved. They are a reflection of the interest, the commonsense interest and intentionality, of every man. They are not a result of sophistication or argument. The analysis of them is the subject matter of philosophy. To introduce the interest factor surreptitiously is the fault of some of the major metaphysicians; to deny the interest factor altogether and content oneself with non-teleological categories is the fault of those whose thought must remain pure. To bring the two together, an interest in one's own existence and a logical talent, is to invest one's thought with the characteristics of actuality. But one thing more, it means being as negative as one is positive, aware, that is, of the objective uncertainty while asserting on behalf of common human subjectivity what is the major human conviction.

This finally marks Socrates' greatness for Søren Kierkegaard. Unlike most philosophers Socrates reflected upon that which he had in common with his fellows. This made him a philosopher of the marketplace. But oddly enough, "Socrates . . . was the most unpopular man in Greece, precisely because he said the same thing as the simplest man, but attached infinite thought to it."[29] The philosopher, the existential philosopher, that is, finds that the content of everyday existing is sufficient material for a lifetime of cogitation. Although the content is common, the philosopher's form of reflection may be aristocratic and rare, but after all, Kierkegaard was, like Socrates of old, quick to note that the content was what mattered.

IV

We began this chapter by suggesting that Kierkegaard does not disparage philosophy. It should be clear by now that he could hardly afford to do so for, in that case, he would leave his own literature, and the very views here noted, unaccounted for. Here again Kierkegaard seems to have anticipated his critics by noting the fact that (a) the

28. *Postscript*, 282–83.
29. *Stages*, 377.

reality question is an immediate and non-cognitive issue; (b) the sentence in which this is said is mediate and cognitive (a possibility); (c) nonetheless, the sentence is true rather than false.

To say that such a sentence is true and yet of limited importance is another way of marking out the issues very carefully. The reality principle, in contrast to the aesthetic and intellectual principle previously mentioned, is that no possibility is understood until each *posse* has really become an *esse*.

> In our age everything is mixed up together: the aesthetic is treated ethically, faith is dealt with intellectually, and so forth. Philosophy has answered every question; but no adequate consideration has been given the question concerning what sphere it is within which each question finds its answer. This creates a greater confusion in the world of the spirit than when in civic life an ecclesiastical question, let us say, is handled by the bridge commission.[30]

The intellectual scrutiny protests every *esse* which is not a *posse* but the reality-interest protests every possibility which is not actualized. Therefore disinterestedness and the possibles are lower than reality to the man who makes his existence his own infinite interest; but with Aristotle, who in the *Poetics* ranked poetry higher than history because it commanded the possible, Kierkegaard likewise avers that disinterestedness and possibility are higher than reality and actuality from the intellectual standpoint.[31] Therefore his own sentences about these matters are philosophical only in a strict and very limited sense, i.e., they are sentences about the status of sentences concerning non-cognitive reality. As such they do not like some bad poetry desert lofty disinterestedness "in order to reach out for reality" and thus confound the confusion.[32]

But this standpoint does not condemn all metaphysical enterprises. As previously alluded to, the fact that reflection can also be teleological and brought into relation with the life of interests, is also a mode of interpreting the metaphysical sentences. Kierkegaard believed that disinterestedness was the characteristic toward which

---

30. *Postscript*, 288. This is the burden too of remarks about the fault of Adler, cf. *On Authority and Revelation*, 164–65.

31. *Postscript*, 282.

32. Ibid., 283.

all cognitive activity approximated. He was as clear as anyone could be that such an ideality for reflection was not easily attained and he would have had little sympathy with the critics who by discovering that much of knowledge is interest-oriented, then go on to deny the possibility or the relevance of objectivity and intellectual neutrality. Kierkegaard is in opposition to neither non-teleological disinterested reflection nor the teleological and interest-ful use of reflection. His point is rather that philosophers, by refusing to admit the significance of interests, have brought them surreptitiously into a supposed disinterested speculative effort. They then deny the interest factor, ostensibly to claim greater cognitive authenticity for their efforts. But the other extreme is equally reprehensible, for here men deny the possibility of objectivity and neutrality of reflection in order to assert the intellective primacy of interests. Kierkegaard chose instead a *via media* between these extremes. He admits a disinterested logico-philosophico standpoint from which everything cognizable can be unified but only when the neutrality and the detachment are rigorously assured. On the other side, thinking is also an instrumentality and everything really neutral can be turned to a use. He denies a cognitive bridge between the two. Reflection can only predispose the world to those forms in which communication can take place but it can do nothing directly to resolve the conflict between interests. There is no science of interests which tells one which is correct; for interests again are not propositions and are not subject to intellectual criteria. The truth of sentences about interests does not decide the quality or the intensity of any interest nor, furthermore, whether I ought or ought not to be simply interested or disinterested.[33]

Briefly and in conclusion, philosophy seems to be understood by Kierkegaard in two senses, compatible perhaps with two long-established practices of philosophers. On the one side, philosophy is the conceptualizing, articulating, and systematization (and completion) of common sense. This is how one can account for teleological and metaphysical schemes of existence and the world. Kierkegaard believed that reference to purposes, even if the chemistry and the physiology of brain states were unknown, was unavoidable. Teleological behavior was essential and rudimentary and, furthermore, there are

---

33. *Either/Or*, II:178.

teleological explanations for the non-teleological and mechanical things and science of things but there is no non-teleological explanation for the teleological character of thought and existence. That philosophies should reflect this character of existence is their honor; that philosophers should seldom admit the anthropomorphic and commonsense point of departure is reprehensible.

But, on the other side, philosophy is also analysis. Philosophy includes also the highly aristocratic kind of inquiry into the means and rules of conceptualization. Metaphysical analysis can then be understood as the inquiry into the commonsense beliefs, not with an eye to providing substitutes for them, but rather showing their scope and necessity. Furthermore, the aim would be to get the categories straight and to see to it that no teleological explanations were being used to fill out causal accounts of nature and history or *vice versa*.

It seems to be Kierkegaard's conviction that any fact whatever may receive an explanation of its existence in two different and mutually supplementary ways, one a cognitive and causal account (today perhaps to be discussed in terms of a hierarchy of generalizations, laws, and theories), the other, a teleological and ethical account. The one account is relevant to the disinterested observer, the other to each of us insofar as we share a subjectivity and a common ethical passion. But, to forsake our common language which always attaches an "of" or an "about" to the naming of concrete mental functions, such as consciousness "of," or thought "about," or perception "of," is to miss the teleological character of human existence. To miss this, advertently or inadvertently, is to miss one's dignity. Kierkegaard, therefore, insists upon both kinds of explanation.[34]

A distinction, drawn as a warning to the reader, may also be in order. As impressed as Kierkegaard is with the transcendent function of common sense, still he wishes to limit the significance of com-

---

34. This is what theology is, apparently (viz., religious teleology) to Kierkegaard. But, religious language presupposes an inward transition, which gives it religious meanings; it looks otherwise metaphysical. *Works of Love*, 169. In a remarkably lucid comment, Kierkegaard notes that Spinoza attributes teleological explanation to the universal ignorance of men (*Ethics*, the end of the first book). But Kierkegaard contends that Spinoza gives a teleological and purposeful account of why teleological views are what they are. Spinoza refuses to believe that his views are the result of an efficient cause, and that only. His views are true, in another sense than "effected." *Papirer* VII A, 30 (*JP* 1, 930).

mon sense primarily to this circumscribed epistemological function. Insofar as common language also reflects common values, so too common sense may be said to include a sense of values at its core. But this language and sense of values are not normative but are optimal. The "customary speech of man" is said by Kierkegaard to reflect "the worldly mind."[35] Abraham's act of faith described in *Fear and Trembling* is without the necessary language counters and he cannot communicate his exceptional decision. Also, Kierkegaard contends that the Kingdom of God language is altogether different, on the value side, from that of common sense.

This does not deny the centripetal character of common sense, referred to earlier. For, once again, common sense unites the various ethical and religious languages of humanity, giving objective reference and believefulness to the existential claims within varying qualitative evaluations of existence and its tasks. In the Kierkegaardian literature, the aesthetic, ethical, and religious views of life are relevant to the same existing world. The transcendent function in all form of meaning and intention, memory, hope, perception, knowledge, and belief is equally presupposed. But only the aesthetic stage accepts the commonsense values. The ethical and the religious, and, we should add, the Christian most of all, repudiates those values.

The place of contrary evaluations is the subject matter of philosophy. There are differences between sciences, for some evaluate objects, while others make evaluations their objects. But to draw these and other distinctions is the subject matter and function of philosophy. To philosophize in this manner is to permit one's thought to become invested with moral content and fervor. In spite of the sophistication of his reflection, Kierkegaard knew how to speak the language of the simple with the meaning of the simple. Unlike Spinoza, for whom God became the sum of logical predicates, and Hegel, for whom existence became of interest only when it was past, Kierkegaard reflected his way out of such sophistication and back into the commonsense matrix of social life.[36]

---

35. *Edifying Discourses*, vol. IV, "Man's Need of God . . . ," especially 13–15, 23–25.

36. Cf. Swenson, "Editor's Introduction," Geismar, *Lectures*, xlviii–xlix.

CHAPTER 11

Indirect Communication

PROBABLY BECAUSE KIERKEGAARD COMMANDED so easily both the passions and a dialectic, because he expressed both his poetic and argumentative talents almost equally in his literature, he was able also to consider so richly the problems of communication. Writing as he did in several styles and with variant moods and intents, he had to be very clear about the limits of communication in order to give some semblance of order to what he did. His personal papers are, on these issues, almost too full; they defy summary.[1] One book, the *Postscript*, develops in detail a theory about communication. Some of the most interesting asides in his pseudonymous literature, and even the religious literature, concern language and its relations to logic, music, poetic values, and its contrasting uses in, for example, a lecture as over against a sermon. Again, it is incumbent to note that Kierkegaard writes a variety of pieces and then withdraws, gathering it together anew in a theory about communication. This is another illustration of the reflective thoroughness by which he always sought to account for himself and his literature.

Considerations of the problem of communication are linked by Kierkegaard invariably to those of style and artful production. Because he believed his literature to be an artful production, intentionally designed though like everything historical and contingent, both a little more and perhaps a little less too, Kierkegaard was always aware of the need for a correspondence between the form and the content. In fact, this distinction taken over from previous writers is given a new twist by Kierkegaard. He discovers that there is no content, or at least

---

1. He even projected a lecture series on "the dialectics of communication" (1847).

Indirect Communication

no body of results available for certain kinds of discourse and that the "*kunst*," the artful form, is neither optional nor supervenient. Against the peculiar view which said that all philosophy, religion, and even science were only discrepant modes of communicating the same rational content, Kierkegaard insists that the form of communication is intrinsic and, if well done, singular to what is being expressed. These judgments are made on behalf of his own authorship and are said by Kierkegaard to distinguish it from other writings.[2]

In a day when so much philosophy is written in a barbaric simulation of scientific writing, it is pleasant to find a writer not only praising style but achieving it and knowing why as he does so. For style has no casual ground in the Kierkegaardian authorship. Kierkegaard argues that style, at least in his case, is a teleological matter and that it must so be judged.

This points to a difficulty not always happily handled by the scholars. It has become a custom among the incidental readers as well as the scholars of literature to explain everything causally. With Kierkegaard this is great sport. His life was a strange one, his relation to Regine so self-conscious, his acknowledged debt to her so enduring, that finally everything seems to fall into a pattern which says, "strange causes (Regine, deep feeling for her, a queer man anyway) make for strange books (pseudonyms, no results, unsystematic, polemical, queer books)."[3]

---

2. F. J. Billeskov Jansen, *Studier i Søren Kierkegaards Litteraere Kunst*, is an astute piece of writing, but for all of its adeptness, it fails to get at the feature noted above. Jansen does, however, describe very clearly what English translations often blur, namely, the differences in style between the various genres of Kierkegaard's literature. E.g., note his remarks in the philosophical works (44–51) and *Either/Or* (13–21). Although the remarks are casual, Kierkegaard does say that ethical matters have an artful form and no results, and, furthermore, that this is what great ethical writers like Plato sought and accomplished. *Papirer* VIII 2 B, 81 (*JP* 1, 649). Brandes' encomiums of Kierkegaard's style are still another matter. He believes Kierkegaard's prose to be the norm for Danish literature. Cf. *Kierkegaard*, 160–61, where he refers to "the literature within the literature, a language within the language," etc.

3. This is not a quotation, but Emanuel Hirsch (*Kierkegaard Studien*), Walther Rehm (*Kierkegaard und der Verführer*), and Walter Lowrie (especially his *Kierkegaard*) so stress the psychological peculiarities of the author and the supposed relations of these to the texts that they tend to neglect (a) the validity of what is said, irrespective of its causes and what it may be representing, in part only, psychologically; (b) the formal stylistic and argumentative (the teleological) factor of the literature. In fact, if Kierkegaard is right, the way to understand any text is to

Because Kierkegaard doubted the validity of indirect communication, as he calls his own style and method, in some instances, some scholars are inclined to interpret this recognition as a denial of its importance and necessity in all instances.[4] However, Kierkegaard never did forsake a set of philosophical convictions in virtue of which he explained logically why his style was required. He simultaneously did not deny all kinds of causes, the broken engagement, the affair with the *Corsair*, the reading of Hegel, Adler's deposition, but even if these were causally efficacious, he does not assert that this admission is incompatible with another kind of explanation of the literature. That is, neither explanation is exclusively or exhaustively correct.

It is the mark of Kierkegaard's philosophical competence that he refuses all reductionist views. Furthermore, even if his own literature is not what he says it is, namely a form of indirect and artistic communication, the theory about that kind of communication can still be addressed, and on altogether independent grounds. Here too Kierkegaard was alert to the danger of inferring from the conceivability of anything to its actual existence. But in his own case, even though there was no logical means of anticipating or deducing from actuality to possibility or from possibility to actuality, he argues the fittingness of a theory of indirect communication to the literature he had penned.[5] It is with this in mind that we once again look at his literature to trace the lineaments of his own account of indirect communication.

---

plunge into these and let the author stand outside (*Postscript*, 289, e.g. "Precisely in the degree to which I understand a thinker I come indifferent to his reality...").

4. Walter Lowrie, e.g., interprets Kierkegaard's concern about not expressing Christianity "definitely" as a retraction of the pseudonyms and the whole elaborate apparatus of "indirect communication" (*A Short Life of Kierkegaard*, 225). This is going too far. Kierkegaard admits something socratic about himself. He says: "Indirect communication was my natural qualification" (Dru, *Journals*, entry 1000; *Papirer* X 2 A, 195) and several other places in his papers admit strong psychological and historical causes for their use. Even his later discussions (Dru, *Journals*, entry 1250; *Papirer* X 4 A, 558) do not deny the causes while they continually reassert a transitional and teleological and educative role to such a procedure.

5. This is directly asserted in *Point of View* and *On My Work*, 25 and 148 respectively. Also note *Postscript*, 250.

I

The *Concluding Unscientific Postscript* has a kind of deft appropriateness as a title that one might not assume upon first encounter. The book is unscientific because it is not, strictly speaking, a descriptive study nor is it systematic and detached. It is full of humor and irony and combines these with a generous sweep of argument. Furthermore, the book is an "*Efterskrift*," a postscriptal piece, a commentary in another medium upon materials already covered in earlier literature. It gives definition and articulation to issues that are only passionately adumbrated in earlier works.

But why a concluding postscript? Besides being the summary and completing work of a lengthy authorship which moved from the aesthetic through the ethical and into the religious, this book concludes matters by putting them into forms which in principle were final and irrevocable. Kierkegaard appreciated as well as anyone ever has that every intellectual effort, if it claimed the truth, was also on the same ground possibly false. He claims no finality for his own expressions. But on the other hand, he does also admit that here the issues are being dealt with in a non-empirical and dialectical fashion, where evidence and quantity of evidence is not conclusive. The passional variety that the early literature is, could have been proliferated almost indefinitely, and without repetition. But there are fewer options open once Kierkegaard begins reflecting on the logic of what he has done. The *Postscript* is a conceptualization and a logicizing of the material already in hand.

Therefore his author, Johannes Climacus, a student of philosophy, says:

> All honor to learning and scholarship, all praise to the man who can control material detail, organizing it with the authority of genuine insight, with the reliability that comes with acquaintance with the original sources. But the life of the problem is nevertheless in the dialectical issue. If the presentation of the problem fails in dialectical clarity, while exceptional learning and great acumen are expended upon the details, it becomes only increasingly difficult for the dialectically interested inquirer to find his way about. In connection with this problem there have been produced undeniably, many excellent works of thorough scholarship, revealing both critical acumen and

powers of organization, on the part of men for whom the present author feels a deep respect . . . But there came a time when be believed himself to have discovered, with mingled feelings of admiration for the distinguished authorities and of dejection over his own isolated doubting situation, that in spite of the meritorious labors of the scholars, the problem was not being advanced but retarded.[6]

Although the *Postscript* ostensibly puts the problem of the *Fragments* into "an historical costume," it does not attempt as the author terms an empirical argument, "to construct a quantitative approach." Instead it becomes an essay on the propriety of redefining the issue in such a way that "fearless dialectical positions and movements" will be apparent.[7] The peculiar issue is put by the author as follows:

> I, Johannes Climacus, born in this city and now thirty years old, a common ordinary human being like most people, assume that there awaits me a highest good, an eternal happiness, in the same sense that such a good awaits a servant girl or a professor. I have heard that Christianity proposes itself as a condition for the acquirement of this good, and now I ask how I may establish a proper relationship to this doctrine.[8]

The question is not the truth of Christianity but, rather, the issue of how one relates oneself to Christianity. The issue is defined in this way by the pseudonymous author to accord with his preceding volume, *Philosophical Fragments*, and somewhat less closely, all of the earlier pseudonymous works. These, as was previously noted, are then oriented to the purpose of the *Postscript* in a peculiar appendix, peculiar because it comes in the middle of the book and is one pseudonym's judgment upon other ostensibly unrelated pseudonymous writings.[9]

All of this literature is about the very general question of how one ought to live. Only the *Fragments* and its sequel, the *Postscript*, deal directly with Christianity. The earlier literature develops a dozen or so varieties of Epicurean and aesthetic answers and a few less but

---

6. *Postscript*, 15. While this is said it must be remembered how thorough Kierkegaard was, even to the finest detail of punctuation. Cf. Dru, *Journals*, entry 643 (*Papirer* VIII A, 33).

7. Again, *Postscript*, 14–15.

8. Ibid., 19.

9 *Postscript*, 225–67.

more detailed statements of a Kantian-like duty view. Ostensibly these views of life are exclusive in reference to one's existence—that is, one cannot become or be all of them in the same moment, but they also have something in common.

In Kierkegaard's estimate all of this early literature, for reasons which shall be noted later, and the later religious writings too, cannot be described by any theory of direct communication. To read any of the literature therefore without recognizing its *differentia* in form and style was to admit to having missed its distinctiveness. Therefore, his penman and editor, Climacus, writes out, in effect, an explanation of its style in a theory of indirect communication. Suffice it to say here that Kierkegaard's fears that in communicating directly about indirect communication he would thus destroy the indirectness are unfounded; for he protects his back by showing clearly that the one mode of communication cannot replace another, and that learning directly that there is indirection afoot does nothing to mitigate the latter's effect.[10]

Kierkegaard's literature from first to last is concerned with the task of becoming moral and religious. But if anyone were to approach his writings and expect answers or results, as he called them, by which one would know the good or know that Christianity is the truth, nothing is forthcoming. He simply does not offer any truths to live by. Or rather, one should say that the truths to live by are present in such profusion and variety that the directness of any one communicating author is balanced by the equally persuasive and clear message of another. The literature, in other words, balances direct communications about moral ends so that one becomes as skeptical and unable to move toward a moral end in a knowledgeable state as one was unable to move in a state of innocence. This is the literature on the direct side. Even considering the most pronouncedly religious and Christian works, still the urbanity and flexibility and indifferentism of an objective reader is not disturbed by either the argument or whatever else is directly communicated. If there is a disturbance, it is rather a disquietude concerning oneself, but this cannot be a result of argument.

---

10. *Postscript*, 247.

Hence Kierkegaard found it incumbent to acknowledge on behalf of his sophisticated reader the possibility of misinterpreting the communication involved. He was not trying to soften his audience, but rather he found that the theory of direct communication was inappropriate when considering moral and religious matters. He is not denying the possibility of all ethical theory—this might well be a direct expression in propositional form of the nature of ethical statements or, for that matter, of the relationship between reflection and being moral. But what his entire literature denies is the possibility of propositions which are directly communicable ever being both moral and true. He denies that ethical theories or religious doctrines even if true and believed will, by being believed, make people moral or faithful. His case for the denial is his entire literature. The theory of communication reflects this error also. Kierkegaard attacks the issue from many angles and this is only one, and seemingly a lesser one to him at that. His argument seems to be that one does communicate concerning moral and religious matters but that the moral and religious efficacy lies in the receptor, the subject who receives the sentence.[11] The skill of the communicator is to occasion the response in the subject, the movement in subjectivity by the use of a neutral objective sentence. To impute to conversation, lectures, and sermons immediate and direct moral values is to mistake both the provinces of morality and religion and that of language. This is the confusion of categories noted repeatedly in earlier chapters.

It is therefore Kierkegaard's particular quality as a thinker, first, to have written a body of literature that concerns itself with these issues and, secondly, with great detail, to have proposed a theoretical account about indirection. His explanation is a consequence of his logicizing and formalizing all of the issues with which he ever concerned himself. But this was not in order only to perfect his own reflection. He found—as most philosophers always profess to—confusions and ambiguities everywhere, but once he had understood the confusions introduced by an exaggerated opinion of the efficacy of reflection in moral and religious matters, he was free to devote his energies to a moral and religious enthusiasm uninhibited by an

---

11. The business of the receiving subject, the recipient, is discussed in *Papirer* VIII 2 B, 81 (*JP* 1, 649).

Indirect Communication 245

alien and unfruitful intellectualism. He became a philosopher who no longer had to believe that philosophy was provident of the good, the beautiful, and the true, but who had simultaneously more courage than most of his decriers and was content not to claim more for clarity and exactness than these values could bear.

But, of course, the theory of communication, direct and indirect, is again a part of philosophy, the technical and aristocratic branch of philosophy. Kierkegaard knew the limitations of this kind of philosophizing very well indeed. But to communicate indirectly, with maieutic art and style, beginning with the aesthetic and using religion as a *telos*, proportioning everything to the dimensions of actual existence, this was philosophy in the democratic and generic sense.[12] This combination of talents describes philosophy as requiring both direct and indirect skills, logicality and aesthetic sensitivity. To practice in this complex mode is to be a philosopher of existence.[13]

II

But, is this to deny all direct communication? Kierkegaard is very clear on this point, more so than one would ever guess from the numerous hasty accounts of his arguments one can now read. He does not deny the possibility of intersubjectivity nor does he in any wise mitigate its importance. If anything, he is at pains to show that it is impossible to deny its importance. His literature presupposes both a direct and an indirect communication from author to reader. However, Kierkegaard's judgment of his own writings was that their indirect communication was more important and significant than their direct communication. All disinterested and objective knowledge, all knowledge of logic and mathematics, everything in scholarship, presupposes communicability.

Of all knowledge that is objective and claims nothing ethical for itself, the task of communication is fulfilled when the words mediate the meanings. Thus Kierkegaard finds it to be a failure on Hegel's part to write seventeen volumes of direct communication and neverthe-

---

12. "On My Work," in *Point of View*, 148–49.

13. *Postscript*, 279, 295. "If the content of thought were reality . . ." is explored in this connection on 302. "The subjective thinker is an artist" (ibid., 314).

less admit that there was only one man who had understood him, and that he had misunderstood him.[14] The man who communicates directly strives to make himself understood and does not need artistry. Instead he wants and needs assent on the part of others as the token of his own success.

In all intellectual endeavors where true sentences or propositions, be they empirical or intuitively derived, are the results, there must also be complete objectivity and direct communication. "Objective thinking is wholly indifferent to subjectivity, and hence also to inwardness and appropriation; its mode of communication is therefore direct. It goes without saying that it need not on that account be at all easy."[15] It is well to remember that Professor Swenson could write: "I have never seen any passage in Kierkegaard in which he shows scorn for objective *validity*. His respect for workmanship in the objective sciences—logic, mathematics, the historical disciplines, the natural sciences—is frequently expressed."[16] The same can be said of direct communication. Any effort in which truths are being sought, theology, philosophy, or the sciences, must issue in propositions or sentences. The disinterestedness and indifferentism of the knowing subject is the psychological condition essential to both the dissemination of truths and their reception.

All intellectual endeavors presuppose that truth is a quality not of the subject but of the sentence. Therefore to convey the sentences between subjects is also to convey its quality. When truth is claimed to be objective, its communicability is thereby also described, for no characteristic of the communicator or of the act of reflection in which truth is grasped characterizes its truth.[17] The objectivity of truth for Kierkegaard does not mean that one must posit a metaphysical realm in which it pre-exists. That truth does pre-exist, and that it is only discovered, not made, he does not deny, but, on the other hand, he does not affirm it either. He is content to mean by the objectivity of

14. *Postscript*, 65–66.
15. *Postscript*, 70.
16. Swenson, op. cit., 237.
17. Again *Papirer*, especially the discussion about the dialectics of communication, e.g., why ethical communication must be an art, because we all know it already and the task is to realize it, not know it, whereas in *"videnskab"* (knowledge and science), this is not true. *Papirer* VIII 2 B, 81 (JP 1, 649).

Indirect Communication 247

truth that it is a characteristic of communicable "objects," sentences or propositions, which are in turn referable to an anoetic world.

Kierkegaard understands all knowledge to be properly propositional. And every cognitive truth is communicated when the set of symbols by which one person understands and states what he knows is made another person's. But this is not simple. Kierkegaard believed that simple linguistic units were actually a part of a system of language and meanings and therefore to have the word for a thought or a thing was already to share the universal.[18] Therefore all cognition, all knowledge other than insight, all knowing which presupposes naming and describing, is inter-subjective in virtue of being linguistic. Among other meanings that Kierkegaard gives to the concept "universal," one is always paramount, viz., that a universal is anything whose significances can be given linguistically. That all knowledge presupposes an anoetic intentional act in order to be about things and places and persons is likewise Kierkegaard's assertion.[19] In this respect knowledge is a synthesis of reals and ideals but the medium of knowledge is an order of universals, and the use of language brings universals immediately into play.[20] Language, therefore, is not only a communicative instrument. A linguistic symbol is the mode of getting particulars and objects into cognitive and reflective forms. Communication and reflection, language and thought, are not finally separable.

Direct communication takes place whenever any use of symbols becomes another's use of the same symbols. Knowledge as Kierkegaard understands it—and here he is surely one with the philosophic tradition—presupposes an exacting translation of non-communicable experience into common and communicable linguistic forms. That logic described the structure of meaning that knowledge possessed has already been insisted to be Kierkegaard's point. Language is a social system, a set of noises and sounds that are aesthetically idiosyn-

---

18. *Enten-Eller*. The English translation, *Either/Or*, is not as happy here as it might be. Kierkegaard's author says: ". . . *forsaavidt som ethvert Udtryk for Ideen altid er et Sprog, da Ideens Væsen er Sproget*," and this should read: ". . . insofar as every expression for the idea is always speech, so the being of an idea is language." Compare *Either/Or*, English translation, I:53ff.

19. *Fragments*, "Interlude," 59–73. Note previous chapter also.

20. *Either/Or*, II:56. *Fear and Trembling*, 176.

cratic and particularized, but meaning-wise and already systematic. To translate a private and idiosyncratic "given" into a public language is what knowledge presupposes. Knowledge and communication are so intimately connected that one of Kierkegaard's authors can exclaim: "So soon as I talk I express the universal, and if I do not do so, no one can understand me."[21] And in explanation of the dreadfulness of Abraham's silence produced by his being an exception and hence *incommunicado*, we read: "The relief of speech is that it translates me into the universal."[22]

In comparing language with music and sculpting and painting, all according to Hegel modes for expressing the Absolute Idea, one of Kierkegaard's aesthetes argues that language is most clearly communicative and reflective because its sensuous and physical media are depressed to mere instrumentalities. He writes:

> If a man spoke in such a way that one heard the movement of his tongue, he would speak badly; if a man on listening heard the vibration of the air instead of the words, he would hear badly; if on reading a book he constantly saw the individual letters, he would read badly. Thus language becomes the most perfect medium when everything sensuous in it is negated.[23]

In the context of Kierkegaard's literature, with its several points of view, it becomes appropriate for the aesthetes who value immediate satisfactions above all else to argue that music is superior to language. Music is sensuous; it stimulates and provokes immediate response in the hearer. On the contrary, language as we have noted fails as language if it does this. It fails as communicative prose if it causes immediate responses. Poetic language may indeed even approximate music in eliciting immediate and imaginative response but this is a special case.

Language involves reflection and cannot, therefore, express the immediate. But, from an intellectual standpoint, this aesthetic limitation and poverty, is, as Kierkegaard well knew, also the wealth and province of linguistic expression.[24] Everything negated within a linguistic expression is negated with an interest to making what is in-

21. *Fear and Trembling*, 89.
22. Ibid., 176.
23. *Enten-Eller, Samlede Vaerker*, I:50. Compare *Either/Or*, I:54.
24. *Either/Or*, I:56.

accessible and incommunicable—and both inner states and physical objects are on parity in this respect—accessible and communicable through ideal logical constants.

Although the art media certainly do bring stimulation and besides stand related to the reflective life in both the artist and the appreciator, still it was Kierkegaard's contention that art forms, including music, were not solely or even principally noetic. Against those who believed that the Absolute Idea, or if not that much, something propositional was being communicated in every cow's moo, or, "that which perhaps makes greater pretensions," in the song of the nightingale, Kierkegaard would have their hearers listen closely and then remember that *qua* knowledge it is all a case of "tweedledum and tweedledee."[25] One hears but does not know, and Kierkegaard found the endeavors to translate everything sensuous into something communicative and cognitive simply ridiculous. The philosopher or the clergyman who was not content to stick to language and ideas and books, but who made nature into a book,[26] everything immediate into a mediating agent, who professed to find a logical reflective factor or universals anywhere and everywhere, such were maudlin sentimentalists and poor thinkers.

Cognition and communication have limitations in two different directions. There is a sensuous immediacy that is individual and cannot be communicated. Feelings, pains, and pleasures, the sensation in the moment it is possessed, the emotion and passion—all of these are not communicable in their immediacy. One may communicate about them and one may seemingly produce something analogous in others. That language could be used aesthetically Kierkegaard did not deny but he found this to be a lesser function of words. That knowledge began in immediate expression, he also insists, but as we have seen the use of language destroys the immediacy. Language brings meanings relevant to certain immediacies, but it does not create the immediacies. Poetry may succeed, as music does, in producing in a

---

25. Ibid., 55.

26. Ibid., 53. The notion that poetry properly creates passion in its reader, and that great poetry does this by juxtaposing passions is explored in *Fear and Trembling*. That book is called "a dialectic lyric," because it lyricizes at length, but yet the opposition within is subject to a dialectical and formal categorization. There is a *logos* in the passions. "Only passion against passion provides a poetic collision . . ." *Fear and Trembling*, 140 fn.

large number of people the same immediate responses. This is not to communicate but it is to create. That language communicates is to assert that there is an identity in the immediacies, something mediated by the immediacies, be they words or sounds or other experiences, but this identity is not then an immediacy itself. It exists only when reflection takes place.

But this is only one limit of cognition. There is another limit in another direction. Cognitive assertions do not communicate the immediacies that are extra-linguistic. But likewise, statements cannot communicate morality and religiosity. But here too there is a limit. It may be described as a limit within language or as a limit within religious and ethical existing. In any case, the endeavor to make religion and morality cognitive is for Kierkegaard as great an error as the endeavor to make all forms of art cognitive. For just as cognition and communication negate the sensuous, so too does language negate the immediacy of morality and religion.[27]

Today these matters are discussed in another set of terms. It has been fashionable to say that poetry and religious dogmas and ethical sentences (whatever their form) are not cognitive but emotive. Recent philosophy is deemed distinguished for producing a chorus of qualifiers who now agree that this is too sweeping. One by one the professors of philosophy, scanning the journals, screw up their courage and tell each other on the best of authority that this went too far. It is interesting to note that Kierkegaard saw this problem in days when it took courage to isolate it. He decried the endeavor on the part of philosophers to construe every human endeavor as cognitive and every kind of language claim as if it were amenable to the same set of norms. Instead of making his point like the recent propagandists, first the contradictory opposite, then the next twenty years in mitigating admissions, Kierkegaard distinguished differences before he made his denials on two counts: one, to save the ethical and the religious from emasculation by philosophical abstraction, and, two, to save philosophy and cognition from the extravagances into which it was catapulted once elementary distinctions were neglected.[28]

27. This is the complaint in the essay *The Present Age*, viz., that people have forgotten what it means to exist morally and religiously because they are so reflective. They have words for everything—as if this were the responsibility.

28. Kierkegaard says somewhere (I have lost the reference) that the quality of

That there is a certain kind of ethical theory, a meta-ethics, and even a kind of direct communication possible in respect to religion, Kierkegaard does not deny. Nonetheless there is a limit. Being ethical and being religious are not the same as knowing about ethics and religion. Neither ethicality nor religiosity are attitudes of belief toward, for example, "reality." For to assert in this fashion would be a way of arguing for the primacy of the cognitive and contending, in turn, that morality and religiosity are derivative. The religious problem is like the moral problem to Kierkegaard in this respect, namely, that the problematic does not lie in our ignorance of what the good is nor will the accomplishment follow immediately upon learning what the elusive good really is. This too disguises a delusion respecting the importance of knowledge. Climacus writes:

> And as for the relationship of the subject to the truth when he comes to know it, the assumption is that if only the truth is brought to light, its appropriation is a relatively unimportant matter, something which follows as a matter of course . . .[29]

Supposing that there is no object corresponding to the ethical and religious truth which can be known, supposing that there is nothing to communicate directly, then Kierkegaard argues, an ethico-religious literature must have a function, partly communicative, partly eliciting, but the problem is not again an easy one. It is at this point that Kierkegaard refuses to lump the difficulties and say that the issue is simply emotive or simply anything else. His doctrine of indirect communication accounts for his own literature, which does already exist, and also the considerable body of moralistic and religious literature besides his own. Is it only poetry? Does it only elicit emotion? Immediate responses? Images and fantasy? He thinks not. Therefore, we turn herewith to see what sense he makes of it as an indirect communication.

---

a thinker is to be measured by the care with which he draws distinctions and the courage he has to stick to those distinctions.

29. *Postscript*, 24.

III

All direct communication is itself disinterestedly formulated. It presupposes ideally equal disinterestedness in the communication as in the learner. If Kierkegaard's position is correct, there is no disinterested knowledge of the good or of God. Every metaphysical and/or ethical assertion that claims to be a cognitive claim about God or the good is an assertion reflecting the interest of the asserter and is not an account solely of something objective. This is not to assert that there is nothing objective to which such language corresponds for this again says too much. Neither is it to say that everything is subjective, that every ethico-religious truth is only a wish fulfillment or an expression of desire.

Kierkegaard considers his own literature to be an ethico-religious communication, but precisely because it is ethical and religious to learn what it says is not enough. All direct communication presents that which is to be affirmed or denied and such responses are enough. But a response to the truth of a proposition is not itself an interest in one's own existence. Being ethical and becoming religious is precisely to have an interest in one's own existence. Such an interest, such subjectivity, is inimical to the life of learning and is rightly to be excluded from the knowing act.

To generalize from this it would seem that Kierkegaard's diatribe is against any effort to define the assertions of ethics and religion as simply objective. If they were objective only, then the act of assent to them must be an ethical or religious act. But then Kierkegaard does not understand how interest can follow from disinterestedness. If the conditions for the apprehension of cognitive truth are detachment and objectivity, then how can knowledge claims produce subjective passion and concern?

But still, one does have ethical and religious literature, and, further, one has claims made about them. Kierkegaard was enough of a commonsense philosopher not to wish to deduce the objects of knowledge, not even if they were language claims—he chose instead to begin with what there was. Philosophers had enough to talk about in the judgments about things without bothering to create everlastingly new judgments. And the judgments about these kinds of literature are invariably to the effect that they too are objectively true, cognitively incremental, and that the recognition of their truth is a moral and religious act. Thus it was (and still is for many) respecting the Bible. Kierkegaard records high regard for philological scholarship but, as his Johannes Climacus says concerning the philologist's painstaking work on the texts of Cicero: "... when he has finished, nothing follows except the wholly admirable result that an ancient writing has now through his skill and competence received its most accurate possible form." But the moralists and the theologians in respect to their chosen literatures, after doing the same sort of scholarly and scientific work want to draw another conclusion: "ergo, now you can have your eternal happiness on these writings."[30] Kierkegaard's point is that such a conclusion does not belong to any kind of learned inquiry.

Kierkegaard finds that ethical and religious language claims are peculiar. They presuppose something in their user that is not evident in the objective sentence. But instead of admitting this, the race seems to have conspired against clarity by introducing notions of inspiration,[31] of intuition, of self-evidence, all of these being, according to Kierkegaard, testimony to the need for external guarantees against doubt. These posited limits, not intrinsic to the objectivity of the sentences but clearly persuasive extra-linguistic factors, are superstitions, aimed to keep dialectical and reflective doubt away.[32] Rather than looking to the externals to describe their difference Kierkegaard again looks to the subjectivity of men and suggests that ethical and religious sentences reflect subjectivity.[33]

But another distinction is in order. Literature that addresses itself to human interest is directly communicative only about possibilities, not realities. The good and God, if we limit ourselves only to these, are not, in virtue of their respective characteristics, known as objects. Even the cognitive relation to an empirical object turns out to be a relationship to the conceived object and the latter is also

30. Ibid., 26.
31. Ibid., 25–35.
32. Ibid., 43.
33. A most interesting discussion of Kant's notion that supernaturalism does not provide theoretical knowledge of God is found in one of Kierkegaard's early papers (1837). Here he already suggests that Schleiermacher was wrong in suggesting that his version of faith was similar to Kant's. Kierkegaard argues that Schleiermacher was operating at another level of consciousness, or as we would say, on another level of discourse, to Kierkegaard, one of inwardness. *Papirer* II C, 48 (*JP* 2, 2252).

a possibility. But minds are intentional and a kind of commonsense interest refers some possibles to an extra-mental existence. But communication with possibles about actualities is feasible and, as was noted earlier, when common sense comes into play. In any case we can neither prove nor disprove the transcendent claim.

The difference between ethical and religious claims on the one side, and empirically descriptive claims on the other is precisely that the former are always present to consciousness, in principle if not in fact, in plural number. The latter, noetic claims, are in principle singular. Plural hypotheses, or possibles, about matters of fact are an indication of an imperfection in the knowledge process.

Therefore, intellectual descriptions, religious literature, and moral theory permit no disinterested mode of limiting the number of possibilities. Logical consistency and the existential reference of such claims, both, are compatible with multiple possibles. To make one's intellectual grasp most complete and most embracing, most objective and detached, is precisely to multiply ethical possibles. This is another clue to the infinity of reflection which comes to no stop by itself.[34] Kierkegaard's own literature is a correction of the philosophical tradition and Hegel in particular at this very point. For his early writings multiply alternatives and give no results. So too he finds that neither Lessing nor Socrates offered results, either, that were communicable and at once of ethico-religious interest. But their works as well as his do communicate something directly: they disclose directly the possibilities that face every person who has an interest in his own existence. However, they conclude nothing; they do not stand in any argumentative and logical relation with their observer.

Kierkegaard therefore does not deny religious and ethical cognition but when he affirms it, he affirms it much less than Hegel. Only the possilbles can be directly communicated and in respect to an ethical interest, this is not enough. And therefore Kierkegaard is quick to point out that something must be addressed but the question is, how?

Ethical and religious communication ought properly then be indirect for the direct communication is not communicative of an ethical result anyway, but only of an ethical possibility. This means

---

34. In respect to action, reflection shows as many possibilities "pro" as "contra." Cf. Dru, *Journals*, entry 871 (*Papirer* X 1 A, 66).

Indirect Communication　　　　　　　　　　　　　　　　　　255

that there ought to be two reflective movements entertained, a double reflection, in both the communicator and the recipient of the communication.[35] First, to think and to communicate one's thought at all is to think the universal, the possible. This both can do easily enough. But any possible (even another man's ethicality is only a possibility to one, the observer) which is ethical has its significance *qua* ethical or religious when it becomes a matter of the recipient's interest, i.e., when he strives to exist in it. Thus, there are two movements: one out of the particular into the universal, out of passion and interest into disinterest and possibility, and the other movement which is to reinvest the possible with interest and thus make it an actuality.

If ethics and religion is, on the intellectual side, a confrontation with possibilities, then on the passional side it is an endeavor to make the possibility an actuality. To communicate directly in religion or ethics means to communicate the possibles. Kierkegaard is very astute, however, on the numerous innuendoes that the history of culture provides here. He acknowledges that few moralists and religious teachers have been so delicately ordered to the issues. They have tried to concretize and to secure actualization too by making their reflection empirical. But whatever the circumlocutions within cognitive categories, they have been hard pressed to show that there is any subjective significance to the contemplation of possibilities.

Kierkegaard's point appears somewhat oblique here but actually is not: he insists that the man who wishes to communicate religious and ethical truth must be artful. He must destroy his own authority, he must let nothing slip into the communication that mitigates the objective uncertainty posed by the possibles, or attenuates the need for passionate enthusiasm on the part of the learner, or trivializes the striving of the recipient.[36]

Kierkegaard's point can be put in other categories. If being a moral man means having enthusiasm for one's own existence, then how can one communicate enthusiasm? Kierkegaard insists that enthusiasm cannot be communicated. When anyone addresses another on these matters he conveys the form of interest and enthusiasm, the forms of the subjective and inner life and these objectively, and then,

---

35. *Postscript*, 68.

36. *Postscript*, 293, and the section titled, "The Subjective Thinker—His Task, His Form, His Style," 312ff.

in addition, he does it so artfully and non-authoritatively as to leave the learner in a free relation to alternative possibles. Furthermore, nothing objective can be adduced in virtue of which one possible rather than another is to be chosen. This leaves the subjectivity of the individual, granted that the description is clear, logical, unambiguous, systematic, etc., at the court of appeal. Unlike a truth claim, there is then no evidence, nothing outside the subject, which aids the decision.[37]

A word about the artfulness of this mode of communicating might now be in order. Kierkegaard believed that subjective thinkers, existential thinkers, would have a philosophy to convey but a manifold of requirements would have to be met. They would seek "to transform themselves into an instrument that clearly and definitely expresses in existence whatever is essentially human."[38] He must use the poetical, ethical, and religious, i.e., his concrete subjectivity, to indicate the difference, indirectly to be sure, between thinking existence and living it. His scenery is the inwardness of himself, not "beautiful valleys and the like."[39] The point is then that everything must be done to reduce the contemplative suspension of action and, simultaneously, to accentuate the possibility of an ethical requirement.[40] But the point, again, is to let the possibility itself become the requirement for the subject.

Indirect communication is direct then on the one side and yet sufficiently candid and artistic to create passion, and this lessens the importance of the dispassionate directness. A direct communication on such matters of subjective interest is not an epistemological falsification but it does mean an ethical falsification. That is, the possibles do not distort the actual, but in this instance the difference between the possible and the actual is the difference between an ethical theory and being ethical. The communication that proposes to possess directly an ethical significance (in virtue of the truth of that which is

37. A good example of this is found in the *Stages* where the author says, "Language, arts, handicrafts, one man can teach another, but in an ethico-religious sense one man cannot essentially benefit another," (316) and then explores the artfulness of learning to communicate and yet leaving the important decision to the recipient.

38. *Postscript*, 318.

39. Ibid., 315.

40. *Papirer* VIII 2, 8, 82–83. *Postscript*, 319–20. On these matters E. Hirsch has many interesting things to say; op. cit., vol. II, 751–67.

communicated) is a deception when the issue is not to assent but to become.

Furthermore, the objectivity is not open to reference. If the religious and ethical man understands that interest and passion constitute him as a man, the proposition stating that fact is not creative of that passion. Furthermore, even that proposition is not probable or improbable as hypothetical assertions are; neither is it tautologous as are logical or mathematical sentences. It fits all the facts simply because it is phrased, as are all ethical and religious propositions, so that all the facts fit. Verification both works and does not work. There is sufficient amplitude so that several teleologies can describe all that is; and the test is not decisive in the external world. The decisiveness is in the inner man. Therefore the ordinary cognitive criteria are not relevant. Everything counts or nothing counts for such impressive and sweeping claims. All of them may be compatible with all of the facts—this is probably more problematic than Kierkegaard believed—but they are certainly not compatible with all of human interests.

To refer the issues therefore by communicative devices back to the arena of the self, to take the thought about (universal) possibles and push them back upon the subjective, this is the aim of indirect communication. The kind of inconsistency found in his day, and which is current within contemporary philosophical circles again, is satirized wonderfully in the following story:

> Suppose thus, that it happened to be the view of life of a religiously existing subject, that no man ought to have any disciple, that having disciples is an act of treason to God and man; suppose he also happened to be a little stupid . . . , and asserted this directly, with pathos and unction: what would happen? Why then he would be understood; and he would soon have application from at least ten candidates, offering to preach this doctrine, in return merely for a free shave once a week.[41]

Kierkegaard's point is that zeal for this doctrine, moving not only those who perspire easily but also the hard-boiled temperaments, is a misunderstanding. To know this becomes ethically significant only as one shuts up and seeks no disciples. So too, he understands the matter of philosophers making philosophy practical. There is needed

---

41. *Postscript*, 30.

an "art enough to vary inexhaustibly the doubly reflected form of the communication, just as the inwardness itself is inexhaustible."[42]

Whenever the cognitive objects stand related to the subjective life and whenever what is conceived must be appropriated and enacted, there the communication becomes artful. There too the reflective process must not allow two persons "to fuse or coagulate into objectivity";[43] for one man's disinterested communication must be so stated as to heighten interest and passion in another, but again not directly. To do so directly would be to stimulate and to cause. The trick is not to be another's *telos*, but to let the *telos* arise in the other person.[44] There must be knowledge first. But it must be so stated as to occasion a double reflection, a thought and the passion to become what the thought pictures. This is all that one person can do for another in areas of most significance.

IV

Kierkegaard's theory of direct communication is addressed to the error into which philosophers have fallen who wish to be pontiffs and provide wisdom to the world. Whether in religion or in ethics, the endeavor to provide objective truths in analogy with the sciences and scholarship is a mistaken one. The recent history of philosophical criticism bears out Kierkegaard's point here. Propositions about God and values are grammatically analogous to other language claims, but their pragmatic functions are different. This Kierkegaard intends to note by using the word "indirect." But the Danish philosopher also addresses his own literature, and his theory in a very limited sense explains it. As he ironically says in a comment that can safely be said to apply in detail to his own literature, there are two ways in which to produce an indirect communication: one is to reduce oneself, the communicator, to an objective nobody but then incessantly compose qualitative opposites into a unity, a dialectical knot, and then force

---

42. *Postscript*, 72.

43. Ibid., 73.

44. Rhetorical speech is artful but it does not introduce dialectical factors. It strives for immediate subjective effect and does not properly orient the subject to his own internal teleology.

Indirect Communication

the reader to untie the knot himself. The other way is so to neutralize the argument that the most zealous partisans and most rabid enemies can use the same argument.[45] Certainly Kierkegaard's literature is sufficiently neutral so that anti-pathetic passions, the happy ones of faith and the unhappy ones of offense, are both compatible with the argument.[46]

The knot that Kierkegaard tied and which his readers had to untie was composed for religious purposes. The multiple oppositions were an endeavor to beguile a person into the recognition of what an ethical and religious decision meant.[47] The literature maieutically began with the aesthetic works, for these were the means of getting in touch with men. But as one reads along, one moves out of the aesthetic, through the directly communicative ethical works, and "headlong into contact with the religious."[48] This at least was the intention. The performance is perhaps more complex than this statement of plot indicates. The illusion against which the entire literature is directed is the one which has translated the subjective life, the moral and religious life, into terms of reflection and direct communication. Kierkegaard makes the movement a double one: out of the subjective and non-reflective into the reflective and objective, and then back into the subjective and passional. He writes:

> And in a Christian sense this means that—simplicity is not the point of departure from which one goes on to become interesting, witty, profound, poet, philosopher, etc. No, the very contrary. *Here* is where one begins (with the interesting, etc.) and becomes simpler, attaining simplicity. This in "Christendom" is the Christian movement: one does not reflect oneself into Christianity; but one reflects oneself out of something else and becomes, more and more simply, a Christian.[49]

---

45. *Training in Christianity*, 132–33.
46. *Fragments*, 39–43.
47. *On My Work*, 148.
48. Ibid.
49. Ibid.

CHAPTER 12

Kierkegaard and the Sermon[1]

KIERKEGAARD'S IMMENSE LITERATURE DOES two different things: it offers instances of all kinds of literature, argumentative prose, rhapsodies on music, love and art, aesthetic criticism, religious discourses, and secondly, a literature about all of these. In the first genre, the Danish author expresses his passions and feelings and these are aroused by and commensurate with everything from a sensitivity to music and the sublimities of nature to equally passionate and feelingful enthusiasm for the ethical and the Christian ways of life. As any of his readers well know, Kierkegaard invented pseudonymous authors to state this passionate content, partly as a precaution against the reader's temptation of imputing the author's authority to the numerous and contrary views coming from his pen,[2] and partly as a tactic aimed to get his reader out of an objective and contemplative mood.

The second kind of writing, i.e., the literature about the literature, finds Kierkegaard commenting in a spirit of detached objectivity about the same matters otherwise given passionate representation. To speak to the matter at hand, Kierkegaard writes not only numerous religious discourses (quite a number of these were delivered as sermons in the churches of Copenhagen) but also about this mode of communication.[3] Thus, he is not only a singular creator of the ser-

1. Editors' note: This chapter, slightly revised, appeared in *Journal of Religion* 37 (January, 1957) 1–9.

2. In 1851 he says that anyone who lumps a lot of quotations "hurly-burly together . . . as if they were my words" would make him out to be a lunatic. Dru, *Journals*, entry 1238 (*Papirer* X 6 B, 145).

3. Excellent illustrations of his sermon-like addresses are to be found in his *Edifying Discourses*, vols. 1–4, and *Christian Discourses*.

monic discourse but is the rare example of a man who reflected long and fruitfully on the purpose, form, style, and limits of the sermon.

He provides on this subject, as upon almost every other one in which he has an interest, actual examples and illustrations and then a more ideal and abstract delineation. This essay concerns principally his specifics, his homiletic lore, rather than his more generic reflections. The latter are to be found in more extended form under the rubric of "indirect communication" and their analysis is to be found elsewhere in these papers. Undoubtedly it would be instructive also to examine Kierkegaard's religious discourses in order to isolate the rules of his actual practice but such an inquiry demands more objectivity than this writer can command when reading such stirring writings. Suffice it to note that Kierkegaard usually does what he says ought to be done and that here as elsewhere his literature both reflects and is his own education.

Kierkegaard was a constant listener to, and reader of, sermons. He went to the downtown churches and heard the reputable preachers. His many personal papers record an almost continuous give-and-take with sundry sermons.[4] He was a sharply critical, yet a worshipful, listener. He was never slow to spot difficulties, the lapses of thought, the drop of sweat trickling down his Reverence's nose as his voice quavered and arms flailed the air. But he knows also on the occasion of a preached sermon seriousness, joy, and even the dread and sense of guilt which belong to a man in the presence of God.

Even though Kierkegaard's papers are a rich source on this topic, I have chosen intentionally to stay within his published and translated works for citations. For these provide usually a better developed context for his remarks than do the papers. But, anyone who wishes to read more can be certain that both will augment and substantiate what is here fragmentarily quoted.

In what follows, four abuses of the sermon are noted. A single word has been chosen to characterize each of the four. These are the author's, not Kierkegaard's, but, if they summarize the argument,

---

4. Remarkable insight into Kierkegaard's early concern about the limits of sermonizing can be gained by examining the report of the homiletical overseers who had to review Kierkegaard's efforts. He acted as critic for another's sermon on December 1, 1840, and was heard in January, 1841 and duly criticized, etc. *Breve*, I:13–16 and *E.P.*, I:273–74.

their use is probably justifiable. The four abuses are to be found respectively when the sermon is: (a) a "deductive" argument; (b) an "aesthetic" object or stimulus; (c) "palliative"; (d) "ethical" rather than religious and/or Christian. It will be apparent, too, that all of these abuses are so defined in virtue of more abstract considerations, some of which have been earlier noted.

I

One of Kierkegaard's pseudonyms speaks scornfully of the confusion of the day which demands that the theatre be didactic and education stimulating, and that philosophers be edifying and professors be in the pulpit.[5] And if it is the case that some men, let us say the parsons, are supposed to be prosecuting attorneys for Deity, then, and then only, is the marshaling of evidence and drawing of proofs really essential.[6] Or, if it could be shown that anyone becomes religious and Christian by getting in on a demonstrable conclusion, then it might be proper that every priest should be a philosopher intent upon necessary conclusions. But this Kierkegaard finds to be a confusion, a mixture, as he says, of scholarship and edification. Anyone who has lived in the shadow of theological seminaries and particularly of those with faculty of great repute cannot but relish Johannes de Silentio's ironic remarks about the state of affairs:

> If scientific scholarship is overestimated, not only the students but the clergy are ranked according to a possible relation to this maximum of being able to become or to be a theological professor...[7]

But, the author goes on, suppose one experiments by asking the theological professor to deliver a sermon. Whether one learns directly from the professor that he cannot do it or infers it while listening to

---

5. *Either/Or*, I:121.

6. *Concept of Dread.* Kierkegaard in his *Journasl* for 1847 argued that the difference between a discourse and a sermon was this: The discourse or Christian address was directed toward doubt, and it could be by a layman, while the sermon had authority, was declarative and delivered by an ordained man. *Papirer* VIII A, 6 (*JP* 1, 638); some of this is translated by Dru, *Journals*, entry 629. Note the comments of Fr. Roos, *Søren Kierkegaard and Catholicism*, 20–25.

7. See the appendix to the *Stages on Life's Way,* 448.

his sermon, is it not in order for the professional and scientific type of Christian to admit that a sermon does not belong to the same genre as a scholarly effort?[8] The hypothetical professor is quoted to the effect ". . . but I understand very well that it may take the whole time and diligence of a distinguished man to prepare and deliver a sermon just as scholarly learning does mine."[9] The point is, obviously, that a sermon does not have to be a proof at all and both the pew which expects it and the pulpit which gives it are equally mistaken.

The sermon does not establish certainty for the listener. But it presupposes certitude and authority on the part of the preacher. Religious authority is in consequence of the Church's ordination of a man to the priesthood and, also, and this latter point was stressed from 1850 on, in virtue of the religiousness and intensity of the speaker. The pastor, supposing then that he is the deliverer of the sermon, speaks out of the character of his thought. Kierkegaard found it ludicrous to behave as the Swedish priest, who, becoming disturbed by the effect his address was having upon his hearers, said: "Children, do not weep; the whole thing might be a lie."[10] To use either the certainties or the uncertainties reflecting the degree of evidence, learning, and argument, in order to create or dispel enthusiasm and passion is an irreligious matter. Religious certitude is not a consequence of proofs; it is not a resolution of reflective doubt. Pastors are not required to show which sentences can be believed and which cannot. Religious certitude and incertitude are a reflection of the despair or confidence one feels concerning the validity of his own personality. A sermon which produces by deductive reasoning the conclusion that every listener is a sinner because all men are sinners is a capital instance of the substitution of cleverness on the part of the pastor for the sense of personal invalidity, the sense of guilt and repentance, on the part of the auditor.[11] Not only the auditor suffers, but the pastor

8. *For Self-Examination*, 203.

9. *Stage on Life's Way*, 449.

10. *Attack upon Christendom*, "Instant," no. 6, 181.

11. *Concept of Dread*, 100. This is almost as bad as the pastor saying: "Thou shalt die unto the world.—The fee is five dollars." *Papirer* X 4 A, 267. Another example of a confusion of categories is explored within his book on Adler. There he notes that a lot of religious addresses defend Christianity in erroneous categories and his example is a bishop who says that the Bible solves great human riddles. *On Authority and Revelation*, 114–15.

is also deluded. Anyone who believes that premises and an argument predispose the sense of guilt has forgotten that it is the quality of one's life in relation to God that is the occasion for the guilt.

But more subtle and infinitely more pervasive, especially among the highly literate clergy, is the conviction (certainly as widespread today as it was in Kierkegaard's day) that it is essential to be certain and clear upon fundamental philosophical matters in order to have a proper Christian confidence and sermonic aplomb. The awful cry today among the seminarians and other religious leaders about logical positivism and the *malaise* of metaphysics is a case in point. It seems that the destruction of philosophical certainties will again mean the end of faith. Kierkegaard saw the other side—the situation in which philosophical and metaphysical claims were widely admissible and sermons were frequently a kind of ecclesiastical and popular redundance of them. As a philosopher Kierkegaard remarks upon the unhappy experience of watching the pastor, whose certainties were secondhand and those of the last generation, adding in bumbling fashion a few extemporaneous and conceding remarks—after being thrown a meaningful glance! Certainly Kierkegaard was not the last man of learning whose very presence challenged the premises and disturbed the deductive serenity of a sermon. A sermon that is successful only because the hearers are more ignorant than the pastor is not Christianly successful. Neither is fawning before a learned pastor humility before God.

The other side of the matter, the huge stake some clerics have in metaphysical certainty, is equally ludicrous. The poor man must always be fighting the philosophers or at least reading them in order to get his permission to be faithful. The onus of Christian responsibility for the sermonizer gets to be more learning rather than the reduplication of Christ's life in his own.

A sermon that is the work of "a guaranteeing clergyman,"[12] is it not a misunderstanding? What about the man who with three solid reasons will bring prayer into good repute, and not only that, but as he warms up a little, will prove again by three reasons that to pray is a bliss surpassing all understanding—and do it with the understanding—is this not absurd?[13] Kierkegaard is convinced that such sermons

---

12. *Postscript*, 378.
13. *Sickness Unto Death*, 167–69. Another example explored by Kierkegaard was

are the explanation of something else, namely, the spiritlessness of the Christian pulpit and the pew. Against these suspicious admixtures of reasons, whimpers, and ingratiating appeals, this misuse of learning and false eloquence, Kierkegaard proposes a sermon born out of one's own life, lived in the thought and discipline of Christianity. He writes:

> No, just as in a well-appointed house one is not obliged to go downstairs to fetch water, but by pressure already has it on the upper floors merely by turning the tap, so too is it with the real Christian orator . . .[14]

III

But then there is the finely timbered soul, the refined pastor who has taste and poetic qualities—too many perhaps for his congregation. What about his sermon? One of the aphorisms in *Either/Or* tells us about Reverend Jasper Morten, probably a sensitive lover of the beauties of nature, who insisted that: "A man should never lose his courage; when misfortunes tower most fearfully about him, there appears in the sky a helping hand."[15] The listener, a habitual traveler, had never seen anything like this but a few days later he saw a queer cloud that looked somewhat like an arm. Ah, perhaps this was it—if only the Reverend were here to decide the matter! But then someone came along with the warning that it was a storm cloud. After taking to his heels, the traveler can not help wondering what the Reverend would have done in his place!

The Reverend's retort might well have been only a figure of speech. But this is to draw attention to another difficulty in sermonizing. When is a sermon ever literal? If one kind of preachment is a misplaced argument, then another kind is surely these stirring aesthetic effects which induce aesthetic enjoyment and wonder, excite the imagination, and even cause admiration for the inordinate flow of words.[16] The latter kind of sermon can be very serious sounding.

Magister Adler who transposes all the religious meanings by the help of Hegelian philosophy. *On Authority and Revelation*, 146–48.

14. *For Self-Examination*, 36.
15. *Either/Or*, I:21–22.
16. *Sickness Unto Death*, 122.

It can be confessional sounding, too, if that happens to be the mode of the hour. But its aesthetic character is evident most clearly when it occasions greater regard for the possibilities by which Christianity is described rather than a concern about realizing that possibility. Christian enthusiasm is in the direction of realizing with and by one's existence the possibility there is in Christ Jesus. This does not mean luxuriating in the thought of the Christian life, of admiring Jesus, of being the spectator to a divine drama, or of agreeing that martyrdom is most exhilarating. Kierkegaard believed most ardently that the principle cause of unbelief was not intellectual doubt, but the reluctance to obey and "to be" what Christianity asked. The scholarly business, even theological and Biblical studies, could reflect this, he suggests, just as the entire population's interest in interpreting and translating and collating and analyzing a royal command might mean a lack of conscientiousness.[17] He observes:

> A remarkable change comes over them all: they all become interpreters, the office-bearers became authors, every blessed day there comes out an interpretation more learned than the last, more acute, more elegant . . . Everything became interpretation—but no one read the royal command with a view to acting in accordance with it.[18]

But then consider the clergyman. He too is rebellious but his way out is not scholarship, it is affectation and elegance. And he uses trivialities: dress, rolling his R's, forceful gestures, leaps of religious enthusiasm, but above all, he keeps insisting that it is all very, very profound. He gets acceptance for Christianity for the wrong reasons just as the parent would who pleads his genius or cleverness or profundity as the grounds for his son's obedience.[19]

When the pericope text calls for the sermon about the ten lepers, "The priest protests that he too has felt as if he were a leper—but when there is typhus."[20] While the terrors of leprosy are sketched with all the powers of a well-trained orator, the worshippers hear their

---

17. *For Self-Examination*, 64.

18. Ibid., 58.

19. This paragraph is an abbreviation of Kierkegaard's remarks in *On Authority and Revelation*, 116–18.

20. *Stages*, 222.

beloved pastor say with feeling that he is as one of them—indeed it is enough to make anyone weep. And this is Kierkegaard's point. The test of a sermon's power is not the pathos it produces in church, not the immediate emotional responses it quickens. Even if everyone's thoughts become pleasant and his spirit warmed, Kierkegaard would caution the homiletician of the danger of accepting immediate responses at face value. A sermon is not Christian unless it awakens self-reflection, strengthens resolution, and brings the life of the Christian into actuality.

Kierkegaard goes so far as to say that even if the sermon re-creates Jesus' crucifixion and its cruelties, even if every last listener shudders over the injustice and yearns to redress the wrongs, still there is nothing intrinsically Christian in all of this. The ease with which some pastors talk about those who have sacrificed their life for the sake of the truth makes him wonder whether the obligation and duty, the paradigmatic element, has really been recognized.[21] There is a profanation of holiness in pleasant talk, in praise if you will, as well as in harsh condemnatory speech. Where preaching pleasantly is made a duty, an entire land, with the help of constant sermonizing, can lose all notion of solemnity and dread, and, instead can be led to believe that God and truth need man rather than the other way around. Soon everybody is led to believe that:

> One renders an exceedingly great service by going once in a while to church, when one is praised for it by the parson, who on God's behalf thanks one for the honor of the visit, confers upon one the title of pious, and on the other hand, taunts a bit those who never do God the honor of going to church.[22]

How amazed Kierkegaard would have been to hear Christianity praised and church worship enjoyed because they would conspire to keep America free of communism and the world a better place.

The constant use of aesthetic devices, of rhetorical flourishes, serves then to make something else higher than the Christian life. Nothing is more ironic than the effect in Protestantism where the notion finally grows up that the sermon is really the major religious effort and accomplishment. Then holiness and virtue, and a life won by

---

21. *The Present Age*, 100.
22. *Sickness Unto Death*, 190.

losing, seem trivial and talk about being faithful becomes the highest expression of faithfulness. At this point Kierkegaard knew that there might be all kinds of motives, including base ones, for letting sermons redound to the minister's glory. The worshippers find an excuse in their lack of talent for not being as faithful (really as eloquent) as the minister; the minister finds an excuse for not being like the Apostles in having a congregation like his, simple and trusting people, who are already so inspired by what he says! Suppose that one Sunday the pastor preaches a glorious sermon about the gloriousness of faith. Then, warns Kierkegaard's pseudonym there is a possibility that believing in God becomes identical with believing that the sermon was really glorious, or if not that, then that faith is a glorious thing.[23] All the while, the aim ought not to be anything less than the increase of glorious faith.

Clearly the point that Kierkegaard makes in all of this is that immediate responses to sermons are neither to be sought nor trusted. The parson who wills the immediate responses, for example, the familiar remark of his hearer about never forgetting that sermon, would do a lot better seeking the seriousness which would cause the listener always to remember it. The sermon would then rest with him like an obligation, always eliciting earnestness of life. The sermon which is so clear and plain that it encourages everybody to talk, and makes everyone an expert in theology, is also a pitiable effect, especially if the mark of religion is in one's deeds, not in one's words. The hazard in attractive and enticing sermons, full of literary values and light learning, is that they too easily become the means whereby the listener secures himself against Christianity by the very energy and enthusiasm by which he responds to the sermon. By admiring the sermon, or even the preacher, and perchance God too, the hearer misses the obligation laid upon us all to be Christians.[24]

---

23. *Postscript*, 304. Note the remarks about preaching now becoming a "heathenish and theatrical thing" and that now something should be done about getting preaching back into the streets. Dru, *Journals*, entry 764 (*Papirer* IX A, 39).

24. *Judge for Yourselves*, 153. This is what Kierkegaard said about Grundtvig's preaching, that it was his weekly evacuation, and an excursion in historical prolixity. Dru, *Journals*, entry 313 (*Papirer* II A, 542).

III

But then there is another kind of sermon, which in the interest of putting first things first, and seeking to get to the heart of the matter, the main point as it were, tends to attenuate the Gospel. It palliates, it abbreviates the Christian cause in the interest of getting the would-be believer to the terminal point. Such a sermon need not be short; in fact, it may be inordinately long. The crux of this kind of sermon is not served by the length; rather it is the well-meaning intention of helping the worshippers to the precious essence of the text. Thus when one of Kierkegaard's authors describes the sermonic adaptations of the story of Abraham and Isaac, he notes that the temptation is to hurry over the troublesome three days' journey to the Mount, the knife in the outstretched hand, and get too soon to the ram tangled in the bush.[25] Here the critical issue can be stated in a rhetorical question: Ought a sermon make the costs of faith cheaper? Does the preacher have the right to recite the conclusion without noting the taxing conditions permitting it? Is this the meaning of grace?

To put the question thus is to make the negative answer too easy. Kierkegaard notes the fact that a sermon governed by the laudable desire of making faith readily accessible also omits frequently the genuinely religious dimension. If one moves to the Christ child and forgets Mary's mortification and dread, if one moves to Paul's victorious sayings and omits his many sufferings and struggles, then is there not the possibility that the sermon helps create the illusion that what one man got by toil and distress another one gets by reading—and the help of an exegete?[26] Is this not to misunderstand faith, grace, and Christian living? Surely such preaching vitiates even the Scripture, despite its use of lofty categories.

Kierkegaard knew what "the fruits of the spirit" were. He was an assiduous reader of Scripture and sought diligently to effect what he read in his life. But he learned that these "fruits" were conditional

---

25. *Fear and Trembling*, 76. In a perceptive passage in his papers, Kierkegaard asks whether it is right to train the clergy to the degree that they introduce Christianity so artfully that it hides the wound which it is supposed to elicit, probe, and then heal. (*Papirer* XI 1 A, 69; *JP* 6, 6860.) According to Kierkegaard, they become like the barbers who take off the beard without the customer knowing it.

26. Ibid., 36–37.

upon repentance, seriousness, a sense of guilt, and personal concern. He suspected preaching that tried to smuggle Christianity into the world by doing away with these personal but necessary conditions.[27] Repairing to the clergy to be set at ease, letting him do away with your fear and trembling by getting to that ram in the bush—these seem proper and consoling, but Kierkegaard asks whether this is not the consolation which omits Christianity?[28] There is even the possibility that "the prodigious quantity of consoling thoughts the physicians of the soul prescribe only make the sickness worse."[29]

Kierkegaard came to feel that Protestantism, and not least the Lutheranism he knew best, was especially prone to the superficial preaching of consolation. The Protestant insistence upon faith, often at the expense of works, gave motivation to the slighting of human concern and effort. To admit that Christianity wounds before it cures, that faith presupposes something within the human creature, seems to verge toward the one-time polemically opposite view that works are efficacious in God's sight. The emphasis upon faith was indeed a corrective in a situation where works were already given emphasis.[30] But the sermon which can presuppose no works, no concern with them even, falsifies faith, even cheapens it, by everlastingly defining it by reference to that which no longer exists.

Kierkegaard insisted that there were no secondhand disciples. This was his way of saying that there is no discipleship via other disciples. The faith relationship is, for every believer alike, early or late, a matter of contemporaneity with Jesus Christ.[31] Faith is not then a matter of profiting on another's life, a quick way to conclusions about how to live. Even Scripture is no shortcut to faithfulness. Others and the Bible teach us what are the personal prerequisites and consequences of contemporaneity with the Savior. The sermon has no right

---

27. Ibid., 109.

28. *Training in Christianity*, 69–71.

29. *Sickness Unto Death*, 184. This is the contention made over and over again in the pages of the pamphleteering literature against the Church. Note the *Attack Upon Christendom*.

30. *For Self-Examination*. Note especially the opening sections. In other places Kierkegaard notes that it is much easier to preach indulgences in Protestantism than the preacher admits. Dru, *Journals*, entry 1097 (*Papirer* X 3 A, 72).

31. This is the argument of *Philosophical Fragments* and *Training in Christianity*.

to remove these. To improve upon grace by omitting the inner life and its difficulties is something like the doctor's wonderful cure—everything was fine about it except that the patient died.

A point to be noted here is that this matter has nothing whatever to do with orthodoxy and liberalism. Theological positions do not safeguard sermons. Here the issue is not the theological position so much as it is knowing the limits of one's helpfulness. Even the most austerely sounding Biblical sermon, one which uses all of the strenuous categories, can still delude the person of responsibility if there is a trivialization of faithfulness going on. And, on the other side, the mildest sounding sermon can still energize human beings if it suggests with appropriate passion the conditions that men must meet in order to be faithful.

IV

In a discourse, actually delivered before Holy Communion, Kierkegaard says that it ". . . would merely give thee pause for an instant on the way to the altar," but then adds a pregnant comment:

> It is true that a sermon should also bear witness to Him, proclaiming His word and His teaching; but for all that a sermon is not His voice.[32]

This remark signals a peculiar failure of the sermon. It is not that past pastors believe that their voice is that of God's but, rather, it is that the pastor gets himself snarled up in a sequence of notions. If what he says is true, if God is truth, then the sermon (if true) must be His voice. But this is to fail to distinguish the sermon from a lecture. In the latter, agreement or disagreement is the aim. What the lecturer asks is that the hearer recognize and cognize for himself what has been said. If the sentences in a lecture are true, they are then worthy of being learned. The immediate assent is accordingly important. But when a sermon is professed to start in an analogous relation to the worshipper the categories are confused. For a sermon is not something to be learned even if, like the occasional lecture, it may be true. The religious response is not an assent to the truth of the sermon. This

---

32. *Christian Discourses*, 278.

is why Kierkegaard's authors say over and over that a sermon is not His voice and that one is not saved by the discourse.[33]

When the sermon omits God's imperative mood and when it becomes the indicative, when it becomes truth to be believed, then the sermon creates the obligation to hear more sermons and a trivializing ethicality is a result. Some sermons may not err in any other way than by putting the stress in the wrong place. As lofty as the church's role in God's economy may be, it nonetheless is a serious error to create by a sermon more religious importance for sermons. This is a kind of spiritual deprivation occasioned by sermons which claim too much for themselves.[34]

Kierkegaard was troubled by the fact that sermons did not make clear that the parish register was not the book of life.[35] Neither did most sermons reveal the ethical drama in the life of faith if they fostered the belief that the present existing church was already God's triumphant and victorious elect. To Kierkegaard, this was all of one piece. If no one introduced the ethical distinctiveness into the sermon, namely that Christianity meant a new synthesis of the subject's life in virtue of the existence of Jesus Christ, then it would not be introduced either in respect to the church's activity and parish life. The sermon could introduce the Christian ethic only by denying its own intrinsic Christian significance and by making clear that a relation to the sermon, even affirmative, was not *ipso facto* a relation to God.[36]

Of course, everybody admits this upon a little reflection. But nobody admits this while they are talking, while the sermon is going on. Again, the pastor may laudably enough be trying to save Christianity from abstractness, he may want to give the faith some "bite"—a few requirements, proximate to the lives of ordinary men. But the discourse which makes a Christian requirement of the hearing of more discourses errs on the side of appropriateness.[37] It is a matter again

---

33. *Stages*, 419.

34. *Stages*, 74. Also note *Training in Christianity*, 214.

35. Likewise Kierkegaard says that it is unfair to change Christianity in order to make people more ready to pay the teacher of it. Dru, *Journals*, entry 1112 (*Papirer* X 3 A, 173).

36. Kierkegaard says that in eternity ministers will not preach, they will be judged like everyone else. *Papirer* X 1 A, 320 (*JP* 6, 6395).

37. *Stages*, 168.

of fitting Christianity to the requirement of the times.[38] An example from Kierkegaard's literature follows:

> Everybody wants to work for others. This is the conventional theme of the patriotic or moral address, where it is easier to understand; but it is also a conventional feature of the rhetorical form of the religious address. I do not doubt that it is found in the printed instructions for preachers . . . If the sermon is about preparing the way of the Lord, the first topic has to do with the duty of every Christian to do his part in spreading Christianity—"not only we priests, but also everybody," etc. That is *charmant*. ". . . it is not only I and we priests who should labor thus, but you should all labor thus!" How? Yes, this is the only thing that is not made clear in this serious address . . . Now the first topic is finished; the priest wipes off the sweat, and the hearers do likewise, at the mere thought that they have thus become missionaries.[39]

The sermon is specific but it tends to identify the Christian's performance with sermonizing, with what goes on in the church, and this surely is not enough. There is a narrow way between believing the sermon to be God's voice and hence as close as we ever get to heavenly things and believing it to be just another expression of opinion. But to find this way was the task of the pastor and Kierkegaard again did not hold that anyone could find it for anyone else.[40]

V

In conclusion it ought to be remarked that these are but a few of the ways in which Kierkegaard reminds his readers that talking is not sermonic, nor Christian, simply because God's name is in it. Against the pew he notes that there is so little attention paid that the most pagan homilies with a few proper name changes would seem properly religious and Christian. Against the pulpit he warns that not everything

---

38. *Christian Discourses*, 172. In another vein, Kierkegaard says most sermonizing is "poetry with a corroborating addition of ethics." Dru, *Journals*, entry 821 (*Papirer* IX A, 312).

39. *Stages*, 314–15. Note a comparison between the poet and the pastor in the respect noted above in *Papirer* X 1 A, 11 (*JP* 6, 6300).

40. *Training in Christianity*, 88.

concocted by a clergyman is therefore religious.[41] Both the speaker and the auditors must remember that the church is not a theater in which there is one performer, the preacher, and many spectators and critics, the worshippers. Christianity is the correction of such an illusion. It tells us that all of us are on stage and that there is only one spectator and He is God.[42] The sermon that does not correct the pride of its preacher or the expectancy of the hearers by referring both to God does not introduce the Christian "decisive difference" to which Kierkegaard's author refers:

> ... there will always remain a decisive difference between the poet and the religious speaker, in that the poet has no other *telos* than the psychological truth of his description and the art of his presentation, while the speaker has at the same time the "principal" aim of transforming everything into edification. The poet loses himself in the delineation of passion, but for the religious speaker this is but the first step; the next step is for him the decisive one, namely, to force the obstreperous individual to lay down his arms, to soften, to clear up; in short to translate everything into terms of edification.[43]

---

41. *Postscript*, see especially 405ff. See also 430, *passim*.

42. *Training in Christianity*, 229.

43. *Postscript*, 230. Note a remark made years later, in 1850 or 1851, in which he concludes that poets are in fact doing the job better than the pastors. His theme then is: "No, the parsons canonize bourgeois mediocrity." Dru, *Journals*, entry 1134 (*Papirer* X 3 A, 463).

CHAPTER 13

Faith and Christianity[1]

IN THIS CHAPTER I propose to indicate first what Christian faith is not. In the second and third sections I shall indicate what Kierkegaard believes it to be. In both instances, negatively and affirmatively, it will be seen, however, that the passional and non-noetic interests are important. But Christianity presupposes a new object, a new terminus for interest and consequently there are similarities and differences.

I

It is clear first, that Christian faith is not a native endowment, not in the author's word, "a stronger or weaker spontaneity (immediacy)."[2] Thus it is distinguished from a happy-go-lucky attitude, from naive optimism that everything will turn out all right in the end. It is an inexact use of words, we are told, to call the power of resistance that some men have against disappointments and failures Christian faith. For,

> This power of resistance, this vital confidence in oneself, in the world, in mankind, and (among other things) in God, we

---

1. Editor's note: The first seven pages of this chapter are missing in the manuscript.
2. *For Self-Examination*, 101. In his *Christian Discourses*, 182, Kierkegaard says: "But the assurance of faith is not something one is born with, the youthful trustfulness of a joyous mind; still less is faith something we grasp out of the air." All of this echoes too his earliest ruminations on this subject as recorded in his papers for the years 1836–1838; cf. *Papirer*, vol. I, and passim.

call faith. But this is not using the word in a strictly Christian sense.³

Whatever the merits of such an attitude, it has "only human nature" as its assumption and is indistinguishable from other kinds of aesthetic immediacy.⁴ For example, the poet, who can take refuge in imaginative reconstructions of the human scene and who seems to adjust to the world via his own constructs, can easily masquerade for the multitude as a man of religious faith. And as is noted, especially if he moves away from the theater and into the church as a clergyman, then he brings about a confusion.⁵

A Napoleon who abounds in confidence and carries the age with him was a favorite Kierkegaardian example. But it was only inviting ambiguity to construe his magical touch in political and military affairs as a religious faith.⁶ For again, although he might feel himself fated for victory and this against overwhelming odds, and, though the most heroic of deeds might ensue, still Kierkegaard finds neither the intensity of accomplishment nor the duration of courage, the testament of religion, and more specifically, of Christian faith.⁷ Whatever sense can be made out of the concept of genius—Kierkegaard uses it to demarcate not spiritual superiority or qualitative difference but rather a kind of quantitative and individual difference—it is this that is more relevant to such immediacy rather than religious and Christian conceptions. Genius is immediacy as such, "with the subjectivity preponderating,"⁸ without the limitations and perhaps advantages too of mediated and cognitive controls.

The confusion on matters of faith is analogous to that which Kierkegaard noted in an essay penned in 1847 in which, distinguish-

3. Ibid., 101. Another discussion of this issue is to be found in Dru, *Journals*, entry 1084 (*Papirer* X 2 A, 592).

4. *Postscript*, 496. Also note "Existential Pathos 2," 386–468, and especially the discussion therein concerning the fortune-misfortune distinction as over against the religious idea of suffering. See also *Stages*.

5. *Postscript*, 348.

6. Ibid., 356ff.

7. On this point, see particularly the pseudonymous work *The Concept of Dread*, 86–92. Despite the fact that this book needs to be retranslated, I refer the reader to the present English translation for it still is superior to either the French or the German translations.

8. Ibid., 88. *Stages*, 441ff.

ing between "a genius" and "an apostle," he asserts that the Christian categories are always qualitative whereas those of the aesthetic sphere are properly quantitative. The genius has an immanent teleology just as do the wish-fulfillments that so often pass for faith.[9] Just as the genius may become an Apostle but not because of his talents, so the hearty confidence of men may eventuate in faith, but not in virtue of maturation.

What has been said seems to imply that faith is not related to subjectivity at all. But this is not so. Kierkegaard's description always seeks at once to distinguish it from the immediate interests in happiness, in longevity, in everything childish and seemingly natural and indigenous to us as creatures, but only for the purpose of showing that all of these reflect and are the interest in one's own existence. All that he considers under aesthetic immediacy is the unabashed and untaught interest in one's own existence. Kierkegaard does not allow that it is wrong to be interested in existing. In fact in a very moving letter, written in 1848 to a young relative, he says that it is a duty to love oneself, literally to have an interest in one's existence.[10] But as we shall note again, Christianity is not an interest-less existence; rather it presupposes the subjectivity and interest which the aesthete evinces but it also proposes a new object mediated to the individual, Jesus Christ. Christian faith is a form of subjectivity, of passion and interest, but not an immediate and native interest. This is also why there are no Christian children. Even granted the richest of native endowment still "no one starts by being a Christian, everyone becomes such in the fullness of time . . . if he does become such."[11]

Secondly, faith is not either an intuition of a cognitive sort. In the interest of an epistemological inquiry Kierkegaard has also distinguished between certain kinds of quasi-cognitive immediacies and the noncognitive attitudes and interests, also immediate. These, the

---

9. "Of the Difference Between a Genius and an Apostle," included in *Present Age*, 139–63. (This essay is included also in *On Authority and Revelation*.)

10. *Breve og Akstykker vedrørende Søren Kierkegaard*, vol. I, letter no. 196, 220–21. For an explanation of peculiar and relevant circumstances, see the editor's comments, ibid., II:39–40. See also Rikard Magnussen's *Søren Kierkegaard set udefra*, 167–72.

11. *Postscript*, 523. Also note the entire section, "Childish Christianity," 20–537. For a contrast in another key between aesthetic immediacy and religious faith, see the discussion in *Fear and Trembling*, esp. 40–46, and relevant comments in "On Authority and the Individual," 95, 132, passim.

ingredients of common sense, were noted in an earlier chapter. But, again, he does not grant that faith is an immediacy, neither a confidence in the good nor pre-rational noetic certainties. Without here attempting an exhaustive analysis of Kierkegaard's many comments upon these issues, I should instead remark only upon two kinds of immediacy, as it were, kinds of intuition, which he does find essential to all knowledge. First every knower has an immediate relation to a sensation. There is in other words sensory intuition. And here there is absolute certainty providing that one reports only what is seen and providing that "seen" does not connote an object or that something has occurred independently of the sensory manifold.[12] But, Christian faith is not a form of sensory intuition, for Christianity introduces something historical and nothing historical can be given immediately to the senses.[13] The point of saying that an event is historical is actually conveyed by the tenseful language we use to describe it. The transitions, for which our language tenses are a sign, are the very transitions that cannot be immediately sensed. Kierkegaard's point is, then, that the language of sensory intuition is present tense language. To make it more than this is to introduce uncertainty, and also means destroying the intuitive immediacy.

There is another kind of intuitive immediacy admissible to the cognitive enterprise. In all instances of conceptual existence, for example, there is an immediate and intuitive relation between the thinker and the objects of his thought. Here thinking is creation, it can give existence, albeit conceptual existence. In every instance where the being or existence of a thing means the same thing as being thought, it is a mistake to interject mediating questions.[14] Kierkegaard continues:

> But existence as a particular human being is not a pure ideal existence; it is only man in general who exists in that manner, which means that this entity does not exist at all. Existence is always something particular, the abstract does not exist. From this to draw the conclusion that the abstract is without valid-

12. *Fragments*, 66–67.

13. Ibid., "The Apprehension of the Past," 64–73. Frequent developments of this view are given in the papers too. Note Dru, *Journals*, entry 1044 (*Papirer* X 2 A, 406).

14. *Postscript*, 293. *Stages*, 39: "Ideality I know by myself." Also note *Papirer* X 2 A, 439 (*JP* 1, 1059).

ity is a misunderstanding; but it is also a misunderstanding to confound discourse by even raising the question of existence, or of reality in the sense of existence, in connection with the abstract.[15]

On the other hand, it is equally ridiculous to introduce grounds for the certainty that any idea exists for one's thought, because it is quite sufficient to insist that an idea exists when it is thought. All of skepticism can admit this kind of abstract certainty and never give up its skeptical case, providing that there is no existential interpretation of the abstract certainty.[16]

The latter kind of immediacy is presupposed apparently by Kierkegaard in order to account for the existence of logical rules. For him there is logical insight and there are no valid and meaningful arguments for ultimate logical principles. And here, too, there is a kind of certainty, limited to those having the intuitive awareness.

But in neither instance, of sensory intuition and of the intuition of essences, does Kierkegaard see any resemblance to Christian faith. He argues that the significance of both of these is limited to the knowledge enterprise. These are then pre-cognitional immediacies, endeavors to relate religion to cognition as pre-science to science that he believes rests on a mistaken analysis of religion. Instead of understanding faith as pre-cognitional as, say, Hegelian philosophers described immediacy, Kierkegaard's thought always is in the direction of denying that religious faith is pre-anything. If it is an immediacy at all it stands related to an aesthetical and ethical immediacy, not pre-cognitive intuition.[17] If it stands related to reflection and mediation at all, it is post-reflection, "after reflection" as the authors say.[18] Furthermore Kierkegaard was a kind of empiricist and denied the notion that reflection "abrogated" the sensory immediacy. The idealist philosophers' reconstruction of the acts of knowing he found to be a falsification. For against the assertion that reflection and ideas constructed the world and enhanced the existential certainties,

---

15. *Postscript*, 294.

16. Ibid., 299. Skepticism has to do with the relation between conceivability, ideal being or intentional existence, and actuality, not with either alone.

17. Ibid., 310, footnote. This is why Abraham is compared in *Fear and Trembling* to great passional figures of Greek tragedy, not to the Greek philosophers or theologians.

18. *Papirer* VIII A, 650 (*JP* 5, 6135).

Kierkegaard insists that the existents of the real world are brought into consciousness by virtue of interest, of the commonsense concern that characterizes every man. If anything, reflection can destroy this interest, but it can never correct it or abrogate it, not on the side of certainty at least. But this is not an intuitive matter—it is a passional matter and matter of interest.

Religious faith is not an intuition of God nor is it an intuitive certainty that God exists. No erstwhile immediacy can resolve a genuinely cognitive doubt and, insofar as a thinker raises questions which demand answers, intuition is no answer. Considering Christianity, Kierkegaard finds that it posits a relation to God via the historical. This means that any person who stands in a faith relationship must stand also in an historical relation with Jesus of Nazareth. All historical relations are non-immediate and are cognitively mediated only.[19] But the historical relation is itself cognitive, and not religious; however, it is essential for the later relation of faith. Immediacy without the historical relation is religion without a mediator. The judgments of the aesthete author in the second volume of *Either/Or* express what were also Kierkegaard's later judgments in other contexts, namely:

> ... one cannot acquit the mystic of a certain intrusiveness in his relation with God ... There is always an inconsistency implied ... he chooses himself abstractly and therefore lacks transparency... For the mystic teaches that it (finite reality) is vanity, illusion, sin. But every such judgment is a metaphysical judgment and does not define ethically my relation to existence ... Consequently, just as he misunderstood reality and construed it metaphysically as vanity, so, too, he misunderstands the historical and construes it metaphysically as unprofitable labor.[20]

In his papers for the year 1848 we read Kierkegaard's own words to the effect that a relationship to God must be dialectical in order to be spiritual, that uncertainty is the dialectical condition herein ob-

---

19. *Fragments*, 64–73. "The historical cannot be given immediately to the senses, since the elusiveness of becoming is involved in it" (66). Also, note the detailed discussion about the relation between anything historical and "ideality" (or teleology) in *Stages*, 397–402.

20. *Either/Or*, II:204–9.

Faith and Christianity 281

taining, and that immediate certainty in a God relation "is something which I cannot acquire."[21]

In respect to these first two modes of defining faith we can now summarize by saying that faith is not an immediacy. It is neither a feeling nor an intuition. To say either would make faith admittedly non-cognitive, or at least non-propositional, but for Kierkegaard both of these conclusions were mistaken. But, neither is faith, therefore, a noetic act of belief. Knowledge is only mistakenly given immediate religious and ethical significance. Instead of analyzing linguistic expressions to locate the source of error, Kierkegaard finds the difficulty in pragmatic considerations. Knowledge is handled and used deceitfully and dishonestly. An immorality in the user rather than an ambiguity in the linguistic expression is also responsible for imparting more to knowledge than it can possibly bear. He writes:

> What really is the shrewd secret of mistrust? It consists in an abuse of knowledge . . . The secret and the falsity lies in the fact that, without further ceremony, it transposes this knowledge into faith, pretending it to be nothing, pretending that it was something that need not even be noticed, "since everyone who has this knowledge must 'necessarily' decide in the same way": as if, consequently, it were externally certain and absolutely decided that if a man has knowledge, then it is also known what conclusion he will reach . . . whereas, from the same knowledge, by virtue of belief, a man can infer, assume and believe exactly the opposite.[22]

Where knowledge is credited with religious meaning, there is misunderstanding, first of the neutral character of knowledge, and, then of the nature of the cognitive act of belief in contrast to the religious act of faith. All that was said in previous chapters about objectivity and subjectivity is germane to this consideration of faith. But it becomes incumbent herewith to turn to Kierkegaard's affirmations on this subject.

---

21 *Papirer*, vol. IX, especially the first sections. Cf. Dru, *Journals*, entry 763ff.

22. *Works of Love*, 183. Kierkegaard insists over and over upon the fact that in respect to a decision of what one should do, knowledge, much or little, is "congeries of data" (*Stages*, 398), raw material, nondeterminative, neutral, etc.

II

For this analysis we turn to the *Training in Christianity*. This book together with *The Sickness Unto Death* construes the content of Christianity, insofar as it permits, from a philosophical standpoint. But while admitting that such a standpoint is severely restricted in scope, it must also be admitted that it permits clarity. The possibility of knowing what Christianity is without being a Christian is a presupposition of Kierkegaard's entire effort as a literary writer. It is also a conclusion following from the argument of the *Postscript* and the *Fragments*, as he has already noted.[23] It is, therefore, also possible to know what faith is without being a Christian. It is another question whether this understanding and knowing may not be an evasion of the principal task. Again, it is important to remember that Kierkegaard thought Christianity rather easy to understand and extremely difficult to effect and to become, and that the duplicity of organized religion and also of theological scholarship was to make it almost as nothing to become a Christian but very difficult and laborious to understand it.[24] Therefore, he was not inclined to credit his own or his reader's understanding with any particular religious merit. But neither does he deny that his view is objectively correct.

If we remember again the relationship which Kierkegaard discovered between the aesthetical and the ethical, between the interests of a man and the categorization and formalization of these in obligations and acts of duty, then we can also reconstruct Kierkegaard's case for an understanding of faith. Faith is not knowledge any more than a statement of duty by itself is my interest or inclination. Knowledge is propositional. The act of believing a proposition is not a religious act of belief. But why? According to the argument already noted all cognitive belief is an attempt to make realities intelligible. But cognition is limited to the acknowledgement of disinterested and detached possibles, which in order to be cognized, are already translated into linguistic and cognized forms. Events or things in their actuality are not knowable.

---

23. *Postscript*, 332. "It is a difficult question whether a man can know what it is to be a Christian without being one, which must be denied."

24. Ibid., 330–40. The particular point is made again on 332.

The past becomes contemporary to a present knower by being translated into possibles. And the possibles can include both the imaginary and the poetized, on the one side, and what really occurred, history and all kinds of past events, on the other.[25] But the contemporaneity of possibles is a contemporaneity obtaining between the objects of thought and the thinker. That this contemporaneity presupposes immediate relations to sensory objects and immediate relations to idealities—these go without saying. In ways which were intentionally described as extra-cognitive and volitional, Kierkegaard argued that such possibles as those used in the historical and natural sciences could be affirmed to be disclosures of the real existing world. But our point here is not the general epistemological one but the specifically religious one. That Christian faith was not a matter of believing that some possibles, whatever they might be, were actually descriptive of God and man is his specific point.

For Christian faith is another kind of contemporaneity. It is the kind in which I can have a more than intellectual interest and to which I can stand related by more than "possibles." It is in this latter sense that Christian faith is a kind of contemporaneity, one of interest, in which the object of the interest and passion, is the existence and reality of another person.[26] This is a non-noetic relation, a relation of passion, of concern, and of interest. But it presupposes that a reflected and cognated content has been given before the interest ensues.

Because Jesus Christ was a historical person, it is necessary that some sentences about his existence must be known. But the facts about His life, whatever they might include, would not be constitutive of Christian belief. For it was the possibility of a transformed life in his hearers that was the aim of His preaching, if not of His entire existence. Therefore to the sentences about His existence there would have to be also a few to the effect that He was believed in. Climacus writes:

> If the contemporary generation had left nothing behind them but these words: "We have believed that in such and such a year God appeared among us in the humble figure of a ser-

---

25 *Training in Christianity*, 87.
26. *Postscript*, 290. Also note again, 280.

vant, that he lived and taught in our community, and finally died," it would be more than enough.[27]

The irony is that the immediate contemporaneity with Jesus as an historical figure did not credit cognitively or argumentatively the hypothesis that they ought to make Him an object of interest. Furthermore, there were no cognitive transitions, no logical transitions, leading from immediate sense impressions to a conclusion that He was God, for to say the latter means that His existence is of more interest than my own. And thus once the object of faith is dead and gone, we have not only the report that he lived but a testimony which goes to the effect that He was God. This latter statement is the statement of another kind of possibility, namely, that He being God for them might be God for me. But both the sentences about His historicity and those about His significance to others lack religious content in their cognitive form.

For admitting that he existed is to assert what any historian might. Even agreeing that the possibility of finding salvation in him was in fact realized by others turns out to be an assent without further effect and obligation. So, assent to his existence as a historical figure and assent to another person's actualization of the possibility he declared still leaves us within the rubric previously marked, that is to say, that all attempts to think another person's reality, even God's, can only be achieved by translating it into possibility.

Interestingly enough, though, Kierkegaard insists that Christianity presupposes reflection because, first, it is a relation to an historical person and, whether it was the first generation or any subsequent generation, such a relation is always cognitive; secondly, the possibility of a new quality of personal life must be cognitively conveyed before it will be widely conceived. Kierkegaard did not believe that the Christian mode of life was in continuity with the aesthetic life of wishing and willing. He therefore would have been dismayed to see so great and sensitive a genius as Sigmund Freud summarily dismiss all of religion by subsuming all of it under categories of illusion and wish-fulfillment. For certainly what Freud missed was the fact that by far the best ground for rejecting religion, and perhaps most particularly Jewish and Christian faith, is the very fact that it is

---

27. *Fragments*, 87.

scandalous to one's preferences and contrary to general expectation and desire. Kierkegaard roots the paradoxicality of Christian faith in this latter contrariety. But this is all the more reason for saying that without it being conveyed, "preached" is the religious word for the mode of communication, from Jesus to His disciples and thence to subsequent generations, it would not survive at all. Even at that, it has its difficulties, particularly from those who "naturalize the fact" by trying to make religious faith simply a matter of cognitive assent.[28]

The possibility which is truly Christian is the one then proposed by the existence of Jesus Christ as an historical figure. Kierkegaard was careful at this point; he knows as well as any contemporary reader that descriptive language is not the language of obligation and that it will never become that. But the task of communication which is religious in intent, is to present the subject matter so that neither admiration nor critical connoisseurship is a consequence but rather so that a requirement is defined.[29] The possibility in the person of God is an ethical requirement, ethical because it refers to one's future behavior.[30] The purpose of religious communication is primarily to effect the transition from statements of historical fact to statements of possibility in such a wise that one will move from cognitive assent to Jesus' historical existence to a resolution and new passion for one's own future existence.

It is in this latter sense, therefore, that this possibility must become a reality. The "for Thee" note marks the difference between the cognitive grasp of possibilities in poetry and that in religion and ethics.[31] The determinant of difference is one's passion and concern. This is the inwardness which is the spring of all religiousness. The God-Man as Kierkegaard describes Him can be known "about" but

---

28. Ibid., 80.

29. *Stages on Life's Way*, 398. Faith, it is urged, is the ideality within a person that resolves an "*esse*" into a "*posse*," even a "*non-posse*," and then believes. "There is therefore nothing more foolish in the religious field than to hear the commonsense question asked when something is taught, 'if the thing actually happened thus, for if so we would believe it.' The question whether it actually happened thus, whether it was as ideal as it is represented, can only be tested by ideality, but this does not come conveniently bottled in history."

30. *Postscript*, 320–21.

31. *Training in Christianity*, 67–68. Again note this distinction in the context of the *Stages*, 399–402.

always by leaving the God-quality out; for the God-quality is not evident, is not objective at all.[32] The God-quality is incognito—it is the part hidden by the masquerade that is human history. Thus it is impossible to assent disinterestedly to His God-quality for disinterestedness belongs to cognition but one cannot cognize His God-quality. Kierkegaard has only satire for the pseudo-empiricists who try to compound Godliness out of the miscellany of facts that might be available. He believes the effort misguided both epistemologically and religiously.[33]

There is, nonetheless, another kind of contemporaneity. This is the kind which means making the possibility that Christ's life was and is (cognitively and objectively) a present ethical reality (passionally and subjectively). This is not a matter of believing something more but is instead a matter of willing to make a possibility an actuality. Granting that the possibility might be objectively uncertain—no, must be objectively uncertain providing the question is correctly asked—then the only question which matters is, does it interest me? If so, then one wills it and becomes it—this is a new contemporaneity with Christ's life on earth.[34] If not, one declines it because of adverse passions, but with no better or no worse cognitive grounds.

What then is faith? It is an immediacy after reflection. But this does not mean that it is an intuitive certainty which comes after

---

32. Ibid., 28. Or, to put it perhaps more accurately, Kierkegaard admits that the God-quality objectively obtains: but again the external scene is not our arena. "... the scene is laid in the interim, in thoughts and the mind which one cannot see ... The principle of the spirit is that the outward and the visible ... exist in order to test faith, and hence not to deceive, rather that the spirit may be put to test by setting all this at zero and withdrawing itself" (*Stages on Life's Way*, 400).

33. *Training in Christianity*, 28–35. Note Dru, *Journals*, entries 513, 514, 752, 753, 754, etc.

34. *Training in Christianity*, 68. An entire book has been written on "contemporaneity" in Kierkegaard: Lønning, *Samtidighedens Situation*. Although the book does not evince marked reflective powers on the part of the author, it has the merit of gathering a lot of literature and focusing it at a single point. Kierkegaard reflected at great length about contemporaneity, and especially about the priest, Adler, who claimed to have a direct revelation and an immediacy with Jesus that was startling enough to get him deposed from the Danish Lutheran ministry. But here Kierkegaard draws a distinction: he believes that Adler is confused by making the contemporaneity noetic, Hegelian, philosophical, etc., instead of ethical and passionate. E.g., see *On Authority and Revelation*, 63ff. and 132ff. where Adler's "dizziness" and lack of ethics is explored.

Faith and Christianity 287

years of discursive reasoning. As Kierkegaard understands the religious situation, there is no mitigation of objective uncertainty with the passage of time. The uncertainty is not rooted in idiosyncratic subjective differences nor in the accidental quantitative differences between more or less intelligence or more or less probability. Instead it is rooted in the objective facts and these do not change. The immediacy after reflection is therefore passional and non-cognitive. It is a doing and an activity following reflection that faith really is. Faith is a return to the immediacy of attitude, of emotion, of love, of caring, of feeling—but all of it as modified and ordered not by an obligation or law or duty—this would be ethics—but rather by an historical figure's existence upon earth and a reflective awareness of this existent. Religion is not the native immediacy but it is a "new" immediacy. It has, says a pseudonymous author, "reflection betwixt it and the first immediacy—otherwise paganism would be really religion, and Christianity not."[35]

"Faith is: that the self in being itself and in willing to be itself is grounded transparently in God."[36] The opposite of sin is not virtue but is faith, for both sin and faith are here defined as broadly as nets—to embrace, as the author says, all forms. But the point for our purposes is clear enough; faith and sin are forms of subjectivity, forms of passion, not kinds of judgments.

Kierkegaard breaks with the philosophical believers who wish to rescue Christianity from its historical critics by insisting that Christianity is a matter of believing timeless truths. But for Kierkegaard such truths, if they exist at all, could only exist for God. Those which seem timeless for men are so only in virtue of being non-existential. Faith is not principally an intellectual act though it presupposes cognition. Neither is faith the opposite of doubt, the latter considered as an expression of intellectual uncertainty. Intellectual certainty and uncertainty are dependent upon talent, upon training, brains, and insight. But faith, because it is a form of subjectivity, is also the expression of something purely human

---

35. *Stages*, 159. *Papirer* IV A, 108 (*JP* 1, 5).

36. *Sickness Unto Death*, 132. Faith is not then an attempt to get "sensible certitude of the fact that God exists" (*On Authority and Revelation*, 109). An excellent summary (and in Kierkegaard's words) of the faith-concept is to be found in *Samlede Vaerker*, vol. XV, "Register."

"which is the essential possibility of every man"[37] and can be possessed equally by every man.

III

Kierkegaard broke with the entire philosophical system which used such strong and magnificent words as "absolute." But there was still one point at which he used it and this was to describe the object of faith. Oddly enough, although faith has an object, and having an object means also having knowledge, it is still not as a predicate that Kierkegaard uses the word "absolute." Faith is the immediate relation in which Christ's historical existence (not only the fact that He existed, which fact is a cognitive event) becomes an individual's interest. "I live no longer but Christ liveth in me" means not a transposition of souls, of immaterial substances from one body to another, but the process of making contemporary another's existence by having an interest in it. A non-cognitive passion is qualitatively distinct from a cognitive interest and it is an ambiguity in terms that invites our opinion that all interest is a piece with whatever it is we name when we refer to an intellectual interest. By a non-cognitive interest Kierkegaard means to insist upon that which permits a person to effect a transition within his own subjectivity. His example is chosen from a relationship between lovers. When one asks the other whether she loves, she communicates directly by responding. But suppose that he should make himself the interrogation by posing as a deceiver rather than as a faithful lover. Then she may still recite the same propositions but her love may well be in other directions. To Kierkegaard the latter instance is a more fundamental way of eliciting love and, furthermore, dialectically understood, is more proper. Although he denied anyone's moral right to use deception with others he found this analogous to the requirement in Christianity for faith.

To have an absolute means then to have a constant interest. That to which one is contemporary in an interest relation is reality; that to which one is contemporary cognitively is possibility.

---

37. *Christian Discourses*, 121. Note the discussion on 242 of the same book of the relationship between cognition and faith. Dru, *Journals*, entry 763 (*Papirer* IX A, 32).

Faith and Christianity

Contemporaneity can be interestedly encountered in two things—the age and environment in which one lives, and Christ's life on earth—for both exist as actualities to the extent that they are objects of intentional and purposeful activity. Human existing is a kind of dialectic between interests. All of those implicit and resident within any individual can be expended upon the numerous particulars which come one's way, but this is to give no order to one's own life. The pursuit of character means chasing an object and making it absolute—or psychologically it means focusing one's passion so that one interest dominates all the rest.

There is no science of the absolute, either metaphysical or theological, which validates the absoluteness of any kind of claim. There are competing absolutes, which means literally, that from a disinterested standpoint they are all relative.[38] When therefore a person becomes a man of faith and relates himself to what he calls the absolute, he is in a position that no language or thought categories can successfully mediate. An absolute relation to the absolute is the Christian's relation to the historical Jesus and this means that all other particular interests are then relegated by this supreme one. All cognitive predication is within universals and stays within universals. And Kierkegaard finds no warrant in correct thought and speech for discovering the absolute.[39] In fact, the absolute and reflection are incommensurables. One can only be contemporary and commensurate with an absolute in passion and faith is a passion.

Faith is not then an aesthetic emotion.[40] Nor is it what Kierkegaard finds modern philosophy calling an "opinion" or what in everyday speech is "believing."[41] It is not opining where there is no evidence, it is not a "hunch" nor is it believing logical contradictions. With all the emphasis upon paradoxicality and reason "beating its brow until the blood comes," still one cannot say that Kierkegaard ever argues that Christian faith is believing the meaningless or avowing what detached judgment might call with justice, nonsense.

---

38. This is the point of saying that from a logical disinterested standpoint there are only competing alternative "*stadier.*"

39. *Fear and Trembling*, 82.

40. Ibid., 97. Note the *Journals*, entry 763 (*Papirer* IX A, 32), for a discussion of the theme that faith is not immediate certainty.

41. *Training in Christianity*, 140.

Jesus Christ is the paradox for two major reasons. First, the language about him is of two kinds, historical-cognitive and what appears to be, according to tradition at least, a kind of theological-metaphysical doctrine. But upon analysis the latter is not significantly true or false—it remains objectively uncertain; the historical-cognitive truths are like all propositions about matters of fact, probable truths. But something else remains. Depending upon the individual and the state of his own regard for himself, there is also something of passion, reported and elicited. Depending again upon the earnestness a person can muster for the issue of what he is ethically and what he shall be, the knower is also asked to be a believer.[42] This is paradoxical only because it involves for the knowing person, the subject, both a cognitive awareness and yet a decision about one's own life. The paradoxicality lies in the fact that two movements, two kinds of acts, are solicited—disinterested and interested, detached objectivity and yet subjective anxiety. Hence, the doctrine offered at once places personality and personal concern above the doctrine.

This first kind of paradoxicality exists then because there is nothing propositional, nothing as the author says in "direct communication," that requires the belief. The interest factor is not a consequence directly of the knowing, yet it is, or at least can be, present with the knowing. The direct communication is meaningful but religiously trivial, but the fact that He is called Savior and Lord and numerous other things, indirectly draws attention to the fact that He is not understood religiously at all in the true sentences. So then one does in fact have sentences which, indirectly only, convey a requirement. It conveys this because what *He* is objectively is that actualized subjectivity, that kind of person, reduplicated and imitated, which can be any observer or listener. But there is no

> ... transition brought about little by little, to the point of accepting it, of regarding oneself as convinced by it, of being of the opinion, etc. No, an altogether distinct sort of reception is required—that of faith. And faith itself has a dialectical qual-

---

42. Ibid., 185–87. Also, 140ff. Note, *Papirer* X 2 A, 312 (*JP* 3, 3218). A journal entry for 1850 suggests the difficulty, yet necessity, of putting the historical objectivity of Jesus' existence together with a (Christian) subjectivity. *Papirer* X 2 A, 336 (*JP* 4, 4553).

Faith and Christianity

ity—and the receiver is the one who is revealed, whether he will believe or be offended.[43]

The God-quality is something which thought cannot think because it is not a predicate to be added to the subject.[44] There would be no paradox if Christianity were a doctrine about the God-Man and if believing were admitting that the doctrine was so. The God-aspect is paradoxical because it refers to a non-cognitive reality, which is real only when realized in an individual's future. The interest in one's own existence is an interest, cognitively in a possibility, and the only response to God as a possibility is not to think about Him but to become what He was. This is the reality to which it stands related. And the relationship to one's future existence is not cognitive—it is an interest in one's existence. God as an object cannot be known as object but He exists only to be imitated within one's own subjectivity. This is why Christ is the paradox about which historical knowledge can never provide anything of direct religious import, which can never be converted into a syllogism, because at once He is one who says, "Come unto Me," and, on the other side, from all the historical records there are, is nothing deserving of such universal attention as He seems to suggest.[45]

But there is a more sharply articulated reason which can be given for His paradoxicality. This lies in the fact that the kind of interest which Christianity produces is antithetical to the interests of immediacy, "the instincts of the heart."[46] There is an opposition of interest, of passions, which Christianity presupposes. Kierkegaard is convinced that the dialectic of the passions is as lawful and orderly as that described by logic, and infinitely more important. The passional life, too, has its oppositions and conflicts, none of them, however, as violent as that produced by the God-Man. For here the immediate and unreflectively grounded enthusiasm that men have for their own existence is opposed by the demand to live by dying away to this inter-

---

43. Ibid., 110. Note the delicate account of "the movement of faith" in *Fear and Trembling*, 43ff.

44. The argument of the *Fragments*, chapter 3. Another discussion of this is found in Dru, *Journals*, entry 1027 (*Papirer* X 2 A, 328).

45. *Training in Christianity*, 28–35.

46. *Fear and Trembling*, 67. This we have noted previously as an instance of Christianity negating the commonsense ethicality of daily life.

est and living in virtue of the interest in the God-Man. Furthermore, the subjectivity of the self is called sin and is adjudged to be wrong. Therefore an act of "infinite resignation" of all that one is originally, of all of one's interest objects and easy dedications, is demanded before one's passions can again accord with the object of faith.[47]

Faith is then the happy passion ensuing when a cognitively mediated object, Jesus Christ, and a man come together in a mutual understanding of their unlikeness. The other kind of response is "offense," when the object and a man's passion are opposed and the difference is disdained. Faith and offense are related passions. The first is called by Kierkegaard's author, Johannes Climacus, the happy passion; the second is the unhappy passion. The conflict of interests is the ground for saying "*quia absurdum*" and for saying that acceptance of the paradox is impossible. And a pseudo-cognitive language is used:

> The reaction of the offended consciousness is to assert that the Moment is folly, and that the Paradox is folly; which is the contention of the Paradox that the Reason is absurd, now reflected back as an echo from the offended consciousness.[48]

An obvious reason for saying that the language of the Christian faith, and most particularly about God, must include the word "paradox" is that it talks descriptively about a man who is God, by which it is meant that the proper response to cognition about Him is to make "a leap," another kind of movement, one of reconstituting one's personality in virtue of His existence. There is no answer to the question: why? Because the motives for the leap are not cognitively imparted, for they are not reasons; they are, instead, hid within the individual (and maybe within God's purposing?). The leap is an expression of an inner teleology. But secondly, there is a paradoxicality in being asked to be interested in that which is against your interests. Here is the rub indeed. In the first instance it is a public life which demands a private and personal response; in the second, my understanding of decency and order and everything in the interest of myself and family is confronted by the possibility of another interest. Cognition brings me to what I cannot effect and this is the paradox which can only be

---

47. *Sickness Unto Death*, 60–61.
48. *Fragments*, 41. See also *Sickness Unto Death*, 200 and *passim*.

Faith and Christianity

believed. But to believe means a compatibility of interests and these are in fact incompatible, hence more of the paradox.

Professor Swenson is certainly correct in noting that Kierkegaard's antithesis between Reason and the Paradox (the capital letters are used following the translator's and Kierkegaard's idiosyncrasies) is an antithesis not between reflection "in an abstract intellectual sense" and the Paradox but rather between "the reflectively organized common sense of mankind including as its essential core a sense of life's values."[49] This means, also as Swenson noted, that faith is not antithetical to scientific cognition, to self-consistency, to logicality, or to orderly thoughtfulness. Kierkegaard's point is precisely that the aesthetic components in human nature are our interests and passions and that these constitute and define subjectivity. Christianity is the truth but the truth is subjectivity, not objectivity. To argue that Christian truth is objective truth obligates one to argue that objectivity is superior to subjectivity much as Plato argued that knowledge was superior to opinion. On this issue Kierkegaard would agree, providing the discussion is limited to cognition. But suppose that Christianity is not cognition? Faith surely is not, then, opinion and aesthetic immediacy? No, but according to Kierkegaard's analysis, Christian faith is a new immediacy, the subjectivity qualified by a heterogeneity, on the one side, with one's immature wishings and longings and also those of society and the age and of the best people; on the other side, that subjectivity is qualified by an heterogeneity which means that after looking for what no reflection can ever bring about anyway, one breaks with the calculating wisdom of the world, the "wait and see" and the dallying with a decision.[50] Faith follows reflection in time and follows aesthetic immediacy also in time.

To say this much is still to admit considerations of great importance. Kierkegaard does not wish to describe faith in even these epistemological categories without drawing attention to the fact that Christ is the pattern and that the sign of faith is not only the happiness of the passions but the degree of *imitation* that characterizes one's life.[51]

---

49. Swenson, "Editor's Notes," 99–100, *Fragments*. The mistakes in judgment of Kierkegaard's writings here are almost as numerous as there are scholars.

50. *Fear and Trembling*, 59.

51. For a summary of Kierkegaard's Christian ethical views, see Holmer, "Søren Kierkegaard," in Beach and Niebuhr, *Christian Ethics*, 414–43.

But, for these further developments which would tend to correct the abstractness of this elucidation, the reader is referred to Kierkegaard's later religious writings, especially *Training in Christianity* and *Judge for Yourselves*.

All of this is also by way of saying that subjectivity is the truth, that subjectivity is faith, and that Christ is the Truth.

> Christ is the truth in such a sense that to *be* the truth is the only true explanation of what truth is . . . That is to say, the truth, in the sense in which Christ was the truth, is not a sum of sentences, not a definition of concepts, etc., but a life. Truth in its very being is not the duplication of being in terms of thought, which yields only the thought of being, merely ensures that the act of thinking shall not be a cobweb of the brain without relation to reality, guaranteeing the relatedness of thought, that the thing thought actually is . . . No, truth in its very being is the reduplication in one, in you, in him, so that my, that your, that his life, approximately, in the striving to attain it, expresses the truth . . . is the very being of truth, is a life, as the truth was in Christ, for He was the truth . . . And hence, Christianly understood, the truth consists not in knowing the truth but in being the truth.[52]

Faith is never secondhand or derived.[53] It is always as individuated as the person who has it. It is only an historical question whether another person has faith or does not. All knowledge that others have it or do not have it is historical knowledge and, even if true, is not faith. For all knowledge leaves the knower unchanged, except that his imagination may be richer. But to become a creature of faith means that the "I" who thinks is changed and is changed not necessarily from a state of ignorance to one of intelligence, but rather from one kind of immediacy to another. It is a kind of synthesis of the personality—the "divine joining in a man."[54]

---

52. *Training in Christianity*, 200–201. Also, *Postscript*, 118, where the theme is developed that faith is the highest passion.

53. *Christian Discourses*, 242–43. See also, *Fragments*.

54. *Gospel of Suffering*, 72. Also note the second discourse called "How the Burden Can Be Light . . . ," ibid., 21–44. Note the difference that Kierkegaard draws between a religious faith for this life and religious confidence that the future will be well and that constituted by common sense, or "human understanding." *Papirer* IV A, 108 (JP 1, 5).

Faith and Christianity

Christian faith is a mode of achieving happiness (Kierkegaard thus keeps the aesthetic note paramount) in time though something historical. As historical it is an object of cognition but still includes a dialectic factor, as Kierkegaard and his authors call it. This means that there are true sentences to be had. But the relation to human happiness, which itself is a happy relationship is a passional relation and not a cognitive one. Therefore there is a pathetic factor which must be represented also. But the pathetic factor, the pathos and passional factor, is not an historical object to be cognized but is a pathos and passion to be achieved. The dialectic factor neither abrogates nor supplants the pathetic factor but the latter is instead "the essence," the aim and goal of the dialectic and cognitive factor too. The difficulty of the problem is "precisely in its being thus composite." And the pathos and the cognitive factor must be united in "the simultaneity of existence." Christian faith is existential and its description, let alone its imitation and realization, makes more demands than do most subject matters. It would require:

> ... an existential inwardness adequate to an apprehension of its pathos, passion of thought sufficient to grasp the dialectical difficulty, and concentrated passion, because the task is to exist in it.[55]

The Christian faith is the active transformation of an individual's entire mode of existence in conformity with the object of his interest, the person of Jesus. It is not an object or a thing that can be had regardless of the way in which it is acquired.[56] On the contrary, not being a thing, not being a sentence or a doctrine, it is the way it is acquired. It is not propositional truth for this can and must be held in a passionless way. Faith instead is a passion.

---

55. *Postscript*, 345. The above quotes are also from the same section, 345–46.
56. *The Instant*, no. 2, contained in *The Attack upon Christendom*, 100.

Afterword

Paul L. Holmer

Self-Effacing, Swaggering, Nonpareil

AN INKLING. AN INKLING, surely, but perhaps more as I attended Paul Holmer's Tuesday evening lectures on Kierkegaard at Yale Divinity School, spring semester, 1966. Perhaps I knew how very special this opportunity was, how fortunate I was. On Tuesday evening, April 12, Holmer said he was going to address again the "certainty / uncertainty" issues in Kierkegaard "because last week was such a travesty on my part." I had never heard a professor say anything like that. But I had never heard a professor like Paul Holmer. On May 17, he concluded the course by saying, "I hope the lectures haven't failed the quality of the man." I was sure the lectures had not.

Professor Holmer also remarked during that semester that "theology can only be communicated directly with a loss." With manifold indirections, he pitted himself against such loss. At Richard Bell's splendid symposium at The College of Wooster, March 1987, in honor of Paul Holmer, "The Grammar of the Heart: Thinking with Kierkegaard and Wittgenstein,"[1] many tributes were paid Paul Holmer. Mine was a reading of this passage from Johannes Climacus' *Philosophical Fragments*:

> ... the fact that I have been instructed by Socrates or by Prodicus or by a servant-girl, can concern me only historically; or in so far as I am a Plato in sentimental enthusiasm,

1. See Richard H. Bell, ed., *The Grammar of the Heart: New Essays in Moral Philosophy and Theology* (San Francisco: Harper & Row, 1988).

> it may concern me poetically. But this enthusiasm, beautiful as it is, and such that I could wish both for myself and all others a share of this εὐκαταφορία εἰς πάθος, which only a Stoic could frown upon; and though I may be lacking in the Socratic magnanimity and the Socratic self-denial to think its nothingness—this enthusiasm, so Socrates would say, is only an illusion, a want of clarity in a mind where earthly inequalities seethe almost voluptuously.[2]

Professor Holmer was appreciative of the selected passage and probably also of the irony that the celebration of a celebrated teacher be marked by a wariness of such celebration.

Yet there was swaggering, a polemical swagger; and that, of course, added to the interest. Professor Holmer concludes his "Preface" to *The Grammar of Faith*:

> It would be most surprising if my debt to colleagues and teachers, students and authors, was not apparent. But a remark of Scipio's, the statesman and conqueror of Hannibal at Zama (202 B.C.), is appropriate. He said that he was never less idle than when he had nothing to do, and never less lonely than when he was by himself. The reflections in these pages have mostly come about when attempts were being made to make sense for and by myself.[3]

In an "interview" with Paul Holmer at St. Olaf College, June 1988, I asked Professor Holmer to retell a story he had mentioned in an earlier public address:

> Well, she [Lillian Marvin Swenson] came with this letter [from Norman Malcolm]. She didn't know who Norman Malcolm was. He was a young graduate student, actually, at Cambridge University. And he had written to her because he had found out about the translation of Kierkegaard's *Works of Love*. She wanted to know who he was, and she wanted to know who Wittgenstein was, who was referred to in the letter. . . . I knew about Wittgenstein, but I didn't know Norman Malcolm. So I assured her that Wittgenstein was worthy of getting a copy of the book. And so Mrs. Swenson sent the volume, a new translation from Princeton Press, of Kierkegaard's *Works of Love*. And then some time later, almost within a

---

2. Kierkegaard, *Philosophical Fragments*, 14–15.
3. Holmer, *Grammar of Faith*, xii.

month, I think, Malcolm wrote back and said about this
... that ... [Wittgenstein] had received the book and read the
book and so on. Mrs. Swenson referred him [Malcolm] to me.
... He then corresponded further with me. I asked Malcolm
outright what Wittgenstein thought of Kierkegaard's *Works of
Love*. He told me that Wittgenstein had already read it in the
German translation, didn't like the German, had tried it in
Danish and, because of his knowledge of Norwegian, he was
able to read it; but it wasn't clear to him. So he wanted to try it
in English translation. But Malcolm told me that Wittgenstein
said it was much too high for him. And so I wrote to Malcolm
and said, "What does he mean by *that*?" And then he wrote
back and said, "It was as if he [Wittgenstein] couldn't manage those intense passions and feelings that were involved in
Kierkegaard's volume." And then Malcolm pointed out to me
that the lovely thing about Wittgenstein was that he didn't
blame Kierkegaard for that. He thought it was his own weakness. And I thought that was a right and true remark.[4]

Swagger (by indirect implication) seems eclipsed by self-effacement. Paul Holmer lived and *was* a dialectic of earnestness and irony. Irony perhaps had the edge—perhaps because of earnestness. His mouth was a runaway, somewhere between a scowl and a smirk—or not between but *both*.

At the end of our time at Yale Divinity School, my wife Marlyne and I invited Paul Holmer over to the Canner Street apartments for a lunch to say thank you. This was May 31, 1967. I know because he dated the guestbook and wrote: "Only the truth which edifies is truth for you."

David Cain
Distinguished Professor of Religion
University of Mary Washington

---

4. Cain, "Appendix" to "Appreciation of Roger Poole," 480–81.

Appendix

Paul L. Holmer: A Select Bibliography

Books by Paul L. Holmer

Philosophy and the Common Life. Tully Cleon Knoles Lectures in Philosophy, 1960; College of the Pacific. Philosophy Institute Publications, vol. 10. Stockton, CA: Fitzgerald, 1960.

Theology and the Scientific Study of Religion. The Lutheran Studies Series. Minneapolis: Denison, 1961.

Youth Considers Doubt and Frustration. Youth Forum Series. Camden, NJ: Nelson, 1967.

C. S. Lewis: The Shape of His Faith and Thought. New York: Harper & Row, 1976.

The Grammar of Faith. San Francisco: Harper & Row, 1978.

Making Christian Sense. Spirituality and the Christian Life series. Edited by Richard H. Bell. 1984. Reprinted as *Making Sense of Our Lives.* Minneapolis: MacLaurin Institute, n.d.

Other Resources

Bell, Richard H. *The Grammar of the Heart: New Essays in Moral Philosophy and Theology.* San Francisco: Harper & Row, 1988. Based on the March 1987 symposium, "The Grammar of the Heart: Thinking with Kierkegaard and Wittgenstein," to honor Paul L. Holmer, held at The College of Wooster, Wooster, Ohio.

———, and Ronald E. Hustwit. *Essays on Kierkegaard and Wittgenstein: On Understanding the Self.* Wooster, OH: The College of Wooster, 1978. Based on the October 1976 symposium, "Søren Kierkegaard and Ludwig Wittgenstein: Philosophy as Activity and Understanding Forms of Life," held at The College of Wooster, Wooster, Ohio.

Cain, David. "Appendix" to "An Appreciation of Roger Poole." In *Kierkegaard Studies Yearbook 2005*, edited by Niels Jørgen Cappelørn and Hermann Deuser, with K. Brian Söderquist on behalf of the Søren Kierkegaard Research Centre, 480–81. Berlin: Walter de Gruyter, 2005.

Carlson, Bruce. "Tribute to Paul Holmer." *Pietisten* 19 (Fall 2004). No pages. Online: http://www.pietisten.org/fall04/paulholmer.html.

Cathey, Robert Andrew. *God in Postliberal Perspective: Between Realism and Non-Realism*, 49–82. Farnham, England, and Burlington, VT: Ashgate, 2009.

Lindbeck, George A. *The Nature of Doctrine: Religion and Theology in a Postliberal Age.* 25th Anniversary Edition. With a New Introduction by Bruce D. Marshall and a New Afterword by the Author. Louisville, KY: Westminster/Knox, 2009.

Sherry, Patrick. "Learning How to be Religious: The Work of Paul Holmer." *Theology* 77.644 (1974) 81–90.

Dissertations on Paul L. Holmer

Rollefson, Richard. "Thinking with Kierkegaard and Wittgenstein: The Philosophical Theology of Paul L. Holmer." PhD diss., Graduate Theological Union, 1994.

Stewart, T. Wesley. "Paul L. Holmer and the Logic of Faith: A Utilization of Kierkegaard and Wittgenstein for Contemporary Christian Theology." PhD diss., Southern Baptist Theological Seminary, 1991.

On Holmer as a Teacher

Hauerwas, Stanley M. *Hannah's Child: A Theologian's Memoir.* Grand Rapids, MI: Eerdmans, 2010, pages 53, 58, 59–60.

———. "How to Go On When You Know You Are Going to Be Misunderstood, or How Paul Holmer Ruined My Life, or Making Sense of Paul Holmer." In *Wilderness Wanderings: Probing Twentieth-Century Theology and Philosophy*, 143–52. Radical Traditions: Theology in a Postcritical Key. Boulder, CO: Westview, 1997.

Holmer, Phyllis. "Holmer and Students." *Christian Century* 122.9 (May 3, 2005) 45.

Horst, Mark. "Paul Holmer: A Profile." *Christian Century* 105.29 (October 12, 1988) 891–95.

Roberts, Robert C. "A Little Protector." In *God and the Philosophers: The Reconciliation of Faith and Reason*, edited by Thomas V. Morris, 113–27. Oxford: Oxford University Press, 1994.

Willimon, William H. "Hard Truths." *Christian Century* 122.4 (February 22, 2005) 25–28.

Online Resources

The "Guide to the Paul L. Holmer Papers" (Record Group No. 195) may be accessed electronically from Special Collections, Yale University Library, Divinity School Library. Online: http://www.library.yale.edu/div/colgpers.html.

The Holmer Lectures

The Holmer Lectures. Since 1996, The MacLaurin Institute, Minneapolis, MN, has sponsored annual Holmer Lectures, inaugurated in 1996 by Professor Holmer. Other Holmer lecturers have been George Marsden, Nicholas Wolterstorff, Glenn Tinder, Bruce Reichenbach, Jean Bethke Elshtain, Alvin Plantinga, Gilbert C. Meilaender, Dallas Willard, Richard John Neuhaus, Richard Swinburne, Stanley Hauerwas, David Gushee, J. Budziszewski, James K. A. Smith, and C. Stephen Evans. Online: http://www.maclaurin.org/home.

Bibliography

Bärthold, Albert. *Noten zu Sören Kierkegaards Lebensgeschichte*. Halle: Fricke, 1876.
Bell, Richard H. *The Grammar of the Heart: New Essays in Moral Philosophy and Theology*. San Francisco: Harper & Row, 1988.
Bense, Max. *Hegel und Kierkegaard*. Köln and Krefeld: Staufen, 1948.
Berlin, Isaiah. *Historical Inevitability*. London: Oxford University Press, 1954.
Blanshard, Brand. "Current Strictures on Reason." *Philosophical Review* 54 (1945) 345–68.
Bohlin, Torsten. *Søren Kierkegaard*. Stockholm: Svenska kyrkans diakonistyrelses bokförlag, 1939.
Brandes, Georg. *Søren Kierkegaard*. Copenhagen: Gyldendal, 1877.
Brandt, Frithiof. *Den Unge Søren Kierkegaard*. Copenhagen: Levin and Munskgaard, 1929.
Brandt, Frithiof, and E. Rammel. *Søren Kierkegaard og pengene*. Copenhagen: Levin and Munskgaard, 1935.
Butterfield, Herbert. *Christianity and History*. London: Bell, 1949.
———. *Christianity in European History*. London: Collins, 1952.
———. *The Englishman and his History*. Cambridge: Cambridge University Press, 1944.
———. *Man on his Past*. Cambridge: Cambridge University Press, 1955.
Carnap, Rudolf. *The Logical Syntax of Language*. London: K. Paul, Trench, & Truber, 1937.
Climacus, St. John. *The Ladder of Divine Ascent*. Translated by Lazarus Moore. New York: Faber and Faber, 1959.
Collins, James. *The Mind of Kierkegaard*. Chicago: Regnery, 1953.
Croxall, T. H. *Glimpses and Impressions of Kierkegaard*. New York: J. Nisbet, 1959.
———. *Kierkegaard Commentary*. New York: Harper, 1955.
———. *Kierkegaard Studies*. London: Lutterworth, 1948.
Descartes, René. *Principles of Philosophy*. Translated by John Veitch. London: Dent, 1953.
Diem, Hermann. *Die Existenzdialektik von Sören Kierkegaard*. Zürich: Evangelischer Verlag, 1950.
Eller, Vernard. *Kierkegaard and Radical Discipleship: A New Perspective*. Princeton: Princeton University Press, 1968.
Findlay, J. N. *Hegel: A Re-examination*. London: Allen & Unwin, 1958.
Geismar, Eduard. *Søren Kierkegaard*. Copenhagen: Gad, 1926.

Gemmer, Anders. *Sören Kierkegaard und Karl Barth*. Stuttgart: Strecker and Schröder, 1925.
Gilson, Étienne. *Being and Some Philosophers*. 2nd ed. Toronto: Pontifical Institute of Medieval Studies, 1952.
Haldane, E. S. *The Wit and Wisdom of a German Philosopher*. London, 1897.
Hansen, P. G. *Søren Kierkegaard og Bibelen*. Copenhagen: P. Hasse, 1924.
Hegel, G. W. F. *Encyclopädie der Philosophischen Wisssenschaft*. Leipzig: F. Meiner, 1920.
———. *Lectures on the Philosophy of History*. Translated by J. Sibree. London: Bell, 1890.
———. *Science of Logic*. New York: Allen and Unwin, 1951.
Heinecken, Martin. *The Moment Before God*. Philadelphia: Westminster, 1956.
Henriksen, A. *Methods and Results of Kierkegaard Studies in Scandinavia*. Copenhagen: Munksgaard, 1951.
Himmelstrup, J. *Søren Kierkegaards Opfattelse af Sokrates*. Copenhagen: A. Busck, 1924.
Hirsch, Emanuel. *Kierkegaard-Studien*. 2 vols. Gütersloh: Bertelsmann, 1933.
Høffding, Harald. *Søren Kierkegaard som Filosof*. Copenhagen: Philipsen, 1892.
———. *Mindre Arbejder*. 2 vols. Copenhagen: Gyldendal, 1905.
Hollander, Lee. *Selections from the Writings of Søren Kierkegaard*. Austin: University of Texas, 1923.
Holm, Søren. *Søren Kierkegaards Historiefilosofi*. Copenhagen: Arnold Busck, 1952.
Holmer, Paul L. "Review of Walter Rehm, *Kierkegaard und der Verführer*." *Philosophical Review* 61 (1952) 270–73.
———. "Review of Walter Rehm, *Kierkegaard und der Verführer*." *Philosophy and Phenomenological Research* 12 (1951–52) 307–11.
———. "Søren Kierkegaard." In *Christian Ethics*, edited by Waldo Beach and H. Richard Niebuhr. New York: Ronald, 1955.
Hyppolite, Jean. *Logique et Existence, Essai sur la Logique de Hegel*. Paris: Press Universitaires de France, 1953.
Iljin, Iwan. *Die Philosophie Hegels*. Bern: Franke, 1946.
Jansen, F. J. Billeskov. *Studier i Søren Kierkegaards Litteraere Kunst*. Copenhagen: Rosenkilde og Bagger, 1951.
Jaspers, Karl. "Was Philosophie für Schelling Bedeutet." In *Schelling: Grösse und Verhängnis*. Munich: R. Piper, 1955.
Kabell, A. *Kierkegaard-Studiet i Norden*. Copenhagen: H. Hagerup, 1948.
Kelly, *Liberating Faith: Bonhoeffer's Message for Today*. Minneapolis: Augsburg, 1984.
Kierkegaard, Søren. *Af Søren Kierkegaards Efterladte Papirer*. 9 vols. Edited by H. P. Barfod and H. Gottsched. Copenhagen: Reitzel, 1869–1881.
———. *Breve og Aktstykker vedrørende Søren Kierkegaard*. 2 vols. Edited by Niels Thulstrup. Copenhagen: Munksgaard, 1953–54.
———. *Christian Discourses*. Translated by Walter Lowrie. Oxford: Oxford University Press, 1939.
———. *The Concept of Dread*. Translated by Walter Lowrie. Princeton: Princeton University Press, 1944.
———. *Concluding Unscientific Postscript*. Translated by David F. Swenson and Walter Lowrie. Princeton: Princeton University Press, 1941.

———. *Edifying Discourses: A Selection*. Edited with an introduction by Paul L. Holmer. Translated by David F. and Lillian Marvin Swenson. New York: Harper & Row, 1958.

———. *Edifying Discourses*. Translated by David F. and Lillian Swenson. Introduction by Paul Holmer. 2 vols. Minneapolis: Augsburg, 1962.

———. *Either/Or*. 2 vols. Translated by David F. and Lillian Marvin Swenson and Walter Lowrie. Princeton: Princeton University Press, 1944.

———. *Fear and Trembling* and *The Sickness Unto Death*. Translated with an introduction and notes by Walter Lowrie. Princeton: Princeton University Press, 1941.

———. *For Self-Examination*. Translated by Howard and Edna Hong. Minneapolis: Augsburg, 1940.

———. *Fortegnelse over Dr. S. A. Kierkegaards efterladte Bogsamling* (1856). Edited by Niels Thulstrup. Copenhagen, 1957.

———. *The Gospel of Suffering*. Translated by David Swenson and Lillian Swenson. Minneapolis: Augsburg, 1948.

———. *Johannes Climacus*. In *Philosophical Fragments, Johannes Climacus*, edited and translated by Howard V. Hong and Edna H. Hong, 113–72. Princeton: Princeton University Press, 1985.

———. *Johannes Climacus, or, De Omnibus Dubitandum Est*. Translated by T. H. Croxall. London: A. & C. Black, 1958.

———. *The Journals of Søren Kierkegaard*. Selected and translated by Alexander Dru. London: Oxford University Press, 1938.

———. *Kierkegaard's Attack upon Christendom*. Translated by Walter Lowrie. Princeton: Princeton University Press, 1944.

———. *The Last Years Journals 1853–55*. Translated by Ronald G. Smith. London: Collins, 1965.

———. *On Authority and Revelation*. Translated and edited by Walter Lowrie. Princeton: Princeton University Press, 1966.

———. *Philosophical Fragments*. Originally translated and introduced by David F. Swenson. New Introduction and commentary by Niels Thulstrup. Translation revised and commentary translated by Howard V. Hong. 2nd ed. Princeton: Princeton University Press, 1962.

———. *Philosophische Brocken*. Translated by Emanuel Hirsch. Cologne: Diedrichs, 1952.

———. *The Point of View for My Work as an Author: A Report to History*. Translated by Walter Lowrie. London: Oxford University Press, 1939.

———. *The Present Age*. Translated by Alexander Dru and Walter Lowrie. London: Oxford University Press, 1940.

———. *Repetition*. Translated by Walter Lowrie. Princeton: Princeton University Press, 1941.

———. *Samlede Vaerker*. 15 vols. Edited by A. B. Drachmann, J. L. Heiberg, and H. O. Lange. 1st ed. Copenhagen: Gyldendal, 1901–1936.

———. *Samlede Vaerker*. 20 vols. Edited by A. B. Drachmann, J. L. Heiberg, and H. O. Lange. 3rd ed. Copenhagen: Gyldendal, 1962–1964.

———. *The Sickness Unto Death*. Translated by Walter Lowrie. Princeton: Princeton University Press, 1941.

———. *Søren Kierkegaard's Journals and Notebooks*. 4 vols. to date. Edited by Niels Jørgen Cappelørn, Alastair Hannay, David Kangas, Bruce H. Kirmmse, George

Pattison, Vanessa Rumble, and K. Brian Söderquist. Princeton: Princeton University Press, 2000–.

———. *Søren Kierkegaard's Journals and Papers*. 7 vols. Edited and translated by Howard V. Hong and Edna H. Hong. Bloomington: Indiana University Press, 1967–1978.

———. *Søren Kierkegaards Papirer*. 16 vols. Edited by P. A. Heiberg, V. Kuhr, and E. Torsting. 2nd ed., augmented by Niels Thulstrup. Copenhagen: Gyldendal, 1968–1978.

———. *Stages on Life's Way*. Translated by Walter Lowrie. Princeton: Princeton University Press, 1940.

———. *Thoughts on Crucial Situations in Human Life*. Translated by David F. Swenson. Minneapolis: Augsburg, 1941.

———. *Training in Christianity, and the Edifying Discourse which "Accompanied" It*. Translated with introduction and notes by Walter Lowrie. London: Oxford University Press, 1941.

———. *Works of Love: Some Christian Reflections in the Form of Discourses*. Translated by Howard and Edna Hong. Preface by R. Gregor Smith. New York: Harper & Row, 1962.

Kuhr, Victor. *Modsigelsens Grundsaetning*. Kierkegaard Studier. Edited by P. A. Heiberg and Victor Kuhr. Copenhagen: Gyldendal, 1915.

Leibniz, Gottfried Wilhelm. *Logical Papers: A Selection*. Translated and edited with an introduction by G. H. R. Parkinson. Oxford: Clarendon, 1966.

Lindhart, P. G. *Grundtvig*. London, 1951.

Lønning, Per. *Samtidighedens Situation*. Oslo: Forlaget Land og Kirke, 1954.

Löwith, Karl. *Von Hegel bis Nietzsche*. 2nd ed. Stuttgart: Kohlhammer, 1950.

Lowrie, Walter. *Kierkegaard*. London: Oxford University Press, 1938.

———. *A Short Life of Kierkegaard*. Princeton: Princeton University Press, 1942.

Mackey, Louis. "Kierkegaard and the Problem of Existential Philosophy," in two parts. *Review of Metaphysics* 9:3–4 (1956) 404–19, 569–58.

Magnussen, Rikard. *Søren Kierkegaard set udefra*. Copenhagen: Munksgaard, 1942.

McTaggart, J. M. E. *Studies in Hegelian Cosmology*. Cambridge: Cambridge University Press, 1901.

———. *Studies in the Hegelian Dialectic*. Cambridge: Cambridge University Press, 1922.

Minear, Paul, and Paul Morimoto. *Kierkegaard and the Bible: An Index*. Princeton: Princeton Seminary Pamphlet, No.9, 1952.

O'Flaherty, James. *Unity and Langauge*. Chapel Hill: University of North Carolina Press, 1952.

Pelikan, Jaroslav. *From Luther to Kierkegaard*. St. Louis: Concordia, 1950.

Rehm, Hermann. *Kierkegaard und der Verführer*. Munich: Hermann Rinn, 1949.

Rindom, Erik. *Samtaler med Harald Høffding*. Copenhagen: Nyt nordisk forlag, 1918.

Roos, Heinrich. *Søren Kierkegaard og Katolicismen*. Copenhagen: Munskgaard, 1952.

Ruttenbeck, Walter. *Sören Kierkegaard: Der Christiche Denker und sein Werk*. Berlin: Trowitsch & Sohn, 1929.

Shestov, Lev. *Kierkegaard et la Philosophie Existentielle*. Translated by Tatiana Rageot. Paris: J. Vrin, 1936.

Stace, W. T. *The Philosophy of Hegel*. London: Macmillan, 1924.

Bibliography

Swenson, David F. *Kierkegaardian Philosophy in the Faith of a Scholar*. Philadelphia: Westminster, 1941.

———. *Something about Kierkegaard*. Minneapolis: Augsburg, 1941.

Thomte, Reidar. *Kierkegaard's Psychology of Religion*. Princeton: Princeton University Press, 1948.

Thust, Martin. *Sören Kierkegaard, Der Dichter des Religiösen*. Munich: Beck, 1931.

Wahl, Jean. *Études Kierkegaardiennes*. 2nd ed. Paris: J. Vrin, 1949.

Weiland, J. Sperna. *Humanitas Christianitas*. Groningen: Van Gorcum, 1951.

Wright, J. R. C. *"Above Parties": The Political Attitudes of the German Protestant Church Leadership, 1918–1933*. New York: Oxford University Press, 1974.

Wittgenstein, Ludwig. *Philosophical Investigations*. Translated by G. E. M. Anscombe. 3rd ed. New York: Macmillan, 1958.

Index of Names

Abraham, 212, 237, 248, 269, 279
Adler, Adolph Peter, 113, 153, 194, 200, 213, 234, 240, 265, 286
Andersen, Hans Christian, 195
Aristotle, xi, 48, 183, 184, 196, 211
Augustine, 6, 118

Barrett, Lee, xv–xxiii
Barth, Karl, 76
Bauer, Bruno, 62
Bell, Richard, 296
Bense, Max, 85
Berlin, Isaiah, 94
Blanshard, Paul, 1
Böhme, Jacob, 159
Boesen, Emil, 34
Bohlin, Torsten, 44, 63, 158, 159
Brandes, Georg, 57, 61, 182, 196, 239
Brandt, Frithiof, 41
Brunner, Emil, xxi
Butterfield, Herbert, 82–84

Cain, David, xxiii, 296–98
Carnap, Rudolf, 79
Cassirer, Ernst, 22
Cicero, 253
Climacus, Johannes, 4, 11, 14, 18–19, 35, 53, 56, 62, 75, 88, 89, 92, 105, 120, 171, 175, 241–43, 251, 253, 283, 292, 296

Collins, James, 61, 158, 159
Comte, Auguste, 61
Croxall, T. H., 41, 175

Daub, Karl, 41, 46
De Silentio, Johannes, 30, 262
Descartes, René, 9, 80, 114, 150, 167, 169, 171, 175, 180, 183, 196, 209
Diem, Hermann, 222
Diogenes, 226
Dostoyevski, Fyodor, 32
Dru, Alexander, xxi, xxii

Eliot, T. S., 94
Eller, Vernard, x

Feigle, Herbert, xviii
Feuerbach, Ludwig, 62
Fichte, Johann Gottlieb, 41, 46, 170, 223
Freud, Sigmund, 284

Geismar, Eduard, 41, 176, 224
Gemmer, Anders, 76
Gilson, Etienne, 222
Grundtvig, N. S. F., 46, 195

Hamann, Johann Georg, 10, 14, 62, 223
Hansen, P. G., 76
Hauerwas, Stanley, ix–xiii

Index of Names

Hegel, G. W. F., xi, 4, 7, 8, 14, 32, 33, 38, 41, 43, 45–48, 50, 84–86, 93–100, 101–4, 106, 109, 110, 112–14, 118–20, 128, 164, 169, 170, 171, 173, 177, 181, 196. 198, 200, 204, 205, 210, 211, 213, 225, 226, 229, 237, 240, 245, 248, 254
Heiberg, J. L., 195, 215
Heineken, Martin, 109
Himmelstrup, J., 223
Hirsch, Emanuel, 24, 41, 222
Høffding, Harald, 159, 195
Hollander, Lee, 61
Holm, Søren, 10, 19, 85, 90, 94
Hong, Howard and Edna, xxi, xxii
Hume, David, 9, 10, 14, 66, 113, 227
Hyppolite, Jean, 95

Iwan, Iljin, 96

Jacobi, Friedrich Heinrich, 171
James, William, 229
Jansen, F. J. Billeskov, 239
Jesus, 150, 188, 220, 264, 266, 269, 270, 280, 283–95
Judge William, 97, 101, 121, 230

Kant, Immanuel, xi, 4, 10, 26–29, 35, 38, 48, 59, 79, 93, 99, 113, 128, 170, 171, 173, 181, 182, 211, 212, 225, 226, 243, 253
Kierkegaard, Peder, 20, 34
Kuhr, Victor, 176

Leibnitz, Gottfried Wilhelm, 80, 118, 178
Lessing, Gotthold, Ephraim, 171, 224, 254
Locke, John, 10, 174, 228
Lovejoy, Arthur, 89
Lowrie, Walter, 24, 41, 239, 240

Lønning, Per, 286
Lund, P. W., 12, 202
Luther, Martin, 76

Magnussen, Rikard, 277
Malcolm, Norman, 297
Mann, Thomas, 33
Martensen, H. L., 119, 176
Marx, Karl, 61
McTaggart, J. M. E., 95
Mill, John Stuart, 26, 61
Minear, Paul, 76
Moore, G. E., 89
Morimoto, Paul, 77
Moses, 206
Mozart, Wolfgang Amadeus, 33
Mynster, Jakob, Peter, 203

Napoleon, 83
Newman, John Henry, 16, 62
Nielsen, Rasmus, 15
Nietzsche, Friedrich, xvii, xxvi

Olsen, Regina, 20, 40, 239

Papini, Giovanni, 22, 24
Pascal, Blaise, 10
Paul, Apostle, 99, 126, 129, 269
Plato, xi, 6, 7, 10, 43, 54, 109, 114, 118, 128, 129, 177–79, 184, 196, 198, 211, 239, 293

Rehm, Walter, 22, 239
Roos, Heinrich, 70, 262
Rousseau, Jean-Jacques, 6, 49
Russell, Bertrand, ix
Ruttenbeck, Walter, 159
Ryle, Gilbert, 113

Santayana, George, 6
Sartre, Jean Paul, xxi
Schelling, Friedrich, 159, 169, 171, 181, 196, 208, 209, 223
Schleiermacher, Friedrich D., 62
Schopenhauer, Arthur, 198

Index of Names

Sibbern, F. C., 203
Socrates, 43, 44, 52, 54, 72, 95, 102, 129, 157, 166, 177–79, 212, 223, 225, 233, 254
Spinoza, Baruch, 9, 10, 112, 167, 169, 171, 236, 237
Stace, W. T., 96
Strauss, D. F., 62
Swenson, David F., xvi–xviii, xxv–xxvii, 3, 7, 13, 44, 81, 179, 222, 227, 246, 292
Swenson, Lillian Marvin, 297

Thulstrup, Niels, 41
Thust, Martin, 223
Tillich, Paul, xxi
Trendelenburg, Friedrich, 10, 159, 223

University of Minnesota, xvi–xvii

Yale University, xv–xvii, 296, 298

Weiland, J. Sperna, 227
Wittgenstein, Ludwig, ix, xii, xix, 107, 112, 151, 161, 168, 183, 207, 296, 297, 298
Wolff, Christian, 112

Zeno, 171

Index of Subjects

Aesthetic, Aesthetics, 26–28, 82, 265–66, 277
Apostle, 277
Approximation, 64, 70, 71, 124, 162, 186
Authorship, 18–36, 37, 41–44, 48–49, 245, 258–60

Being, 46, 65, 206, 207
Belief, 182–83
Bible, xx, 56, 62–78, 148, 155, 211, 253, 263, 269, 270

Certainty, Uncertainty, 142–49, 152–58, 161–66, 177–90, 279
Christendom, xii
Christianity, xvii, xx, 112, 146, 242, 243, 264–95
Church, 199–201, 263, 272
Common Sense, 224, 226, 230, 236–37
Communication, xviii, xx, xxi, 16, 238–59, 290
Concepts, xix, xx, 4, 76, 81, 112, 119, 126, 130–31, 204–13
Consciousness, 180
Contemporaneity, 284–89

Dialectic, Dialectics, 16, 32, 68, 88, 93–97, 101–11, 113, 115, 143
Doctrine, 116, 160

Doubt, 170–76, 180–90
Duty, 26–29, 243

Ego, 135–37, 157
Emotion, xvii, xx
Empiricism, 61–62, 227
Epicureanism, 112, 242
Epistemology, 2, 3, 158–92
Ethics, the Ethical, 5, 9, 11, 26–30. 86–89, 91–103, 121–23, 244, 251–59
Evil, 46–47
Existence, 174, 205–9, 223–35
Existentialism, xi, xvii, xxi, 41, 52, 54–55, 135, 218

Facts, 74–75, 83–84
Faith, xxv, 60, 61, 71, 138, 166, 182–83, 189–91, 269–70, 275–95

Genius, 276–77
God, xii, xix, 34, 46, 63, 66–69, 74, 96, 98, 99, 104, 107, 115, 121, 141–49, 167, 186, 187, 188, 190, 211, 220, 232, 252, 253, 258, 264, 268, 270, 271–74, 280, 281, 284–92

Happiness, 106, 253, 295
History, 79–100

"How," 111–17, 129, 133, 138, 142, 145, 149, 150–54, 158, 173, 210
Humor, x, 51

Ideal, 172–76, 181–82
Idealism, 62, 146, 179, 200
Ideas, 228–29
Immanence, 147
Immediacy, 171, 249–50, 275–81, 287
Immortality, 130–32
Indirect Communication, 16, 238–59, 261
Individual, 39, 50, 135–42
Inspiration, 65, 67–68
Irony, x, xxv, 14, 22, 51

Knowledge, 104, 138, 140–43, 163, 176, 189–92, 214, 278–79, 281

Language, xx, 81, 111, 112, 136, 150–52, 168, 209–12, 247–48
Leap, 73, 194, 224
Logic, xvii, 2–5, 75, 96, 114, 133–49, 205, 219, 222
Love, 138

Meaning, 151–52
Metaphysics, 2, 7, 10, 11, 61, 80–85, 158, 193–220, 221–26, 234–36
Movement, 210–11

Objectivity, 50, 59, 70–71, 92, 105, 117–21, 130–34, 142–43, 151–58, 231, 246, 256–58

Pantheism, 146
Paradox, 290–93
Passion, xvii, xix, xx, 4, 14, 16, 26, 71, 73, 91–99, 101–6, 183–85, 191, 192, 249, 256, 289–95
Philosophy, xi, xii, xvi, xvii, xix, 1–17, 31–32, 37–55, 89, 95–97, 105–7, 110, 113–20, 134–39, 157–59, 178–79, 203, 212–37, 245, 252
Positivism, xvii, xviii, 164, 264
Possibility, 101–2, 133–34, 140, 148, 231–34, 255
Probability, 124, 156, 183–85
Pseudonymity, 30, 31, 36, 45, 239, 242, 260

Rationalism, 146
Rationality, xvii, 25–26
Real, Reality, 53, 140, 160, 169, 172–76, 181–82, 194, 200, 202, 207, 208, 214–19, 234
Reflection, 102–3, 105
Religion, 33–35, 126–27, 251–59, 263

Science, 79–84, 202, 209–10
Sermons, 260
Sin, 210
Skepticism, 170, 184, 189
Stages of Life, 54, 114, 194
Stoicism, 112, 198
Subjectivity, xi, xxvi, 13, 16, 25, 26, 56–58, 60, 73–75, 105, 108–11, 113–57, 166, 220, 226, 231, 246, 256–58, 294
System, 105, 128, 198

Teleology, 93–89, 233–235
Theology, xvi, 74–75
Truth, x, 11, 12, 25, 26, 53, 56–60, 99, 104, 108–11, 115–57, 246, 251, 294

Verification, 152, 155, 168, 257

Wonder, 183–85

www.ingramcontent.com/pod-product-compliance
Lightning Source LLC
Chambersburg PA
CBHW020106020526
44112CB00033B/970